Horse Racing

On the dirt at the Keeneland fall meeting

Horse Racing

COAST TO COAST™

THE TRAVELER'S GUIDE TO THE SPORT OF KINGS

By
Michael Walmsley and Marlene Smith-Baranzini

BOWTIE
P R E S S®

Irvine, California
A Division of BowTie, Inc.

Karla Austin, *Business Operations Manager*
Nick Clemente, *Special Consultant*
Jarelle S. Stein, *Editor*
Mark Simon, *Consulting Editor*
Jill Dupont, *Production*
Allyn A. Salmond, *Interior Design*
Curtis Boyer, *Cover Design*
Bocu & Bocu, *Interior Layout*
Melody Englund, *Indexer*

Library of Congress Cataloging-in-Publication Data

Walmsley, Michael.
  Horse racing coast to coast : the traveler's guide to the sport of kings / by
Michael Walmsley and Marlene Smith-Baranzini.
      p. cm. — (Coast to coast)
  ISBN 1-931993-52-1
  1. Racetracks (Horse racing)—United States—Guidebooks. 2. Racetracks
(Horse racing)—Canada—Guidebooks. 3. United States—Guidebooks. 4.
Canada—Guidebooks. I. Smith-Baranzini, Marlene. II. Title. III. Series.

  SF324.3.W35 2006
  798.4'006'873–dc22

2005021897

BowTie Press®
A Division of BowTie, Inc.
3 Burroughs
Irvine, California 92618

Printed and bound in Singapore
10 9 8 7 6 5 4 3 2 1

TABLE OF CONTENTS

FOREWORD 7
PREFACE 11
ACKNOWLEDGMENTS 15

THE NORTHEAST

DELAWARE 18
MASSACHUSETTS 19
NEW JERSEY 25
NEW YORK 30
PENNSYLVANIA 42

THE SOUTHEAST

KENTUCKY 74
MARYLAND. 89
VIRGINIA 94
WEST VIRGINIA 96

THE SOUTH

ARKANSAS. 122
FLORIDA 124
LOUISIANA 131

THE MIDWEST

ILLINOIS 156
INDIANA 162
MICHIGAN 165
MINNESOTA 166
OHIO 168

THE GREAT PLAINS

IOWA 194
KANSAS 195
NEBRASKA 199

THE WEST

COLORADO 214
MONTANA 215
WYOMING 216

THE PACIFIC NORTHWEST

IDAHO 228
OREGON 229
WASHINGTON 231

THE SOUTHWEST

ARIZONA 244
NEW MEXICO 247
OKLAHOMA 251
TEXAS. 255

CALIFORNIA

TRACKS. 282
COUNTY FAIRS 294

CONCLUSION. 315
APPENDIX: CANADA. 317
PHOTO CREDITS 323
INDEX. 325

Bugler, Gulfstream Park

FOREWORD

*E*very railbird and most casual horseplayers remember their favorite horse, favorite race, or ultimate racetrack experience as if it were etched in granite. Racing fans are eager to talk about the day grandma and grandpa took them to a track for the first time, or the race in which they bet on the gray mare and she waxed the boys down the stretch, or the sad moment when their favorite equine champion succumbed to the ravages of time. Racing fans also remember the cerulean color of the sky, the glistening coat of a Thoroughbred in the sun, the sound of hooves on spring grass. Horseplayers love the rituals and pageantry of their sport—the bugle call to post and the flash of silks on the far turn.

The racetrack is the quintessential fertile environment for this poet and former English teacher turned newspaper columnist. For starters, the backstretch and grandstands are a never-ending resource for human interest stories to excite an imagination already prone to poetics and hyperbole. Just an alphabetical listing of the names of some of these individuals—Jimmy the Hat, Jimmy the Greek, Blind Jimmy from Chicago—is an invitation to sit down over a double Coca Cola and tell stories.

I have one or two of my own.

I was born beside the jade gurgle of the Yakima River in the state of Washington, in Prosser, a sleepy, two-horse hamlet barely clinging to its riverbank by the knurled roots of cottonwood trees. Above the town towered a great knoll of land from which a boy could gaze east or west for miles down the Columbia Gorge. And away and up a box canyon perched on that arid shoulder of earth was Horse Heaven Hills, where my grandfather said one of the last herds of wild horses ran free.

We lived in a fruit picker's shack on the prairie floor. My bed was an empty packing crate. At night, bits of tarpaper flapped in the constant wind that ripped upriver through the gorge. Above the tiny shack loomed huge silos of grain that turned pewter in the moonlight. Nightly I dreamed about those wild horses until they came down from Horse Heaven and circled the silos, wild-eyed and snorting, hooves drowning out the madness of the wind.

Dad got a job on the other side of the mountains, and we moved away. I grew up in the big city of Seattle. I forgot about the wild horses. Then one lazy summer's day not so long after graduation, my friends talked me into going to Longacres. I saw my first horse race all in a blur because those forgotten dreams of wild horses flooded my senses. I ran down to the far turn in a frenzy and listened to the slap of leather on flesh and the snort of horses still wild in the bewildering world of man.

What I believe I saw that first day I still believe—when a horse is at full speed, he returns for a brief moment in time to the high mesas and plains where he was unfettered by human desire and free in the simple wind of the natural world. To see a horse in full flight is to understand at once why the human imagination invented Pegasus, the horse with wings.

I am a lucky man. I have seen great and wondrous things. I have seen Secretariat destroy his three-year-old brethren by a widening 31 lengths, still considered by many to be the greatest athletic achievement of modern times. I have seen John Henry, the people's choice (the son of Ole Bob Bowers) will himself to a Grade I turf victory, again at Belmont, at the age of nine. And I have seen Personal Ensign nip Derby winner Winning Colors in the 1988 Breeder's Cup Distaff, making her the first major horse in 80 years to retire undefeated.

I have lived to see the globalization of Thoroughbred racing. The best of the best now compete in faraway lands: Dubai, Japan, the Happy Valley Racetrack in Hong Kong (where upwards of $25 million dollars is wagered on each card). Racetracks are changing hands like the walnut shell infra-structures of corporate conglomerates. I have also lived to see Thor-oughbred horse racing in America suffering recurring nightmares brought about by unfair and unbridled gaming statutes both local and national in ori-gin. The racing industry has suffered a failure of national lobbying coalitions to properly present the economic plight of forgotten horsemen and horse-women in America. Racing has also lost fans, men and women who have cat-egorically tuned out the "sameness" of racing's everyday cards.

And yet major events such as the recent Belmont Stakes still draw upwards of 100,000 fans.

Make no mistake—the sport of kings, as Thoroughbred racing shall be forever called, endures. It does so because it is the harbinger of the myth of our human future. Each crop of two-year-old maidens sparks new hope in the barns of both the Thoroughbred racing elite and the most obscure ranches of North America. Optimism is a virus that endures. My teacher John Logan, a noted poet, once said that people live for the "hope of change." Cross-culturally the horse is a symbol of hope and regeneration. I predict that like the phoenix, the mythic bird that rises from its own ashes, Thoroughbred racing will emerge from its downward economic spiral to assist in the revitalization of confidence in American sporting events at a period in our history when that confidence is sorely tested.

Horse Racing Coast to Coast: The Traveler's Guide to the Sport of Kings is a blue-print for the rediscovery of our nation's most venerable sport. Even a casual survey of modern day hippodromes reveals that—just as there are "horses for courses"—there are racetracks in America uniquely suited to almost all fans of flat track Thoroughbred racing. Whether it's the heart-pumping pageantry and thunder of hooves on sod at one of the premier tracks in Kentucky or California, or the up close and personal venue of "bull rings" and small town Americana—no matter—most likely there is a racetrack in your neck of the woods exciting enough to make your socks roll up and down. Many of the tracks are national treasures. World-class meet or ten-day county fair circuit, they are all presented in this long-overdue regional tour guide and novitiate's handbook, with photographs, feature stories, historical vignettes, and accounts of racing's best and worst moments. The golden days of tracks now vanished—Longacres, for one, modeled on the grand French Longchamps–are recalled and celebrated in these pages.

In undertaking a comprehensive compendium of racetracks in the United States, *Horse Racing Coast to Coast*—in its sweep across the scores of active North American Thoroughbred tracks of the twenty-first century—does much more than fill an information void long neglected—it provides an insightful peek behind the backstretch and shedrows to reveal a collective nostalgia for the golden era of Thoroughbred racing. In an era when regional travel seems more preferable than ever before, this book does much to put Americans back in touch with the pageantry, rituals, and fascinating histories that have revolved around racetracks in our country for more than 250 years.

Larry Lee Palmer
Seattle, Washington

On the turf at Keeneland

PREFACE

*I*t was the best of times. As wine was being poured, the conversation turned again to the sport that has long captured our passion: horse racing. Michael had the floor. As a professional photographer and connoisseur of all things fast and furious, he had been going to the racetracks, shooting pictures, and playing the ponies for thirty years. He loved the spectacle of racing, the crowds at the rail, the chance to win. Horse racing, he reflected, is one of the only sporting events where everyone gets along. Everyone wants the same thing, roots for the same thing. From the Turf Club to the grandstand, a winner is a winner. The guy who can throw $200 on a horse and the guy who plays the $2 voucher—if they win, the elation is the same. But at the end of the day, Mike wanted more. He wanted someone to take racing *beyond* the track. Any time he left town for an unfamiliar track, he did his homework. He found the great places to stay and where to party after the races, and everything else one might do that would maximize the racing sabbatical in an unknown spot. There were guides for nearly everything on the planet. Why wasn't there a traveler's guide to the racetracks of America, to tracks around the world?

This book is his brainchild. For a decade it incubated, until, impelled by the harmonic convergence of longtime friends (photographer and writer) it began taking form in scribblings on a stack of cocktail napkins—provided by Santa Anita's clubhouse restaurant, the Frontrunner. Sir Barton Press was founded that day. Immediately, we began consulting racing schedules across the country, talking to media people at the tracks, studying maps and calendars, and trying to pack lightly. Although only one of us did the physical writing of the book, we traveled together as often as our schedules permitted. (The editorial "we," used for ease of reading, sometimes refers to just one of us.) Ultimately, we spent three years preparing this guide, visiting all of the major and most of the minor racing venues of North America. We had no idea that it would become such an adventure for *us*.

Whether you reached for this book because you're curious about Thoroughbred racing but have never watched a live race or because you're compiling a life list of racetracks you've visited, we think you'll find it valuable. Organized geographically, it covers the entire Thoroughbred racing scene across the United States as well as Canada. Regional maps and opening vignettes orient the reader and track the history of the sport of kings, from its colonial beginnings to the present. For every track, we've begun with a portrait that includes some of the unique features of place and suggests the lay of the land. Each racetrack SnapShot includes the essential rundown: track description, general meet dates (we recall that as in life, nothing in racing is constant), useful phone numbers, nearest airport information, Web sites and addresses, as well as some of the extras the race fan and family may enjoy at that track. Accompanying every feature are photographs that spin a kaleidoscopic portrait of the track and premises.

Leaving the racetrack behind, the travel sections include our recommendations for nearby fine lodging, dining, and nightlife. More importantly, we present a sampling of unique regional attractions not to be missed, along with a splash of history and regional photographs both iconic and fresh. Our goal is to arm you with the right information, providing everything you need to plan a racing adventure that's memorable from check-in to cash-out. In addition, we've included sketches of a few people in the industry—those who race and those who make racing possible, whether they're jockeys, owners, Thoroughbred breeders, track personnel, or keepers of the sport's history. We explore the symbolism and mystique of the horse in art, from prehistory to the present. We also let animal activists know how they can participate in equine welfare. When describing our experiences and impressions, we have striven to walk that fine line between awe and irreverence.

Horse Racing Coast to Coast appears just as domestic travel is on the rise and our citizenry is restless to reclaim all that is wonderful about America. Steeped as it is in tradition, pageantry, legend, and lore, and touching the very roots of our collective soul, Thoroughbred racing offers that hope. It has endured through the ages and carries the promise of a brighter tomorrow.

A Note to the Reader
The information in this book was accurate and complete to the best of our knowledge at the time it was written. Because of the fluidity of the marketplace, we recommend that you confirm all prices and details with the establishments involved. We traveled anonymously and have not accepted gifts of accommodations, meals, discounts, or other favors that might have influenced our selection of hotels, restaurants, or entertainment spots. Lodging rates are usually based on double occupancy per night; prices for meals usually refer to dinner entrées.

Handicapping legend Andy Beyer at Gulfstream Park

Seabiscuit bronze, National Museum of Racing

ACKNOWLEDGMENTS

*W*ithout the contributions, support, and encouragement of a number of people, this book would never have seen the light of day. Sir Barton Press especially thanks the following individuals for their particular contributions and assistance with the guide: Stephanie Funk, whose fine and generous help kept us from the brink; Randy Robinson, for initial graphic designs, watercolors, and cartography; award-winning turf writer and poet Larry Lee Palmer; writers and researchers Chanel Studebaker, Heather Jacobs, Zac Baranzini, Lindsey Creighton, and Cassie Hamman. Special acknowledgment goes to horsewoman and author JoAnn Guidry, our first reader, who set wheels in motion and whose friendship and spirit have been deeply sustaining from the start.

So many people in the Thoroughbred racing industry welcomed our project and made their facilities totally accessible to us, answered questions, sent media guides, and helped with photographs when we could not get to the finish line or the rain got there first: we say thank you. Especially to Michele Blanco, Vince Brun, Martha Claussen, Jim Claypool, Suzie Conger, Nina Earll, Tom Farrell, Margo Flynn, Vince Francia, Darlene Guenther, Dave Johnson, Tammy Knox, Dan Leary, Amy McNeil, Paul Nicolo, Jesse Parsons, Rick Pickering, Sherry Pinson, Darren Rogers, Dan Smith, Joe Tannenbaum, Frances Carr Tapp, Fran Taylor, Terry Tony, Melody Truitt, Terry Wallace, Dan White, and Bruno Zabulil. The contributions of track photographers, tourism associations, and cultural institutions have been essential. The knowledgeable staff at Keeneland Library, Phyllis Rogers and Cathy Schenck, and at the National Museum of Racing, Tom Gilcoyne, Richard Hamilton, and Beth Sheffer, have generously supported our research. Several people we met (or dragged) along the way shared insights—and a glass or two—that we would otherwise have missed: Chris Venis, Benny Lafever, David Sirucek and Lu Kizer, John Hemling, Peter Williams, Dale Day, and Bob Dunn. Thanks also to Cory Bourdeau, who practices the art of not picking winners, and to Phil Gladstone, handicapper extraordinaire.

Special thanks for ongoing support to Mark Simon, *Thoroughbred Times*. This would be a much lesser work if not for our talented editor at BowTie Press, Jarelle Stein, whose fine skills improved it and whose patience and unfailing goodwill helped us over many a hurdle. Thank you to Karla Austin, Barbara Kimmel, Jill Dupont, Jennifer Dodd Perumean, and April Balotro, who dedicated countless hours to endless details.

On the home front, we'd have gone nowhere were it not for the total support of our clans: JB "Sir Lucky," Zac, and Spc. Nick Baranzini; sage woman Dottie Walmsley, head cheerleader Barbara J. Walmsley, and promising student in the School of Fun, Shannon Walmsley.

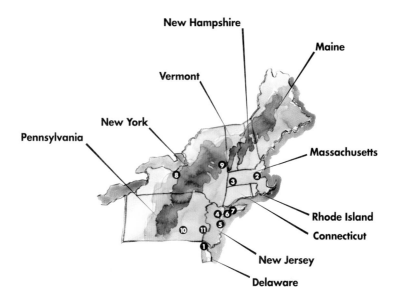

NORTHEAST MAP LEGEND

Delaware
❶ Delaware Park
(Wilmington)

Massachusetts
❷ Suffolk Downs
(Boston)

❸ Three County Fair
(Northampton)

New Jersey
❹ Meadowlands Racetrack
(East Rutherford)

❺ Monmouth Park
(Oceanport)

New York
❻ Aqueduct Racetrack
(Jamaica)

❼ Belmont Park
(Elmont)

❽ Finger Lakes Gaming and
Racetrack
(Farmington)

❾ Saratoga Race Course
(Saratoga Springs)

Pennsylvania
❿ Penn National Race Course
(Grantville)

⓫ Philadelphia Park
(Bensalem)

THE NORTHEAST

British colonists brought their horses—and their passion for horse racing—to the New World. No sooner had the Dutch surrendered New York when, in 1665, Governor Richard Nicholls approved the first formal horse racing course in America. Laid out on a grassy plain on Long Island, the course was named New Market, after the familiar British site. Nicholls awarded a silver cup to the winners of the spring and fall meets and decreed that the prize was intended for the "bettering of the breed." Those acts earned Nicholls his title Father of the American Turf.

Long Island, and soon Manhattan, became dotted with racecourses. Spreading rapidly along the mid-Atlantic seaboard, the sport flourished. Upper-class gentlemen spent heavily to improve their stock, set formal race conditions, and sponsored now-extraordinary contests that offered the young nation both leisure and recreation.

In 1715, a Boston newspaper announced the town's earliest known race: a hopeful challenger boasted that his black gelding could take on "the whole country," either on the commons or on the beach. But such enthusiasm along the New England seacoast was discouraged by Puritan forefathers, who frowned on such "unholy" pleasures as horse racing. He who dared to race a horse in the street was levied a fine—or spent time in the stocks. Though more lenient attitudes crept in and a number of courses cropped up from Massachusetts to Maine, the sport never took a robust hold.

DELAWARE

DELAWARE PARK (WILMINGTON)

Delaware Park is a survivor. This venerable track has staved off threats from competing tracks in neighboring New Jersey and has weathered the winds of change. Built in an era when racing was the sport of kings, the park exudes a feeling of grand tradition. One threat from New Jersey is gone now, plowed under with the grandstand at Garden State Park. Today, a casino is attached to the building, pumping new blood into the track. The acres of parking lots are full. Shuttle buses run back and forth from the far end, depositing people at the entrance. You must pass through the casino—with its jangling bells, pulsing music, and neon lights—to get to the track.

Delaware Park casino area

In the stands, the noise recedes and warm wood ceilings with mirrored panels replace the garish neon. Bronze statues of horses dot the interior, which holds massive wooden Victorian furniture. The park's simulcasting theaters offer a comfortable retreat for the horseplayers.

The grounds are immaculate, with lots of red brick walls and flowers draped over every area. The long stands are open fronted, clearly made for summer racing. A closer look, however, reveals the neglect of the past decades. Entire sections of seats have been removed, leaving empty concrete tiers forlorn behind plastic construction netting.

The jewel of Delaware Park isn't its grandstands or nicely groomed racing surface but a saddling paddock to rival the finest in the country, a lush oasis of lawn and flowers enclosed by a red brick wall, just to the right of the stands. Impressively built, it provides the sleek Thoroughbreds with the setting they deserve.

Behind the paddock, the stewards and jockeys share a brown-shingled colonial building, complete with white

Delaware Park Paddock in spring

Delaware Park horses before the race

MASSACHUSETTS

SUFFOLK DOWNS (BOSTON)

Pari-mutuel (French for "among ourselves") wagering was approved by Massachusetts in the winter of 1935. By summer, Suffolk Downs opened as the state's first new racetrack in decades. Proving that post-Depression Bostonians were ready again for the sheer excitement and recreation of horse racing, a crowd of 35,000 came out on opening day in July. The circular driveway at the entrance was thronged as clubhouse patrons filed between a pair of thoroughly modern art deco Pegasus pillars and into the pristine facility. The building itself, the first American racetrack built of concrete, was viewed as a marvel of modern construction.

columns soaring into the trees. Pots of petunias and American flags adorn the front of the building and the boxes in the saddling paddock. To the left of this lie the picnic grounds, a wonderful area of massive trees, volleyball courts, and playgrounds overlooking the first turn. The smell of hamburgers grilling on charcoal drifts by, along with the smell of freshly crushed grass. Children run and shout, playing kickball as their parents set out lunches on picnic tables.

In the coming decades, Suffolk Downs would know many great moments. There, on June 29, 1936, trainer Tom Smith and a three-year-old colt named Seabiscuit first laid eyes on each other. Smith later recalled that when he nodded at the intelligent-looking animal, the 'Biscuit nodded back.

All in all, Delaware Park has made the marriage of casino and racetrack work, without compromising the track's storied past.

SNAPSHOT - DELAWARE PARK

Description: The highlight of the track is the gorgeous saddling paddock and walking ring, redolent with the smell of cedar and shaded by dozens of ancient trees. A 1-mile track with two chutes encompasses a 7-furlong turf course. The main track's homestretch is 995 feet from last turn to the wire.

Season: Late April to early November

Address: 777 Delaware Park Boulevard, Wilmington, DE 19804

Phone: 302-994-2521/(fax) 302-994-3567

Web site: http://www.delpark.com

Nearest airport: Philadelphia International Airport (PHL) and New Castle Airport (ILG)

Getting there: Exit 4B off I-95, located on Routes 7 and 4

Admission: Free; children under sixteen must be accompanied by an adult; only twenty-one and older allowed in the slots area

Parking: Free; valet parking is extra

Fine dining: Dining Terrace, on the third floor clubhouse level, open on live racing days, dress code; Racing Legends, Victorian décor, second floor, dress code

Casual fare: On A Roll Deli, Del' Cap Room, Beefstro. Check out the picnic grove, acres of tree-covered lawns with playgrounds, volleyball, and basketball courts.

Spirits: Rooney's Deli and Bar

Extras: Annual Breakfast at the Park (with handicapping seminar), handicapping tournaments

PERFORMANCE CATEGORIES

As with any sport, racing has performance categories. Most basic is whether the horse will be run on dirt, the outer oval track, or turf (grass), the inner track. Turf racing is primarily favored for horses with wide hooves. A second racing distinction is the maiden race, contested by a horse who has not yet won his or her first competition. *Breaking the maiden* means the horse has had that first win and can go on to compete against other winners. Most important for wagering, races are organized by experience level and perceived ability, and for some races, by the animal's age. These races fall into four categories:

Claiming races: Every horse entered is for sale at a similar price; prospective buyers put cash on the line before the race. Winning and placing horses split the purse. The seller keeps the claimed horse's winnings; the buyer (claimer) takes the horse. Claiming races equalize the opportunity for registered owners and trainers to purchase racehorses at fair value.

Handicap races: Each horse is made to carry a specific weight so that more competitive horses cannot automatically dominate the race.

Allowance races: These races are for horses who have broken their maiden but are not for sale. Written for various conditions, such as a previous earnings' level or number of wins, the allowance race attracts horses of similar abilities and at similar places in their careers.

Stakes races: These are the most significant big-money races; only the best horses run. The very top stakes nationally are graded (G1, G2, or G3), with only about 450 of the 2,500 total stakes races attaining such lofty status. A horse is nominated ahead of time by the owner through payment of entry and starting fees. The racetrack adds big dollars to the purse; these races give Thoroughbred racing its glamorous reputation.

Fusaichi Pegasus wins the 2000 Kentucky Derby in 2:01.12 minutes.

The following summer, Seabiscuit beat a field of twelve others to win the third running of the Massachusetts Handicap. Five years later, after running last in the early stages of the race, Whirlaway pulled ahead of the pack to take the eighth renewal of the "MassCap," displacing Seabiscuit as the top money-winning American Thoroughbred of all time. In 1997, famed Skip Away, at age four, won the MassCap; when Skippy took the prize again in 1998, he set an all-time race record of 1:47.27 for 1 ⅛ miles, with Jerry Bailey in the saddle.

Not surprisingly for a racetrack that sits on reclaimed mudflats, there have been sea stories, too, over the years. Beyond the 130-acre grounds, the land runs eastward for a mile to the beaches on the Atlantic Ocean. On the afternoon of September 21, 1938, the seventh and remaining races were called when hurricane devastation up and down the mid-Atlantic coast leveled thirteen barns on the backside. Since then, coastal storms have caused

Midseason racing

cancellations from time to time, but such adversities have been setbacks, not derailments.

The tides of fortune have also crashed periodically over the regional equestrian community that revolves around Suffolk Downs. During the early 1990s, the track closed for a spell. Gradually, the Massachusetts summer fair racing circuit, once lauded and robust, has dwindled to one site, in Northampton, though three counties consolidate to race there. When Rockingham Park in New Hampshire canceled Thoroughbred racing in 2002, the impact on Suffolk Downs was jangling. Threatened now by a political tsunami called Indian gaming, Suffolk Downs steels itself for the latest tempest. History suggests that it will ultimately prevail.

Almost seventy years after its opening, Suffolk Downs underwent its requisite face-lift, emerging, according to some standards, stripped and utilitarian; according to others, the look is clean and restrained. On opening day of the 2004 Spring Meet, which coincided with

Suffolk Downs

the running of the Kentucky Derby at Churchill Downs, the Turf Club dining tables were all set, the stadium seats fresh in deep rose and greens, complemented by a tasteful, green-patterned carpet. In the clubhouse, with its mirrors and colorful neon drink signs, Legends Sports Bar anchored the activity. The simulcast audience engaged in boisterous and dangling conversations as they watched other races from other cities, their necks craning toward the windows overlooking the track and back to the screens overhead. From the enclosed grandstand area on the main floor, the true fans of live racing spilled onto the apron in front of the track to scream into the wind at the jockeys and horses, beg favor from the racing gods, and exhibit contagious glee for this grandest of sports.

Entrance to Suffolk Downs

The season's biggest day at Suffolk Downs has been the running of the Massachusetts Handicap, inaugurated in 1935 at $35,000 for the 1 ⅛-mile distance. The length of the race has varied and the date has shifted—in 2004, it was run on June 19. (It was cancelled for 2005.) It's been a $500,000 Grade 2 race that draws competition from across the United States and Europe. Another big race, the James B. Moseley Breeders' Cup Handicap, which is a six-furlong, $200,000-race, also guarantees nail-biting finishes.

Suffolk Downs demonstrates a solid commitment to regional activities. In its embrace of good-fun modernism, the racetrack said yes to the Beatles in the summer of 1966, when the Fab Four made it the last stop on their U.S. tour. Today, grand entertainment engagements are back, exemplified by Cirque du Soleil's dreamlike *Varekai* performance in the summer of 2004. Suffolk Downs's support of worthy causes is epitomized by the summertime Hot Dog

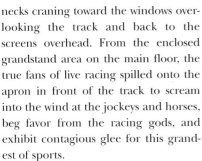

SnapShot - Suffolk Downs

Description: Suffolk Downs, on the eastern outskirts of Boston, a mile from the Atlantic Ocean, is the leading Thoroughbred track in Massachusetts. Opened in 1935, it had the first grandstand in the country built of concrete. The main track is a 1-mile oval with a chute for 6-furlong and 1 ¼-mile races. The turf course is 7 furlongs long and 65–70 feet wide.

Season: Early May through late November. The Massachusetts Handicap is its biggest race, at $500,000.

Address: 111 Waldemar Avenue, East Boston, MA 02128

Phone: 617-567-3900

Web site: http://www.suffolkdowns.com

Nearest airport: Logan Airport (BOS)

Getting there: Located in east Boston at the junction of routes 1A and 145; two miles north of Logan Airport

Admission: Grandstand: $2; clubhouse: $4; senior citizens: $2 (grandstand or clubhouse); children under twelve: free. Admission is free after the seventh race during live programs and when the track is open for simulcasting.

Parking: $2; valet: $4

Fine dining: The Terrace, The Turf Club

Casual fare: Deli Grill; general concessions

Spirits: Legends Bar, beverage stands throughout the facility

Extras: Suffolk Downs presents live in-field entertainment during the summer and offers space for holiday parties and group events.

Safari, sponsored by Eddie Andelman, veteran radio sports-talk host. Wiener concessions of every variety take over the park, and tens of thousands of families spend the day at the races, filling up on dogs and sodas. The Safara raises $250,000 yearly for cystic fibrosis research.

Suffolk Downs is also the scene of weddings—"the only wedding where I've ever won money," says a colleague of ours, whose friends exchanged vows in the winner's circle. The facility was festive with colorful banners and the day's biggest race was named for the couple, who received guests in the Turf Club and appeared in the winning race photo.

Suffolk Downs announcer Larry Collmus, who became the youngest professional announcer in the industry when he started calling races in 1987, nowadays invites aspiring young announcers into the booth to try their abilities on a race or two. It's an honor, bar none, for those lucky young callers. And as a means of cultivating the next generation of racing personnel, it's downright inspired.

THREE COUNTY FAIR (NORTHAMPTON)

The sun stands a little past the zenith as the crowd files through the tunnel running underneath the track at the Three County Fair in Northampton, Massachusetts. Cool air tickles bare arms as people stream out into the grassy infield. The heady scents of a country fair fill the nostrils; fried dough and popcorn vie with the pungent smell of freshly trampled grass. Inside the oval, young girls in shorts run past the horseplayers seated in lawn chairs, the *Daily Racing Form* spread across their laps. Classic fair buildings dot the landscape, some containing concession stands, some lined with betting windows.

The horses for the first race are being saddled in the infield paddock, their riders bright in the primary-colored silks. Across the stretch, the old open-fronted red grandstand is thronged, people filling the seats much as they have since 1943, when the racetrack opened. Originally a harness racetrack, Three County Fair saw

Race finish at Three County Fair

First turn, Three County Fair

its first pari-mutuel Thoroughbred race in 1945.

The horses parade onto the track to whistles from the fans. Narrow and tight-turned, the track is a challenge. Taking a turn on the wrong lead can result in disaster, with the horse heading toward the outside railing. Because of the technical aspects of competing at this bullring track, only experienced riders can compete; apprentices are not allowed.

The result of the tight turns is that the action is fast paced and right there. Dirt clods sail over the fence, rattling off the chain-link that keeps the crowd from the track railing. The horses sweep past, leaning so far over as they round the turns that you can see the tops of their straining backs. Beyond the first turn, the midway rides are in full swing, screams and howls trailing off across the infield.

The Three County Fair is the lone survivor of the once-robust New England agricultural fair circuit, an unusual blend of old and new. The other fairs and small racetracks have melted away, done in by changing political climates and fierce competition from the state lotteries and Indian casinos. The Three County Fair is hanging in there, thanks to a good working relationship with the town of Northampton and a dedicated racing staff. The fair weathered losing a significant portion of its income to competition and has actually seen an increase in handle in recent years, thanks to simulcasting. For color, drama, and good old-fashioned racing, it's well worth the journey in late August.

SNAPSHOT - THREE COUNTY FAIR

Description: As its name implies, Three County Fair is located on fairgrounds property. The narrow, bullring dirt track is particularly challenging with its tight turns.

Season: The season runs for several days in late summer or early September, spread over two weekends. State-bred allowance races are sprinkled throughout the cards of claiming races.

Address: 41 Fair Street, Northampton, MA; send correspondence to P.O. Box 305, Northampton, MA 01061

Phone: 413-584-2237

Web site: http://www.3countyfair.com/

Nearest airport: Bradley International Airport (BDL); Logan Airport (BOS)

Getting there: From central Northampton, where Main becomes Bridge Street, drive east on Bridge Street to Fair Street. Turn right and drive to fairgrounds. Check Web site for directions from I-90 and I-91.

Admission: Adults: free with Fair admission of $7; children ages 7–12: $4

Parking: Several nearby large fields: nominal fee

Fine dining: Bring your own most elegant picnic spread

Casual fare: Standard fair goodies such as corn dogs, cotton candy, and soft drinks

Spirits: Available at some concessions areas

Extras: Carnival rides; craft, livestock, and horse shows

NEW JERSEY

MEADOWLANDS RACETRACK
(EAST RUTHERFORD)

Thoroughbred racing comes to Meadowlands Racetrack in the fall, after its cousin track, Monmouth Park, closes. Meadowlands holds a relatively short Thoroughbred meet with dates that have varied in recent seasons. During the year, the East Rutherford, New Jersey, track is a premier location for Standardbred racing. When it is Thoroughbred time, Meadowlands offers good purses, big stakes, and days and nights of racing filled with fun.

Meadowlands Racetrack is part of a huge sports arena complex of the same name, built in the 1970s. The triangular spread today includes Giants Stadium and Continental Airlines Arena, as well as the racetrack. The glass-and-steel facility offers upper-level dining rooms that look toward the New York City skyline. Pegasus Restaurant, in the penthouse, won a 2003 *Wine Spectator Great Restaurant*

Terraces Restaurant, Clubhouse level

Wine Lists Dining Guide award for its menu and libations.

The biggest event of the season is the Meadowlands Breeders' Cup, a Grade 2, $500,000, 1 ⅛-mile race on the dirt for three-year-olds and up. Capitalizing on autumn's ultimate race competitions, Meadowlands Racetrack invites guest handicappers to instruct the fans before the simulcast of the Breeders' Cup World Thoroughbred Championships.

If you can get here only once, circle the last weekend in October. Make it Halloween, when there are cash prizes

Breaking from the gate, Grey Ghost Handicap

Burning Roma wins the Meadowlands Cup.

for costumes; parties in Paddock Park; giveaways; and, in past years, hay rides and appearances by radio personalities. The racing fun rides in on the Grey Ghost Starter Handicap, with the requirement that all entrants be naturally roan or gray. In 2003 and 2004, the 1 1/16-mile turf race was won by the well-named He Flies. Later in the card comes one for the gals, the Witches Brew Stakes, which is 5 furlongs and also run on the turf.

The eyes of the racing world are focused on New Jersey horse racing. Economic competition comes from the state's casino industry. The New Jersey Sports and Entertainment Authority (NJSEA), a quasi-official state department, regulates the Meadowlands Sports Arena, the racetracks, and the casinos. The good news for now is that those fighting to protect Thoroughbred racing are a tenacious lot. Better news is that purses, attendance, and total handles in the state were up in 2003 compared with the previous year, which bucks a regressive national trend. Field sizes increased to an average of nearly eight horses per race.

MONMOUTH PARK (OCEANPORT)

Monmouth opens its gates in mid-to-late May and offers several high-profile graded stakes. Among the tracks important races are the historic Jersey Derby (G3), celebrated as the oldest derby race in America (though it took a long hiatus), and the Red Bank Handicap, also a Grade 3. The season's biggest race comes round in August: the exclusive, $1 million Haskell Invitational Handicap (G1) for three-year-olds.

SNAPSHOT - MEADOWLANDS RACETRACK

Description: Meadowlands Racetrack, in East Rutherford, New Jersey, is one venue of the Meadowlands Sports Complex, a sports and entertainment complex that was opened in the early 1970s. The Meadowlands Racetrack's main track is a 1-mile oval; the 7-furlong turf track is right inside the main track.

Season: Thoroughbreds run a twenty-eight-day meet in the fall, generally in October and November.

Address: Meadowlands Racetrack, 50 Route 120, East Rutherford, NJ 07073

Phone: 201-935-8500/(fax) 201-460-4042

Web site: http://www.thebigm.com

Nearest airport: Newark Liberty International Airport (EWR)

Getting there: The Meadowlands Sports Complex is located between the New Jersey Turnpike (I-95) and Route 3. Both highways lead to the Sports Complex. It is also accessible from Route 120 (also known as Paterson Plank Road).

Admission: Grandstand and paddock: $1–$1.50; clubhouse: $3; teletheaters: additional

Parking: Free; clubhouse and valet: $5

Fine dining: Pegasus East and West; for groups, the President's Room; the Terrace Suite

Casual fare: Terraces, numerous concessions with dogs, deli fare, sugar treats

Spirits: Sports Bar, International Ale and Beer bar, other stations throughout the facility

Extras: Mane Street gift shop, the Antique and Arts Room. Meadowlands Racetrack's merchandise has included such jaw-droppers as the Dartmoor Gilder, a handmade, 250-pound English mahogany riding horse with a real horsehair mane; an 18-carat Italian gold horse-motif necklace; and rare American and European equestrian antiques and memorabilia.

Everything at Monmouth Park is trimmed in sparkling white and summer greens. There are bubbly fountains, mounds of glorious flowers, a long lane of covered picnic tables, and the shady paddock, where Belgian oaks with broad, arching canopies form a unique, dense grove. Spectators cluster at the paddock, sipping vodkas or icy champagne, assessing the magnificent horses on parade. Encircling the perimeter of the wide track are stands of mature deciduous trees. Great architecture, attractive landscape design, and the deep-rooted pageantry of horse racing seem effortlessly intertwined.

Virtually every weekend features one or two graded races. Fourth of July weekend brings the United Nations (G1), one of America's top grass races, and the Molly Pitcher Breeders' Cup Handicap (G2) for fillies and mares. In late August, the Monmouth schedule showcases the Philip H. Iselin Breeders' Cup Handicap (G3), for three-year-olds and up, and the Sapling (G3), a 6-fur-

Monmouth architecture

long race for two-year-olds. Total purses at Monmouth have grown steadily and now push $4.5 million.

Most celebrated of all the Jersey track's races is the Haskell Invitational, a Grade 1, $1 million race that stands as the richest invitational Thoroughbred competition in North America. The 1 ⅛-mile race draws crowds like a magnet, pricey as it is and falling as it does in early August after Triple Crown fever has cooled. The Haskell has emerged as another thrilling face-off between some of the country's top

Monmouth outer oval

Fans at the Monmouth paddock await the horses.

three-year-olds. In 2003, Peace Rules, with Edgar Prado aboard, stole the show from everybody's favorite, Funny Cide, who had just won the Kentucky Derby and the Preakness Stakes. Similarly, in 1997, after having stopped Silver Charm from winning the Triple Crown at Belmont, Touch Gold went on to claim the Haskell.

The Haskell was established in 1968 to celebrate the memory of Monmouth Park founder and Jockey Club chairman Amory Haskell (1893–1966), who campaigned tenaciously in the

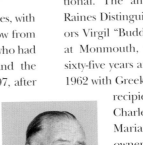

Amory L. Haskell

late 1930s to bring pari-mutuel wagering to New Jersey. His widow, Blance Haskell, awarded the silver trophy to the winning owner for years, a tradition now passed on to daughters Hope Haskell-Jones and Anne Haskell-Ellis.

In 1996, Monmouth launched another proud tradition, that of publicly honoring those whose service to the local Thoroughbred industry has been exceptional. The annual award, the Virgil Raines Distinguished Achievement, honors Virgil "Buddy" Raines, a near-fixture at Monmouth, who trained horses for sixty-five years and won the Preakness in 1962 with Greek Money. The 2003 award recipients were Mr. and Mrs. Charles Hesse III (Charles and Marianne), Thoroughbred owners for thirty years and supporters of Monmouth Park's philanthropic causes. The Hesse racing passion reaches back at least one generation, to Charles Jr., who built the track at the new Monmouth Park in 1946.

SNAPSHOT - MONMOUTH PARK

Description: At this resort racetrack, you can find great racing in a parklike setting. The crown jewel in the stakes lineup is the $1 million Haskell Invitational Handicap, a midsummer event drawing the best of the best by invitation only. Monmouth has a 1-mile dirt oval with two chutes surrounding a 7-furlong turf course with one chute. The distance from the last turn to the finish line is 990 feet.

Season: Opens at the end of May and runs through the end of September

Address: Oceanport Avenue, Oceanport, NJ 07757

Phone: 732-222-5100/(fax) 732-571-8658

Web site: http://www. monmouthpark.com

Nearest airport: Newark Liberty International Airport (EWR)

Getting there: Take the Garden State Parkway to Exit 105 (Route 36). Follow the signs on Route 36 East to Monmouth Park. Transportation by train and boat is also available.

Admission: Grandstand: $2; clubhouse: $4; seniors: (55+) half price; children under twelve: free;

Parking: Free; charge for valet and preferred parking

Fine dining: Parterre Box, the first luxury suites built at a sporting venue, dress code; the Lady's Secret Café, the Garden Room, the Dining Terrace

Casual fare: Monmouth Café; picnic area along the homestretch, charcoal grills welcome, large playground

Spirits: Salvator Bar and Grill

Extras: Monmouth Park hosts many special events, music, and giveaways throughout the summer, including its Ladies Day Luncheon and fashion show.

"Seastreaking" to Monmouth

On our mid-August jaunt up to Saratoga Springs we spent a Saturday at Monmouth Park. Crossing from New York City to the New Jersey shore by water was a spectacular, easy trip. Boarding the *Seahorse Express* in Manhattan, we slipped into vacation/celebration mode right at the pier. The weather was gorgeous, with high puffy clouds sailing across the blue sky—and the fast cruise across the New York Bay delivered amazing cityscape views. Looking up into the Verrazano-Narrows Bridge was astounding. Our stop was the Atlantic Highlands Harbor. A bus met us for a narrated tour, taking us past little summer bungalows, stately Victorians, celebrity mansions, and other exclusive estates.

Leaving the track at day's end, we retraced our morning route via taxi to the pier. Our excursion over the waves was the triple olive in the martini of life. Golden reflections of sunset splashed over everything, illuminating fellow passengers, sails on other boats, and radiant Miss Liberty herself.

Seastreak ferry service operates a special Saturday and Sunday *Seahorse Express* from Manhattan's East 34th Street Pier and lower Manhattan's Pier 11 to Monmouth Park. It returns at sunset. Cost is $30 for adults and $12 for children under twelve, which buys your round-trip cruise and the bus ride, the racing program, and grandstand admission at the track. For schedules and other information, call 800-BOAT-RIDE, or visit the Monmouth Park Web site (http://www.monouthpark.com; click on Visitor's Center and then Directions).

Returning to Manhattan

NEW YORK

AQUEDUCT RACETRACK (JAMAICA)

The day Aqueduct opened in Queens County, Long Island, in the fall of 1894, the Jockey Club of New York branded it an "outlaw racetrack," condemning it for its nonregulation track. Aqueduct came into conformance within a few months by extending the track's length an extra furlong. For spectators and horsemen and horsewomen alike, however, the tough and tenacious attitude that prevailed on that first fall morning of watch-me defiance has never really been abandoned. The Big A is still the venue of choice for city dwellers whose philosophy adapts the postal service creed: "neither rain, nor snow, nor sleet, nor hail . . . will keep us from the rail." The 700,000 fans who go through the gate each year to see some 130 days of racing wouldn't like it any other way.

Old Aqueduct ran its last race in 1955, when the New York Racing Association (NYRA) purchased the state's four Thoroughbred tracks (Aqueduct, Jamaica, Belmont, and Saratoga). The NYRA demolished the Jamaica track for housing and closed Aqueduct for rebuilding. It reopened in 1959. The price tag was $33 million for the huge new Aqueduct, which measures a million square feet, with seating accommodations for seventeen thousand and space for another seventy thousand patrons. Ongoing improvements to the track and facility have added a large dining room, a one-mile winterized inner dirt track, and a weatherized paddock for the comfort of wise players who study the horses before each race.

Spectators at Aqueduct—so named because it stands on the old Buffalo Water Works land—have been rewarded for their diehard loyalty. The roster

Breaking from the starting gate at Aqueduct

Winter racing at Aqueduct

another big series occurs in mid-March. The year's biggest race at Aqueduct is the Grade 1 Wood Memorial in April (first held in 1925), offering a purse of $750,000, and leading up to the grandmother of all race parties, the Kentucky Derby (G1). The winner of the Wood Memorial has gone on to win the Derby eleven times. Race fans who can't get down to Kentucky crowd into Aqueduct to drink a mint julep or two, catch the Derby on simulcast, and maybe take a final look around. Aqueduct closes the following day.

of champions they've seen cross the wire includes such legendary names as Man o' War, Exterminator, Secretariat, Seabiscuit, and more recently Cigar (for whom a Grade 1 race is named) and Empire Maker. They've also seen some amazing finishes, including a triple dead heat in 1944, the only one in stakes racing history.

Aqueduct purses may surprise those who are not familiar with the long and lucrative racing tradition here. The winter meet kicks off in January with $75,000 stakes races marking a sort of baseline for stakes purses, followed by two $100,000 Grade 3 races mid-month;

NYRA manages its trio of racetracks in a unique fashion. When Aqueduct shuts down, the entire NYRA team packs and heads up the freeway a few miles to Belmont Park, also on Long Island, for the next several months. Horses are moved from the stables, and everything goes: all the electronic equipment and computers, pari-mutuel registers, office supplies and paperwork, kitchen equipment, fresh landscaping for the track, and of course, the people. The routine repeats itself when Belmont Park closes in July and Saratoga Race

SNAPSHOT - AQUEDUCT RACETRACK

Description: Aqueduct is a big facility on 192 acres in Jamaica. Aqueduct's main dirt track is 1 ⅛ miles; its inner dirt track—for winter racing—is 1 mile; the turf track is ⅞ mile.

Season: Three meets—winter, spring, and fall—alternating with short seasonal meets at Belmont Park and Saratoga Race Course. Its prominent races include the Wood Memorial, a Grade 1 Kentucky Derby prep race that typically draws The Big A's largest turnout of the year.

Address: 11000 Rockaway Blvd., Jamaica, NY 11417

Phone: 718-641-4700

Web site: http://www.nyra.com/aqueduct

Nearest airport: JFK International (JFK), eight miles away

Getting there: From New York City, take the A line subway train to the Old Aqueduct Station and board the courtesy bus to the track. For driving directions, check the Aqueduct Web site.

Admission: Grandstand: $1; clubhouse: $2; season passes available

Parking: $1; preferred: $4; valet: $5

Fine dining: Equestris Restaurant

Casual fare: Big A Grill, food courts throughout facility

Spirits: Man o' War Sports Bar, Champs, other bars throughout facility

Extras: Free grandstand admission in winter; enclosed paddock; backyard picnic area; eleven-bed hospital

Finishing in a flurry

back at Belmont Park, the year's cycle ends at the Big A, where racing runs again from late October until the end of the year.

In addition to watching live racing in October, crowds pile into Aqueduct to watch the simulcast championship Breeders' Cup matches. During Thanksgiving weekend when the track hosts its Holiday Festival, which includes the Cigar Mile (G1) and the Remsen Stakes (G2), the atmosphere is exuberant. It almost matches the intoxicating excitement felt every April, when twenty thousand fans may be on hand for the Wood, hoping history's next Triple Crown champion is out on the track and that they're sharp enough to spot him.

Course opens. To help with temporary lodging costs during the Saratoga meet, track personnel receive a housing stipend. After a short fall meet

SIR MIKEY'S LAWS OF HANDICAPPING

The venerable Michael W goes to the races for one reason only: to have a great time. While there, he may also quench his thirst, photograph the ponies, watch people, strike it rich. The tried-and-true formula is to arrive at the tracks, look around, take in the space, order a bite, order a cocktail. Play the long shots.

Cornering Sir Michael for more insiders' secrets, we followed him to the bank. And why not? At a simulcast of the 2003 Arkansas Derby, he picked up 10 C-notes on the winner, Sir Cherokee, a long shot at 55-1. His investment: $20. "The Sir Cherokee win," he recalls, "was a simple case of selecting the long shot with just the right name."

Kentucky Derby 128, in 2002, was another pleasant wallet stuffer at $10,000, reaped by splitting $300 into exactas and trifectas. (And had our self-designated lordship bet his favorite combo on a superfecta, the take would have been a mere $66,000. But we digress.) Another fabulous moment, he recalls fondly, occurred at Ascot in 1990, during a jaunt with traveling pal Philly G. Off to the paddock, our players separately zeroed in on one of twenty-seven horses ready to go a 5-furlong race, running the opposite direction (of US of A) on a straightaway. Both took the horse with 40-1 odds and romped it. Mikey literally bagged £2,000.

Sundays of yore often caught our player at the old Longacres, resplendent in turf club attire, a treasured Sir Barton (first Triple Crown winner; wellspring of literary inspiration) pin affixed like a talisman to his Panama hat. Drink in the left hand, cigar in the right, Michael and friend would plunk maybe $120 each on five long shots. When the chosen ponies came in, the rewards were always pleasingly big, often pushing $7,000.

Internationally acclaimed for his gift of maximizing a good time, that 1990 Ascot trip perfectly illustrates Sir M's philosophy. The day was wonderful, the weather beautiful, the Moët et Chandon icy. Unable to cipher the British version of the *DRF*, he picked his winner from the herd. Our victorious travelers went to the cash-out window, where Phil scooped his £6,000 in the last of the cashier's pounds sterling. Just like Ole King Cole, Sir Mikey's payoff in pound coins made three bags full. He walked away with a decided swagger. "Then," he notes gleefully, "we went to the Horse and Groom Pub, bought drinks all around. Had a party. Next stop, France. Where we blew it all on Dom and caviar."

Handicapping? Stick with nightcapping. "Racing," Sir Michael affirms, "is meant to be fun. Have a cigar, have a drink. Take pictures, look at the fillies. Always visit the paddock, and don't bet the family fortune."

BELMONT PARK (ELMONT, LONG ISLAND)

It's raining. The track has been downgraded from fast to sloppy, and it keeps getting wetter. The clubhouse terrace is crowded; people are jostling to avoid the slanting downpour while protecting their views of the track. The crowd is psyched to witness the 135th Running of the Belmont Stakes (G1) later today. The afternoon race will decide the 2003 winner of racing's most demanding threesome. Funny Cide, the chestnut gelding who won the Kentucky Derby and the Preakness Stakes just weeks ago, may become the twelfth winner of the crown following Affirmed, who claimed the coveted prize back in 1978.

Outside the clubhouse, a sea of umbrellas bobs

A packed house

above a school of horse lovers who sidestep the puddles and mud for a look at the paddock parade. Many in this fashionable group of perfectly tailored jackets, gorgeous hats, and curve-hugging sundresses hold fiercely to the notion that it is summer at the Belmont. Not far from this impeccable parade, beside the grandstand entrance, sprawls a refugee city of tents and tarps; survivalists attempt to grill meat in defiance of the elements.

When the rain eases, we venture beyond the stone patio and paddock to the backyard, where the Big Sandy (as the Belmont racing surface is familiarly called) has dissolved into what should be called the Big Muddy. Beyond the hot dog and beer concessions, among keggers and picnic tables heaped with soggy food, Frisbee tossing and mud wrestling proceed apace, free of distractions in the grandstand.

The only flaw on this celebrated race day is that the crowds—and the weather—prevent full appreciation of the history and traditions that define Belmont Park. Fortunately, yesterday was picture perfect, with deep blue skies and big dreamy clouds. The sweeping grounds sparkled in late spring blossoms. The buzz of dress rehearsal filled the air, and we could roam freely, exploring and enjoying this Thoroughbred race park.

Funny Cide and José Santos before 2003 Belmont Stakes start

Belmont sprawls generously over 430 acres (originally 650 acres) in Queens County, Long Island. It was built at the turn of the twentieth century, when undeveloped land was more plentiful. Belmont founders William C. Whitney, his friendly stable rival James R. Keene, August Belmont II, E. D. and J. P. Morgan, and others in their syndicate transformed Foster's Meadow into a magnificent race park, which opened on May 4, 1905. Its main track of 1 ½ miles around, the longest (and widest) dirt track in America, has been praised by many owners and trainers as the best anywhere for horses. Its clubhouse, the exclusive dining rooms, and even the 1,277-foot grandstand excite wonder. The original trees now tower on scale with the grandstand. The showpiece of the paddock, a huge white pine, is more than a century and a

Bailey and Santos

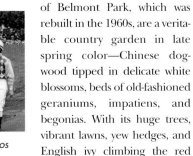

half old, its branches swooping fifty feet or more. Beneath its wide canopy stands a bronze sculpture of the phenomenal Secretariat in full stride above a thick carpet of pure white carnations. The grounds of Belmont Park, which was rebuilt in the 1960s, are a veritable country garden in late spring color—Chinese dogwood tipped in delicate white blossoms, beds of old-fashioned geraniums, impatiens, and begonias. With its huge trees, vibrant lawns, yew hedges, and English ivy climbing the red brick building to frame its high arched windows, Belmont clearly earns its reputation as one of the world's magnificent sporting sites.

A day of lighter attendance is good for reviewing Belmont's chronicle of wealthy and illustrious New York families, with their world-class stables and

SNAPSHOT - BELMONT PARK

Description: Luscious lawns, established landscaping, seasonal flowers, and climbing ivy provide a potent aesthetic to this 430-acre racetrack park. Belmont has the longest track in the United States; its main course is 1 ½ miles. Distance from the final turn to the finish line is 1,097 feet. The Widener Turf Course is 1 ⅜ miles, and the inner turf course is 1 ⅜ miles.

Season: Belmont hosts both spring and fall meets. The spring meet runs from early May until mid-July; the fall meet from early September to late October.

Address: 2150 Hempstead Turnpike, Elmont, Long Island; send correspondence to New York Racing Association, P.O. Box 90, Jamaica, NY 11417

Phone: 516-488-6000

Web site: http://www.nyra.com/belmont

Nearest airport: JFK International Airport (JFK)

Getting there: Skip the driving and parking hassle by taking the Long Island Rail Road from Penn Station in midtown Manhattan or from the Jamaica Station in Queens. For details, pick up the special Spring/Summer Long Island Rail Road timetable for Belmont Park, check the Web site at http://www.mta.info. Round-trip fare in summer 2003 was $10; special boarding gates are announced at the station. To avoid the most crowded time, get there an hour early. A taxi from midtown Manhattan is roughly $45 per person (in 2003), tip included.

Admission: Grandstand: $1; clubhouse: $2

Parking: $1; preferred: $4; valet: $5

Fine dining: The Garden Terrace Dining Room, The Paddock Dining Room

Casual fare: The Belmont Café, The Food Court, Hofbrau, Belmont Grill, backyard picnic area with concessions stands

Spirits: The Saloon, numerous bars throughout the facility

Extras: Twilight Racing Fridays; Breakfast at Belmont on many weekends; Family Fun Day on Sunday afternoons; special giveaways during the meet

appearances in the most prestigious contests in the country, including the Belmont Stakes—oldest of the Triple Crown competitions. The timeless story appears in the photos and portraits lining the walls of this huge facility. Every floor has a gallery displaying trophy presentations for incredible horses, such as Secretariat, who won the 1973 Belmont Stakes by thirty-one lengths; daring and athletic jockeys, such as Eddie Arcaro, who took the Belmont six times; celebrity owners and trainers; and America's unofficial royal families of horse racing. These exhibits underscore the deep sense of celebration, continuity, and significance that Americans—up and down the social ladder—have always attached to horse racing.

Funny Cide Light

This thrill of participating in communal celebrations is just one of the reasons we are nearly 102,000 strong this afternoon. Another is that this weekend's series of races—including the Acorn Stakes, the Manhattan Handicap, the Belmont, and the New York Stallion Stakes—adds up to total purses of more than $2.5 million. Belmont Park's spring and summer meets, running from early May to late July, include thirty graded stakes. The park reopens in September with more high stakes, as interest turns toward two-year-olds who may become next year's superstars. The biggest race of the year is the $1 million Belmont Stakes, and the crowd today is toughing it out, hoping history will be made. If the likeable, unassuming owners of Sackatoga Stables have a Triple Crown winner in their everyday horse Funny Cide, they will split an additional $5 million tossed into the pool by VISA, the king of plastic.

The late afternoon light is dull gray; the temperature has plunged to 55 degrees. The track has gone from fast to muddy to sloppy. As the 11th race approaches, out near the paddock the Harlem Jazz Ensemble strikes up Billy Joel's bluesy urban tribute "New York State of Mind."

The standing room–only crowd, as well as those who have been nibbling away at buffets on tables in private banquet areas, is heading for the exterior doors. The televisions all flash now to the Belmont post parade and display the final odds for this six-horse card: Empire Maker, Ten Most Wanted, Funny Cide, Dynever, Supervisor, and Scrimshaw. As the 135th running of the Belmont nears, race announcer Tom Durkin offers the simple classic lead, "Ladies and gentlemen, you're going to see a horse race."

You would not expect a hush to fall over a crowd of New Yorkers rooting for their state-bred horse, Funny Cide, but it does. Most of all, the fans want a Triple Crown winner, and the energy and emotion channeled into anticipating a Funny Cide victory are mighty. Urgency and hope charge the air, reinforced by the knowledge that horse racing is a chance adventure, an unpredictable contest.

When the gates at last slam open, Empire Maker bolts to a ½-length lead. Funny Cide catches him before the first turn and snatches the lead away. A thunderous roar from the spectators urges him on. Then at three-eighths of a mile to the finish line, Jerry Bailey on Empire Maker overtakes Funny Cide. In two minutes and twenty-eight seconds, with a ¾-length's lead over second-place finisher Ten Most Wanted, Empire Maker crosses the wire. Funny Cide finishes third, 4 ½ lengths back. The crowd is plunged into disbelief and disappointment. Though some losers boo the winner, with a little perspective most will come to admit that the better horse won that day.

SIR BARTON SCORES THE CROWN

The first winner of the Triple Crown was a bad-tempered, undistinguished three-year-old plagued by tender feet who required a strip of piano felt between each shoe and foot. Sir Barton was picked up in 1918 at a Saratoga sale by Commander J. K. L. Ross, a swashbuckling First World War Canadian naval hero who purchased the two-year-old for $10,000.

J. K. M. Ross, the owner's son and author of the book *Boots and Saddles* wrote that "Sir Barton was at times downright evil. It was always advisable to keep well clear of his heels, and even when facing him a handler had to be on guard, for Sir Barton could turn with the agility of a polo pony and kick with the power of a mule."

Sir Barton's only good race as a two-year-old came in the Belmont Futurity, where he placed second. Then, as a precocious three-year-old, he astounded everyone with a show of speed from chute to wire to break his maiden in the mud at the Kentucky Derby. A scant four days later, on May 14, 1919—on a lightning-fast track at Pimlico—the chestnut colt beat favored Eternal to win the Preakness Stakes. Showing stamina and heart, Sir Barton was odds-on at the Belmont Stakes on June 11, winning by 5 lengths and setting a U.S. record of 2:17 ⅘ for 1 ⅜ miles.

At age four, Sir Barton dominated the handicap ranks in the United States, often packing 130 pounds or more. His victories included the Havre de Grace, the Saratoga Handicap, and the Dominion Stakes at Fort Erie. The legendary jockey Earl Sande was aboard when the colt packed 129 pounds at Saratoga, defeating the remarkable Hall of Fame steed Exterminator in record time. Sande called this race "the best performance—time, weight, and class of opponents considered—I have ever witnessed. He gave the best handicap horses of his day a decisive beating while setting his own pace all the way."

Sir Barton was finally bested in a match race at Kenilworth Park in Windsor, Ontario, against the wickedly swift and brilliant Man o' War. In a curious turn of events, young jockey Sande, Sir Barton's regular rider, was taken off his mount just before the race and replaced with the more experienced Frank Keogh. Some say Sir Barton's tender feet were no match for the hard racing surface; whatever the reason, Man o' War crushed his rival by seven lengths. Sir Barton was never the same after the match race, and though he raced three more times that year, he never won again.

Nevertheless, he was the first horse to capture the grueling three jewels of the Triple Crown, in actuality winning four stakes races in a jaw-dropping thirty-two days. In 1930, when Gallant Fox swept the Kentucky Derby, the Preakness, and the Belmont Stakes, the Triple Crown series was born. Archival records showed that only Sir Barton had accomplished the same feat, and he was retroactively honored as America's first Triple Crown winner. —Larry Lee Palmer

Sir Barton, 1919, Thoroughbred racing's first Triple Crown winner

FINGER LAKES GAMING AND RACETRACK (FARMINGTON)

In 1962, the Finger Lakes Racing Association became the new kid brother to the three established NYRA racetracks in eastern New York. Its proximity to New York's Thoroughbred country has allowed the independent track to hold its own into the twenty-first century. In recent years, to keep purses competitive and cards full, Finger Lakes sometimes has trimmed its racing schedule. In a momentous turn of events, those lean days may have vanished. The new name, Finger Lakes Gaming and Racetrack, tells the story.

On a frigid day in February 2004, ten thousand people showed up to play in Finger Lakes's new $10 million gaming hall. As people filled the bold interior—finished in natural stone columns, dark ceilings, and wine barrel motifs—to claim one of the new video lottery terminals (VLTs), one wonders how many of them knew that the live horse racing conducted just beyond those new walls was the reason they could now play casino-type games there.

When the Finger Lakes meet opened in April 2004, the air was abuzz with possibility—not just for the season ahead, but for Finger Lakes racing from here on out. Thanks to projected revenues from its gaming facility, purse money here increased by more than 35 percent: $30,000 races jumped to $50,000. The biggest event of the year, the New York Derby, leg two of the Big Apple Triple for New York–bred three-year-olds (the other two are the Mike Lee Stakes at Belmont Park and the Albany Stakes at Saratoga), went from a purse of $125,000 to $150,000. If revenue estimates continue to be met, the percentage of gaming dollars going to the Finger Lakes track may do more than restore the competitive level of racing in western New York. This is the outcome all tracks that welcome slots, cards, or VLTs are counting on.

Into the first turn, Finger Lakes

Historically, Finger Lakes Racetrack has enjoyed many exciting moments. The most recent of them centered on the two-year-old filly Shesastonecoldfox, who won her first four starts in races at Saratoga, Finger Lakes, and Belmont Park. After she broke her maiden at the Spa, hometown fans cheered her two Finger Lakes victories, the Lady Finger Stakes and the New York Breeders' Futurity, which were run against several males. Only a few weeks later, in late September, she took Belmont's Joseph A. Grimma Stakes by 15 ½ lengths with Jerry Bailey on board.

Other grand moments centered on popular New York–bred Fio Rito, who won nineteen of twenty-seven starts here from 1977 to 1981. In 1980, he won the Wadsworth Memorial Cup, carrying an almost unheard of 138 pounds. The next year, he took the Whitney Handicap at Saratoga, making him the first New York–bred to claim a Grade 1 stakes race. That year, he set two speed records at Finger Lakes in six days. New York horse of the year in both 1980 and 1981, he was also Finger Lakes horse of the year from 1979–1981.

Though 28,000 square feet of space at Finger Lakes is new, the traditional racetrack atmosphere remains, with the Terrace Dining Room still overlooking the finish line and the wonderful pastoral countryside beyond it. The Paddock Room remains a great place to meet and watch the races. The biggest addition to the Finger Lakes racing facility, completed in 2001, is the equine exercise pool, one of a handful of U.S. equine therapy facilities.

Architects of the VLT facility made a substantial change to one area of track space: they created the Sevens Sports Bar, where game players and race lovers just might intermingle. Accessible from the track and casino common areas, it's a contemporary pub that seats one hundred. Designed with rich, natural materials, Sevens provides a grand view of the finish line.

SnapShot - Fingerlakes Gaming and Racetrack

Description: Finger Lakes, in rural western New York State near Rochester, opened in 1962, expanding in 2004 to include a multimillion-dollar casino. The track is a 1-mile oval, with chutes for 6-furlong and 1 ¼-mile races.

Season: 161 days, from mid-April to late November. Its biggest race is the New York Derby, at $150,000, run in July.

Address: 5857 Route 96, Farmington, NY 14425

Phone: 585-924-3232/(fax) 585-924-3967

Web site: http://www.fingerlakesracetrack.com

Nearest airport: Buffalo Niagara International Airport (BNIA); Greater Rochester International Airport (GRIA)

Getting there: Finger Lakes is on Route 96, approximately one-half mile south of the NYS Thruway (I-90). Check map or Web site for specific connector highways between I-90 and Route 96, depending on your approach. The racetrack is five and a half hours from New York City; three hours from Albany; one and one-quarter hours from Buffalo.

Admission: Free

Parking: Free

Fine dining: The (clubhouse) Terrace, Fio Rito Room for groups

Casual fare: The Paddock Room, Vineyard Food Court, Jake's Coffeehouse

Spirits: Sevens Sports Bar, other stations throughout

Extras: Regular racing gift promotions, video gaming

THE ARCHIVIST

"I haven't fed a horse, trained a horse, or ridden a horse," Tom Gilcoyne volunteers. "The only part of me that's ever been on a horse," he says in his smooth, deadpan voice, "is my wallet." But the handsome, fit, six-foot-four octogenarian with the ruler-straight posture of a five-star general has devoted much of his life to Thoroughbred racing. As a result, he has an encyclopedic knowledge of racing history and culture. For almost twenty years after his retirement, this man of genuine warmth and good humor volunteered his time to the National Museum of Racing and Hall of Fame in Saratoga Springs. He knows its historic collections well, and for years he contributed a regular column to the museum's newsletter.

Tom's appetite for all things Thoroughbred began in his childhood. He's been going to the races since 1923, when he was six. His parents took him to his first Travers Stakes at Saratoga in 1924, and he watched his first Belmont Stakes in 1931. "My father was a devout racetracker. His vacation always coincided with the Saratoga racing season, and so a day at the races and dining afterward was what we did." The racing experience became a father-son weekend outing they continued well into the 1930s. They were the best times he has had at the races.

A professional career with a national company meant that Tom traveled extensively. "Wherever there was a track available, I didn't pass it up." He was at Hollywood Park in 1951 when Citation won the Hollywood Gold Cup and became the first Thoroughbred to reach the $1 million mark in earnings. At Arlington Park he watched the future American Triple Crown winner Whirlaway run as a two-year-old. "He didn't win, but I predicted to friends that he *would* be a winner." One of the biggest disappointments he saw was in the 1978 Travers, at Saratoga, when Affirmed won the race but was disqualified, and the prize went instead to Alydar.

Tom's involvement with the National Museum of Racing began not long after his retirement in 1991, when he and a racing colleague were visiting the museum. In the hall of fame room, they spotted a color error in a display of jockey silks. The director overheard the conversation and immediately suggested they come to work at the museum. That invitation launched Tom's tenure at the museum. He spent several years, too, as a placing judge at the Far Hills steeplechase course in New Jersey, "the closest thing to pure sport that's left in racing."

One of the biggest surprises ever for this racing authority centered on the Hall of Fame presentation in August 2002, in conjunction with Saratoga's annual Fastig-Tipton yearling sale. Ten minutes before the presentation, officials learned that the designated speaker would not be arriving. As Tom walked in, "they pulled me aside and said, 'You're on.' I improvised, to get the job done."

Recently, Tom decided to retire from his museum activities. "I turned eighty-eight on my last birthday," he pointed out. "It was time to leave before they stuffed me and stood me in a corner." Besides, he added with a lilt in his voice, it was time to get serious about his golf game.

Archivist emeritus Tom Gilcoyne

SARATOGA RACE COURSE
(SARATOGA SPRINGS)

In the eighteenth century, the Mohawk Indians, who revered the local springs and geysers for their spiritual powers, introduced the British to *Saraghtoga*, the "place of swift water." After Americans took this land for themselves at the end of the Revolutionary War, the affluent also began taking the cure here, trusting in the power of the healing drink and the therapeutic soak in the hot mineral waters.

In the nineteenth century, because of its healing waters, Saratoga Springs became the premier resort in America. In 1863, Saratoga Race Course opened and soon became the vital organ of this small community. Almost a century and a half later, the oldest existing racetrack in America stands essentially unchanged, tradition preserved and historic ambiance protected. The grandstand itself, though modernized over the years, is the original one.

To its patrons, Saratoga is the mecca of horse racing. Prominent Saratogians support the horse racing industry and the cultural arts and fill the season with private dinners and parties. The exclusive

Opening day 2003, Saratoga Race Course

annual Fasig-Tipton Thoroughbred yearling sale runs for several days and is held at the Humphrey Finney Pavilion, next to the National Racing Museum and across from the Saratoga training track. This annual auction is just one of many interesting events the public can attend. All in all, this is the undisputed summertime scene for anyone who takes horse racing seriously. It spotlights some of the highest-caliber Thoroughbreds in the country.

For a fleeting period each summer, all eyes in Saratoga Springs turn toward the track, with its familiar turreted grandstand; its clubhouse and pavilions trimmed in crisp green and white stripes; and its white rail fences colorful with hanging baskets of flowers. Many in the

Jockeys and horses in Saratoga's walking ring

racing circle keep their private spectator boxes for decades, even generations. With the entire community passionate about the races, dressing up to attend them daily, and greeting each other with warmth and excitement, the atmosphere says country club.

Beginning in late July when the meet opens, Saratoga's schedule offers more than $11 million in purses, with big stakes and handicaps featured nearly every day during the six-week meet. The Travers Stakes, most celebrated of Saratoga's dozen-plus Grade 1 races, annually draws some of the nation's top three-year-olds to compete for its $1 million pot, and leading jockeys from across the country are also on the scene. Many of these horses and riders will go on to compete in the championship Breeders' Cup races later in the autumn.

We arrived in Saratoga Springs on Sunday of opening week. By the time we had checked in and walked to the track, it was raining. In spite of intermittent thunderstorms, with lightning and rain coming down in buckets at times, a very large crowd was already here. During the warm afternoon, the official track condition went from sloppy to muddy to good. After a break for sunshine, it poured again, and

Saratoga's popular picnic area

the track was downgraded once more to sloppy; more heavy rain followed. But even the sticky humidity did not subdue the excitement of racing. The picnickers were not deterred by the weather; they huddled under canopies with their assortments of sandwiches, gourmet temptations, and barbeques. It's clear that the outdoor lunch, carried in a traditional wicker picnic basket and cooler, and served up under deep green or striped tents and umbrellas, is popular with Saratoga fans.

Wet or dry, we can't say enough about Saratoga Race Course. The setting is wonderful and we had a grand time. As we bet on Moët et Chandon champagne to drive away any lingering thunderclouds, we went on record saying that everyone should experience this elegant venue at least once in a decade.

SnapShot - Saratoga Race Course

Description: 350-acre racetrack. The main course is 1 ⅛ mile long; turf course is 1 mile.
Season: Six-week meeting in the summer beginning in July
Address: Saratoga Race Course, 267 Union Avenue, Saratoga Springs, NY 12866
Phone: 718-641-4700/516-488-6000
Web site: http://www.nyra.com/saratoga/
Nearest airport: John F. Kennedy International, New York (JFK)
Getting there: At press time, Amtrak leaves Penn Station in New York City twice daily; from the stop at Saratoga Springs, taxis deliver passengers into town. Check the Web site, http://www.amtrak.com, or phone 888-USA-RAIL, for further information.
Admission: Grandstand: $3; clubhouse: $5; children under age twelve: free with parent or guardian
Parking: Free; Oklahoma preferred parking: $5
Fine dining: The Turf Terrace Dining Room, strict dress code
Casual fare: The Porch, Club Terrace, At the Rail Pavilion, The Carousel, the Paddock Tent (check with track or Web site for dress codes)
Spirits: Travers Bar, Jim Dandy Bar

PENNSYLVANIA

PENN NATIONAL RACE COURSE (GRANTVILLE)

Late night travelers on Pennsylvania's I-81 must wonder why the sky glows so in the north. Steel light posts loom above the dark ridge, each bank of bright lights encased in a swirling cloud of insects. The lights form an oval shape, the mystery of what is beneath them concealed by the forest that lies between them and the highway.

Turning off the highway at the Grantville, Pennsylvania, exit, the traveler heads north on a country lane for a short distance. A colorful wooden sign announces the answer to the question that brought him to this place. Penn National Race Course lies nestled against one of the long shale ridges that march down this central Pennsylvania valley, its tan stone exterior blending with the iron rich soil in the Susquehanna River valley. Behind the low, square grandstand, the

Penn National, Grantville, Pa.

racetrack is visible, lit up as if it were noon instead of nighttime.

Built in 1970, the stands are comfortably arranged, with the typical glassed-in front overlooking a tight, fast racing surface. The saddling paddock is a brightly colored oasis, tucked in against the left side of the grandstand. Upstairs, diners relax in the dining room overlooking the track.

Action around the first turn, Penn National

Simulcast players flick through the TV menu of races as the horses are led to the paddock below. On a hot July night, the moon rises behind the backstretch, bloated and orange, tremendous in the summer atmosphere. Horses being led up to the saddling paddock emerge into the light like stars on a stage, feet prancing and necks arched.

A look at the program reveals a varied race card, with conditions ranging from races with nonwinners of a race within the past year competing for $2,500 to allowance and stakes races carrying as much as $50,000 purses. With Pennsylvania on a fast track to slots, the industry is poised for a renaissance, with trainers from all over the East Coast looking to race here.

Checking the competition at Penn National

At last, the final race of the evening is run, and the lights are extinguished. In the stable area, horses shuffle and snort as they settle down for the night, the long fingers of light from the moon their nightlight.

SNAPSHOT - PENN NATIONAL

Description: Penn National has grown up in a big way since it opened its doors in August 1972. It has simulcasting facilities at six Pennsylvania locations. Racing is held at night on the 1-mile-long dirt track or on the 7-furlong turf course. Two chutes open onto the main track, one at the quarter-mile pole and one at the three-quarter-mile pole. The horses battle to the wire at the end of a 990-foot homestretch.

Season: Penn National races year-round, braving winter storms where snowfall is measured in feet instead of inches. It begins its season with the Mountainview Thoroughbred Racing Association Meet, running from January until the end of August. After a brief break, racing resumes with the Penn National Turf Club Meet from the beginning of September until the end of December.

Address: 720 Bow Creek Road, Grantville, PA, 17028; send correspondence to P.O. Box 32, Grantville, PA 17028

Phone: 717-469-2211/(fax) 717-469-2910

Web site: http://www. pennnational.com

Nearest airport: Harrisburg International Airport (HIA)

Getting there: From Philadelphia, take the Pennsylvania Turnpike north to exit 19 (Harrisburg). Proceed north on I-283 to I-81 North. Take I-81 North to exit 80. At the top of the ramp, turn left. The track is approximately one-half mile ahead on the right. From Harrisburg, follow I-81 North to exit 80. At the top of the ramp, turn left. The track is one-half mile on the right.

Admission: $2

Parking: Included in the admission

Fine dining: Mountainview Terrace

Casual fare: Various concessions available throughout the grandstand for sandwiches, hamburgers, and other light fare

Spirits: Numerous bars throughout the stands

Extras: VIP party rooms, casino gaming activities

PHILADELPHIA PARK (BENSALEM)

Just before the 2004 Kentucky Derby's double starting gates slammed open, a commentator at Churchill Downs reviewed the lineup and casually described Philadelphia Park as off the beaten path. He had Pennsylvania-bred colt Smarty Jones in mind. Smarty was working class, people said, all blue collar, even though he was six for six in his short racing life. But by 6:15 on Derby evening, Smarty Jones was sporting the coveted blanket of red roses, and Philadelphia Park had become Main Street, USA.

Short field out of the gate, Philadelphia Park

The race park Smarty called home came into existence in 1984. It is the reincarnation of Keystone Race Track, which was built in 1972 on this now-suburban site. When the track changed hands and took its present name, a turf course was installed. Management also developed an in-state simulcast-like system that broadcast betting tips and live race coverage from the park. New owners took over again in 1990 and expanded off-track wagering sites into the greater Philadelphia area. Though Philadelphia Park races year-round, its management direction aims as much toward promoting the convenience of visiting what it calls its Turf Club sites as it does toward drawing new patrons to the live sport at the facility.

Philadelphia Park rang in the millennium by undergoing a major over-

Rounding the final turn at Philly

haul. The two-story facility has become a comfortable and inviting destination, its corporatelike interior featuring marble and native stone, large round columns, bold colors, and geometric carpet designs. A full-size horse sculpture and a two-tier fountain enhance the bright new lobby. The Sports View Bar and Grill, designed with contemporary curved lines and marble finishes, is a sleek, busy gathering spot, filled with tables and chairs and lots of large-screen TVs. Special luncheons and other celebrations are held in the Pennsylvania Derby Dining Room, also on the second floor. In this room, the Cella family, owners of Oaklawn Park, presented Smarty Jones's $5 million Centennial Bonus check for winning three Oaklawn Park races along with the Kentucky Derby to his owners, Roy and Patricia Chapman. The covered grandstand and horsemen's boxed seating in greens and violets complete the mix of seating options for patrons. In

Philadelphia Park picnickers

nice weather, horseplayers can spread out in the large new picnic grove, shaded by tall trees, and kick back at several watering-hole cabanas and cafés.

Two of Philadelphia Park's most popular races are the $750,000 Pennsylvania Derby (G2), at 1 ⅛ miles for three-year-olds, and the $300,000 Cotillion Handicap (G2) for fillies. The seven-furlong season finale is the Pennsylvania Nursery Stakes, which of course "Smartypants" Jones won in 2003.

SnapShot - Philadelphia Park

Description: In 1999, the track underwent extensive renovations to the grandstands, raising the level of fan comfort. Today, the track is proud of its simulcasting and telephone wagering systems. A 1-mile track with two chutes surrounds a 7-furlong turf course. The homestretch is 974 feet from last turn to wire.

Season: The season runs from January 1 to December 31, with summer steeplechase events. The park's popular races include the Pennsylvania Derby (G3), a 1 ⅛ miler for three-year-olds, and the Pennsylvania Nursery Stakes, run in mid-November.

Address: 3001 Street Road, Bensalem, PA 19020

Phone: 215-639-9000/800-523-6886/(fax) 215-639-8330

Web site: http://www. philadelphiapark.com

Nearest airport: Philadelphia International Airport (PHL)

Getting there: Take I-95 to Route 132 West (Street Road). The track is three miles from the highway. From Route 1, take Route 132 (Street Road). The track is three miles ahead. Check the Web site for more details.

Admission: $3

Parking: Free; valet parking is extra

Fine dining: Pennsylvania Derby Room, televisions on every table, upscale menu, reservations are suggested

Casual fare: Finish Line Café, tables with TVs and personal wagering terminals; Horseman's Café; Finish Line Deli; Paddock Deli; My Juliet Café

Spirits: Finish Line Bar, Ultimate Sports View Bar

Extras: Special live music events; track and sponsor giveaways; gift shop

NORTHEAST TRAVEL SECTION

BELOW, YOU'LL FIND A MILEAGE CHART LISTING THE DISTANCES BETWEEN THE REGIONAL RACETRACKS AND ALL THE CITIES DISCUSSED IN THE FOLLOWING TRAVEL SECTION. THE CITY OR CITIES CLOSEST TO A TRACK ARE INDICATED BY AN X.

COAST TO COAST	Boston, Mass.	Fingers Lakes Region, N.Y.	Harrisburg, Pa.	New York, N.Y.	Northampton, Mass.	Philadelphia, Pa.	Saratoga Springs, N.Y.	Wilmington, Del.
Aqueduct Racetrack (New York)	210 miles	320 miles	95 miles	**X** 15 miles	160 miles	110 miles	195 miles	135 miles
Belmont Park (New York)	210 miles	325 miles	105 miles	**X** 20 miles	160 miles	115 miles	195 miles	145 miles
Delaware Park (Delaware)	340 miles	340 miles	55 miles	130 miles	290 miles	40 miles	310 miles	**X** 10 miles
Finger Lakes Gaming and Racetrack (New York)	375 miles	**X** 30 miles	330 miles	315 miles	300 miles	325 miles	205 miles	340 miles
Meadowlands Racetrack (New Jersey)	220 miles	300 miles	85 miles	**X** 15 miles	165 miles	95 miles	175 miles	125 miles
Monmouth Park (New Jersey)	265 miles	340 miles	70 miles	**X** 55 miles	215 miles	85 miles	235 miles	110 miles
Penn National Race Course (Pennsylvania)	380 miles	230 miles	105 miles	**X** 55 miles	355 miles	100 miles	315 miles	95 miles
Philadelphia Park (Pennsylvania)	295 miles	310 miles	**X** * miles	80 miles	240 miles	**X** 20 miles	250 miles	45 miles
Saratoga Race Course (New York)	200 miles	195 miles	255 miles	190 miles	125 miles	265 miles	**X** * miles	310 miles
Suffolk Downs (Massachusetts)	**X** * miles	370 miles	305 miles	220 miles	110 miles	315 miles	205 miles	345 miles
Three County Fair (Massachusetts)	105 miles	285 miles	245 miles	160 miles	**X** * miles	260 miles	125 miles	285 miles

*The racetrack is located inside or within 10 miles of the city limits.

MUST SEE / MUST DO

DELAWARE

WILMINGTON

Sitting at the confluence of the Brandywine and the Christina rivers in the Brandywine Valley, Wilmington was the first permanent settlement in Delaware. The Civil War brought the city's most important social legacy as the last stop on the Underground Railroad.

Wilmington's—in fact, all of Delaware's—past and present is rooted in the ambitions of a remarkable family of French immigrants, the duPont de Nemours clan, who settled there in the early 1800s and established a gunpowder mill beside the Brandywine. Supplying explosives during the War of 1812 and the Civil War (and supplying 40 percent of the Allied forces' firepower in World War I), the duPonts commanded a fortune that they expanded into synthetics. They made Wilmington their world headquarters, and along with shipbuilding, cotton mills, railroad cars, and other manufacturing industries, the city flourished. In the twentieth century, politically influential duPont heirs supported liberal state incorporation laws that especially attracted major banking institutions, making Wilmington the financial-electronics capital of the country today.

Wilmington is the state's largest city, with a population close to 75,000. Its unique political and industrial history and the philanthropy of its leading families have made it a culturally significant New England destination. Redevelopment has revitalized both riverfronts, making the city youthful and touristy again.

Explore the city's museums and its Grand Opera House on Market Street, and maybe catch a theatrical performance. Wilmington is restoring the riverfront, so hop on a water taxi and cruise the Christina River from Market Street. Take a microbrew break. Tour the duPont mansions, whose interior spaces and gardens are historical treasures.

The **Riverfront Market Street at the Christina River** (302-425-4454; http://www.riverfrontwilmington.com), is an old shipbuilding and factory district, accessible by a long landscaped promenade. Parks, shops, specialty foods, pubs, and other businesses are moving in. Explore it all, have lunch, have a brew at the **Iron Hill Brewery** or the **Washington Street Alehouse** (see listings), and then hop aboard *Le-Roy*, the Water Taxi (302-530-5069). Stop and reboard at numerous locations for just one ticket.

The **Winterthur Museum and Country Estate** (800-448-3883; http://www.winterthur.org), on Route 53, six miles northwest of Wilmington in Winterthur, is called the premier museum of American furniture. It was built by Henry Francis duPont (1880–1969), an antiques collector and gardener, who amassed some 85,000 items representing major American furniture styles and crafts from 1640 to 1860, now displayed in numerous period galleries. The sixty acres of gardens surrounding the mansion create a pageant of color throughout the growing seasons. It's open Tuesday through Sunday, 10:00–5:00; admission ranges from $15–$30, depending on tour.

The Conservatory, Winterthur

DuPont dining room, Winterthur

The **Hagley Museum and Library** (302-658-2400; http://www.hagley.lib.de.us) can be found just past the junction of Routes 141 and 100, at 298 Buck Road East, eight miles northwest of Wilmington. Hagley is the ancestral home of the duPont family and the site of the original gunpowder works founded by E. I. duPont in 1802. The 235-acre grounds include restored mills, the family's lavish five-genera-tion home, a laborers' community, gardens, and a research center. The Hagley Library on the grounds is an archive and modern scientific research center for the preservation, study, and advancement of technolo-gy. Several tours are available. Special events include an annual auto show, and there are hands-on exhibits, such as duPont's NASCAR no. 24, which you can sit in but not race. March 15 through December 31, 9:30–4:30 daily/call ext. 259 for winter hours and tour schedules. Admission for adults is $11; students and seniors, $9; and kids 6–14, $4.

MASSACHUSETTS

BOSTON

Eleven ships carrying Puritans crossed the Atlantic from England in 1630 and put in at Massachusetts Bay. They brought a charter granting them the land between the Charles and the Merrimack rivers, extending from the Atlantic to the Pacific oceans. The immigrants scattered; some 120 of them settled along the Charles River, on a rise they named Boston, reminis-cent of one of their English villages. When they found the soil too rocky and poor for farming, they turned to the sea. A fortune awaited them in the deep, frigid waters, rich with cod. Robust sea trade among the West Indies, England, France, and Spain brought the immigrants rum, molasses, slaves, and wine in exchange for fish. Soon Boston was the premier port in the colonies.

A wealthy new merchant class elbowed in alongside the town's pious Puritan founders. Grand homes rose up, and Boston proper took form. In 1635, America's first public school was founded here; Harvard University opened one year later. During the cen-tury that Boston thrived as the most important center in the New World— earning its distinction as Hub of the Universe—colonial resistance to English authority, oppression, and heavy taxation grew until the water-shed moment when Paul Revere and

Paul Revere bronze, Boston

Skaters on the Frog Pond, Boston Common

other patriots crept onto Griffin's Wharf disguised as Indians and silently dumped a cargo of British tea into the harbor.

In Philadelphia, the Second Continental Congress voted in 1775 to raise a colonial army. Six long, bloody years later, the British were defeated and a new nation was born. That a handful of struggling little colonies huddled at the edge of a continent could unite with a dedication so powerful they would overcome one of the world's mightiest armies is one of the great stories of history.

Our early March weekend here fell in the hollow between winter's dull edge and spring's lusty budding. Although not lush and lovely in leaf or flower, the city was nevertheless starkly handsome. Its acclaimed architectural lines and angles, a strong marriage of old and new design, stood in bold focus. The grass on **Boston Common**—America's oldest public park—lay matted and brown, trees lining the footpaths pointed barren branches toward the steely gray sky, and lightly bundled ice skaters spun smooth, graceful orbs on frozen Frog Pond. Framing the whole was a wide square of regal churches, brick apartment buildings, shops and pubs in solid rows, and the tall, private homes on Beacon Street, once called the most prestigious address in America. Boston, cradle of the American Revolution, where courageous people and pro-

State House

found events sculpted the young face of freedom, remains a living stage.

To show us the vitality of Boston's history, the city has literally mapped out the essential Freedom Trail, a three-mile walk that takes you to sixteen of the most historic spots in Boston's—and the nation's—colonial and revolutionary history. Walk the Freedom Trail, marked on most tourist maps, in a full day or in a weekend, or choose the sites that interest you most. The "trail," marked with a red painted line on the sidewalks, goes from Boston Common to Charlestown.

Starting your walk at Charlestown puts the geography of land and sea into perspective. It was here that John Winthrop and his Puritans first settled before moving across the river to Boston. Go early to the **Charlestown Navy Yard** for an uncrowded tour of the *USS Constitution* ("Old Ironsides"), the oldest commissioned warship in the world, launched in 1797 and used against the British in the War of 1812. Visit the museum next door as well. **Bunker Hill Monument**, the next stop, actually puts you on Breed's Hill, the scene of one of the first battles of the war. **The Old State House** (Boston Historical Society, 617-720-3292), site of the Boston Massacre, is a National Historic Site in the financial district on Washington and State streets. Right across the street at 15 State Street is the **National Park Visitors Center** (www.nps.gov/bost), where the staff can answer questions and load you up with informative brochures to your heart's content. The tour also takes you into the North End, boyhood turf of the original Midnight Rider.

See some of Paul Revere's silver work pieces at the **Museum of Fine Arts** (465 Huntington Avenue; 617-267-9300; http://www.mfa.org). His sterling silver Sons of Liberty bowl, called

The Museum of Fine Arts, Boston

one of America's three most cherished historical treasures, is here. The MFA is one of the nation's very best, for American as well as international paintings and objects, with many Bostonian portraits by Gilbert Stuart, John Singleton Copley, and others, and fine collections of folk art and impressionist art. MFA also has an airy little restaurant and a nice big gift shop.

Boston offers tours of every sort, some free, by many groups. For architecture, the elite Beacon Hill neighborhood is one of dignified homes, some designed by America's first professional architect, Charles Bullfinch, who went on to design the U.S. Capitol. Walk Chestnut, Mount Vernon, and Pickney streets, and check out the works of other architects, including Henry Hobson Richardson and I. M. Pei.

A **literary tour** opens the worlds of Henry David Thoreau, Henry Wadsworth Longfellow (his home in Cambridge was Washington's headquarters during the first months of the war), Louisa May Alcott, and other eminent writers. Get your bearings at http://www.searchboston.com and http://www.bostonbyfoot.com.

Boston's waterfront, essentially stretching from the mouth of Fort Point Channel up to the Inner Harbor, is lined with expensive condominiums and small marinas. It is also filled with stunning views and relaxing, fun places to go to, including the **New England Aquarium**;

Christopher Columbus Waterfront Park, with its Rose Kennedy Rose Garden; whale watching; harbor cruises; and historic wharves. In the channel at Congress Street Bridge are the **Boston Tea Party Exhibit**, a small museum (closed until at least the fall of 2006), and a replica of the *Beaver II*, one of the three fateful ships that carried the tea—90,000 pounds of leaves—into the harbor, all of which became iced tea on the night of December 16, 1773.

We accidentally stumbled upon high-end shopping. Taxiing east from the Museum of Fine Arts, we passed tall thickets of wheatlike reeds, reminding us that this area was once shallow marshland. Now reclaimed, the Back Bay area isn't what we expected. (In *The Bostonians*, Henry James may have said it first: "Don't you hate the name?") With a bit of municipal engineering and a grand, ambitious design, Back Bay is now likened to the Champs-Elysées. It is first-class shopping along wide Newbury and Boylston streets, where bold, handsome buildings house exclusive stores and designer boutiques offer the best labels in clothing, gifts, and housewares.

Boston is home to the Boston Red Sox, who play at **Fenway Park** in the Back Bay. The Bruins fire the puck and the Celtics sink hoops, both at TD Banknorth Garden (formerly named FleetCenter; 617-624-1000) at 1 Fleet Center Place. Fenway Park (617-226-6666) is open for tours in the off-season. And, of course, the Boston Marathon beckons the fleet footed on Patriot's Day, every April. The New England Patriots, champs of both the 2002 and 2004 Super Bowls, play in Foxborough, MA (800-543-1776 for info). Catch up with Boston teams and see about tickets by visiting http://www.bostonsportsmedia.com, http://www.boston.com/sports, and http://www.bostonmarathon.org.

ROBIN BLEDSOE, BOOKSELLER

Downtown Cambridge, noontime. Gaggles of college students stroll the sidewalk, sipping on lattes. Traffic is a constant metal throng. Overhead, a departing jet from Logan Airport thunders by, obliterating the street noise. We pass trendy little shops filled with designer clothing and turn in at a blue banner hung perpendicularly to the building. A few steps from the street we pass through an arched gate of white latticework and come upon a neat little garden. Street noise is muted here, and the trees cast dappled shade against pools of midday sunlight. At the far length of the building, a modest green sign, Books, hangs above a basement door. Inside, the stairs drop into small, rambling rooms packed floor to ceiling with equestrian, art, and architecture books of all sizes, shapes, and ages.

Proprietor Robin Bledsoe, an equestrian bookseller for more than thirty years, has distinguished herself in the antiquarian horse book world, bridging the gap between the backside life and the illustrated coffee-table book. A native of northern California, she studied art history at Wellesley and Columbia and in 1973 began to indulge her dual love of all things art and equestrian, collecting and selling volumes part time. In 1983, she opened her shop, dedicated to locating and stocking rare and hard-to-find books. Her inventory ranges from secondhand books on basic equine knowledge to scarce limited editions, sometimes in foreign languages. Of the hardest to find books, Bledsoe tells us, the first edition of *Black Beauty* by Anna Sewell, published in 1877, ranks among the rarest. Another rarity: *Notes on the Thoroughbred from Kentucky Newspapers* by John L. O'Connor (np, 1926), in an edition of fewer than ten copies, came into her hands just once and quickly left the shop.

The bookshop is located at 1640 Massachusetts Avenue, Cambridge, MA 02138. Call ahead to confirm hours or to arrange an appointment. (Phone 617-576-3634; fax 617-661-2445; robin.bledsoe@verizon.net.) Bledsoe's new acquisitions are announced in her regular catalogs; communications with collectors fly over the Internet; and she regularly exhibits selections from her inventory at equestrian trade shows. Yet nothing beats exploring the shelves of her shop for the simple joy of leafing carefully through a priceless tome or a sleek, crisp first edition.

Bookseller Robin Bledsoe

NORTHAMPTON

The rural, old-fashioned flavor of horse racing at the Three County Fair reminds you that the Connecticut River valley's beginnings are agricultural. The ambiance changes from country to cosmopolitan when you venture into Northampton, leaving behind horses and the squeals of children on fast carnival rides. The city, home to Smith College for women, emits its energetic liberal streak, obvious in its eclectic shopping, great museums, fine theater and literary evenings, and spirited nightlife. With architectural styles dating back to the 1700s, the historic business district, the residential neighborhoods, and the lovely Smith campus make it a great walking town. You can't go far without bumping into significant cultural history everywhere. Our favorite Web site for information about the city of Northampton is http://www.northamptonuncommon.com.

Revisit that old college spirit with a walking tour of the **Smith campus**, entering through the ornate iron gates on Elm Street. The campus's **Museum of Art**, in the **Brown Fine Arts Center**, holds a world-class collection, and CK's Café in the atrium serves lunch. The entire campus is an arboretum designed originally by Frederick Law Olmsted. Stop at the **Smith Botanic Garden** at the Lyman Conservatory on College Lane and catch the waterfall at the edge of campus. Check

http://www.smith.edu for current activities, day and evening events, and directions.

Northampton isn't just a hotbed of intellectualism. It's also a vigorous center for artists and writers, with dozens of galleries and author readings at downtown bookstores. Stroll the energetic business district (Main Street, for starters), and stop for window shopping and drinks along the way. Take in Thornes Marketplace (150 Main Street), a historic building renovated into several floors of specialty stores, galleries, bookstores, salons, crafts, a live theater, and more. Investigate at http://www.thornesmarketplace.com.

NEW YORK

FINGER LAKES REGION AND NIAGARA FALLS

After leaving either the U.S. or the Canadian track, start your tour with a stop in historic Seneca Falls, then drive south through the Finger Lakes region and enjoy the wine country in the hills. Spend time in Ithaca, home of Cornell University. End your excursion in Buffalo, with a day or two at Niagara Falls.

Take to the waters of Canandaigua Lake on a boat tour narrating the geology of the Finger Lakes. In Seneca Falls, tip your hat to Elizabeth Cady Stanton, mother of women's rights, with a visit to the **National Women's Hall of Fame** and the **Women's Rights National Historic**

Hotel Northampton

Niagara Falls

Park, which includes the restored **Elizabeth Cady Stanton House**.

Dotting the hills along the highways between Cayuga and Seneca lakes are a number of wineries; some in Finger Lakes have rated 86 on the *Wine Spectator* scale. From the southern lakes region head west to Corning, where several glass museums display the technology that has developed both industrial and exquisite glass items. Returning to the shores of Lake Erie, walk the handsome, historic city of **Buffalo**. Everything that you need to know about the area is yours at http://www.tripadvisor.com. In the search window, enter the city and state.

Widmer's Wine

Top off your getaway with the spectacular sights and roaring sprays of Niagara Falls. "[T]he Universe does not afford its Parallel," Franciscan missionary Fr. Hennepin wrote in 1687, after he watched the waters of the falls roar and "foam and boil" in a "hideous manner." Millions of visitors have followed him to the site of America's oldest state park, established in 1885. The wild water's fresh, natural beauty lures you away from the hokey tourist traps. Niagara's abundance of parks, trails, and paths lets you feel as if you're alone in the world, at least for a little while.

Niagara Falls is best navigated by public transportation from outlying areas, such as Buffalo, where you can arrange round-trip transit via bus. The visitors' center at the **Niagara Falls State Park** (called Niagara Reservation State Park on the New York side) is open year-round, though hours vary seasonally. From the park, hike out to the American and the Luna falls; take a ride on the legendary *Maid of the Mist* excur-

sion boat below the falls (716-284-8897), boarding it at Prospect Point in the park. If you have time, pack a lunch and walk through the **Cave of the Winds**, behind American Falls. (Get to it via the elevator from scenic Goat Island in the Niagara River, which separates the Canadian and U.S. sides of the falls.) Return at night to enjoy the lights on the water, which infuse the falls with a mystical, magical glow. Take in the history of the Niagara Falls area at Old Fort Niagara State Park, at the mouth of the Niagara River. Before you go, use the following Web sites for Niagara Falls State Park and Niagara County to get maps, make your list of places and sights not to miss, and check seasonal dates, hours, and rates of tourist sites: http://www.niagarafallsstatepark.com; http://www.niagara-usa.com.

NEW YORK CITY

New York City feels endless. It's an energetic metropolis and one of the most exciting destinations in the world. Whatever you seek—art, architecture, history, sports, shopping, theater, dining—it awaits you. If you go for a three-day weekend, with two full days at Belmont Park, Aqueduct Racetrack, Monmouth Park, or even Saratoga Race Course, you'll have two free evenings and a Sunday for the city that never sleeps. What follows is our recipe for twenty-four unforgettable hours in the streets of Manhattan.

Love, New York City

We flew in from San Francisco on a Thursday evening in early June and took a cab from JFK airport to our hotel in midtown Manhattan, where we checked in, caught our breath, and then set out to wander the almost deserted streets. We stopped often to appreciate the artistry of urban architectural lines on inspiring nineteenth-century churches that stood elbow to shoulder beside soaring art deco or ultramodern skyscrapers. Five blocks from our hotel, we happened upon La Vineria, which served up a soothing Italian dinner and robust wines that capped our long day.

Friday morning kicked off the big stakes weekend at Belmont Park. Returning to in Manhattan that evening, we told our cabbie simply, "Take us to the Village." Hopping out on West Broadway, we walked a wide grid around **Greenwich Village** that took in Broome, Mott, Bleecker, and several side streets. Sidewalks and stairwells were a crush of animated people enjoying the first warm summer evening. Slender trees in new leaf, tiny street-side gardens, and rows of streetlamps added charm and color to this celebrated counterculture district of coffeehouses, bars, shops, eateries, and old row houses.

On Saturday, we waited all day through the cold rain, sorry that Funny Cide lost this final Triple Crown race. Back in mid-town Manhattan, we had a nightcap at the Plaza Hotel's storied Oak Bar (closed now during the Plaza's extreme makeover, but we hope it lives again), where we heard squealing and commotion from the dark leather corner booth and soon spotted actor and city dweller Bruce Willis and entourage outside the window.

A serious tour of the sidewalks of New York was our Sunday morning plan,

Greenwich Village

Central Park

Grand Central Terminal

beginning with **Central Park**. Strolling into the 843-acre park via 7th Avenue (opting for a piece of the whole rather than a hike around the six-mile perimeter), we followed an ungroomed wooded path past the Hecksher Playground, uphill and through a terrain of huge granite boulders, around the Pond, eventually leaving the park at East 59th Street at the Pulitzer Fountain, the centerpiece of the Grand Army Plaza. The fountain, donated by Joseph Pulitzer and located at 59th and 5th Avenue, was placed in the Plaza in 1916. It features round granite basins that catch cascading water, and a bronze statue of Pomona, the Roman goddess of abundance.

Next, we went to **Grand Central Terminal**, at East 42nd Street at Park Avenue. *Grand* is a modest description of this structure, once the center of the universe for rail travelers. Restoration, completed in 1998, has returned it to its awesome Beaux Arts beauty. We marveled at breathtaking details of the zodiac constellations in the ceiling, the gorgeous brass clock in the center of the terminal, and pillars of marble everywhere, and we peered into the windows of the Campbell Apartment, the famous cocktail lounge upstairs on Grand Central's east side.

It was Puerto Rican Independence Day, and by brunch time, a huge parade and crowds were overrunning midtown Manhattan. We escaped into a cab to SoHo and began walking—from West Broadway up, down, and around a rectangle completed by Grand, Broadway, and Houston—past galleries, boutiques of clothing, jewelry, and home design shops. Soon the street morphed into a bazaar of art vendors at tables and racks teeming with souvenir New York scenes, rock star portraits, CDs, you-name-its. On Greene Street we studied the intriguing architecture in SoHo's unique Cast-Iron District, a neighborhood of nineteenth-century ornate and detailed iron-beamed industrial buildings. They've been resurrected as lofts, galleries, and artists' spaces.

By early afternoon, we had left SoHo to experience colonial New York at **Battery Park**. That meant a ride on the subway. Down we went, under the city, and into the station, where we studied the (easy) map and bought all-day metro passes for $7 each. We emerged at the tip of lower Manhattan, at bright and breezy Battery Park, canopied by dappled sycamore trees, where the city began as the Nieuw Amsterdam colony in 1626. A long esplanade of statues, monuments, war memorials, and the red-block **Castle Clinton**—built to hold off the British in the War of 1812—

Statue of Liberty

anchor this historic square at the edge of the water. Off in New York Harbor stands the **Statue of Liberty**, rising majestically on Liberty Island. We then went east to the **U.S. Custom House**, a magnificent Greek Revival monument to free trade. On the way we halted before the ravaged remains of the World Trade Center's signature sculpture, *The Sphere*, by Fritz

TITANS OF THE TURF CLUB

On East 52nd Street, in New York City, behind a tall, ornate wrought iron fence, jockey statues in silks the colors of Monet's palette line the steps and window ledges. There, in the heart of Manhattan, an important group of "jockeys" gathers regularly. They carry a lot of weight, though less than they did a hundred years ago, and you'll never catch them in a racing saddle. The horseplayers in this winner's circle are the elite members of The Jockey Club.

In the beginning, jockey clubs were scattered like leaves across the land. One of the earliest was the prerevolutionary Philadelphia Jockey Club, begun in 1766, by seventy-one men who each anted up £275 for annual membership. The New York–based club was founded in 1894 by a group of men who patterned it after the Jockey Club in England. Until these men took charge, each American track independently set its own race dates, made its own rules, and imposed its own penalties for violations—usually ignored by the other tracks. Chaos reigned in the naming of Thoroughbreds. (In the earliest volumes of the *American Stud Book*, the official registry of blood horses and bloodlines, there were 139 horses with John in their names and 102 fillies or mares named Fanny!) The Jockey Club stepped in, some say iron-fisted, to bring consistent racing rules and regulations to the sport.

Members of The Jockey Club were and are giants of the industry. Powerful, prominent, and wealthy, they're Thoroughbred owners and breeders, winners of countless racing awards—and their ranks now include women. Teaming up with several corporate partners, they've expanded into a Kentucky office, and they continue as an influential advisory group concerned with all Thoroughbred matters. They still keep the stud book, but today most regulation decisions are in the hands of state racing associations and commissions.

Tour boat under the Brooklyn Bridge, East River

Koenig, which had stood for thirty years in the fountain at the twin towers, until September 11, 2001.

Across the street from the Custom House, we toured Trinity Church, founded by the Church of England in 1698 and destroyed and rebuilt three times in its history. Walking up Trinity Place to Liberty Street, we stood briefly behind the crowds staring through the chain-link fence that guarded the excavation pit of Ground Zero, so recently the twin towers of the World Trade Center. Though *The Sphere* left a haunting taste of what New Yorkers endured in the 9/11 attack, the shock for us was seeing this cavern of emptiness.

In the quiet financial district, we walked the city's first and narrowest thoroughfares—**Maiden Lane**, **John Street**, **Water Street**. We stopped to stare in amazement at an encrusted grid of huge iron pipes exposed in the earth below the street. A massive project to replace the city's oldest water mains was under way there. At 26 Wall Street, at Nassau Street, we climbed the stairway to the **Federal Hall National Memorial**, a reminder that New York was the first center of the federal government and that George Washington had been sworn into office on this site. From beneath his huge statue we looked toward the venerable New York Stock Exchange, now at 20 Broad and Wall streets, a handsome neoclassical revival structure completed in 1903,

with NYSE fully spelled out in big gilt lettering above its massive front doors. At the end of Wall Street, we emerged at the New York harbor and crossed to Pier 17—a tourist magnet of candy and souvenir shops and crowded with hawkers selling disposable trinkets. Upstairs at the nautical **Harbour Lights Restaurant**, we chose an outside patio table overlooking the East River and the majestic **Brooklyn Bridge**.

We had walked as far as possible, but the evening stretched before us with landmarks still to visit. A cab returned us to midtown, to the infamous **P. J. Clarke's**, where we chatted with the bartender, swapping stories of bookies and Belmont. Our warp speed tour of New York City wrapped up with a late, animated dinner at **Gallagher's Steak House**.

In the cab going to JFK, we made a list of all the places we'd had no time for—art museums, galleries, shopping, theater, harbor tours. We're watching http://www.orbitz.com daily and planning to return at the drop of a lucky horseshoe.

SARATOGA SPRINGS

Traveling north to Saratoga Springs by Amtrak train from New York City is an enjoyable three-hour ride into the celebrated Hudson River valley. Romantically painted by the Hudson River School artists, the valley is just as beautiful now as it ever was. As the train sped north, we newcomers were fascinated by such grand

Fox 'n' Hound B&B, Saratoga Springs

icons of American history as West Point Military Academy, one of the Vanderbilt mansions, the Roosevelt's Hyde Park residence, and Gore Vidal's home.

With more than a dozen warm mineral springs bubbling naturally from the ground, Saratoga Springs first flowered in the early 1800s as a health resort. In 1863, along came Saratoga Race Course to seal its fate as a destination for the wealthy and indulgent. Soon a wonderful gambling casino followed. As the town grew, grand homes with fine architectural detail rose up on wide, tree-lined streets, and the high cultural arts and pleasures that sustain affluent society followed quickly. For more than a century, the city has remained the playground of the rich, the royal, the socially elite, and occasionally, the wanton. Today, more than a thousand homes and public buildings are listed on the National Register of Historic Places. Yet for all its cultural sophistication, Saratoga Springs remains small town friendly.

Visitors are welcome in this city of 25,000 people. Horseplayers find ready racing conversations and can buy the *Daily Racing Form* almost any place. Everywhere, the passion for horse racing is apparent, and during the racing season the sport seems to dominate all else in life, except, perhaps, the parties. With the population doubling or even tripling during the summer meet, advance reservations for lodging are critical. Saratoga Race Course is just a few blocks from downtown, and several hotels and bed-and-breakfasts are easily within walking distance.

An endless card of day and evening activities surrounds the race season at Saratoga, as you'll discover when you arrive. Many cultural events are fund-raisers—public and private—for various organizations, so your ticket buys more than an evening out. Sample the history,

The National Museum of Racing

music, culture, art, and shopping at your leisure, all featured in many of the keepsake tourist magazines you'll find in Saratoga Springs. The *Saratogian* newspaper (http://www.Saratogian.com) puts out a thorough little city guide.

In Saratoga Springs's **Congress Park** (the intersections of Broadway, Circular, and Spring streets) are the city's information center and the Historical Society of Saratoga Springs, housed in the Canfield Casino, built in 1870 by boxer John Morrissey. The stylish gambling casino is now a history museum, and in the park you can sample the mineral waters at the dome-covered Columbian Spring and the Congress X Spring.

Start one morning of your racing vacation at the **National Museum of Racing and Hall of Fame** (191 Union Avenue; 518-584-0400/800-JOCKEY4; http://www.racingmuseum.org), across from the racetrack. Racing fans will enjoy the museum's cool, rich interiors and gardens as well. Plan to take the museum's exclusive walking tour of the Oklahoma horse training track, just

Saratoga Automobile Museum

across from the Saratoga course. The museum's annual Hall of Fame awards ceremony, staged in the huge tent of the Fastig-Tipton yearling horse sales, is a wonderful public celebration. Honoring those recipients—one jockey, one trainer, and a couple of Thoroughbreds—is the bedrock on which the racing museum was founded. The museum itself winds you through

Saratoga Monument, dedicated in 1882

three centuries of Thoroughbred history and artifacts, leaving you feeling that you've just seen everything there is to see about racing. Admission for adults is $7; for seniors/students, $5; for children five and under, free.

For the speed that horsepower inspired, visit the **Saratoga Automobile Museum** (Saratoga Spa State Park, enter at 110 Avenue of the Pines; 518-587-1935; http://www.saratogaautomuseum.com), where the exhibition changes to feature the most exciting vehicles ever designed, from Ferraris to muscle cars. Admission for adults is $7; for seniors, $5; under six, $3.50.

Finally, witness Saratoga's role in our Revolutionary War at **Saratoga National Historic Park** (Route 9-P east of Saratoga Springs; 518-664-9821; http://www.nps.gov/sara/). Its 2,800 acres include the 1777 battlefields where British general John "Gentleman Johnny" Burgoyne was defeated by General Horatio Gates and his American troops in the first major American victory of the war (called one of the fifteen most decisive battles in world history). Historic markers, trails, and the visitors' center are open year-round. Admission if you come by car is $5; by foot, bike, or horse, $3.

PENNSYLVANIA

HARRISBURG AND HERSHEY

Freshly mown grass, hot blue skies, ice cream cones at the amusement park—this is summer in Harrisburg, Pennsylvania, near Penn National. The fields are dotted with cattle and baby Thoroughbreds; tourists love this destination for the fishing, the pristine woodlands, and the nearby entertainment. Perched at the edge of Amish country, the architecture is interesting and hex signs grace the peaks of the stone barns.

The Hershey Hotel, Hershey

While away the summer days at Hershey, enjoying one of the many adventure and sports theme parks. Pick your destination at http://www.hersheypa.com. Take a drive through the town that chocolate built, where the streetlights are shaped like Hershey's Kisses and the air is redolent with the smell of cocoa. In Harrisburg, the state capital, enjoy the Susquehanna River from the banks of **Riverfront Park** and **City Island**. Or take a trip to the **Mount Hope Estate and Winery**, home of the Pennsylvania Renaissance Faire. Go to http://www.parenaissancefaire.com for directions and more information. For more information on the area, request your free thirty-two-page visitor's guide at http://www.visithhc.com.

PHILADELPHIA

If Boston was the scrimmage field for the American Revolution, Philadelphia was the front office, where the rules of sovereignty were sketched on parchment. With Philadelphia Park racing all year long, you can visit anytime. For this city that cherishes its colonial red brick and thick gray stone beginnings, consider visiting during the crisp weekends of autumn, when leaves begin to blush and fires crackle in historic hunkerdown taverns.

Downtown Philadelphia is beautiful and grand. Visionary Quaker William Penn designed the city in 1682, planning riverfront vistas on the Schuylkill and the Delaware rivers, public greens flanking a central square, and wide streets that would become handsome avenues. Young Benjamin Franklin arrived in 1723 and put his signature on civic design, federal politics, and every document issued by the young nation in the city's meeting halls.

In its greatest era, Philadelphia was the largest and most important place in the country—in banking, communications, and trade. The heart of downtown, **Center Square**, is at the intersection of Market and Broad streets, where **Philadelphia City Hall**, a gorgeous French Renaissance structure with Penn's likeness at its crown, dominates five acres. Stroll Market Street, stopping at 1300-1326 Market to take tea at **Lord & Taylor** (formerly the John Wanamaker Store), whose five-story interior court holds a one-ton bronze eagle created in 1904. Wanamaker's office on the fifth floor is now a museum. On Broad Street are many of the city's cultural institutions, including the **Academy of Fine Arts**, the renowned **Academy of Music**, and the magnificent **Masonic Temple**, one of the world's finest.

East of the Delaware River is **Independence National Historic Park**, marking the section now called **Old Town** or Old City. It includes twenty-six historic buildings operated by the National Park Service (Visitor's Center at 143 South Third Street, at 6th and Market). For maps and all questions about sites, phone 215-965-2305. Most sites are free, open 9:00–5:00 daily, longer in summer.

The centerpiece of the park is **Independence Hall** (500 Chestnut Street), where the Declaration of Independence was signed on July 4,

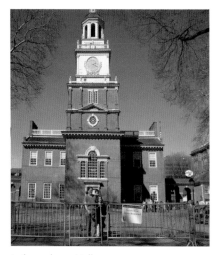

Independence Hall

Benjamin Franklin bronze

1776, and the U.S. Constitution was drafted. Meticulously restored, the hall is a national shrine.

On Independence Mall, on Market Street, between Fifth and Sixth, you'll find the **Liberty Bell Pavilion**, which houses the famous bell. The original bell was sent from London in 1752 to mark the fiftieth anniversary of the successful Pennsylvania Colony. It cracked soon after it arrived and was recast by John A. Pass and John Stow, local craftsmen, in 1753 using metal from the English bell. Who would have guessed it would come to symbolize independence from its makers?

Liberty Bell

In the park at 316–322 Market between Third and Fourth lies **Franklin Court**, which holds an underground museum covering Benjamin Franklin's life. Above it on the street level stands a unique steel skeleton depicting the house he built. With very few accurate details to refer to, the park service opted for this unconventional memorial.

Nearby on the Delaware River is Penn's Landing, a thirty-seven-acre site where ships of various sizes and eras are displayed, including the USS *Olympia* from the Spanish-American War; a seaport museum, and a sculpture garden. Call 215-925-5439 for hours and fees.

Northwest of downtown in nine-thousand–acre Fairmount Park is the **Philadelphia Museum of Art**, built for the nation's 1876 centennial. It has expanded into a massive neoclassical yellow marble monument designed to complement the city waterworks below it. Its collections make it one of the finest in the world. Located on Benjamin Franklin Parkway at 26th Street, the museum (215-763-8100) is closed on Mondays, and admission is free on Sunday mornings.

WHERE TO STAY

DELAWARE

WILMINGTON

Hotel DuPont
11th and Market Streets
Wilmington, DE 19804
302-594-3100/800-441-9019
http://www.hoteldupont.com
$179–$309 (suites higher)
The hotel is downtown Wilmington's crown jewel, an experience that delivers the best of the past along with the sophisticated perks we appreciate. With a lobby lounge, the Green Room bar's extended hours, and a concierge staff just waiting to please you, it promises to be a memorable stay. Member of Historic Hotels of America.

MASSACHUSETTS

BOSTON

The Fairmont Copley Plaza
138 St. James Avenue
Boston, MA 02116
617-267-5301/866-540-4417
http://www.fairmont.com/copleyplaza
$159–$429

A Back Bay alternative to staying downtown, the Fairmont offers total sophistication and splendor overlooking architecturally exciting Copley Place. Home of the Oak Room, a premier steak house; the Oak (martini) Bar; the intimate Wine Room; and several other fine dining options. Bed and breakfast packages are available.

The Hyatt Regency Boston
One Avenue de Lafayette
Boston, MA 02111
617-422-5500/800-233-1234
http://www.bostonfinancial.hyatt.com
$109–$345
Request a business floor with views of Boston Common, the Charles River, or the harbor. We chose the Hyatt especially for its indoor pool. There is live entertainment regularly in the bar off the lobby; breakfast and Sunday brunch in the dining room.

The Omni Parker House Hotel
60 School Street
Boston, MA 02108
617-227-8600/800-843-6664
http://www.omnihotels.com
$110 and up
Historic, restored, with ornately carved interiors, the Omni offers weekend museum and other specialty packages. Charles Dickens held literary seminars here.

NORTHAMPTON

Hotel Northampton
36 King Street
Northampton, MA 01060
413-584-3100/800-547-3529
http://www.hotelnorthampton.com
$155 and way up, depending on amenities
Just off Main Street, this Colonial Revival–style hotel was built in 1927. It's the city's only hotel on the National Trust for Historic Preservation's list; with its fine architectural details and antique furnishings it's *the* place to stay.

NEW YORK

FINGER LAKES REGION AND NIAGARA FALLS

Adam's Mark Hotel
120 Church Street
Buffalo, NY 14202
716-845-5100/800-444-ADAM
http://www.adamsmark.com
$100–$400
Overlooks Lake Erie, with stunning city views

Crowne Plaza Rochester
70 State Street
Rochester, NY 14614
585-546-3450/hotel@rcpny.com
$149 and up
With its convenient downtown Rochester location, the hotel's amenities include 362 standard rooms and suites, on- and off-site exercise facilities, complimentary morning newspapers, and special weekend packages, including tickets to the Rochester International Jazz Festival, launched in 2001.

Four Points by Sheraton Niagara Falls
114 Buffalo Avenue
Niagara Falls, NY 14303
716-285-2521/800-325-3535
http://www.fourpoints.com
$109–$270
Overlooking the Niagara River, the upscale Four Points is within a ten-minute walk to the falls and other tourist activities.

The Mansion on Delaware Avenue
414 Delaware Avenue
Buffalo, NY 14202
716-886-3300
http://www.mansionondelaware.com
$145–$275
This elegant hotel dates to 1867, features contemporary amenities, and puts you near Buffalo's art, antique, and entertainment districts.

The Statler Hotel at Cornell University
130 Statler Drive
Cornell University
Ithaca, NY 14853

607-257-2500/800-541-2501
http://www.statlerhotel.cornell.edu
$135–$299

At the south end of Lake Cayuga and the wine country, the Statler is operated partly by students of the hotel administration program. With three fine restaurants and excellent service, it is rated one of the top hotels in the region.

NEW YORK CITY

The Algonquin
59 West 44th Street
New York, NY 10036
212-840-6800/800-555-8000
http://www.thealgonquin.com
$200–$400

In the 1920s, the storied Algonquin was the gathering-and-watering place of New York's shining literati, including acid-witted Dorothy Parker and humorist Robert Benchley. Recently restored, its historic architectural details sparkle. *Historic Traveler* magazine rates the hotel among its top ten favorites.

Hotel Chandler
12 East 31st Street
New York City, NY 10016
212-889-6363
http://www.concorde-hotels.com
$170–$350

Two blocks from the Empire State Building and Madison Square Garden, this intimate, elegant hotel with a gleaming marble lobby offers lovely rooms, an inviting cocktail lounge just off the entrance, and a fitness center and sauna for staying in shape.

The Swissôtel New York, The Drake
440 Park Avenue
New York City, NY 10022
212-421-0900/800-372-5369
http://www.newyork.swissotel.com
$199–$400

The Swissôtel New York, the Drake, in the heart of midtown Manhattan near Central Park, is well located for sightseeing, dining, and shopping. It has a sophisticated European atmosphere, with plush, quiet guest rooms. Located off the lobby for morning and evening convenience are a pastry shop and a contemporary cocktail lounge.

SARATOGA SPRINGS

The Aldephi Hotel
365 Broadway
Saratoga Springs, NY 12866
581-587-4688
http://www.adelphihotel.com
$115–$475, depending on season

This high Victorian hotel on Broadway, an architectural achievement built in 1877, is centrally located in Saratoga's restaurant and shopping area. Period antiques fill the interior, with historic Saratoga photos and eclectic art decorating the walls.

Chestnut Tree Inn
9 Whitney Place
Saratoga Springs, NY 12866
518-597-8681/888-243-7688

http://www.chestnuttreeinn.net
$110–$295, depending on season
Cozy and Victorian, serves a continental breakfast; walkable distance to the racetrack.

Fox 'n' Hound Saratoga Springs Bed and Breakfast Inn
142 Lake Avenue
Saratoga Springs, NY 12866
866-FOX-1913/518-584-5959
http://www.foxnhoundbandb.com
$95–$335, depending on season
Our first four-poster canopy bed experience! We loved its English country name, so we stayed at the Fox 'n' Hound Bed and Breakfast Inn, situated in the heart of Saratoga Springs only four blocks from the racecourse. It is owned by Marlena Sacca, a wonderful hostess and former chef instructor at the Culinary Institute of America. Every morning we feasted on her gourmet European-style breakfast in this spacious Victorian home.

Gideon Putnam Resort and Spa
Roosevelt Spa and Baths
24 Gideon Putnam Road
Saratoga Springs, NY 12866
518-584-3000/800-732-1560
http://www.gideonputnam.com
$105–$550, depending on season
In 1789, Mr. Putnam established an inn in Saratoga Springs and laid out Broadway, securing the town's future. At the historic Gideon Putnam, you can arrange for a variety of pampering treatments at the Roosevelt Spa, during a day visit or as a guest. (Contact the spa directly at 518-226-4790.) The hotel and spa are both within the 2200-acre Saratoga Spa State Park.

PENNSYLVANIA

HERSHEY

Hotel Hershey
1 Hotel Road
Hershey, PA 17033
800-HERSHEY/717-533-2171
http://www.hersheypa.com
$198 and up
It's on the pricey side but comes with a lot of features. Enjoy fine dining and sweets right in the hotel. Guests can enjoy access to the Hershey Golf Club private courses, Hershey Gardens (seasonally), and Hershey Museum. Shuttle transport to local attractions is provided.

PHILADELPHIA

Loews Philadelphia Hotel
1200 Market Street
Philadelphia, PA 19107
215-627-1200/800-235-6397
http://www.loewshotels.com
$154–$304; seasonal rates may vary
Sleep in the world's first skyscraper, right in the heart of the city. Totally futuristic when it was built in 1932, it has now been luxuriously renovated. Two blocks west and you're on Broad Street, also called Avenue of the Arts, with cultural sites including the Pennsylvania Academy of the Fine Arts (118 N. Broad, 215-972-7600), the oldest art museum in the country, its first art school, and a nineteenth-century architectural wonder of black, white, and pink marble.

The Omni Hotel Independence Park
401 Chestnut Street
Philadelphia, PA 19106
215-925-0000/800-843-6664
http://www.omnihotels.com
$105–$269

A luxurious AAA-rated, four-diamond hotel in downtown Philadelphia's prestigious Society Hill, it has all the usual frills, plus the Azalea Restaurant for hotel dining, indoor lap pool, marble bathrooms, fluffy bathrobes, and twenty-four-hour room service. Horse-drawn carriage rides are available at the front door. Overlooks Independence National Historic Park with its famous landmarks.

WHERE TO WINE & DINE

DELAWARE

WILMINGTON

Iron Hill Brewery
710 S. Madison
Wilmington, DE 19801
302-658-8200
http://www.ironhillbrewery.com
Lunch: $7–$11; dinner: $15–$20

Relax with a microbrew and a steak and watch the brewing process in this restored riverfront warehouse.

The Green Room
Hotel DuPont
11th and Market Streets
Wilmington, DE 19804
302-594-3154/800-338-3404
http://www.dupont.com/hotel/dining.htm
Entrées from $34

An opulent Victorian space, true to its French heritage, the Green Room serves haute French cuisine. Delectable entrées include prime meats, poultry, and seafood presented with culinary flair. Musicians accompany dinner. Jackets on weekends. Open for breakfast and lunch as well.

Sienna
1616 Delaware Avenue
Wilmington, DE 19806
http://www.delawareonline.com
302-652-0653
$12.50–$26.00

Sienna's old-world touches accompanied by Continental and Mediterranean entrées make it another special dining spot. It is fun, friendly, with nightly entertainment and a trendy upstairs martini-cigar lounge. Upscale casual attire.

Washington Street Alehouse
1206 Washington Street
Wilmington, DE 19801
302-658-2537
http://www.wsalehouse.com
$9–$19

Have a drink here while exploring the Riverfront Market Street at the Christina River.

MASSACHUSETTS

BOSTON

Caffé Vittoria
290-296 Hanover Street
Boston, MA 02113
617-227-7606
http://www.vittoriacaffe.com
Under $20; average: $12; desserts from $3.75
The oldest Italian café in Boston, with three full liquor bars, Caffé Vittoria has nooks and crannies that ramble up, down, and around. It offers rich desserts, grappas, and the best cappuccino we have ever sipped. Downstairs, at 292 Hanover, you'll find Stanza dei Sigari, a traditional cigar parlor.

The Harborside Grill
Hyatt Harborside
101 Harborside Drive
Boston, MA 02128
617-568-6060
http://www.harborside.hyatt.com
Most entrées $20–$25
Sparkling and contemporary, the Hyatt delivers the seagull's view of Boston by day, the glitter of lights at night, and always fresh, delicious seafood.

Les Zygomates
129 South Street
Boston, MA 02111
617-542-5108
http://www.winebar.com
$8.50–$29.00
This French bistro and wine bar with a microbrew menu and live jazz nightly offers delectable gourmet plates with total eye appeal and wines by the bottle, glass, or taste. We liked the wine menu for listing labels by their predominant grape first, in order of robustness. Don't leave the table without sharing the butterscotch pudding.

Lucca Restaurant and Bar
226 Hanover Street
Boston, MA 02113
617-742-9200
http://www.luccaboston.com
$9–$30
Everyone loves Lucca, from Zagat to *Wine Spectator* to *Best of Boston* to us, with its traditional fine dining in an elegant setting. Our *agnello con patata* (lamb with garlic potatoes) was totally *divino.*

South Street Diner
178 Kneeland Street
Boston, MA 02111
617-350-0028
http://www.southstreetdiner.com
$4–$10
A nice alternative to elaborate hotel morning fare, the diner, a retrofitted streetcar of sorts, serves breakfast and brews 24/7. Long on neighborly conversation.

NORTHAMPTON

Spoleto
50 Main Street

Northampton, MA 01060
413-586-6313
http://www.fundining.com
$14.95–$20.95
This superb dinner spot, a favorite among co-eds, is too much fun! Named for the Spoleto Festival in Charleston, South Carolina, the interior is a riot of color and art; entreés are Italian with unexpectedly nice twists.

Sylvester's
111 Pleasant Street
Northampton, MA 01060
413-586-1418
http://www.sylvestersrestaurant.com
$5–$13
Have breakfast in the very building where in 1829 Sylvester Graham created that old familiar snack the Graham cracker. He baked it up hoping nineteenth-century Americans would switch to a healthier, whole grain diet. Alas, they wouldn't.

Wiggins Tavern
Hotel Northampton
36 King Street
Northampton, MA 01060
413-584-3100/800-547-3529
http://www.hotelnorthampton.com, click on Dining
$16.95–24.95
End the evening with dinner and a nightcap at the early American Wiggins Tavern, est. 1786, where celebs such as Jenny Lind and JFK dined. Its unusual history includes its move, piece by piece, from its hand-hewed beams to the hearth stones, to its present site in the Hotel Northampton.

NEW YORK

FINGER LAKES REGION AND NIAGARA FALLS

Lincoln Hill Inn
3365 East Lake Road
Canandaigua, NY 14424
585-394-8254
http://www.lincolnhillinn.com
$8.95–$26.95
This centennial farmhouse-turned-restaurant, surrounded by gardens, is adjacent to the Finger Lakes Performing Arts Center. You may find yourself dining near a party of visiting celebrities.

Ristorante Lombardo
1198 Hertel Avenue
Buffalo, NY 14216
716-873-4291
http://www.ristorantelombardo.com
$7.95–$28.95
Quiet, elegant, and romantic, serving haute Italian cuisine, with dining in two cozy rooms or on the intimate outdoor patio. No checks or credit cards, please.

Top of the Falls Restaurant
Terrapin Point on Goat Island
Niagara Falls State Park
Niagara Falls, NY 14303
716-278-0340

http://www.niagarastatefallspark.com
$8.95–$26.95
Offers spectacular views of the American Falls in its tiered dining rooms, cocktail lounge, and espresso bar. Open May through September.

NEW YORK CITY

Boom
152 Spring Street
New York, NY 10012
212-431-3663
Average: $35
With its dark, intriguingly decorated walls, Boom is both hip and rustic. At the bar we had a perfectly arranged plate of tuna carpaccio, Sunday brunch beverages, and an enjoyable conversation with the Italian barkeep.

Carpo's Café
189 Bleecker Street
New York, New York 10012
212-353-2889
$5.95–$10.95
Informal with great food, this landmark Greenwich Village café has outdoor seating in good weather and live jazz on weekends. We shared a generous platter of delicious calamari, freshly baked bread, pomodoro caprese, and a nice bottle of something red.

Gallagher's Steak House
228 W. 52nd Street
New York, NY 10019
212-245-5336
http://www.gallaghersnysteakhouse.com
$17–$51
Founded by Helen Gallagher, one of the beautiful 1920s Ziegfeld dancers, and her bookie-comedian husband, this comfy restaurant has fed every New Yorker who's anyone—their pictures adorn the walls—and hundreds of regular guys, too. Classic red-checkered tablecloths, dark wood walls, a bold curved bar in the corner, and great food and wine selections make this an excellent spot for late-night dining and people watching.

Harbour Lights Restaurant
South Street Seaport, Pier 17, 3rd floor
New York, NY 10038
212-227-2800
http://www.harbourlightsrestaurant.com
$8–$57
This is the perfect touristy spot (cherished by New Yorkers) for light refreshments, lunch, or dinner featuring American cuisine. Overlooking the East River, with its endless stream of water traffic, Harbour Lights commands the city's most spectacular view of the Brooklyn Bridge.

La Vineria
19 W. 55th Street
New York, NY 10019
212-247-3400
http://www.lavineriarestaurant.com
$11.50–$34.50
When only Italian will do, this small, cozy restaurant, with its friendly waitstaff, serves a wide menu of excellent regional cuisine and desserts.

The Oak Bar, Plaza Hotel
768 5th Avenue at 59th Street
New York, NY 10019
212-759-3000
Appetizers from $7.50
Closed until fall 2006 while the Plaza is refurbished, hotel management says the Oak Bar will remain structurally unchanged. The new Plaza, with condos and more upscale shopping, will surely be worth a visit too. Celebrate the reopening of this world-renowned bar overlooking Central Park with our favorites: a glass of bubbly and a double Blanton's manhattan.

P. J. Clarke's
915 Third Avenue at 55th Street
New York, NY 10022
212-317-1616
http://www.pjclarkes.com
$12–$30
Established in the 1860s, this Irish pub, dwarfed by surrounding high-rises, clings to its dark paneled interior and historic architecture and only occasionally straightens the pictures. Originally a sailor's hangout, since the 1940s it's been a retreat for writers, now often in company with sports and media people. Sinatra had a regular table and singer-songwriter Johnny Mercer composed "One for My Baby" here. *The Village Voice* recently gave it the Best Manhattan award. Open late.

Zoë
90 Prince Street
New York, NY 10012
212-966-6722
http://www.zoerest.com
Dinners $14–$45
At Zoë, we sat on buff-colored stools at the black granite bar and enjoyed champagne and French chardonnay, paired with crispy calamari and breadstick straws served up in a tall glass.

SARATOGA SPRINGS

Bailey's Café
37 Phila Street
Saratoga Springs, NY 12866
518-583-6060
$4.95–$8.95
A restored centennial hotel with tin ceilings, stained glass windows, and Tiffany lamps, Bailey's serves casual lunches and dinners and hosts great live music on the outdoor deck about four nights a week during the summer.

43 Phila Bistro & Bar
43 Phila Street
Saratoga Springs, NY 12866
518-584-2720
$6–$26
Robert Redford frequented 43 Phila with a small entourage during the filming of *The Horse Whisperer*. It's a wonderfully friendly bar, at which we spoke with the owner's wife and several of the restaurant employees. Passing up the duck in port wine cherry sauce, we split an excellent sirloin steak au poivre covered with mushrooms.

Siro's Fine Dining
168 Lincoln Avenue
Saratoga Springs, NY 12866
518-584-4030

Dinners average $100
Called party central since the 1930s, Siro's, just outside the racetrack, is *the* place for drinks and fine dining after the races. Chef and co-owner Tom Dillon says the veggies on your dinner plate were in the ground that morning. Open during the race season only; reservations only, well in advance.

Springwater Bistro
139 Union Street
Saratoga Springs, NY 12866
518-584-6440
http://www.springwaterbistro.com
$5.95–$22.95
Race fans can order picnic baskets from the Springwater, two blocks from Saratoga Race Course, to take to the track. It is the favorite spot of our innkeeper Marlena, who loves Springwater's local ambience. The chef varies the gourmet menu regularly. We had wonderful tapas here while staying out of the rain at the track.

Wheatfields
440 Broadway
Saratoga Springs, NY 12866
518-583-0534
$12.95–$23.95
Upscale yet casual and friendly, Wheatfields makes nearly two dozen different fresh pastas daily and turns them into delicious "homemade" dishes. They also have steaks, a nice wine selection, desserts, and espresso drinks. If you bring your racing party, call ahead about reserving a private room.

The Wine Bar of Saratoga
417 Broadway
Saratoga Springs, NY 12866
518-584-8777
http://www.thewinebarofsaratoga.com
$6–$22
Offers fifty wines by the glass, a full bar, a cigar lounge, tapas plates, and fine dining.

PENNSYLVANIA

HARRISBURG AND HERSHEY

Appalachian Brewing Company
50 North Cameron Street
Harrisburg, PA 17101
717-221-1080
http://www.abcbrew.com
$8–$22
Located in one of the historic Hershey buildings downtown, Appalachian Brewing Company was the area's first microbrewery, established in 1951. Today, it combines an array of flavorful beer varieties with a varied menu, creating a unique eating and imbibing experience.

Cantone's Southern Italian Restaurant
4701 Fritchey Street
Harrisburg, PA 17109
717-652-9976
http://www.cantones.net
$4.95–$23.95
With more than thirteen veal dishes, homemade soups, broiled crab cakes, and fresh seafood specials daily, this family-owned restaurant will satisfy the hungriest traveler. Voted the Number 1 Favorite Restaurant in 1999 by the *Patriot News*.

Circular Dining Room
Hotel Hershey
Hershey, PA 17033
717-534-8800
$28–$39
This classic, elegant restaurant offers exquisite country American cuisine in a smoke-free setting. Rated four diamonds by AAA. Reservations are required, proper dress for dinner.

The Cocoa Beanery
Hotel Hershey
Hershey, PA 17033
717-534-8800
$2–$4
Start your morning or end your night at this mouthwatering spot, located in the hotel lobby. Choose from an array of delicious pastries or chocolate confections, and wash it down with a specialty coffee drink or a shot of espresso.

PHILADELPHIA

Bistro Romano
120 Lombard Street on Society Hill
Philadelphia, PA 19147
215-925-8880
http://www.bistroromano.com
$16.95–$24.95
Immerse yourself in the night scene at this traditional Italian restaurant, located in an early 1700s sea merchant's house that was also an Underground Railroad station. Exposed beams and brick walls tell the tale. Best of Philly award winner. On Friday and Saturday nights, enjoy an evening of dinner followed by mystery theater. One price, $36.95 per person, includes preshow hors d'oeuvres, special chef's menu, and ticket. Box office at 215-238-1313.

City Tavern
138 S. 2nd Street at Walnut
Philadelphia, PA 19106
215-413-1443
http://www.citytavern.com
$17.95–$23.95
From the time it opened in 1773, City Tavern was the unofficial Philadelphia gathering spot for political strategizing. Destroyed by fire in 1834, it was authentically rebuilt in 1976. Today's menu, tableware, and ambience closely replicate period dining. Taste Martha Washington's turkey pot pie, filled with mushrooms, peas, and potatoes in a sherry cream sauce, and served with noodles and fried oysters; or sample the Tavern lobster and shrimp pie, baked in a pewter casserole.

The Fountain Restaurant at the Four Seasons Hotel
1 Logan Square
Philadelphia, PA 19103
215-963-1500
http://www.fourseasons.com/philadelphia
Entrées from $39; dinner for two, $125
In a setting of pure European elegance, with grand floral arrangements and sparkling chandeliers, executive chef Martin Hamann is renowned for creative, surprising entrées of French inspiration and regional German touches. Start with venison carpaccio garnished with grapes in a juniper marinade and proceed to the amazing braised Alaskan salmon in a Pernod cream sauce. Save room for possibly the best chocolate mousse this side of Paris. Jackets and reservations required.

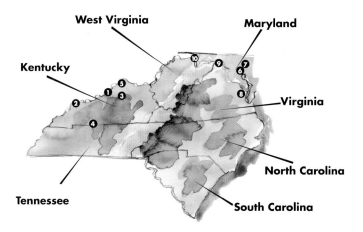

SOUTHEAST MAP LEGEND

Kentucky
1 Churchill Downs
(Louisville)

2 Ellis Park Race Course
(Henderson)

3 Keeneland
(Lexington)

4 Kentucky Downs
(Franklin)

5 Turfway Park
(Florence)

Maryland
6 Laurel Park
(Laurel)

7 Pimlico Race Course
(Baltimore)

Virginia
8 Colonial Downs
(New Kent)

West Virginia
9 Charles Town Races and Slots
(Charles Town)

10 Mountaineer Race Track and Gaming Resort
(Chester)

THE SOUTHEAST

With prominent breeders in colonial Virginia supporting the early racing hubs in Richmond and Williamsburg, Virginia was looked upon as the New World's Thoroughbred capital. North Carolina, too, developed early, excellent breeders—in 1734, Carolina colonists in Charleston had founded America's first jockey club. In frontier Tennessee, settlers' passion for racing was championed by Andrew Jackson, the only president to keep a racing stable during his administration. Seeds of a shift in the Southeast were sown in 1769, when Daniel Boone broke the first non-Indian trails into rugged "Kaintuckee" and opened the way to the founding of Lexington, on a rolling plateau covered with natural springs and abundant meadow grass. Enriched by an underlying vein of mineral-laced limestone, the land proved superb for raising livestock. As Virginians spread into Kentucky, their horse breeding spread, too, and by the early 1800s, the Kentucky Bluegrass region was the premier breeding ground of the racehorse.

KENTUCKY

CHURCHILL DOWNS (LOUISVILLE)

January 1 is the official birthday for every American Thoroughbred. Even as Churchill Downs still hibernates under a wet, gray winter cloak, the venerable racetrack in Louisville, Kentucky, is foremost in everyone's thoughts. The previous year's two-year-olds have come of age, and on the first Saturday in May, the unofficial opening of the summer racing season, the best of them will meet on the Kentucky track as they have since 1875. The Kentucky Derby (G1), the oldest continuous horse race in the United States, kicks off the Triple Crown chase and is also the equestrian world's biggest social event.

Bartender E. Crouch

We were not planning to attend Churchill Downs for the 2004 Kentucky Derby, but Lady Luck rang us up and we answered. Friends hooked us up with a corporate party searching for additional magnetic personalities. We flew east and met our Derby mates at the hotel bar. It seemed right to offer a get-acquainted round of mint juleps, the perfect ice-breaker. Much too soon a pair of limos squired us off to Churchill Downs in the rain. Having experienced the deluge at the Belmont Stakes 2003, we weren't fazed one driblet by the rare wet Derby, and even the crowd of 140,000 felt familiar.

We sat in a box overlooking the track and the soggy spectators in the open grandstand seats and in the infield, who were taking cover under green and blue and white plastic tarps. Gusts of wind whipped at the tents. Clouds rolled in and out, dumping buckets of rain and then teasing with glimpses of sunshine. Still, the crowd was boisterous, eager for the day's momentous race to get underway.

Sitting in a box at Churchill Downs, you're looking out over the sporting field that's defined horse racing for more than a century. The Derby Winner's Circle, in the infield, with its red-and-white flowers, curved white railing, boxwood shrubbery,

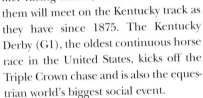

Funny Cide wins the 2003 Kentucky Derby

Churchill Downs fall meeting

and raised platform on which the winning owners are greeted by the governor of Kentucky, is used only for this special race. Beyond the green infield and the far side of the track are the backside café, the green-roofed stables where horses board, the jockey dormitory above the Paddock Pavilion simulcast center, and a fleet of pickups, hard evidence that far removed from the corporate suites, the world of horse racing is one of pure physical activity.

With its periodic expansion to accommodate larger crowds and to endorse bigger corporate checks, Churchill Downs has evolved into an architectural puzzle. The track opened in 1875; the

Racing in the rain

first clubhouse was a wooden Victorian structure with arched columns supporting its porch roof and a tall, slender spire capping every peak. The present grandstand was built in 1894. In the mid-1900s, more seats were added at the north end of the grandstand, and later the museum opened. The paddock was rebuilt in the 1980s, and more clubhouse and Skye Terrace improvements were made.

In the twenty-first century, the most dramatic changes yet are taking place. A

new Olympian-size entrance, exclusive corporate suites, premium box seating, a ballroom, a new press box and media compound, and a new central kitchen are either finished or in the works. The famous twin spires, the core of the old wooden grandstand, and the interior lower-level food courts retain their now-humble yesteryear character, dwarfed by the weighty proportions of the $121 million renovation and expansion.

During an interlude between races, we waded through the soggy crowds to tour the museum and its gift shop. At the north end of the grounds, near Gate 1, the Kentucky Derby Museum, with its dark, dramatic interior, is chock-full of racing treasures. On display are historic silks and saddles and prize-winning, wedding-bouquet Derby bonnets from several fashion eras. Everywhere are eye-catching displays and interactive stations. A video library houses all of the Derby races since 1918. Press the screen, watch, and listen. We were most struck by the horse pyramid chart that illustrated what happens from the time thirty-five thousand Thoroughbred foals are born to the day three years later when no more than twenty will ride in the Derby. Fewer than half of the original crop will win a race of any kind, and fewer than five hundred will eventually win a graded stakes race—graded earnings being one determining factor for Derby qualification. Every three-year-old has exactly four months to figure it out.

Back at the clubhouse, we wagered on our two favorites: Smarty Jones, the people's choice, and Master David, one of the mid–long shots. Settling in with a fresh julep and a southern ham sandwich in hand, we were ready to win.

Despite the weather, the race itself was unforgettable, and the human-interest stories were compelling this year. There was Someday Farm, which after its trainer was murdered sold off its stable, except for two horses who seemed special. The new trainer, Pennsylvanian John Servis, was here for his first Derby. He wouldn't go, he'd said in earlier days, unless he had a horse there. In April 2004, his colt Smarty Jones—the one they were calling blue collar, the one who nearly died as a two-year-old after smashing his skull on a starting gate—made the Arkansas Derby (G2) his six-for-six win. So here he was in the 2004 Louisville lineup, which had been an unpredictable and second-guessing exercise that left sports pundits shaking their heads all winter.

When the double starting gates at last flew open, Lion Heart broke fast, followed by a pack of five, with twelve more trailing. Smarty Jones, in post position fifteen, moved into fourth on the sloppy track, then into second down the backstretch, staying competitively off the pace. At the three-eighths pole, he began moving up, a powerful locomotive. He flew past the finish line post, winning the race in 2:04.06, with an air and a bearing that said, "I would keep running if necessary." Lion Heart finished second; Imperialism took third. A few in our party collected our winnings. Others were disappointed that favorite jockeys, such as José Santos on Limehouse and Edgar Prado on Birdstone, hadn't done better. We, however, loved it that Smarty had outsmarted the pack. Off to a rowdy dinner we went, where every one of us, appropriately, became a smart aleck on this most fantastic of days.

SnapShot - Churchill Downs

Description: The Kentucky Derby is the most famous horse race in the world. Run at Churchill Downs, in Louisville, Kentucky, the race itself is identified with the track's signature twin spires, graceful white-and-black spears that rise above the historic oval. Less recognizable are the boxy new suites that have risen alongside them to dwarf the spires, as part of Churchill's massive renovation project. The main track is 1 mile long, with one chute. On Derby Day, the best three-year-olds in the country battle to the wire, located at the end of a 1,234 1/2-foot stretch. Inside the main track is a 7-furlong turf course.

Season: Churchill Downs holds two seasons, a spring/summer meet from the end of April until the beginning of July, and a fall meet from October into November.

Address: 700 Central Avenue, Louisville, KY 40208

Phone: 502-636-4400/(fax) 502-636-4479

Web site: http://www.churchilldowns.com

Nearest airport: Louisville International Airport (SDF)

Getting there: Churchill Downs is located in south central Louisville, approximately three miles from the downtown business district and two miles from Louisville International Airport (Standiford Field). Greater Louisville is encircled by I-264, with Churchill Downs in the south central section of the loop. From downtown, go south on Third Avenue to Central, and turn right. At Taylor, turn left and find parking.

Admission: Weekdays: free; children under twelve: free; weekends: $2; seniors: $1; Kentucky Derby and Kentucky Oaks days: extra charge

Parking: Free; valet and preferred parking: extra charge

Fine dining: On-track dining in the Jockey Club Suites, the Central Avenue Deli, and several concessions catered by Levy Restaurants

Casual fare: Central Avenue Deli, Thrill of the Grill, Sweet Finishes, and other concessions located throughout the grounds

Spirits: Best Bets Bar, kiosks and carts throughout the facility

Extras: Kentucky Derby Museum and Gift Shop (http://www.derbymuseum.org); throughout the year, the Downs hosts concerts and promotions.

FROM LASCAUX TO TROYE: THE ART OF THE SPORT

Sporting art is as old as the renowned horse paintings in the ancient cave at Lascaux, France. Englishman George Stubbs (1724–1806) was considered the first equine artist of the Western world. His book *Anatomy of the Horse* (1766) established his reputation for rendering the correct anatomical form and creating fine, precise etchings. He painted the most famous English and European horses of the upper classes, works that now hang in public and private collections throughout the world. French impressionists Edgar Degas and Édouard Manet painted scenes of racing that are particularly prized today. Perhaps the most exacting of the British nineteenth-century artists was Sir Alfred Munnings, who had a lifelong love of all animals, especially the horse. His artistry, blending realism and impressionism within a single canvas, his facility as a landscape painter, and his eye for equine form and musculature made him, according to art historian Lorian Peralta-Ramos, perhaps the finest equestrian artist of all time.

America's most celebrated nineteenth-century sporting painter was Swiss-born Edward Troye, the son of French artists, who immigrated to the southern United States in 1830, at age twenty-two. His outstanding talent as a blood horse artist drew him to the region's foremost owners, and his best-known works include such great Thoroughbreds as Lexington, Lecompte, American Eclipse, Dixie, and Black Maria. He lived until 1874. A number of his works are held by Bethany College, West Virginia, and by the National Racing Museum, Saratoga Springs, New York. Alexander Keene Richards, Troye's patron and owner of Blue Grass Park, designed the monument to his life that stands at his burial place in Georgetown Cemetery, Georgetown, Kentucky.

For many people today, urbanites especially, the horse has become an abstract figure, signifying grace, freedom, power, and perfection in the animal world. Artistic interpretations of the horse, whether as companion or sport figure, flourish as never before.

Paleolithic cave horse, Lascaux, France

ELLIS PARK RACE COURSE
(HENDERSON)

Not every racetrack in America plants a cash crop, but during the summer race meet an infield soybean crop sprouts up, earning Ellis Park Race Course the affectionate nickname "the Pea Patch." The race course sits beside the Ohio River at Henderson, Kentucky, on a low spot mostly protected by levees. In November 2005, a tornado struck Ellis, seriously damaging the entire facility. Simulcasting was suspended. At our press time, Ellis officials had expressed hope that repairs could be completed in time for the 2006 season, which will presumably run from July 19 to September 4.

Founded by the Green River Jockey Club in 1922, the track (then named Dade Park) almost immediately closed because of financial troubles. James Ellis came

Soybeans ripening in the infield

along two years later and bought it at a bankruptcy sale. He owned the park—renamed after him in 1955—until his death in 1956. Churchill Downs Incorporated has owned Ellis since 1998.

Though the track, which had been retrofitted years before the tornado hit, hadn't shown robust economic growth, the handle had increased slightly and attendance kept rising steadily. One marketing

EDGAR PRADO: THE JOCKEYS' JOCK

Peruvian-born jockey Edgar Prado makes no bones about it: his favorite trainers are the ones who use him. And he has been used aplenty. In 1997, 1998, and 1999, he was the country's winningest jockey, and in 2002, 2003, and 2004, he ranked second nationally by earnings. In March 2003, Prado received the coveted George Woolf Memorial Jockey Award, a peer vote for the jockey who is regarded as demonstrating high character and success.

Son of a trainer and a leading rider in his native Peru, Prado began racing in the United States in 1986. Earning a name as the leading Maryland rider in the early 1990s, Prado switched to the New York tracks, where he was challenged by stiff competition. In 2002, Prado rode in the Kentucky Derby on favored Harlan's Holiday but finished a disappointing seventh. In the Preakness Stakes, again on Harlan's Holiday, he took fourth. War Emblem won both of the races and was favored by many to sweep the Triple Crown in the Belmont Stakes the following June 8. That would have made the colt the first Triple Crown winner since Affirmed took the prize back in 1978. But in the Belmont, Prado challenged War Emblem on Sarava, a 70-1 long shot, and won. His winning mutuel ($142.50) was the largest in Belmont history. In 2004, Prado again proved a spoiler in the Belmont Stakes, riding 36-1 long-shot Birdstone to victory over Derby/Preakness winner Smarty Jones.

Edgar Prado

When talking of horses and races, Prado is passionate. He would rather ride a good horse and lose than take a bad horse first across the wire. After the 2002 Belmont Stakes, he was sorry War Emblem didn't sweep the coveted crown. His reason? The sport needs the excitement of a Triple Crown winner. And he'd be glad to ride him. Does he do it for the money? If he won the lottery big time, he swears it would not change his racing routine. "If I did," he told columnist Steve Anderson in March 2003, "I'd still be back in the morning."

strategy that may have contributed to this is the track's creative public relations campaign: every household within a seventy-five-mile radius sometimes receives free passes to the park. Ellis's purses topped $1 million going into the 2004 meet. Every weekend includes a race with a pot between $75,000 and $150,000. In the first week of August, the Gardenia Stakes (G3) for fillies and mares—with its exquisitely fragrant winner's wreath—is the meet's biggest race. The purses may keep Ellis from competing directly with Keeneland, but the racetrack is an essential part of mainstream regional racing. If most of the Pea Patch crew isn't getting rich off racing, they're doing what they know and love, and they're getting by. Recent leaders have included jockey Jon Court, trainer Bernie Flint, and owners Richard Klein and family. Female riders have put their mark on the track as well. In 1970, sixteen-year-old Paula Herber broke the gender barrier at Ellis, finishing sixth on Moon Fair. In 2002, the leading apprentice jockey was Valerie

Home stretch from the far turn

Nagle, with twenty-six wins. This down-home wooden racetrack has the further distinction of being the only one where a jockey temporarily switched professions during a pause in the racing. Jockey Shane Sellers entertained the crowd with his repertoire of country songs on 2001 Gardenia Stakes Day, when a heavy storm temporarily knocked out electricity at the track.

New fans at Ellis are quick to see that loyalties here span decades. When it's time to acknowledge greatness in the ranks, a bobble head in the likeness of an honoree is a very big deal. In 2003, a bobblehead was made in the

Parade to post

Jockey Jones

likeness of R. A. "Cowboy" Jones, a three-time champion rider at Ellis Park. He noted that he prefers the toy's face to his own, with its slightly more weathered lines. Others, such as jockey Jon Court and owner Mike Pegram, have also basked in their bobble-head days in the sun, and it's a sure bet that a few more modest heroes will someday make great bobble models.

KEENELAND (LEXINGTON)

In the heart of the Kentucky bluegrass stands a racetrack characterized by timeless elegance and tradition. It is neither the oldest nor the largest track on the American racing scene, but it stands as one of the world's most exclusive, most treasured. The track is Keeneland, an English-style country estate shaded by stately trees and defined by stone walls and lantern-crowned pillars. East of the race park, across a rolling sweep of meadow, stands the Keeneland Library, unmatched for its historic and contemporary holdings, including eight thousand volumes, a quarter-million photo negatives, stud books, stallion directories, Thoroughbred registers, chart books, and more, some dating from as far back as the eighteenth century. Beyond the Keeneland acreage in every direction are found the storied Thoroughbred farms, whose names we hear when their horses run in the country's top races. The ambience is unique; nowhere but here can one experience total immersion in the world of Thoroughbred horse racing.

SNAPSHOT - ELLIS PARK RACE COURSE

Description: Clambering over the wooden seats in the historic old grandstand, the race goer might pause to wonder why the infield lacks the usual decorative landscaping found at other racetracks. If you look closer, you might notice that the grass in the infield isn't grass at all; it's soybeans. Racing is conducted on a 1 ⅛-mile dirt track with a 1,175-foot stretch and two chutes. The turf course is 1 mile.

Season: Early August to Labor Day weekend

Address: 3300 US Highway 41, N. Henderson, KY 42419

Phone: 812-425-1456/(fax) 812-425-0146

Web site: http://www.ellisparkracing.com

Nearest airport: Louisville International Airport (SDF)

Getting there: Ellis Park is located on US 41 N., on the north side of the Ohio River in Henderson. From I-164, take the US 41 N. exit.

Admission: $2, free on Sunday; clubhouse: $2; Sky Theater: $3; grandstand boxes: $9

Parking: $1; valet: extra charge

Fine dining: Sky Theatre, Gardenia Room, Clubhouse Terrace

Casual fare: Clubhouse Deli, Thoroughbred Room

Spirits: Available in all dining areas and at grandstand concessions

Extras: Education and community-related activities include scholarship awards, art at the races, support for Habitat for Humanity and many other civic groups; Junior Jockey Club.

The Keeneland Library

Keeneland was created with that very philosophy incubating in the mind of its owner, John Oliver "Jack" Keene, who began building on this property in 1916. Having traveled the world as a young trainer following his racing passion, he envisioned his future estate with stables, a morning exercise track that friends would share, and a mansion in which guests could stay comfortably. A fine dining hall and a ballroom for parties were in order as well. The 1 1/16-mile-long track had been completed, and the barns and other buildings were underway when the Great Depression and cost overruns halted construction. The stone barn stood idle until a small group of private investors decided they needed what Keene had built. They purchased the property and completed Keeneland at last. Jack Keene eventually resurrected his finances and constructed a new private home nearby.

Racing began here in 1936; in the mid-1940s, the seasonal Thoroughbred sales that put Keeneland on the international map began, and in the mid-1950s, current owner Keeneland Association, Inc., assumed management of both the sales and the racetrack.

The Keeneland clubhouse is a two-story space with a large ground-floor entrance, its interior designed by legendary decorator Billy Baldwin. The west wall is dominated by a stone fireplace; above it hangs a large oil painting of a festive European race gathering. Chairs of green and yellow chintz, a red leather sofa, and mahogany end tables holding ceramic lamps are arranged on a bold red-and-green-patterned area rug, and potted living ficus trees fill the corners near the white French doors. Above, dark

Racing for home, Keeneland

crossbeams in the high ceiling lead the eye up to the wide mezzanine, which opens onto the clubhouse dining rooms and executive areas. The landing is decorated by a stunning floral arrangement of autumn flowers and greens, accented with antique pieces. To complete the classic decor, period side tables stand against walls, which display fine equestrian art.

Throughout Keeneland, we noted the same attention to aesthetics and upkeep, from the landscaping at the entrance gates to the barn area on the backside. With a largely middle and upper-middle class clientele, the no denim policy in specific areas of the facility is not an issue for patrons. Navy blazers and neckties prevail.

Keeneland bugler

Keeneland's race meets, featuring some of the world's most expensive and pedigreed horses, are held in the spring and in the autumn, averaging one month each. Fans love to argue about which of the seasons at Keeneland is prettier, and though we're inclined to say it's fall, we cannot speak against April's creamy dogwoods and pastel fruit blossoms or bright tulips and daffodils. The walking ring is fenced by a boxwood hedge and vibrant bedding flowers and shaded by its signature tree, a grand, leafy sycamore. Even the parking is sheltered by dappled groves of

SNAPSHOT - KEENELAND

Description: Green rolling grounds and tree-lined drives sweep you toward a setting that's more country estate than racetrack. The elegant stone grandstand and clubhouse, with their decorative wrought ironwork, are truly fit for the sheiks and kings who make the journey here. The main track is 1 1/16 miles with two chutes opening onto it. The homestretch is 1,174 feet from last turn to the wire. The turf course is 7 1/2 furlongs, with a 1,190-foot homestretch.

Season: Keeneland holds only about thirty live race dates per year: a spring meet during April and a fall meet during October.

Address: 4201 Versailles Road, Lexington, KY 40510

Phone: 859-254-3412/ (fax) 859-288-4348

Web site: http://www.keeneland.com

Nearest airport: Blue Grass Airport (LEX)

Getting there: On Route 60 (Versailles Road), about twelve miles west of Lexington

Admission: $3; children under twelve: free; reserved seating: extra charges; clubhouse: members only

Parking: Free; valet: extra charge

Fine dining: Phoenix Room, Lexington Room, Kentucky Room, all open to the public, reservations recommended

Casual fare: Equestrian Room, the Track Kitchen (located in the barn area, open to the public), Blue Cactus Cantina, Brats n' Brew, Clocker's Corner, 16th Pole Grill, other concessions throughout the grandstand

Spirits: Many concessions and beverage stations throughout the facility

Extras: Keeneland is the site of major Thoroughbred sales during the year, which are open to the public. During the race season, Breakfast with the Works offers a chance to watch morning workouts while enjoying a hearty breakfast. On nonrace days, preplanned tours of the facilities may be available to nonprofit groups only. The fine Keeneland gift shop carries everything from tiny diamond stud earrings to original art and large pieces of furniture. It reopens in December as an exclusive Christmas shop.

Queen Elizabeth II greets Keeneland jockeys.

the lawn and across to the grandstand or the clubhouse.

If your budget can take you only to one racecourse beyond your home turf, save it and splurge when you arrive here. From the classic setting to the graciousness of Keeneland personnel, who strive to make the racing experience here unforgettable, from research librarians with help at the ready to elevator operators poised with a lighthearted greeting (even for a one-floor ride)—everything reflects the high standard of a racing association destined to continue being the yardstick by which all others are measured.

trees. This pleasing first impression only gets better as you enter the grounds and ascend the wide steps, flanked by stone pillars and big pots of riotous red geraniums, that lead onto

PAINTER IN THE PADDOCK

The tall sycamore beside the paddock spreads its illuminated shade over the figures on the oval below. A wash of blue autumn sky filters through the branches. In the background, dappled spectators look down from the grandstand balconies. Jockeys appear in the oval, ready to mount for the post parade.

Standing before the easel that captures this scene, brushes in hand and driving cap pulled down to screen the sun, the painter commanding the paddock hesitates, studying the canvas he is brushing to life.

"I wonder if the branches need more black. What do you think?" he asks, turning to engage an observer.

Artist Peter Williams, in the enviable position of interpreting the energy, the pageantry, the carnival of colors, the beauty of horse racing, clearly enjoys his plein air work. Selected as the official artist of Breeders' Cup 2005, Williams has painted America's leading Thoroughbred racecourses, from Del Mar to

Artist Peter Williams

Saratoga. His paintings hang in premier hotels and private estates; Queen Elizabeth, William Farish, and Ogden Phipps are among his collectors. Williams, a self-taught artist, was a sheepherder and rancher in his native New Zealand when he began exhibiting in New Zealand and Australian galleries. Eventually, his patrons lured him to New York to paint Thoroughbred racing scenes at Belmont Park.

Though equine anatomy might seem to be a sporting artist's biggest challenge, it isn't so for Williams. The form of the horse was imprinted in his imagination from his ranching days. "I think of movement—its gait—rather than anatomy," he says.

Impressionism, with its spontaneous use of light and color to quickly capture form and mood, is especially suited to the tempo of the racetrack, where nothing waits for the photographer or the artist. "It's all happening so quickly, my head is so full of horses and things, all trying to get out. Unless you've got a brush in your hand, the moment is lost."

The septuagenarian Williams can be difficult to track down, as his artistic reputation keeps him traveling. It's easier when there's a classic race such as the Derby or the Belmont Stakes; then you'll find him painting in the paddock, ready to say hello.

KENTUCKY DOWNS (FRANKLIN)

Tucked away in southern Kentucky near the Tennessee line is the small town of Franklin, founded in 1819 and named in honor of Benjamin Franklin. Its racetrack, Kentucky Downs, is one of a kind. It is a wonderful anomaly in the world of Thoroughbred racing—a European-style flat race, kidney-shaped turf course, running up and down and around the land for 1 ⁵⁄₁₆ miles. The usual outer oval dirt course is absent. The turf-only track was built rather recently—in 1990—and opened under the name Dueling Grounds, recalling the legendary nineteenth-century duels that took place here. Its token, one-day meeting facilitated the primary focus: simulcasting. In 1996, however, owners changed the name to Kentucky Downs, and the track has

On the grass at Kentucky Downs

since expanded live racing to six days in autumn.

The meet, organized as the Kentucky Cup Turf Series, follows soon after the significant Kentucky Cup Championships at upstate Turfway Park. The Downs's meet is unquestionably too short, but its Kentucky Cup Turf Festival day presents four hefty stakes races, including the center-

Kentucky Downs turf battle

piece, the $200,000 Kentucky Cup Turf (G3), at 1 1/2 miles.

The live racing experience here is unique. Reminiscent of an earlier Keeneland (Keeneland, Turfway Park, and Churchill Downs own Kentucky Downs), there is no infield totalizer board flashing results, though there are simulcast screens in abundance and final numbers are readily available outside as well. The setting is pure pastoral, quiet and green and rolling, and very informal. Some fans bring sandwiches, others set up elaborate picnics beside the track, and still others retreat to the comfort of the clubhouse.

The fields are among the largest anywhere, and because purses are nice and fat, the caliber of racing is almost as good as it gets. If you can get away in September, drive or fly in and treat yourself to this experience. Do the really fun thing and stay in Nashville, Tennessee, just forty-five minutes south of Franklin. Check out Nashville lodging and Grand Ole Opry performers at http://www .nashvillecvb.com. Both Franklin and its neighbor Bowling Green, twenty miles north, offer plenty of motels too; search at http://www.tripadvisor.com.

Turfway Park

TURFWAY PARK (FLORENCE)

Turfway Park, standing in the lush, rolling hills of northern Kentucky, looked handsome in the evening light. On that opening night of the fall meet, everyone was upbeat, and hospitality flowed freely. When we arrived at the paddock entrance, Turfway executives Greg Schmitz and Chip Bach were welcoming returning owners and patrons. Marketing director Brian Gardner, who joined them, aroused our curiosity with the bag of fresh limes he carried. Out on the apron we met Bob Elliston, president of the park. Our warm welcome included a full Turfway tour, hosted by the track's media relations director Sherry Pinson. Foremost on everyone's lips this evening was the nice weather. Mother Nature had finally ended her

SNAPSHOT - KENTUCKY DOWNS

Description: Its European-style flat race, kidney-shaped turf course runs up and down and around the land for 1 ⁵⁄₆ miles.
Season: Open for six days through late September
Address: 5629 Nashville Road, Franklin, KY 42135
Phone: 270-586-7778/(fax) 270-586-8080
Web site: http://www.kentuckydowns.com
Nearest airport: Nashville International Airport (BNA)
Getting there: Located on the central Kentucky-Tennessee state line. From I-65, take Exit 2 and go south on Route 31W, approximately one mile. The track is on the right.
Admission: $2.00
Parking: Free
Fine dining: Sly Fox Restaurant (Turf Club)
Casual fare: Horseshoe Deli
Spirits: No liquor sales on premises; bring-in privileges for Turf Club members
Extras: Simulcasting year-round, with seasonal promotions

Turfway walking ring

seven-day deluge and brought clear skies to the meet.

Turfway Park opened in 1959 as the new Latonia Race Course. Along with an ownership change in 1986 came its present name, though Turfway celebrates its heritage and strong ties to the original Latonia, which stood at nearby Covington, Kentucky, on the Ohio River, from 1883 to 1939. One of America's grand tracks in the heyday of horse racing, old Latonia rivaled Churchill Downs for its high caliber of racehorses and huge crowds. In this modern era, the directors of new Latonia, now Turfway Park, have distinguished the track with daring innovations. Turfway introduced regular night racing to Kentucky in 1968. (With it, in 1974, came the first ever triple dead heat under the lights—only the thirteenth such feat in racing history—

RAFAEL BEJARANO'S EXCELLENT NUMBERS

Peruvian-born jockey Rafael Bejarano may remember thirteen as just one of his lucky numbers. On Friday, March 12, 2004, at Turfway Park, in Kentucky, he recorded seven wins for the day, setting a new track record. On Saturday the 13th, he claimed an early victory in race three and another in the ninth, and then won the day's tenth race, the $50,000 Tejano Run Stakes, astride Ask The Lord. That made it his 112th victory since the winter/spring meet began on January 1, a win that broke Jason Lumpkin's 2003 Turfway record of 111 wins. But it wasn't quitting time for twenty-one-year-old Bejarano. He finished the day with two more victories, making this the third time during the meet that he had won five races in a single day.

It adds up impressively: in a twenty-four-hour period, Bejarano won twelve races, set two records, and became the leading jockey nationwide for number of wins to date in 2004.

when Deleterious, Quipid, and Bob Twinkletoes split the first-place win.) In 1988, Turfway broadcast its races at Ellis Park, launching Thoroughbred race simulcasting in Kentucky. With its recent innovations in electronic wager-ing, the park has again leapt to the fore-front of technology.

Rising five stories, Turfway Park's clean architecture and remodeled interi-or are a pleasing blend of atmospheres. On the upper levels, where the Racing

LEGENDARY LATONIA

On June 9, 1883, a cheering crowd of eight thousand people celebrated the opening of Latonia Race Course, near Covington, Kentucky. For a summer day at Latonia, they dressed in elegant Victorian finery—high-collared dresses with big bustles and sweeping skirts for the ladies; high-buttoned coats, with starched shirts and cravats, or ties, for the gentlemen. With picnic baskets overflowing, the crowd flocked to the new course for a day of music, socializing, and the excite-ment of racing festivities.

From the beginning, horses of the highest caliber raced at Latonia. Some were starters in the Kentucky Derby, the then nine-year-old Churchill Downs race in Louisville, a hundred miles to the southwest. With Thoroughbred racing underway at Latonia, the Kentucky circuit was born. Crowd size and prize money at the two popular tracks were competitive for years.

No horse who raced at Latonia is more remarkable than Exterminator, a chestnut gelding who won his first start as a two-year-old maiden there in 1917. The next year he captured the Kentucky Derby at 30-1 odds as a last-minute fill-in for another horse. Exterminator could win at 6 furlongs or at 2 1/4 miles and ranked as the nation's top handicap horse from 1919 to 1922, earning more than $250,000. He raced a total of one hundred times during his eight-year career, winning 50. In 1957, he was posthumously inducted into the Racing Hall of Fame.

In the 1920s, with Latonia's ownership in the capable hands of Churchill Downs's manager Matt Winn, the racecourse set the national record four times for purse money offered. Then Winn decided to turn his full attention toward promoting the Kentucky Derby. For that and other rea-sons, Latonia began the slow descent to its closing, which came in 1939; the track was subse-quently torn down. Twenty years later Latonia rose anew, ten miles from the original racetrack site, and eventually became known as Turfway Park.

In *The Tradition Continues: The Story of Old Latonia, Latonia, and Turfway Racecourses* (1997), horseman and scholar James C. Claypool tells the story of Latonia's three incarnations—as old Latonia, new Latonia, and modern Turfway Park. He describes their relationship to regional, national, and international events and trends that have shaped the sport of horse racing for more than a century. This is one of the best racetrack histories we have found.

Ben Ali, Kentucky Derby winner 1886

Club hosts private parties and buffets, the rich look of mahogany and green sets a traditional tone, whereas in the more casual Garden Terrace, white lattice and floral motifs frame the large, round tables. Long Shots and Blinkers bars serve spirits on the third and second floors, and every level has enclosed, climate-controlled grandstand seating. On the main floor, a sweep of bright neon energy and several king-size monitors fill the Racebook, where the amazing touch screen Super Carrels are installed. These new individual screens offer every live simulcast race available and videos of any horse's recorded performances (you can choose a head-on or final stretch angle), and include options for self-contained wagering and even touch screen food service.

Mike Battaglia

Turfway's biggest events are its graded stakes, run during the winter/spring and fall meets. Best known is the $500,000 Lane's End Stakes (G2), origi-

nally run as the Spiral, and later as the Jim Beam Stakes. As an important Kentucky Derby prep race, the Lane's End is scheduled annually at the end of March. The fall meet at Turfway Park brings the exciting Kentucky Cup Championships, a $1 million-plus series of Grade 2 and Grade 3 competitions in mid-September, preparing top contestants for the Breeders' Cup World Championships to be held a month later. Highlighting the Cup Day program is the $350,000-guaranteed Classic (G2).

Before settling down to wager and win, we visited the Corona Cabana, quenched our thirst, and met up with Brian Gardner again. We watched as he revealed the secret of the twelve limes still in his possession. He was teaching fans to play Corona Hole, in which a person tries to toss a lime into one of several numbered water buckets, each number representing a horse running in the

SnapShot - Turfway Park

Description: Turfway's white grandstand isn't overly fancy. The dirt 1-mile oval with two chutes has a 970-foot homestretch. There is no turf racing here.

Season: The winter/spring meet runs from early January to early April; the fall meet runs from September to October; and the Holiday meet is held from late November to New Year's Eve.

Address: 7500 Turfway Road, Florence, KY 41042; send correspondence to P.O. Box 8, Florence, KY 41022

Phone: 859-371-0200/800-733-0200/(fax) 859-371-0200

Web site: http://www.turfway.com

Nearest airport: Cincinnati/Northern Kentucky International (CVG); Blue Grass Airport (LEX), Lexington, KY

Getting there: Florence, Kentucky, is just south of Cincinnati, Ohio. From I-75 in Cincinnati, take Exit 182 (Turfway Road).

Admission: Free

Parking: Free; valet: extra charge

Fine dining: Private parties and Racing Club members can reserve private rooms on the fourth floor.

Casual fare: Homestretch Restaurant, Terrace Restaurant

Spirits: Long Shots Sports Bar, Blinkers, Corona Cantina on the apron, open evenings during the fall meet

Extras: Player's Row: $1.50 per seat; pool tables and video games are on the third floor.

upcoming race. By sinking a lime in the bucket, the winner receives a $2 win voucher on that horse in the next race.

Leaving the Cabana, we stopped in for an introduction to longtime track announcer Mike Battaglia, relaxed and friendly even as he worked out technical matters before the first race. (As a young man, Mike called that triple dead heat in 1974, when his father, John, was general manager of Turfway.)

Finally, we settled down, studied the program, and set out to win serious dollars. Two hours later, winnings in hand, we aimed our rental car toward nearby Cincinnati for the final night away. The sky was beautiful, the half-moon rising like a wedge of creamy Camembert cheese. Against the grandstand wall, Turfway's five neon ponies, illuminated in sparkling green, raced across the night.

MARYLAND

LAUREL PARK (LAUREL)

Laurel Park seems as if it is fading away. Literally, it isn't; the acres of glass and banks of televisions are still there. But there is a feeling that it will fade into history without new lifeblood.

Built in 1911 on land that was cow pasture, Laurel Park is reached by crawling along congested two-lane roads off I-95. It is located midway between Baltimore and Washington, D.C., on the very spot that once served it well but now threatens to overwhelm it.

Vestiges of Laurel Park's grand past abound. The stands are slightly L-shaped; the building is faced with an impressive swath of glittering, green-tinted glass. In the junction of the L, perched high above the park, the announcer's stand peers down from a dizzying height. To one side of the stands is a massive round building, built of heavy wooden beams, reminiscent of the roundhouse at a country fair. The saddling paddock is here; the stalls curving around the back of the building. Closer examination reveals that the roof of the structure sags in spots, the windows near the top zigzag up and down.

The field moves into the turn, Laurel Park

Down the backstretch at Laurel Park

Inside the clubhouse, the floor plan is fairly open. The first level is decked out in green and white, with banks of simulcasting televisions providing a dizzying collage of color and sound. A staircase in the front, beneath a massive chandelier, leads to the second floor area. Here the ceilings are lower, and the decor is red and white. Automated teller kiosks and simulcasting theaters are everywhere; track employees are scarce.

The top floor best reflects the grand past of Laurel Park. Glass doors open into the Jockey Club, an exclusive area of carpets and paneled decor with bronze racing statues on display. Along the wall, black-and-white photographs recall Laurel-raced champions of the past, including Spectacular Bid and Affirmed. On this day, live racing is being conducted at Laurel's better known sibling, Pimlico, and the darkened stands are silent. If the clatter of slots one day soon punctuates this silence, then perhaps the glory of Laurel Park will spring to life anew, borne along by the roar of returning spectators.

SnapShot - Laurel Park

Description: Tucked midway between Washington, D.C., and Baltimore, Maryland, Laurel Park held its first live race card on October 2, 1911. Today, Laurel is solidly working class, with simulcasting and everyday racing interspersed with stakes events. The track is 1 ⅛ miles long, with a 1-mile turf course. The dirt homestretch is 1,344 feet to the wire; the turf course homestretch is 990 feet to the wire.

Season: Laurel Park has three meets, an early winter meet from January 1 to the end of March, a midsummer meet from the end of July to the end of August, and a fall meet from early October to the end of December.

Address: Route 198, Laurel, MD; send correspondence to P.O. Box 130, Laurel, MD 20725

Phone: 301-725-0400/(fax) 301-725-4561

Web site: http://www. marylandracing.com

Nearest airport: Ronald Reagan Washington National (DCA) and Washington Dulles International (IAD)

Getting there: Twenty-two miles from either Washington, D.C., or Baltimore, off Exit 33 (Route 198) from I-95. Track is approximately four miles from I-95.

Admission: Seats on weekdays are free, with some exceptions; grandstand or clubhouse: $3; nights and simulcasting: free; active and retired military personnel: free with military ID; local police and firefighters: free with proper ID.

Parking: Free; valet and preferred: extra charge

Fine dining: Maryland Turf Caterers, the official caterer at Laurel Park Several elegant rooms are available for private functions.

Casual fare: Sunny Jim's, Tycoon's

Spirits: Available throughout the facility

Extras: Gift shop, "Live it Up at Laurel Day" and other promotional events, handicapping contests, Pony Pal for kids

PIMLICO RACE COURSE (BALTIMORE)

While enjoying a splendid dinner party in 1868, some sporting fellows up at Saratoga decided to commemorate the evening with a horse race: the Dinner Party Stakes. They'd make it a two miler, open to three-year-old fillies and colts. One member of the illustrious party, the governor of Maryland, set the purse at a jaw-dropping $15,000 and even guaranteed that in two years he'd have a new Baltimore track ready for the race. Thirty nominations quickly poured in and betting began at once!

They inaugurated the new track, Pimlico, in the autumn of 1870. The final field for the Dinner Party Stakes was narrowed to two colts and five fillies. Among them was the Kentucky-bred colt Preakness, running his first race. He was built quite unlike his powerful, legendary sire, Lexington, and many a spectator made fun of him. There was no mocking him after the race, however; he won that huge purse for his owner, M. H. Sanford, who

Breaking from the gate, Pimlico

had been, coincidentally, host of that Saratoga dinner party.

In 1873, the track decided to conduct a spring meet as well and named its biggest race in honor of the track's first winner. Blue-and-white pennants decorated the grand Victorian clubhouse, the grandstand was painted violet, and twelve thousand spectators watched as Survivor took the inaugural Preakness Stakes by 10 lengths.

The Preakness Stakes (G1) is today the crucial middle gem in the elusive American Triple Crown. If the Kentucky Derby winner can't trade the prestigious blanket of roses for the

Maryland-bred La Reine's Terms winning the Maryland Million

Preakness victory blanket of black-eyed Susans, there will be no Triple Crown champion in that season.

For two weeks preceding the Preakness, a long string of parties, dinners, and other events guarantees sumptuous entertainment for Pimlico's aristocracy. Then on the Thursday prior to the race comes the Alibi Breakfast, when the clubhouse fills with some five hundred morning diners who heartily carry on the tradition—trading tales of their greatest losing bets—that led to the naming of the first Alibi Table long ago. The Black-Eyed Susan Stakes (G2) is run on the Friday before the Preakness. The race is for three-year-old fillies, therefore it's the female equivalent to the Preakness.

Come rain or come shine, no one stays away on Saturday. A hundred thousand–plus fans strain Pimlico at the seams, packing the infield Preakness Village Turf Club tent parties and Turfside Terrace buffets, while thousands of professional partygoers and race fans revel in the infield.

In a Preakness tradition that lets everyone see the horses being saddled, jockeys mount their horses on the turf course in front of the grandstand. The bugler trumpets the call to post, and the Preakness theme song, "Maryland, My Maryland," fills the air. In 2004, all eyes were on Kentucky Derby winner Smarty Jones. Smarty, with Stewart Elliott up, went into this race undefeated in a seven-race career. He faced strong competition, especially from Lion Heart ridden by Mike Smith, who had taken second in the Derby, and Rock Hard Ten, a massive black horse with Gary Stevens in the saddle. Almost as soon as they broke from the gate, the second leg of the series looked oddly easy, familiar, and almost predictable.

SnapShot - Pimlico Race Course

Description: Pimlico is on 140 acres within the Baltimore city limits. The glass-fronted grandstand looks out over a mile-long loamy track, one reputed to favor speed horses. Two chutes open onto the racetrack. The stretch is 1,152 feet from last turn to wire. On the ⅞-mile turf course, horses race over a cushion of bluegrass.

Season: Pimlico holds a spring season running from the end of March until the beginning of June, and a brief fall meet from early September until early October. The second jewel of the Triple Crown, the Preakness, is held here in mid-May.

Address: 5201 Park Heights Avenue, Baltimore, MD 21215

Phone: 410-542-9400/(fax) 410-466-2521

Web site: http://www.marylandracing.com

Nearest airport: Baltimore/Washington International Airport (BWI)

Getting there: Take I-95 to 695 West (Baltimore Beltway). Take Exit 83 south to the Northern Parkway West. Follow signs for Pimlico. Transportation by bus is also available; check the Web site for more information.

Admission: Grandstand & clubhouse: $3; active & retired military personnel: free with military ID; local police and firefighters: free with proper ID; reserved box seats: extra charge of $2.50

Parking: Free; valet and preferred parking: extra charge

Fine dining: Maryland Turf Caterers are the official caterers for Pimlico. Several elegant rooms are available for private functions.

Casual fare: The Track Kitchen is located behind the grandstand; numerous concessions for light fare are throughout the facility.

Spirits: Available at several concessions

Extras: Lots of special events and giveaways throughout the season, especially around Preakness Day. Check the Web site or call for specific information.

THE TRIPLE CROWN UNDOZEN

Winning the American Triple Crown series requires amazing performances in rapid succession. The three tracks are so varied, with each race unfolding under different conditions, and the races so close together in time that winning them all is the crowning achievement of a Thoroughbred's career.

Opening the unrivaled series, the legendary Kentucky Derby is a gala affair, a huge, genteel but electric party of big hats and mint juleps—140,000 strong. The field of three-year-olds, most of them running 1 ¼ miles for the first time, is usually jammed—sheer luck sometimes makes the critical difference in this classic race. The Pimlico track is a slightly shorter ¹³⁄₁₆ miles, the turns are a little tighter than Churchill Downs. Ready or not, three weeks later the Belmont Stakes, the oldest of the three races as well as the longest, completes the Crown. Bloodlines and breeding count for everything now. The horses run 1 ½ miles on a track dubbed interminable by writer Elizabeth Mitchell. Its wide, sweeping turns are tough, and the final stretch, the longest in America, makes this race the ultimate jewel in the crown.

In the past seventy years, only eleven Thoroughbreds have claimed the Triple Crown trophy, and more than forty others have won two of the three prestigious races. Only two fillies have competed in all three Triple Crown races. In 1980, Genuine Risk won the Derby and finished second in the Preakness and Belmont Stakes, the best overall performance of any filly to date. Eight years later, Winning Colors, who won the 1980 Kentucky Derby, also competed in the Preakness and the Belmont.

The world of Thoroughbred racing is ready for lucky number 12. The eleven TC winners are Sir Barton (1919), Gallant Fox (1930), Omaha (1935), War Admiral (1937), Whirlaway (1941), Count Fleet (1943), Assault (1946), Citation (1948), Secretariat (1973), Seattle Slew (1977), and Affirmed (1978).

Triple Crown winner Secretariat at Belmont Park

First to the finish at Pimlico

Lion Heart took a quick lead. Smarty moved up in the pack, took to the inside, and in what looked effortless, settled in second, as he had in the Derby. Then on the far turn he moved into the lead and just kept going, farther ahead, ahead, ahead, as the crowd stared in wonder. He flew across the finish line, 11 ½ lengths ahead of Rock Hard Ten, with Eddington, ridden by Jerry Bailey, finishing third.

On a more typical day at Pimlico, when the throng is gone and you can actually appreciate the buildings and grounds, you're left with a sense of nostalgia for the glory days of racing. Touches of yesteryear transport you back in time, such as the simple, old-time metal rail that leans into the edge of the track. Portraits and stories at The National Jockeys Hall of Fame remind you that Sir Barton won the 1919 Preakness a mere four days after winning the Derby and that this is where Seabiscuit beat the great War Admiral in a 1938 match race.

Even the word *wire* was supposedly coined here at Pimlico. According to legend, in 1870 a cord was tied across the track, with the prize money inside a bag wired to the cord. The winning jockey retrieved the purse from the wire at the finish line. Pimlico, a stately racetrack through the ages and one of the pillars of Thoroughbred racing, remains a treasured institution.

VIRGINIA

COLONIAL DOWNS (NEW KENT)

Racing in Old Dominion is legendary. Wealthy gentlemen farmers such as George Washington and Thomas Jefferson contributed much to the turf scene in young Virginia—and in the United States. Washington especially liked legislative meetings that coincided with race meets in Richmond and Williamsburg. During the early days of the republic, Richmond alone boasted three racetracks. In the late 1700s, another Virginian, John Tayloe III, born into the most significant turf family of the Revolutionary War period, imported English Derby winner Diomed, who would become the most successful Thoroughbred stallion of the young American empire.

Despite this glorious start with racing and Virginia's continuing reputation as a notable Thoroughbred breeding state—the legendary Secretariat, for example, was foaled there in 1970 at the Chenery family's Meadow Stable—the commonwealth boasted not one single Thoroughbred track for most of the twentieth century. Finally, in 1997, Colonial Downs, in New Kent, made its long-awaited debut. Attendance, racing days, and purses at the independently owned latecomer have all increased steadily in recent years. Colonial Downs has set a high standard for its racing, which shows in the attention to details. It also doesn't hurt that it has former Monkees member Davy Jones as a spokesman and horse owner on the grounds.

Colonial Downs, which sits at the edge of a large wooded area near the York River halfway between Richmond and Williamsburg, is a medium-size facility of traditional colonial architecture. Its red brick exterior showcases tall, Federal-style windows and bold

Grass race at Colonial Downs

white columns that frame the peaked portico at the entrance. Most of the big races here are run on the 7 ½-furlong turf course, which draws high praise from horsemen. In 2004, daily purses totaled $200,000, though the meet's biggest day (an evening, actually) brings the $500,000 Virginia Derby, along with two other significant races, to the card.

On Virginia Derby Day, the grandstand and clubhouse are decorated with yards and yards of striped red, white, and blue bunting, draped the length of the railing on several spectator levels.

SNAPSHOT - COLONIAL DOWNS

Description: Tucked deep within the pinewoods of Virginia, echoes of Rhett Butler and Scarlett O'Hara can be found at Colonial Downs. A massive red brick and white-columned colonial mansion greets the fans as they stream in from the parking lots. The mansion morphs into a modern glass-fronted grandstand overlooking a massive racetrack. A 1-¼ mile dirt track with a 1,290.5-foot-long stretch surrounds a 7 ½-furlong turf course.

Season: Late June to late July

Address: 10515 Colonial Downs Parkway, New Kent, VA 23124

Phone: 804-966-7223/(fax) 804-966-1565

Web site: http://www.colonialdowns.com

Nearest airport: Richmond International Airport (RIC)

Getting there: From I-64, take exit 214. At the bottom of the ramp, turn left if coming from the west, or right if coming from the east. In approximately three hundred yards, turn left onto Colonial Downs Parkway. Track entrance is about one-quarter mile on the left.

Admission: $2

Parking: Free; valet parking: extra charge; children twelve and under: free

Fine dining: Jockey Club, reservations are recommended; Turf Club, members only during live meet, open to the public during the harness meet, reservations are recommended.

Casual fare: Concessions located throughout the stands

Spirits: The Jockey Club, Home Stretch, Trotter's Tavern

Extras: Beatles tribute bands and fireworks are among the special summer attractions.

Add a throng of picnickers barbecuing on the green beside the grandstand and dressy crowds enjoying buffets in the clubhouse and corporate suites, and the result is a festive, all-American scene. Virginia Derby Day has expanded to include the $200,000 Virginia Oaks, for fillies, and the $200,000 All Along Breeders Cup (G3). All three races are run over the grass course.

Going into the Virginia Derby in 2003, Senor Swinger was the big favorite, though he finished a disappointing fourth. Winning jockey Edgar Prado rode Silver Tree, who had not raced during his two-year-old season, to a 2:01.11 finish. Coincidentally, Prado also won the 2003 Virginia Derby on Silver Tree's full brother, Orchard Park.

WEST VIRGINIA

CHARLES TOWN RACES AND SLOTS (CHARLES TOWN)

Following the signs to Charles Town Races and Slots takes you off Interstate 81 and onto a curving two-lane road, giving you a glimpse of life in rural West Virginia. But at the entrance to Charles Town, it's immediately apparent that change has come to town. The old racetrack has taken on a new life in recent years, attributable to the word *slots* in its new name.

Charles Town Races and Slots is a success story, a graphic example of how tying the fortunes of a racetrack to slots can bring a track back from the dead. In Charles Town's case, the place was old and funky, almost gone. Purses were as small as the number of horses competing in them; when horses here ran for $2,500 claiming tags, purses hovered at $3,000. The installation of slots changed all that. There are still $2,500 claiming races, but the purses for them have jumped to $10,000.

Established in 1933, the West Virginia track was languishing and nearly forgotten when it was taken over by Penn National Gaming Inc. in 2000. Today, the facility is clean and well kept. From the apron in front of the grandstand, the building appears plain: a tan grandstand with a glass front, banks of lights lining the top, an announcer's booth perched precariously on the very top. Fresh paint covers the ironwork fence and the trim on the stands.

Flowers bloom in abundance, and a number of tables are set up on the apron. The track, narrow and tight, is well groomed. Fans can get close to the action here as the horses thunder past into the first turn. There is talk of redoing the track in the near future, expanding it and adding a turf course. Inside, the changes in fortune are even more evident. A casino, styled like a

Charles Town Race Track

Western town, has been added, with costumed waitstaff and huge fake cacti hiding the support columns. The effect is surreal: bells and buzzers, metallic clanking of coins hitting a pan, music thumping overhead, neon blinking and flashing everywhere. Simulcasting theaters abound, with banks of televisions and comfortable accommodations. The inner grandstand has also been retrofitted with plants, bright linoleum flooring, and soft lighting.

From high up in the glassed-in section of the stands, you can see the barns lined up behind the new saddling paddock to the far left of the stands. In red-roofed rows, they have a distinctly military look to them. From the stands, the fans can see the entire track clearly. Here again, evidence of upgrading abounds. Traditional fold-down stadium seats fill one-third of the stands. Another third is lined with long countertops and chairs, inviting you to put down your drink and mark up your rac-

Blinkers on and ready to race

ing form. At the far right, behind glass, is the track's tiered clubhouse restaurant, with a television on every table. With all this new life pumping through its veins, Charles Town Races and Slots promises to be around for a long time.

SnapShot - Charles Town Races and Slots

Description: Bright colors, bright lights, bustling crowds, red roofs, and a red racetrack, that's how Charles Town looks to the new fan. Everything has been renovated, from the stands to the barn area. A fast, 6-furlong bullring track is the centerpiece, with two chutes opening onto it. The homestretch is a fast 660 feet from the last turn to the wire. There is no turf course.

Season: Charles Town holds live races year-round.

Address: US Route 340, Charles Town, WV 25414

Phone: 304-725-7001/(fax) 304-724-4326

Web site: http://www.ctownraces.com

Nearest airport: Hagerstown Regional Airport (HGR)

Getting there: The track is in northeastern West Virginia, in the little crook that borders Maryland and Virginia. Charles Town is about twenty miles southwest of I-70 and fourteen miles east of I-81. From I-70, take Route 340 west approximately twenty miles. From I-81, take Route 9 south. For more information, check the Web site or call.

Admission: Free

Parking: Free

Fine dining: Skyline Terrace

Casual fare: Long Shots Deli, Charles Town Fare, Silverado Buffet, Sundance Café

Spirits: Everywhere

Extras: On Friday and Saturday nights, enjoy live music from the track's new stage, located next to the slot floor.

MOUNTAINEER RACE TRACK AND GAMING RESORT (CHESTER)

The Ohio River meanders through the area, its banks sprouting steel mills and tree-covered banks. Route 2 winds alongside it, curving up and over a metal toll bridge before running through the sleepy town of Chester, West Virginia. At the far end of town, the roadsides open up, fields replace factories, old farmhouses peek out through the trees. The river hooks away from the road, and an unexpected vista opens up: two hotels and a cocktail lounge; a theater. And silhouetted against the low hill on the opposite shore is the grandstand of Mountaineer Race Track and Gaming Resort. This new upscale racing resort is located in the state's northeastern tip, in the finger where West Virginia hooks in between Ohio and Pennsylvania.

The track started life as Waterford Park in the 1950s. On May 19, 1951, when the horses burst from the starting gate for the first time, the track surface was a fine golden sand, and airplanes landed in the infield, delivering jockeys and wealthy patrons alike. Harsh winters

The Mahogany Bar, Mountaineer Park

convinced management to tear out the sand and replace it with a surface that contained pea stone—easier to keep from freezing but harder on the horses. Trainers had to devise strategies to protect their horses, such as using blinker hoods with wire mesh over both eyes for protection against flying gravel. An aircraft accident put an end to the infield landing strip, and the racing in this remote location slowly began to slip away. Attendance and the handle dwindled, and the quality of the horses diminished.

By 1992, Mountaineer was in serious jeopardy. An experiment with slot machines was ending in disaster amid

Mountaineer Park

allegations of mismanagement and the resignation of the state's lottery director. The track was ordered to shut down its slots, and Mountaineer faced the end of the road. That is when Edson "Ted" Arneault became involved. A former tax accountant, Arneault, Mountaineer's CEO, managed to persuade the state not only to leave the terminals in place but also to install slot machines at the state's other racetrack, Charles Town. He successfully argued that the jobs and revenue generated from these gambling sites would benefit the area and the state. (People had been scrabbling to make a living here for decades.) Boy, did it ever.

Today, Mountaineer Race Track and Gaming Resort is one of the fastest growing small companies in the country, generating revenues in the hundreds of millions. Under Arneault's management, more land was acquired; the facility was expanded; a casino, a

Smile for the camera.

golf course, and two upscale hotels were built; and a glittering nightclub opened. Locally, the job market skyrocketed. People are making a living again. Brought back from the brink, Mountaineer is now thriving.

Thousands of people are making the trek to this resort, where the sign at the roadway proclaims, "We'll Leave the Slots on for Ya." When you go, stay on the premises at The Grande Hotel (800-804-0468).

SnapShot - Mountaineer Race Track and Gaming Resort

Description: Tucked along the banks of the Ohio River, where West Virginia juts into Pennsylvania and Ohio, lies one of Thoroughbred racing's biggest success stories. This scenic track is the centerpiece of a multimillion-dollar resort and spa destination. A 1-mile dirt track with two chutes encompasses a 7-furlong turf course. The stretch is 905 feet long.

Season: Live racing is held from early January to late December. The meet's highlight, the West Virginia Derby (G3), runs in mid-August.

Address: Route 2, Chester, WV 26034

Phone: 304-387-2400/800-804-0468/(fax) 304-387-3156

Web site: http://www.mtrgaming.com

Nearest airport: Pittsburgh International Airport (PIT)

Getting there: Off Route 11 from either Route 80 or 90. Go south on Route 11 to the East Liverpool downtown exit, and follow the signs to Mountaineer Park. Cross Newell Toll Bridge. From the WV side, turn right onto Route 2 South. The track is nine miles from the bridge.

Admission: Free

Parking: Free

Fine dining: The Mountaineer Clubhouse Terrace and Dining Room, reservations are suggested.

Casual fare: The Outdoor Café, Big Al's Hot Rod Café, Big Al's Concessions

Spirits: Hollywood Knights Saloon

Extras: Catch a big-name live concert or sporting event at the Harvey "Harv" Arneault Theatre, Mountaineer's performance hall. Spa indulgences are available at the luxurious Grande Hotel. Or catch a round of golf at Mountaineer's own course, the Woodview.

SOUTHEAST TRAVEL SECTION

BELOW, YOU'LL FIND A MILEAGE CHART LISTING THE DISTANCES
BETWEEN THE REGIONAL RACETRACKS AND ALL THE CITIES
DISCUSSED IN THE FOLLOWING TRAVEL SECTION. THE CITY OR
CITIES CLOSEST TO A TRACK ARE INDICATED BY AN **X.**

COAST TO COAST	Baltimore, Md.	Charles Town, W.Va.	Henderson, Ky.	Lexington, Ky.	Louisville, Ky.	Richmond, Va.	Washington, D.C.
Charles Town Races and Slots (W.Va.)	80 miles	**X** * miles	700 miles	500 miles	570 miles	150 miles	**X** 65 miles
Churchill Downs (Ky.)	610 miles	570 miles	135 miles	**X** 80 miles	**X** * miles	565 miles	610 miles
Colonial Downs (Va.)	175 miles	170 miles	715 miles	515 miles	590 miles	**X** 30 miles	125 miles
Ellis Park Race Course (Ky.)	735 miles	695 miles	**X** * miles	200 miles	125 miles	685 miles	730 miles
Keeneland (Ky.)	545 miles	505 miles	200 miles	**X** * miles	**X** 75 miles	495 miles	545 miles
Kentucky Downs (Ky.)	910 miles	665 miles	**X** 125 miles	175 miles	135 miles	650 miles	705 miles
Laurel Park (Md.)	**X** 20 miles	80 miles	740 miles	540 miles	610 miles	130 miles	**X** 20 miles
Mountaineer Race Track and Gaming Resort (W.Va.)	285 miles	**X** 245 miles	500 miles	355 miles	380 miles	380 miles	285 miles
Pimlico Race Course (Md.)	**X** * miles	70 miles	735 miles	535 miles	610 miles	155 miles	**X** 45 miles
Turfway Park (Ky.)	535 miles	495 miles	215 miles	**X** 70 miles	**X** 85 miles	555 miles	530 miles

*The racetrack is located inside or within 10 miles of the city limits.

MUST SEE / MUST DO

KENTUCKY

HENDERSON

Sitting on high (and dry on Sundays) ground overlooking the Ohio River, Henderson is a charming town with a regional reputation. Once one of the wealthiest tobacco ports in the mid-South, Henderson has a population today that hovers around 27,000. Henderson's historic district, especially along Main Street, has dozens of homes and buildings representing architectural styles dating to the mid-1850s. The city supports a vibrant cultural scene. The river, which was once the lifeblood of the town, is a recreational hub of parks, boating, and a Riverwalk, as well as the site of the Henderson Riverfront Amphitheater, where summer concerts are performed. Famed nineteenth-century ornithologist John James Audubon identified this region as a major flyway for bird migration and lived here for several years.

Henderson is also home to that unique genre of folk music that characterizes the hill country of the Southeast, bluegrass. While the horses are racing at Ellis, the annual bluegrass and folklife festival draws big crowds.

"Father of the Blues" William C. Handy spent years here; now the annual, weeklong **W. C. Handy Blues & Barbecue Festival** (www.handyblues.org) is the largest free blues festival in the United States. Bluegrass in the Park (Audubon Mill Park, on the Ohio) kicks off every August for a weekend of concerts; jamming; folklife exhibits such as fly-tying, thumb-picking, and weaving; and general all-around partying. Call 270-827-0016, or email info@downtownhenderson with questions. During the year, the **Henderson Area Arts Alliance for the Arts** (270-826-5916; http://www.haaa.org/) sponsors musical performances featuring the likes of Randy Travis and Dr. John.

Stroll along the **Riverwalk**. At the Second Street boat ramp, watch the small craft come and go, or enjoy a Friday night summer concert at the amphitheater on Water Street. Bring your own lawn chairs, or sit on the benches or the grass and enjoy the vendor temptations. For city and area maps, concert listings, and other events, visit http://www.hendersonky.org/event.htm.

LEXINGTON

Out beyond the city limit signs, past the narrow crossroads with their solitary corner markets and clusters of houses, bluegrass country rolls gently over the hills, down beside the creeks, and up

The Audubon Museum, Henderson

Labrot & Graham distillery

again. The seemingly endless grasses ripple green and shiny in the wind and disappear beyond the horizon in every direction. Such horse-breeding empires as Lane's End, Claiborne, Three Chimneys, and Calumet command the hills and valleys of this picturesque region. Distinctive icons identify the great farms—large black eagles flanking the red entrance gate at Calumet, the natural fieldstone walls and ledges of WinStar Farms—with their large barns and deep lawns shaded by stately magnolias, pines, and oaks. Small herds of horses graze or romp in adjoining pastures, suggesting the genteel, unhurried lifestyle of a bygone southern era. But inside the breeding sheds and business offices is a multi-billion-dollar Thoroughbred industry that rarely sleeps, here in the horse capital of the world.

Downtown Lexington, the economic heart of bluegrass country, is as energetic and industrious as the Thoroughbred farms appear idle. As the city rides the wave of economic revitalization, a big new courthouse complex was recently completed, and nearby Rupp Arena hosts University of Kentucky intercollegiate basketball, concerts, and other events. The UK campus hugs the city's eastern side, and cultural and performing arts events draw suburban crowds into the city for an evening. Fine little restaurants and gleaming martini bars cater to an urban population of students, business travelers, and a solid middle-class population. Encircling the business district are antebellum Victorians of every size, many undergoing handsome restoration, and Civil War markers and monuments are everywhere. We stayed downtown, exploring bluegrass byways and bourbon distiller-

Calumet Farms

ies by day, Keeneland by afternoon, and the urban scene by night.

Lexington is filled with historic sites, small shops, and interesting architecture. It offers great walking neighborhoods with grand Victorian homes. The **University of Kentucky** campus is only blocks away. After an afternoon at Keeneland, tour the scenic countryside and drive past some of the handsome horse farms in the area. Several Thoroughbred farms, including Calumet and Lane's End, offer free tours if you plan ahead. Check their Web sites and email or call for details.

For a real taste of Kentucky, visit the **Woodford Reserve Distillery** outside the town of Versailles (7855 McCracken Pike; 859-879-1812; http://www.woodford reserve.com), open Tuesday through Sunday, with extended summer hours; closed on major holidays. Call for free tour schedule and Picnic on the Porch dates. A tour of the historic buildings explains the pioneering process that long ago set the standard for fine bourbon. Enjoy the large visitors' center, filled with illustrated panels, historic portraits, and authentic equipment that also clarifies the distillery process. A fine gift shop carries quality items, and the distillery offers a simple picnic lunch that can be enjoyed inside or on the large wraparound, white-railed porch and patio overlooking the handsome distillery and holding barns.

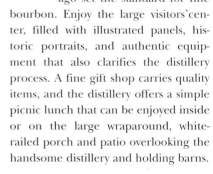
Historical landmark

If you have the time, take a tour of **Mary Todd Lincoln's** beautifully appointed family home in Lexington, the first home of a first lady to be restored for public visiting (578 W. Main Street; 859-233-9999), and the **Kentucky Horse Park** (www.kyhorse park.com; 859-233-4303). The latter is a working horse farm that is home to several retired racing champions, including Cigar, and presents varied activities throughout the year. For more Kentucky tourist information, visit http://www.kytourism.com.

LOUISVILLE

The Ohio River spills out of Pennsylvania and flows across or beside six states on its winding westward way toward the Mississippi. In the late eighteenth century, travelers navigated its long and dangerous course by flatboat, until they reached the only place in the river's 981-mile path where a series of falls formed a treacherous barrier. There, in 1778, Louisville, Kentucky, sprang up.

There is much to see and do in Louisville. When you arrive, head to the **Greater Louisville Convention and Visitors Bureau** (Third and Market; 502-582-3732). If you can't make the Derby, plan to catch a summer race, or

Louisville, Kentucky

be here in October for the huge **St. James Art Show** (502-635-1842; http://www.stjamescourtartshow.com), an annual event that draws hundreds of exhibitors, showing at locations throughout the city. There is also the **First Friday Gallery Hop** (502-585-1234) as well. A dozen downtown galleries are open from 5–9:30 p.m. for enjoying art and socializing with artists. Free trolley transportation gets you around. For a night of good theater, dance, or music, attend **The W.L. Lyons Brown Theatre** (315 West Broadway; 502-584-7777/800-775-7777; http://ww2.kentuckycenter.org). Past performers at the recently renovated Brown include the Moody Blues, the Twyla Tharp Dance Company, and Lyle Lovett. Or take a walk through town to Waterfront Park and Plaza and enjoy some time beside the Ohio River.

Other Louisville discoveries include the **Gheens Science Hall and Rauch Planetarium**, on the University of Louisville campus (Gheens Science Hall; 502-852-6664; http://www.louisville .edu/planetarium); there are several interesting and fun planetarium and laser shows you can see. Those interested in life on the planet, particularly early American history, should stop in at the **Filson Historical Society and Museum** (1310 South Third Street; 502-635-5083; http://www.filsonhistorical .org). The Filson holdings are a nationally acclaimed collection of Lewis and Clark items.

The Bourbon Capital of the World, Bardstown (http://www .bardstowntourism.com), is thirty-five miles west of Louisville. The town hosts the **Kentucky Bourbon Festival** in September (http://www.kybourbonfes-tival.com). Bardstown is also where Stephen Foster was inspired to write "My Old Kentucky Home." If you want to know how bourbon got its start, take a tour at nearby **Woodford Reserve Distillery** (7855 McCracken Pike, Versailles; 858-879-1812; http://www.wood fordreserve.com), a National Historic Landmark (formerly the Labrot & Graham Distillery). Woodford Reserve is the official bourbon of the Kentucky Derby.

MARYLAND/ WASHINGTON, D.C.

Fort McHenry, Baltimore

BALTIMORE

The heart and soul of Baltimore is the wide, meandering Chesapeake Bay, which has given the city its character. On the bay and just south of the Susquehanna River, colonial Baltimore flourished as a port, shipping cargoes across the seas on ships built at its wharves. Until the mid-1800s, Crabtown was the third largest city in America.

Swinging into the twenty-first century, a renaissance of construction is transforming the city's handsome old neighborhoods and hard-working wharf areas into energetic, aesthetic spaces. From the National Aquarium to major league baseball to historic sites, harbor tours, art, music, shopping, and vibrant nightspots, the city of Baltimore has everything to offer. Like Boston, it's the perfect size for spending a weekend discovering its revitalized charms.

Tall Ships Festival

The Preakness Stakes coincides with baseball season. The Baltimore Orioles play at the beautiful Oriole Park, located at **Camden Yards** (not three blocks from Babe Ruth's birthplace, and only fifteen minutes by foot from the Inner Harbor). Check http://www.theorioles.com for the official details.

The **Baltimore Museum of Art** (10 Art Museum Drive; 410-396-7100) has two lovely sculpture gardens, a large collection of Andy Warhol art, and five hundred Matisses in its celebrated collection of impressionist works. Baltimorians defended **Fort McHenry**, est. 1798, and their city from the British during the War of 1812. Watching through the night, 35-year-old Francis Scott Key penned our national anthem. Take time to visit the **Star-Spangled Banner Flag House and 1812 Museum** (844 E. Pratt; 410-837-1793). Learn more at http://www.flaghouse.org.

The very best visitor's approach to Baltimore is via the Inner Harbor, where renovated piers and wharves now feature great shopping, restaurants, galleries, museums, ships of every description, and the acclaimed **National Aquarium** (501 E. Pratt Street; 410-576-3800). Admission for adults is $19.50; for adults sixty years and older, $18.50; and for children three to eleven, $13.50. Hours vary seasonally; call for a schedule.

On Pier 3, the aquarium is an amazing marine and nature center, with its 335,000-gallon coral reef environment, acres of rain forest, educational programs, exhibits, and gift shop. Watch dolphins and sharks in their vast, re-created natural habitats from a 1,300-seat amphitheater. Then stop by **Phillip's Harborplace** (301 Light Street, at the Pavilion; 310-685-6600), to sample the menu of this regional favorite, established in 1916.

Just west of the Inner Harbor, Charles Street is the city's main north-south thoroughfare, running from the harbor all the way to the campus at Johns Hopkins University, bisecting Charles Center and the Mount Vernon neighborhood. A skywalk from the Inner Harbor takes you to Charles Center. Along the route are galleries, bookstores, gift and antique shops, clothing boutiques, cafés, bars, and restaurants. **Mount Vernon Place** is twelve blocks from the base of Charles, where the historic **Washington Monument** stands. The monument and its museum are open 10:00 a.m. to 5:00 p.m., Wednesday to Sunday (699 N. Charles Street; 410-396-0929).

The National Cathedral

Two blocks west of Charles is Howard Street, aka **Antiques Row**, undergoing renovation as the Avenue of the Arts, with new performing art centers and gallery spaces.

WASHINGTON, D.C.

Washington is the grandest city in America, a historic metropolis designed during architecture's golden age, and one of the few places anywhere purposely created as a showplace of government. Whereas New York City is the

The Kennedy Center

mecca of money and merchandise, Washington, D.C., is the pinnacle of power and politics. Both places are sexy and exciting, though it's more fun to eavesdrop in the capital city and imagine that you've been privy to tomorrow's headline news.

When planning a visit to Washington, avoid the tired and sweaty masses pounding the sidewalks on their summer vacations. In a city virtually outlined by its promenades of stately trees, spring and autumn are both seasons of enchantment. And leave the driving to others—what you spend on buses, cabs, and good walking shoes, you'll save in parking headaches and traffic nightmares.

A bird's-eye view of the city, which was designed by the prickly French engineer Pierre Charles L'Enfant, shows an ambitious but easily navigable layout. The district, essentially now the city of Washington, D.C., is a sixty-seven-square-mile plot carved out of Maryland. Almost a rectangle, it points north. Its western edge hugs the Potomac River and separates the district from Virginia, where the landmark resting place, Arlington National Cemetery, can be found. Rock Creek Park fills up the most northerly point of the tract; George Washington's grand estate, Mount Vernon, stands some twenty miles downstream in Virginia.

At the very center of Washington, on a rise once called Jenkins Hill, stands the U.S. Capitol, focal point of the city and the nation. Run two imaginary lines through it, north-south and east-west, and you've mastered the street directions. Streets that end in NW are northwesterly from the Capitol, those ending in SE are in the lower-right quadrant, and so on. Most of the major monuments are clustered on or about the **National Mall**, a two-and-a-half-mile public green stretching west between the Capitol and the Potomac.

Pennsylvania Avenue runs on an east-west diagonal from the Capitol, with the White House about a mile west of it. Downtown Washington fills several blocks running north. West of downtown and north of the White House is Georgetown, full of restored colonial row houses with proper little gardens lining the sidewalk, and an exuberant district of great bars, excellent restaurants, and specialty boutiques.

Getting around the district is fairly easy using metro buses or the Metrorail subway system that runs deep underground. The free metro pocket guide is essential for mapping out which of the five color-coded subway lines will get you to your destinations; most major tourist sites are close to a metro stop. Station entrances are marked by a round brown column with an *M* at the top (get more info at 202-637-7000). Cabs are good for fast and convenient travel, unless it's rush hour, when no one's moving.

Washington, D.C., isn't Boston. Resign yourself to exploring a few sites at a sane pace; even if you sprint everywhere in cardio mode you'll run out of hours before you do all the landmarks. Have a flexible sightseeing plan, and give it up for special programs, tours, or events that present themselves.

Washington is packed with marvelous and interesting monuments and museums. Some memorialize our founding fathers and greatest leaders or honor those who have defended our freedoms. Others display and preserve magnificent collections of art, history, and science. There are many wonderful parks and gardens for relaxing and reflecting. Several of the city's symbols of liberty and democracy seem almost

Interior of the Capitol dome

required viewing on the maiden trip to the capital; beyond that, the days should be filled with discovering unique and memorable sites, and the nights dedicated to the pursuit of happiness. It's your inalienable right.

In the ABCs of American democratic institutions, the U.S. **Capitol** is the *A*. But it rates about *Z* for convenience of touring, unless you go in the off-season, plan months in advance and get passes from your senator, or book a guided tour. Only a few public areas, such as the Rotunda and the Statuary Hall, are open for inspection. Passes are required for all tours of the Capitol. Contact your senator (www.senate.gov) to request free passes, as well as separate passes to visit the Senate gallery. Or try your luck with a free, same-day, timed-entry pass for guided tours beginning at 9:00 a.m. Same-day passes are distributed one per person on a first-come, first-served basis at the Guide Service kiosk located at the southwest corner of the Capitol grounds (across from the Botanic Gardens). Hear recorded information at 202-225-6827. Or, skip the tour and see the Capitol in the evening, when the dome is lit and the surroundings are magical. Climb the steps of the western entrance and stand on the spot where presidents since Ronald Reagan have taken the oath of office. Check out the lineup of softly lustrous monuments illuminating the mall and stroll among them.

Across the street from the Capitol is the **Library of Congress**, the largest library in the world, at First Street and Independence Avenue (202-707-8000). The Library of Congress is made up of three separate buildings; its main entrance hall is a soaring, lavish space of columns, arches, sculptures, and a profusion of carved and gilded detailing. Worth a brief stop if your time is limited.

Southwest of the Capitol, on the mall, is the quaint red brick **Smithsonian** Information Center, "the Castle" (1000 Jefferson Dr.; 202-357-2700), where you can plan which of the Smithsonian's fourteen museums to visit.

Continue west and you'll eventually come to the **Washington Monument**. At 555 feet it was the tallest building in the world when it was completed in 1884. Test your calves and quads on the descent of the 897 steps; no one is allowed to walk up anymore. Call 800-967-2283 for info about reservations and tickets (which are $2.00 per person) or make reservations at http://www.res.nps.gov. If you haven't made reservations, line up early in the morning at the kiosk at the monument (202-426-6841) for free first-come, first-served admission.

At the other end of the mall is the dramatic **Lincoln Memorial**, honoring one of our greatest presidents. An interior wall carries the Gettysburg Address, and the craggy-featured Great Emancipator is enshrined in a 9-foot-tall likeness. Nearby, the somber **Vietnam Veterans Memorial**, *The Wall*, carries twenty-four years of names of servicemen and women who paid the ultimate price of war. Our final recommended site, a bit south of the mall, is the gorgeous **Jefferson Memorial**, a neoclassical, columned rotunda of white marble. Standing at the edge of the Potomac and overlooking the Tidal Basin, it is bordered by Japanese cherry trees, whose pale pink blossoms symbolize the capital in springtime.

Tourists unable to walk the two miles between the Capitol and the Lincoln Memorial can purchase tickets to ride the **Tourmobile** (202-554-7950), which circles the mall throughout the day and stops at all the major sites. You can get off along the way for as long as you like, and then catch it to resume the route. Call the National Park Service at 202-426-6841 for other general questions about the National Mall.

North of the mall is the **White House**, at 1600 Pennsylvania, which has housed every president but George Washington. Self-guided morning tours for groups of ten or more take about thirty minutes and offer quick passes through a few public reception rooms, including the East Room, the Red Room, and the handsome State Dining Room. Visitors must obtain a free admission ticket before entering, by contacting your senators or representatives with your request. Check http://www.nps.gov/whho or http://www.whitehouse.gov/history, or call the NPS at 202-456-7041 for recorded current information and other tourist tips.

A second day of traveling should include **Georgetown**, with its tall, narrow Federal town houses dating from the 1800s, where the famous and powerful, including Ulysses Grant, JFK and Jackie, Henry Kissinger, and Madeleine Albright, have lived. Georgetown is one of the great places for nightlife.

Enjoy a walk along Georgetown's scenic **C & O Canal**. Begun in 1828, the Chesapeake & Ohio Canal (C & O) runs 185 miles along the Potomac River. It was built to transport goods by water from Georgetown into the Ohio River valley, bypassing the falls and rapids of the Potomac. It was declared a National Historic Park in 1971, and today visitors

The Georgetown canal

can boat along the canal (drawn by mule power); canoe it; or walk, run, or bike beside it, enjoying the Great Falls in the river and even going into the Appalachian mountains of Maryland. Visit http://www.georgetowndc.com or call the National Park Service at 202-653-5190 for tour information.

If you have the time, spend an afternoon at lovely **Mount Vernon Estate and Gardens** (http://www.mountvernon.org), sixteen miles south of Washington, and roam the estate where George and Martha lived for forty years. Tour the mansion, kitchen, and gardens; enjoy daily and seasonal programs; and make reservations for lunch or dinner at one of the cozy rooms at the Mount Vernon Inn. Check http://www.mountvernon.org for details, tickets, and directions.

Wrap up your Washington stay with an evening at the **JFK Center for the Performing Arts** (2700 F Street; 202-467-4600 or 800-444-1324; http://www.kennedy-center.org), overlooking the Potomac and only a ten-minute walk from Georgetown. Called the nation's busiest arts facility, this live memorial to President John F. Kennedy presents an endless card of theater, dance, musical performances from jazz to orchestra, black-tie events, balls, and gourmet dining options, with spectacular views from the Roof Terrace levels.

VIRGINIA

RICHMOND

Captain John Smith put New Kent on the map in 1607; the same year, Captain Christopher Newport led an exploration party farther west. Beside the rapids of the James River, Newport's party erected a wooden cross that marked the founding of Richmond. Before long, homegrown tobacco and imported coffee were the crop kings in this powerful southern port.

Three centuries of history are seen everywhere in Virginia's capital city, from monuments to museums to Civil War battlefields. For information, stop in at the Richmond Visitors Center, 405 N. Third (at Clay), in the Richmond Convention Center, or call 800-RICHMOND. You can also go to http://www.richmond.com/visitors/ for information on the city and surrounding area.

On our most recent visit to Richmond, we decided to skip the monuments and go white-water rafting through the city. How many cities offer that kind of adventure? In the evening,

Mount Vernon

Richmond at night

we revived ourselves with fabulous French cuisine for dinner and went dancing in the moonlight to wrap up the day in this warm southern metropolis. As you pack, think dressy, rugged, and waterproof.

The city has been under construction recently, but don't let that stop you from staying downtown near the touristy one-mile Canal Walk, which once diverted watercraft around the rapids in the river. Find hotel deals at http://www.tripadvisor.com and http://www.expedia.com.

Civil War buffs will enjoy **Richmond's battle sites and monuments**. The National Park Service is the keeper of the Civil War flame; you will find information on each site at http://www.cr.nps.gov/hps/abpp/civil.htm parks. Downtown, too, is filled with historical buildings and landmarks; check the Web site noted above. **Capitol Square** is the historical heartbeat of the city, anchored by the neoclassical state house designed by Thomas Jefferson and a sixty-foot equestrian monument of George Washington.

Stop in at the **Virginia Museum of Fine Arts** (200 N. Boulevard; 804-340-1400, http://www.vmfa.state.va.us/). The museum holds twenty thousand works in its permanent collection, including one gallery exhibiting Mr. and Mrs. Paul Mellon's British sporting art series. Other treats are the English silver and jeweled Fabergé objects and some of the nation's finest (and most unusual) Asian, African, and Himalayan art and cultural artifacts. The museum is open Wednesday through Sunday, 11:00 a.m.

Robert E. Lee, Richmond

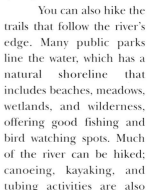

White water rafting

to 5:00 p.m.; a $5 donation is the suggested admission. It offers midday dining in both a casual café and a fine dining room (reservations suggested).

The real discovery is the **James River**, coursing in its natural state through the city. The old cobblestone and brick warehouse sections of the riverfront (now called Shockoe Bottom and Shockoe Slip) have been restored with good restaurants, bars and clubs, and small shops and galleries that line the canal, whose locks allow boats to bypass the falls.

The James River is the only Class IV urban whitewater river in the country. Raft the rapids through the city on one of three different excursions that vary from easy to thrilling, enjoying both wilderness shoreline and urban skyline. The **Richmond Raft Company** (4440 E. Main Street, 800-540-7238, http://www.richmondraft.com) offers three- to six-hour trips, costing $48–$70.

You can also hike the trails that follow the river's edge. Many public parks line the water, which has a natural shoreline that includes beaches, meadows, wetlands, and wilderness, offering good fishing and bird watching spots. Much of the river can be hiked; canoeing, kayaking, and tubing activities are also options. Check out the **Virginia Department of Conservation and Recreation's** Web site on the James River State Park for information on the various activities (http://www.dcr.state.va.us/parks/jamesriv.htm). The site includes maps, lists of seasonal activities, and accommodations.

WEST VIRGINIA

CHARLES TOWN

It's a part of West Virginia like no other. Where the elbow of the state juts up into Maryland's belly, you venture into a land that's at once wild and tamed. Defined by the junction of the Shenandoah and Potomac rivers, this eastern border retains the history and color of West Virginia's past, yet offers the amenities of the present. Many people confuse Charles Town with its better-known brother, Charleston, located on the western side of the state.

A beautiful old town, Charles Town has been revitalized in recent years, with shops and businesses filling the historic buildings that line the sidewalks. Ornate street lamps garlanded in flags and flowers, fresh paint, and new wrought ironworks enliven downtown. A walk through town is an opportunity to appreciate architectural details at every step.

A short drive from town takes you down the hill to the rolling banks of the Shenandoah, a favorite of fishermen,

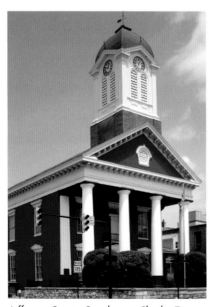

Jefferson County Courthouse, Charles Town

kayakers, white-water rafters, and tubers. Here the river, immortalized in song, is wide and active, with water rolling over long swells of stone. The hillsides plunge to the banks; stone foundations are partly hidden by the trees. It's a tantalizing place, one that invites you to stay and explore.

Most racing takes place at night, leaving plenty of time to explore the area and enjoy the attractions. Harper's Ferry, where abolitionist John Brown staged his unsuccessful raid in 1859, is one of the premier destinations in the country for river activities, and the river presents a cool way to spend a hot afternoon. On a free evening, take in a live performance at the nearby theater festival at Shepard University. Or get in a round of golf at nearby Woods Resort.

The **River Riders** (408 Alstadts Hill Road, 800-326-7238) at **Harper's Ferry** is a licensed professional guide service that offers water rafting, tubing, kayaking, and canoeing. Reservations are required; pay in advance by check or money order.

Although its season is brief, usually four weeks in July, if you're there at the right time, check out the **Contemporary American Theater Festival**, Shepard University in Shepardstown (304-876-3473/800-999-CATF, http://www.catf.org). Visit the Web site or call for productions and times.

If you're a golfer and want to get in a round or two, there is **The Woods Resort**, on Mountain Lake Road in Hedgesville (800-248-2222, http://www.thewoodsresort.com). Lodging and golf packages are available. The resort, approximately one-half hour from Charles Town, offers two eighteen-hole four-star courses, Mountain View and Stony Lick, with a pro shop on the grounds. From I-81 north, the resort is off Highway 9 west.

WHERE TO STAY

KENTUCKY

HENDERSON

John James Audubon State Park
3100 US Highway 41 North
Henderson, KY 42419
270-826-2247 (park)/270- 827-1893 (museum)
http://parks.ky.gov/stateparks/au
$65–$118, depending on season
The park, just south of the bridge over the Ohio, is a 700-acre preserve where Audubon observed the birds and animals he would later paint life-size, in their natural surroundings. This is the perfect way to kick back and learn more about America's most famous ornithologist. Relax after the races here at the lake or with a round of golf in the park. Five fully furnished, lakeside one-bedroom cottages can sleep six each. Kitchens and baths are stocked; you bring food, libations, and personal items. Make reservations up to one year in advance.

LEXINGTON

Gratz Park Inn
120 W. Second Street
Lexington, KY 40507
859-231-1777/800-752-4166
http://www.gratzparkinn.com
$149–$239
This charming sanctuary in the heart of the city's Gratz Park neighborhood features forty-four lovely rooms, each decorated differently in rich warm colors but all featuring handsome antiques, including four-poster beds and fresh-cut flowers. Gas fireplaces add to the historic charm, and period art fills the walls. Don't miss Jonathan's, with its celebrated regional restaurant and terrific bar adjoining the inn.

Hyatt Regency
401 W. High Street
Lexington, KY 40507
859-253-1234
http://www.lexington.hyatt.com
$95–$190
The Hyatt, like the Radisson, is right on Triangle Park, making it a good central location. The Hyatt adjoins the convention center and Rupp Arena and is therefore often very busy. Rooms are spacious and comfortable. Other features include a contemporary lobby bar and restaurant, an indoor pool, and a handy gift shop with a cigar counter.

Radisson Plaza Hotel
369 W. Vine Street
Lexington, KY 40507
859-231-9000/800-333-3333
http://www.radissonlexington.com
$99–$250 depending on amenities
This is the perfect address for walking the city. Sitting in the very heart of downtown, the Radisson is Lexington's largest city hotel, with lots of conference and meeting space. Directly across the street, just beyond Triangle Park with its long, wonderful wall of water spilling noisily down into the channel below, are the Lexington Convention Center and Rupp Arena. The Radisson's amenities include large, bright, tailored guest

rooms; great service; a big, friendly bar; and several gift shops just off the lobby. After a day of winning on the long shots, take a swim in the indoor heated pool.

LOUISVILLE

The Brown Hotel
335 W. Broadway
Louisville, KY 40202
502-583-1234/888-888-5252
http://www.brownhotel.com
$139–$189; call for Derby week rates
J. Graham Brown, the story goes, could not get a room at the Hilton so he in 1923 he built this ornate and beautiful downtown hotel in the grand English Renaissance architectural style. The guest rooms have plush fabrics, period furnishings, and plump, and satiny bed linens. The hotel includes the chic Lobby Bar, the English Grill and the Thoroughbred Restaurant, and the J. Graham's Café, with its southern breakfast buffet.

The Galt House Hotel and Suites
Fourth Avenue at the River
Louisville, KY 40202
502-589-5200/800-626-1814
http://www.galthouse.com
$120 and up; 3-night Derby packages from $1,000
The Galt House soars twenty-five stories and offers 1,300 rooms; many are spacious suites with river and city views. Its humble beginnings in 1835 make it the city's oldest lodging site. Accommodations are designed to attract groups of various sizes and feature comfortable, modern décor. The Galt houses the revolving Flagship Restaurant on the 25th floor.

The Seelbach Hilton
500 S. Fourth Avenue
Louisville, KY 40202
502-585-3200
http://www.seelbachhilton.com
$119–$199; suite rates higher
The Seelbach, downtown as well, is on the National Register of Historic places. Recently renovated guest rooms and suites preserve their historic charm with classic four-poster beds, soft color schemes, and period art on the walls. The hotel includes the acclaimed Oakroom restaurant as well as more casual cafés.

MARYLAND

BALTIMORE

Harbor Court Hotel
550 Light Street
Baltimore, MD 21202
410-234-0550/800-824-0076
http://www.harborcourt.com
$215 and up, depending on season and amenities
The Harbor Court Hotel may offer Baltimore's most luxurious accommodations. Overlooking the water, its roomy rooms are outfitted in elegant tradition. It offers an indoor pool, whirlpool, and racquetball court. It is home to the acclaimed Hampton's restaurant, where jacket and tie are expected dining attire and reservations are essential.

Harbor Inn Pier 5
771 Eastern Avenue
Baltimore, MD 21202
410-539-2000/866-583-4162
http://www.thepier5.com
$179–329, depending on season and amenities
The Harbor Inn on the pier offers views of endless seaport activity; an interior art deco theme sets an artistic tone. A health club and library provide other diversions. The Cobalt Lounge with its martini bar and the Cohibar (your escape for that smoke and a nightcap) offer easy, late-evening relaxation.

The Hyatt Regency Baltimore
300 Light Street
Baltimore, MD 21202
410-528-1234/800-233-1234
http://www.baltimore.hyatt.com
$195–$345, depending on season and amenities
The Hyatt, with its captivating mirrored exterior, established itself at the harbor long before others; its reputation is secure. The glass elevator offers spectacular harbor views, and the rooms are cozy and lovely. The outdoor pool and health club will keep you fit and relaxed.

WASHINGTON, D.C.

WASHINGTON, D.C.

The Capital Hilton
1001 16th Street, NW
Washington, DC 20036
202-393-1000
http://www.capital.hilton.com
$150–$439, based on amenities; some suites have patios
Being two blocks from the White House makes this a great location. Rooms are handsome in Queen Anne period furnishings. The Hilton ballroom hosts the annual Gridiron Club dinner and political roast.

The Four Seasons
2800 Pennsylvania Avenue NW
Washington, DC 20007
202-342-0444/800-332-3442
http://www.fourseasons.com
$285 and up
The perfect Georgetown location, the Four Seasons backs up to Rock Creek Park and the Chesapeake & Ohio (C & O) Canal. Upscale and comfy, its rooms are gorgeous, the lap pool is great, and it hosts a Sunday brunch with live jazz.

The Renaissance Mayflower
1127 Connecticut Avenue, NW
Washington, DC 20036
202-347-3000/800-228-7697
http://www.renaissancehotels.com
$159–$340
Opened in 1925, the Renaissance Mayflower is opulent and furnished with historical pieces. This is where Franklin Roosevelt and his family stayed while the White House was being readied for them and where FDR penned the famous line "We have nothing to fear but fear itself." The endlessly long lobby has become a shortcut from downtown to federal offices, so people watching can be rewarding. Its Café Promenade is also a good place to park and spot favorite political heroes and scoundrels.

VIRGINIA

RICHMOND

The Jefferson Hotel
101 W. Franklin (at Adams)
Richmond, VA 23220
804-788-8000/800-424-8014
http://www.jefferson-hotel.com
$165–$335
This is Richmond's most aesthetic hotel, built in 1895 by the architects who designed the New York Public Library. Its grand central marble staircase, the dazzling Tiffany domed skylight in the Palm Court lobby, and exterior beaux arts details and Italian clock tower will transport you. The hotel has an indoor pool and two fine restaurants: T. J.'s and Lemaire. It is also on the National Register of Historic Places. Oh, and Elvis slept here.

Omni Richmond Hotel
100 South 12th Street
Richmond, VA 23219
804-344-7000/888-444-6664/(fax) 804-648-6704
http://www.omnihotels.com
$119–$300
The Omni is luxurious and great for city access. Its rooms have spectacular views of the James River. Options include turndown service and suite packages; rooms on Omni Club floors have additional exclusive guest services. The hotel includes a casual all-day restaurant and deli. It offers an indoor pool and access to the adjoining cushy Capital Club fitness/spa facility for a fee.

WEST VIRGINIA

CHARLES TOWN

The Carriage Inn
417 East Washington Street
Charles Town, WV 25414
304-728-8003/800-867-9830
http://www.carriageinn.com
$95–$225
Hidden among the lush trees that line Charles Town's main street is this graceful black-shuttered home, now an inn, with its open front porch bracketed by soaring columns. Walking up to it is like stepping back in time. Rooms offer canopied beds and private baths. Stay only three minutes from the track, while journeying back in time.

Washington House Inn Bed and Breakfast
216 South George Street
Charles Town, WV 25414
304-725-7923/800-297-6957
http://www.washingtonhouseinnwv.com
$99–$150
If red brick and soaring turrets are more to your liking, check out this highly acclaimed late Victorian bed-and-breakfast, filled with period furnishings.

WHERE TO WINE & DINE

KENTUCKY

HENDERSON

Wolf's Tavern & Restaurant
31 N Green Street
Henderson, KY 42420
270-826-5221
$6.95–$12.95
As it should, this 1878 tavern with sports TVs can get noisy. The restaurant is praised for its good home cooking, with traditional and regional entrées such as charbroiled chicken breast with shrimp and the famous Kentucky Hot Brown, turkey and ham on toast with a Mornay sauce. Jockey silks from across the nation decorate the walls. The upstairs bar and restaurant are nonsmoking, a little dressier, and quieter.

LEXINGTON

A la lucie
159 N. Limestone
Lexington, KY 40507
859-252-5277
$10.95–$24.95
Charming and funky, A la lucie is a delightful, cozy spot, with white tablecloths and a hammered tin ceiling painted red. The teal blue walls are filled with female portraits in every style, mode, and color imaginable. Art deco fringed lamps illuminate the bar area, and a glitter ball suspended from the ceiling sparkles in the middle of the room. The menu is wonderfully creative; they call it Continental, we call it classic with a twist. We started with a very good steak tartare and a bottle of champagne to celebrate our arrival in the Thoroughbred capital of the world. Our crispy duckling with polenta and steamed baby arugula was heavenly.

deSha's
101 N. Broadway
Lexington, KY 40507
859-259-3771
http://www.deshas.com
$5.25–$19.95
In downtown's Victorian Square, this popular contemporary nightspot and eatery is filled with lots of greenery and hanging pots and warm wood and chrome accents. The bar is big and well stocked, and the food is great. We sampled our first fried green tomatoes here, very tasty. The blackened chicken penne was spicy and satisfying, and our blackberry cobbler a la mode was fabulous.

Nadine's
3955 Harrodsburg Rd.
Lexington, KY 40513
859-223-0797
$12.95–$21.95
Stop in after the races for a martini or glass of wine in this jazzy, energetic restaurant, where horse owners and race fans collide. Choose from a versatile American menu that includes salmon, lamb, veal, and pasta dishes. Friends we met said the white lasagna is terrific. With an extensive, award-winning wine and martini list, you're in for a rousing evening. Reservations suggested on weekend race nights.

LOUISVILLE

The Oakroom
Seelbach Hilton Hotel
500 Fourth Avenue
Louisville, KY 40202
502-87-3463
http://www.seelbachhilton.com
$26–$48; Sunday brunch $24.95
Writer F. Scott Fitzgerald hung out here in the 1920s. The restaurant's dark polished wood columns and carvings and sparkling brass chandeliers hint at its original space as an exclusive billiards hall at the turn of the century. Noted for its haute southern cuisine by *Gourmet* and *Epicurean* magazines, dining in the Oakroom will be memorable. Plan to enjoy the Sunday brunch, with complimentary champagne, dramatic ice sculptures, and light jazz. Reservations recommended.

The Thoroughbred Restaurant
Brown Hotel
335 W. Broadway
Louisville, KY 40202
502-583-1234
Entrées from $14.95
This is the casual brother of the English Grill, a quiet, sophisticated retreat from the day, featuring a lighter menu. Our entrée, Father's Pasta, earned the Lady Barton 2003 Dining Out award; it was her most divine meal of the year. Served over linguini, the rich alfredo sauce carried a subtle note of country ham, with onions and broccoli.

Vincenzo's
150 S. Fifth Street
Louisville, KY 40202
502-580-1350
http://www.vincenzosdining.biz
Entrées from $20
From the five-course traditional Italian dinners to the very nouveau "Euro-spa" lite dining, these two brothers from Palermo do it right in this elegantly European atmosphere. For starters try the *Carciofini marini* (baked artichoke bottoms filled with crabmeat and scallops, glazed with a lime hollandaise), then twirl your fork in the *Spaghetti con aragosta* (spaghetti with chunks of lobster, sun-dried tomatoes, and asparagus tips), or advance to the *Filetto al portafoglio*, beef tenderloin stuffed with Stilton cheese and wild mushrooms, served in a vermouth peppercorn sauce.

MARYLAND

BALTIMORE

Bandaloops
1024 Charles Street
Baltimore, MD 21230
410-727-1355
$6–$18
For happy hour, have drinks and nibbles among the chic at Bandaloops, on historic Federal Hill.

Black Olive
814 S. Bond Street
Baltimore, MD 21231

410-276-7141

$30–$50

The best fresh seafood and gourmet Greek entrées are served in this two-room restaurant in Fells Point; reservations are a must.

The Brass Elephant

924 North Charles St.

Baltimore, MD 21201

410-547-8480

http://www.brasselephant.com

$18–$28

Baltimore magazine says put on your slinky black dress for this *Wine Spectator*–recommended gourmet restaurant, in a handsome retrofitted Victorian house, where the waitstaff don tuxedos. Special events include wine dinners with celebrity chefs; the upstairs Tusk Lounge is the perfect spot for a nightcap or two.

Cat's Eye Pub

891 S. Ann Street

Fells Points, MD 21231

410-276-9034

$5–$10

In the evening, check out this pub at Fells Point, Baltimore's original seaport site; it hosts live music nightly.

Hampton's (in the Harbor Court Hotel)

550 Light Street

Baltimore, MD 21202

410-234-0550

Entrées average $40

Hampton's ranks as one of America's ultimate dining experiences, in the view of *Condé Nast Traveler*; jacket and tie are expected dining attire and reservations are essential.

WASHINGTON, D.C.

WASHINGTON, D.C.

La Chaumière

2813 M Street, NW

Washington, D.C. 20007

202-338-1784

$14–$18

Have lunch or dinner at this very *haute* Georgetown restaurant with its delightful French country décor and award-winning cuisine.

Martin's Tavern

1264 Wisconsin, NW

Washington, D.C. 20007

202-333-7370

http://www.martins-tavern.com

$11–$30

Georgetown is an essential stop on this capital tour, and casual, friendly Martin's is touted as Washington's oldest restaurant. Today's owner is the founder's great-grandson, and the menu's tasty dishes—from steaks and burgers to chowders and seafood—keep even the nation's major politicos coming back for more.

The Palm Steak House
1225 19th Street, NW
Washington, DC 20036
202-293-9091
http://www.thepalm.com
$16.50–$89 (steak for two)
The Palm is the place for lunch or dinner. Its steak and lobster entrées are unbeatable, but you're here for the faces, right? The walls are plastered with caricatures of anyone who's done something, and because of the food and location, political celebrities are everywhere. The Palm's Web site reports Hillary, Rudy, and Larry the King; we haven't been that lucky yet.

Third Edition
1218 Wisconsin, NW
Washington, D.C. 20007
202-333-3700
http://www.thethirdedition.com
$7–$22
Offers live music and dancing several nights a week.

VIRGINIA

RICHMOND

La Petite France
2108 Maywill Street
Richmond, VA 23230
804-353-8729
http://www.lapetitefrance.net
$41 and up
We never pass up superb French cuisine, and this is it. Chef Paul Elberling has been at the helm for more than thirty years. The restaurant's unassuming exterior hides an opulent Parisian ambience inside. If you are lucky, the wild boar carpaccio, dusted with fresh truffles (flown in from France) and garnished with arugula and *citronnelle* essence will be on the menu along with veal, lamb, duck, and fish entrées. The New York sirloin steak is served with a green peppercorn sauce and cognac coulis. Order your chocolate soufflé when you order dinner.

The Tobacco Company Restaurant
1201 East Cary Street
Richmond, VA 23219
804-782-9555
http://www.thetobaccocompany.com
$17.95–$29.95
Along the Shockoe (say shock-oh) Slip section of the waterfront, where tobacco warehouses once stood, this restored city region delivers the nightlife. The Tobacco Company Restaurant is a light, retro-Victorian, atrium space restored with eclectic fixtures and antiques. Come for a mimosa brunch and sample true southern fare, from garlic cheese grits and spoon bread to morning meats, including sausage and ham. Or start the evening with regional treats such as Backbay crab croquettes followed by flounder roulades filled with spicy crabmeat and covered in a creamy lobster sauce. If you've picked at dinner, wrap up with the all-you-can-eat dessert buffet. Burn it off with live music and dancing, here or elsewhere on Cary or Main streets.

WEST VIRGINIA

CHARLES TOWN

Charles Washington Inn
210 W. Liberty Street
Charles Town, WV 25414
304-725-4020
$15–$21.95
A welcoming, casual spot. Enjoy the interior's colonial touches, including several fireplaces, or dine on the garden patio. Entrées on the extensive menu, featuring American cuisine, include veal, duck, seafood, and steak. A good wine selection and a full bar complete the picture.

Jumpin' Java
109 West Washington Street
Charles Town, WV 25414
304-728-0195
http://www.jumpjava.com
$1.35 and up
The old storefront, with the word *Java* prominent in the signage, caught our eye, along with the board listing iced drinks and sandwiches. Once inside the building, with its long brick-walled interior, we weren't disappointed. The sandwiches are tasty, and the drinks well made. Try breakfast, lunch, or light fare here, and sample the baked goodies.

The Jefferson Hotel, Richmond

Arkansas

Mississippi

Alabama

Georgia

Louisiana

Florida

SOUTH MAP LEGEND

Arkansas
❶ Oaklawn Park
(Hot Springs)

Florida
❷ Calder Race Course
(Miami)

❸ Gulfstream Park
(Hallandale Beach)

❹ Tampa Bay Downs
(Tampa Bay)

Louisiana
❺ Delta Downs Racetrack and Casino
(Vinton)

❻ Evangeline Downs Racetrack and Casino
(Opelousas)

❼ Fair Grounds Race Course
(New Orleans)

❽ Harrah's Louisiana Downs
(Bossier City)

THE SOUTH

*I*n the late eighteenth and early nineteenth centuries, racetracks in the South were laid out on private estates in cities such as New Orleans—the City of Pleasure—and in frontier settlements such as Tallahassee, and later Mobile and Natchez in the Deep South. The earliest "tracks" were often little more than long strips cleared through the forest for match races. Sportsmen of means transported their champion runners long distances, by river whenever possible, to match them before thousands of spectators eager to watch the standard 3- and 4-mile heats run during this period. By the mid-1860s, economic hardship caused by the Civil War spread across the South and dealt horse racing a devastating blow, although in New Orleans it managed to survive. As the century closed, the healing thermal waters around Hot Springs, Arkansas, began drawing seasonal health seekers. Horse racing followed, as recreational pleasure. There, as in New Orleans, the resort aspect of the city helped maintain visibility for the sport of kings. By then, however, the national center of Thoroughbred racing had shifted permanently to the north.

ARKANSAS

OAKLAWN PARK (HOT SPRINGS)

If ever a racing destination enjoyed an aura of mystique, this one is it. To be sure, picturesque Saratoga, Del Mar, and Keeneland are worthy of adulation. Their brief, exclusive meets attract royal Thoroughbred lineage and present the sport at its finest. Oaklawn, in the mountains of southwestern Arkansas, is a saddlecloth of a different weave. To those living on the East and West coasts, Hot Springs may seem a little secluded. Driving here, over miles of winding, hilly, two-lane roads, where Queen Anne's lace stirs in the summer breeze and mimosa trees bloom pink and feathery, requires some forethought. Yet the Hot Springs track has stood for more than a century in a spot known even to Hernando de Soto, if legend tells us true. Its history encapsulates the saga of modern Thoroughbred racing with all its glories, tribulations, and everyday bothers. Toss in the geography—world-famous thermal waters, the Ouachita Mountains setting, and the 5,000-acre Hot Springs National Park—and it's a destination worthy of kings.

Horse racing in and around Hot Springs began shortly after the town attracted settlers in the 1850s. In 1904, the Oaklawn Jockey Club organized, and the next year Oaklawn's first meet opened at a track just outside the city. The mayor declared the afternoon a holiday, and three thousand fans turned out for the event. Over the next three decades, however, racing stopped, started, and stopped again while reformers debated the morality of gambling.

When pari-mutuel wagering was legalized in 1935, Oaklawn jumped back in as an important center of racing from winter into spring. Its biggest contest, the Arkansas Derby (G2), was inaugurated a year later. That $1 million race as well as the $250,000-guaranteed

Apple Blossom Cup winner Azeri, Oaklawn Park 2004

Tornado damage at Oaklawn Park, 1916

Rebel Stakes (G3) serve to help narrow the field of Thoroughbreds vying for a Kentucky Derby slot.

Kicking off Oaklawn's centennial celebration in 2004, third-generation owners, the Charles Cella family, offered a $5 million prize to the owner whose three-year-old could combine victories in the Rebel, the Arkansas Derby, and the Kentucky Derby. Smarty Jones met the challenge. Smarty had a greater impact on Oaklawn than any other horse in recent history, though he shared the stage with the gorgeous chestnut mare Azeri, 2002 North American Horse of the Year. They were the bookends starring in Oaklawn's 2004 Racing Festival of the South. The eight-day celebration featured six graded stakes races worth more than $2.5 million.

Azeri kicked off the week and set the pace by winning the $500,000-guaranteed Apple Blossom Handicap (G1). Thirty-one thousand people watched as the six-year-old took this race for her third consecutive year. Peace Rules captured the $500,000 Oaklawn Handicap (G2) later in the day. On the final day of racing, 62,000 spectators watched Smarty Jones win the Arkansas Derby by 1 ½ lengths.

The springtime setting for these races is a perfect Grandma Moses painting. Pale, fragrant blossoms cover the apple trees standing throughout the grounds. Beyond the infield, a forest of pines and tall oaks, with new leaves unfolding green and lacy, surrounds the track. Above the trees, the massive spa hotels on the city skyline stand like sentinels before the national park.

Terry Wallace, media man and track announcer, is a member of Oaklawn Park's Old Guard. He hasn't missed calling a race at Hot Springs track in thirty years. Recapping Oaklawn's past, he showed us photos of the small open-air grandstand in 1905; the racetrack ripped apart by a tornado in 1916; and the backstretch in the 1940s, a scene of horses, riders, old barns, and vintage autos.

Oaklawn's purses draw quality racing all winter. In 2001, management

SNAPSHOT - OAKLAWN PARK

Description: Oaklawn, on Central Avenue, is one of the oldest racing establishments in America. It offers a 1-mile track encompassing a 7-furlong turf course, there are two chutes on the main course, and the homestretch is 990 feet long.

Season: January through mid-April. The fifty-five-day meet features the Racing Festival of the South, a week of stakes races culminating in the $1 million Arkansas Derby.

Address: 2705 Central Avenue, Hot Springs, AR 71901; send correspondence to P.O. Box 699, 2705 Central Avenue, Hot Springs, AR 71902

Phone: 501-623-4411/800-625-6296/(fax) 501-624-4950

Web site: http://www.oaklawn.com

Nearest airport: Hot Springs Memorial Field Airport (HOT), Little Rock Regional Airport (LIT)

Getting there: Located on Highway 7, just south of historic downtown Hot Springs

Fine dining: The Carousel Terrace, The Post Parade, The Oaklawn Club (private club)

Casual fare: The Oyster Bar, The Pony Express Grill, concessions stands throughout

Spirits: The Arkansas Sports Tavern, one among many

Extras: Fantasy Racing contest, special dining events, promotional giveaways

Entrance to Oaklawn Park

made the decision to jump into electronic pari-mutuel horse racing games and opened a dark, flashy casino room. The games have clearly bumped up the dollars that feed live racing. Owner Charles Cella, however, confesses that he can't pass up the real contest on the dirt. The decision to add games boiled down to staying competitive or sitting on the sidelines.

A city with old world flavor, a cosmopolitan attitude, legendary mineral springs, and nationally competitive racing, Hot Springs attracts visitors far and wide. Yet Oaklawn is at heart a community racetrack. Hot Springs is affordable, and the region supports the industry. For townsfolk, horse racing is the social event of the season. Even during the simulcast season, don't go looking for a table on Friday night. Few of the local restaurants can compete with Oaklawn's $8.99 prime rib platter.

FLORIDA

CALDER RACE COURSE (MIAMI)

Afternoon sunlight filters through a broad canopy of Florida oaks, casting soothing shadows on the thick lawn and sandy pathway that cuts to the track. Stripes of raspberry, white, and coral impatiens line the hedge. This signature southern paddock is unmistakably Calder Race Course, which opened in 1971. Across the paddock, a towering wall of windows reflects the ever-changing blue-and-white Miami sky.

Calder's race calendar opens in late April with its summer meet and includes more than fifty stakes races, several at grade 2 and 3 levels, for a total purse of nearly $6 million. The six races in July that form the Summit of Speed mark the richest single sprint stakes day in American horse racing. In 2002, the Smile Sprint Handicap trophy went to Orientate, who then sped forward to claim the Breeders' Cup Sprint (G1) in October and ultimately the Eclipse Award for top American sprinter. Other big stakes are the Festival of the Sun, with a purse upwards of $1.5 million, including the Florida Stallion Stakes. The Needles Stakes honors Needles, the first Florida-bred champion to win the Kentucky Derby (1956), and, some say, the horse who drew major attention to the state as a serious center of Thoroughbred breeding.

Calder's summer meet closes in late October as its two-month Tropical meet begins. Tropical recalls the long tradition of fall and winter racing once popular at Tropical Park (in Coral Gables, twenty-five miles to the south—now a public equestrian park). Tropical's $2.8 million purse offerings include the Florida Million, in November; and in

Calder infield

December, the high-handle Grand Slam I, Grand Slam II, and the Tropical Park Derby (G3).

On this breezy and not-too-warm first Saturday in May 2003, the Calder summer meet is into its third day; its 2002 Hall of Famers were recently inducted, and today is Kentucky Derby day. The fans have each received a 129th Kentucky Derby commemorative glass, and the classic event, with sixteen contenders, will be simulcast at the end of today's racing card. Calder-based jockey Rosemary Homeister Jr. has the mount on Supah Blitz in the big race at Churchill Downs, which creates even more local interest.

Calder has lots of great spaces for settling in and picking the winners, from the Turf Club and Club House facilities on the upper floors to multilevel grandstand seating in private boxes or free seating with general admission. On the second floor, serious bettors may retreat to the Winner's Edge, and the sociable can meet in the Flying Colors Sports Bar on the west side. The recently renovated

first floor feels wide open and light, of course with banks of TVs for simulcast racing. The track's Hall of Fame, on this floor, honors its star riders, trainers, and owners. It also displays three interesting cutaway track views showing how the dirt, the turf, and an experimental man-made track are composed and maintained in this semitropical climate, where rain falls silently down or blows in on ferocious storms and racing goes on nearly the whole year around.

At the east end of the track, the exceptionally handsome paddock, flanked by two outdoor cafés, is an oasis of shade and the essential location for observing the condition of the horses before plotting informed wagers.

Calder, a Churchill Downs Incorporated racetrack, sponsors a number of fund-raisers for children's health-related charities. Enticing to children who visit Calder are a family picnic grove near the parking lot and the Junior Jockey Club, with year-round programs such as learning about track photography and the educational

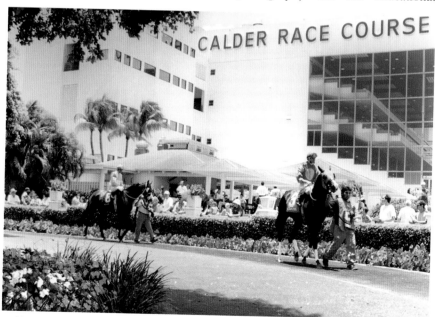

Calder Race Course from the paddock

Rosemary Homeister Jr.

the finale. Most of the fans patiently stay put for Rosemary Homeister, the fifth female in history to ride in the prestigious event. The vivacious thirty-year-old has drawn the first slot and, astride Supah Blitz, leads the long line of horses emerging from the tunnel. The colt Supah Blitz had several good finishes at Gulfstream Park and Calder earlier in the year. With a slight wave to the crowd and a flash of her wide, disarming smile, Rosemary relishes the post parade.

As soon as she broke from the starting gate, Rosie reported later, the crowd and the noise faded and total concentration took over, in a race that lasted a mere two minutes. At the eighth pole, she felt Supah Blitz starting to tire, she knew he had given it his best, and only then did she hear the roar of the crowd again. Supah Blitz finished thirteenth in a field of sixteen. Rosemary flew home that evening. On Sunday, she was back at the Calder track, and back in the winner's circle.

aspects of horsemanship and making everything from jockey silks to helmets. Two miniature horses live at Calder, mascots named Thunder and Lightning, who come out in costume for holidays and parades.

Twelve races fill the day's program, with the simulcast Kentucky Derby as

SnapShot - Calder Race Course

Description: Calder's dirt track is a 1-mile oval with a ⅛-mile chute for 7-furlong and 1 ¼ mile-races, an 80-foot stretch, a 75-foot backstretch, and 990 feet from final turn to finish line. The Bermuda turf track is a ⅞-mile oval, 67 feet wide, with one chute of a ¼ mile (diagonal straightaway), which allows for races of two turns to be up to 1 1/8 miles. The 1 ½-mile turf races begin on the backstretch, pass the stands, and go around the track again for a total of three turns, with a distance from the final turn to finish line of 986 feet.

Season: Late April until late December/early January

Address: 21001 N.W. 27th Ave., Miami, FL 33056; send correspondence to P.O. Box 1808, Miami, FL 33055-0808

Phone: (Dade Co.) 305-625-1311/(Broward Co.) 954-523-4324

Web site: http://www.calderracecourse.com

Nearest airport: Miami International (MIA), Ft. Lauderdale–Hollywood International Airport (FLL)

Getting there: On the Broward/Dade (Miami) county line, accessible via the Florida Turnpike, I-95, US 441, the Palmetto Expressway, and 27th Avenue (University Drive)

Admission: $2; clubhouse: $4; children seventeen and under: free with an adult

Parking: $1; preferred: $2; valet: $5; free parking after 4:00 p.m.

Fine dining: Turf Club, Clubhouse

Casual fare: Blinker's Deli, twelve concessions stands throughout the facility

Spirits: Calder Pub, Flying Colors Sports Bar, beverage stands throughout the facility

Extras: Barbershop, gift boutique, miniature-horse mascots for the children, Junior Jockey Club with many activities, family picnic area

GULFSTREAM PARK
(HALLANDALE BEACH)

Blue skies, whitecaps, and the roar of the surf breaking upon the sand—what could top this? Only horse racing. So to start the year right, we followed the smart money to Hallandale Beach for the kickoff of Gulfstream Park's ninety-day winter race meet. Since our visit, after nearly two years of noise, dust, and temporary enclosures, a total makeover has transformed this park completely. Little of the former elegant old Gulfstream facility remains, and the race park now boasts a 1⅛ mile dirt track, a

New Gulfstream architectural rendering

separate 1-mile turf course, and a four-story grandstand. The Village at Gulfstream Park, a complex including boutique shops, a hotel, condominiums, and a theater, was slated for completion

THE TRACKS HAVE ALWAYS BEEN GOOD TO ME

Jesse Parsons, jockey, jockey's agent, trainer, pari-mutuel clerk, husband, and father, has done about all of it at the tracks. Jesse works the pari-mutuel counter in the press box at Calder Race Course. That's where we met him and learned about his life in the horse racing industry. He grew up on a farm in Idaho, riding as a kid, entering county fairs. He was barely a teenager when an in-law of a family friend came out from Illinois looking for riders. Jesse remembers he and his father were fixing a windmill in the field that morning.

"Benny Creech came up and said, 'I'm lookin' for Jesse, the kid I saw ride yesterday.' "

That afternoon, Jesse and Creech boarded the train to Bloomington, Illinois. After a summer working around the horses at the Chicago tracks, Jesse turned fifteen and began racing at Hot Springs, Arkansas. After a stint at that, he began training horses at Arlington Park. Next he became a jockey's agent. Thirty years ago, when summer racing began in Florida, he headed south.

"It's a tough business," he said of being an agent. "High pressure. You don't show, you don't make it. But now, there's big money in it. But, your good riders train here and then go north for the purses and prestige. We've had most of the top riders here. Alex Solis, [Jorge] Chavez. We had [Jerry] Bailey for a winter here."

While working at Calder, Jesse married. He often talked of the travel adventures he and his new wife, Cheryl, would have. "One day," he recalled, "we were driving to work. I brought it up again. She says, 'Stop the car. I'm so tired of you saying we're gonna do this; we're gonna do that. Got a quarter? Heads we go to San Francisco, tails we stay here.' "

"I've got to have a leave of absence, to go on a working vacation," Jesse told the track manager when he got to work. The next day he called jockey Paul Nicolo, whom he had sent out to ride at Longacres in Seattle. Paul had ridden in the Kentucky Derby on Special Honor that May (1978). Jesse flew west ahead of Cheryl, and met up with Paul on the northern California circuit. They bought sleeping bags. When Paul wasn't racing, they went camping.

"We were the third leading rider at the northern California meet. I roomed with Paul. He and I did everything. Then we decided to go to Longacres. Spent the summer in Seattle. Hiked Mt. Rainier," he remembers. After Cheryl arrived, the adventurers headed east, into Idaho.

At the end of the summer season, Jesse called his boss. "I said, 'I'll be there on opening day of the Tropical Park Meet.' My wife and I drove home. We bought a new house. And then we adopted seven kids."

Looking back on his lifetime of racing and his long career at Calder, Jesse summed it up: "The tracks have always been good to me."

If the tracks have been good to Jesse Parsons, it's likely been a very fair exchange.

in late 2005, just south of the track club-house. Yet even during the ambitious renovation by track owner Magna Entertainment, Gulfstream Park continued attracting the cream of championship horses, owners, and trainers during its tropical meet.

For many promising three-year-olds who will race elsewhere during the year, this is debut time. Huge purses accompany Gulfstream's more than forty stakes races. Biggest of these is the Sunshine Millions series in January, a rousing multirace rivalry between Florida- and California-bred runners; and the early April $1-million-dollar Florida Derby (G1), a regional warm-up for the storied Kentucky Derby (G1). Three-time host of the championship Breeders' Cup Day, Gulfstream Park has had seasonal purse offerings of $8 million and more. Although lighter attendance during construction meant smaller purses and handle, Gulfstream expects to rebuild and even expand its fan base as the race park is completed. Part of the expansion includes new grooms' quarters, where stable hands can live for free during the live meet.

New drama and new records are guaranteed to enhance the history of this racetrack, which opened fleetingly in 1939 (and came back strong in 1944). The popular concert series (which proved a boon to evening attendance) will likely start up again, to the approval of music lovers who poured in for pre-reconstruction headliners, including Cyndi Lauper, Sergio Mendes, America, Air Supply, and the

On the turf at "old" Gulfstream Park

Grand Funk Railroad, live at Gulfstream Park

Gin Blossom. The informative women's luncheon program continues, too, along with Sunday family day and other activities geared toward drawing in the horse fan and attracting new groups to the sport. With the old paddock gardens, gift boutique, nail salon, and barbershop all recalling a grander era, yesteryear's version of Gulfstream Park is already frozen on the sentimental horizon of human memory. But the elegant new venue has plans for attracting more revenues to the sport, locally and regionally.

For the horse lover, the aura of Gulfstream Park will always come down to the equine legends that have raced here, rather than entertainment or merchandising perks. If time proves the sport—and the region—is ready for an ambitious design that wraps housing, horse racing, shopping, and other diversions into one grand complex, we'll pronounce the plan visionary.

TAMPA BAY DOWNS (TAMPA BAY)

Our whirlwind Florida tour wrapped up at this Gulf Coast racetrack under the warmest and sunniest of early May skies on the final day of the Tampa Bay meet. This racetrack sprang to life to fill a regional need after tracks to the south, in languid Tampa and industrious Ybor City (a Cuban cigar-making hub dating to the 1880s), folded in about 1910. Tampa Downs, as it was then known, opened on February 18, 1926. A depressed economy later forced a halt to its racing ambitions, and during WWII, the federal government converted the track to an army training camp. Not until the 1950s and early 1960s (when it was called Sunshine Park) did the racetrack finally experience solid financial footing. In the mid-1960s, Chester Ferguson became the new owner and named his track Florida Downs. Famed New York Yankees

Florida Downs, circa 1960s

SNAPSHOT - GULFSTREAM PARK

Description: Gulfstream has a 1 ⅛ mile dirt track, a separate 1-mile turf course, and a four-story grandstand.

Season: From early January to late April

Address: 901 S. Federal Highway, Hallandale Beach, FL 33009-7124

Phone: 954-454-7000/800-771-8873

Web site: http://www.gulfstreampark.com

Nearest airport: Hollywood International Airport (FLL); Miami International Airport (MIA)

Getting there: US 1 and Hallendale Boulevard

Admission and dining: For admission, dining, and more about new Gulfstream, check the Web site or call the park. (At this printing, the track's Web site was unable to furnish such information, a result of Hurricane Katrina.)

owner and Thoroughbred breeder George Steinbrenner bought the track during the eighties and the name changed again, this time to the present Tampa Bay Downs. His shares were later bought out at auction by Chester's daughter, Stella Ferguson Thayer. Today, the five hundred-acre parcel of land is the largest racetrack-owned parcel in the United States.

The fully air-conditioned facility is open 363 days a year and reported an all-source handle for 2003 of $237 million. Average attendance has been around three thousand on live race days, with double that number turning out for the big stakes events. Twenty-six stakes races, all with guaranteed purses of $50,000 to $250,000, anchor the Tampa Bay meeting. The Florida Oaks, Tampa Bay Derby (G3), the $125,000 Hillsborough Stakes (G3), and the Holiday Inn Express Turf Dash are all contested on Festival Day in mid-March. Don Rice has led the trainer standings eight times since 1995, and Jesus Castanon was the track's top jockey of 2004–2005. Future Racing Hall of Fame jockey Julie Krone scored her first career victory here on February 12, 1981, aboard Lord

Front gate at Tampa Bay Downs

Farkle. Tampa Bay's new turf course opened in 2002 and is reputedly one of the finest in the region.

Approach Tampa Bay Downs via the gleaming brass and glass clubhouse, inside and just up the steps from the canopy at clubhouse (valet) parking. Cool, sophisticated, and jazzy, the clubhouse overlooks the homestretch. Alternatively, from the lobby, it's up the elevator to the Turf Club or out through the clubhouse and into the grandstand concourse, then off to the paddock at the north end of things.

Fast fractions out of the turn, Tampa Bay Downs

Other gathering spots include the Sports Gallery inside the clubhouse, the tropical Clubhouse Garden for private parties, and the Clubhouse Turn for groups. Two little gift shops carry particularly nice racing motif items. An especially fun element here is the Paddock Preview—a rundown on the upcoming race. The whole card is analyzed by Tampa's publicity director Margo Flynn, vivacious, pretty, and a highly spirited turf writer.

Our visit coincided with the track season's wrap-up, Fan Appreciation Day. The staff, attentive to all the details that make a fine race program, was genuinely friendly. In the classically appointed Turf Club, its walls accented in a southern floral of rich blues and greens, a tropical gourmet brunch was laid out, starring a perfectly baked haddock in a heavenly macadamia nut sauce, served with fresh, grilled pineapple. Mary Mikula, manager of the dining room, answered many of our questions and brought us handicapping sheets, helping us pick several winners during the day.

Happy to help commemorate history here, we bet a florinella, a wager introduced by owner Ferguson in 1966: on the day's last race, you choose two horses to win and place, in either order. Nowadays, on any race you wish, it's best known as your basic quinella. We almost won it. All in all, it may not be possible to find a friendlier racetrack and crowd than at Tampa Bay Downs.

LOUISIANA

DELTA DOWNS RACETRACK
AND CASINO (VINTON)
If life is a slot machine, then Delta Downs, a modest little Louisiana track too young to have acquired much history, has hit the jackpot. Slots arrived here in early 2002, and the face of the Downs began changing quickly. In its first two weeks, gamblers fed the casino $7.9 million. This sum was so far beyond the projected figure that money-handling complications temporarily closed the doors. Today, as a testament to the good times, over on

SNAPSHOT - TAMPA BAY DOWNS

Description: Tampa Bay Downs enjoys a rich racing history and tenacious leadership that assures its place on the southern circuit. Friendly and casual, the facility sports a 1-mile oval dirt track with an inner 7-furlong turf course.

Season: December to early May

Address: 11225 Race Track Rd., Tampa Bay, FL 33626; send correspondence to P.O. Box 2007, Oldsmar, FL 34677

Phone: 813-855-4401/866-823-6967

Web site: http://www.tampadowns.com

Nearest airport: Tampa International Airport (TPA)

Getting there: From I-275, approx. 10 miles northwest on Hwy 580 to Oldsmar, then 1 mile north on Race Track Rd.

Admission: Grandstand: $2; clubhouse: $3; children under 14: free when accompanied by an adult

Parking: free; preferred parking: $2.00; valet: $2.00 additional

Fine dining: Skye Terrace Restaurant

Casual fare: Fast-food concessions throughout grandstand area

Spirits: Counters and kiosks throughout facility

Extras: Handicapping seminars, Breakfast at the Downs, golf practice course, TBD cap day, classic car days, family days

The starter lets them fly.

the racing side the winter meet gets going with the Delta Jackpot, now a $1 million graded stakes race (G3) for two-year-olds, one of the richest juvenile competitions in the country. On an average day, the purse total offered may run $160,000 or up, a far cry from former purses, which were mostly low four digits.

Transformation is elsewhere, too. Talk of adding a golf course and movie theaters circulates at financial meetings. At home in their new two-story race quarters, the jockeys have more room and nicer facilities. With it all have come more horses to mount and more races to ride. So far, the grand-

SnapShot - Delta Downs

Description: Delta Downs began life on the banks of the Mississippi River at the farm of Lee Berwick, a quarter horse breeder. The track has seen many transformations along the way, including a move to Vinton in 1973. Since then, the track has changed hands and gained slot machines. Delta has a ¾-mile oval with two chutes. The homestretch is 660 feet. There is no turf course.

Season: Early November to early April. The Delta Jackpot, a $1 million (G3) race for two-year-olds, is the track's first graded race

Address: 2717 Delta Downs, Vinton, LA 70668

Phone: 337-589-7441/(fax) 337-589-2399

Web site: http://www.deltadowns.com

Nearest airport: Lake Charles Regional Airport (LCH); other options include George Bush Intercontinental Airport (IAH) and William P. Hobby Airport (HOU), both in Houston, TX; and Louis Armstrong New Orleans International Airport (MSY) in New Orleans

Getting there: Near the Texas/Louisiana border, off I-10, then north on Highway 109 and east to Highway 3063

Fine dining: Outlook Steakhouse, Triple Crown Buffet

Casual fare: The casino area includes cafés; concessions located throughout the grandstands

Spirits: Many watering holes and kiosks on the premises

Extras: The Gator Lounge, with nightly entertainment

Delta Downs jockeys line up.

stand overlooking the ¾-mile track hasn't moved. The view beyond the sprawling infield lake is of lush pines. Eventually, though, a fancy hotel will fill part of that space, and spectators in the guest suites will be able to watch the races from their windows.

During the fall Thoroughbred meet, we spot jockey names that are very familiar and note others that undoubtedly will become so: Shane Sellers, Victor Espinoza, Terry Thompson, Robby Albarado. This is one of the winter circuits for many of them. Veteran rider Guy Smith, who has raced at Delta Downs for most of a career that began in 1992, charted his one thousandth victory here in February 2004, while Gilbert Ortiz took top rider honors in both 2004 and 2005.

EVANGELINE DOWNS RACETRACK AND CASINO (OPELOUSAS)

In south-central Louisiana, the difference between St. Landry's and Lafayette parishes is the difference between veto and vote yes. Because St. Landry's voters said no to casino gambling, after almost forty years of horse racing in the small town of Carencro, Evangeline Downs moved up the road fifteen miles to Opelousas, where voters made the track part of the country's first racino facility. The casino opened in early 2004, and horse racing celebrated its first season at the new Evangeline Downs in spring 2005.

Old Evangeline Downs has become a training facility, creating additional opportunities for regional horsemen. Yet rickety old Evangeline Downs will be missed by the fans. Night racing in Carencro always brought out the hometown crowd. Everyone knew everyone; newcomers

SNAPSHOT - EVANGELINE DOWNS

Description: The only place where the announcer cries in French, *Ils sont partis* as the horses spring from the starting gate deep in the heart of Cajun country. Known for the fine jockeys that have originated here in Arcadia, this new track hosted its ribbon-cutting ceremony on April 7, 2005. Evangeline Downs's racino anticipates a myriad of supporting entertainment options coming its way soon. The 1-mile dirt track will eventually include an inner turf course.

Season: An eighty-eight-night meet, from mid-April to early September, Thursdays through Saturdays, and Mondays

Address: 2235 Creswell Lane Extension, Opelousas, LA 70570

Phone: 866-472-2466/(fax) 337-574-3166

Web site: http://www.evangelinedowns.com

Nearest airport: Lafayette Regional Airport (LFT)

Getting there: Located on I-49 in Opelousas, Louisiana. Take Creswell Lane exit (no. 18)

Admission: Free; clubhouse: $3

Parking: Free; valet: $5

Fine dining: Silks Dining Room in the clubhouse, appropriate attire expected; Blackberry's Restaurant and Bar

Casual fare: Café 24/7, The Cajun Buffet, concessions located throughout the casino

Spirits: Mojo's Sports Bar, Zydecos

Extras: Horsin' Around entertainment and dancing, cash-prize drawings, other activities

Architect's rendering of new Evangeline Downs

stood out like fireflies in the grass. Despite heat and humidity so thick you could smear 'em on crackers, everybody was outside, crowding the small apron, leaning on the rail, milling about, waiting for the horses; waiting in the easy, patient way that northerners know nothing about.

At the new ED, you get to the racing side by going through the rustic-themed casino entrance and past the food and shopping stalls. The racetrack facility is bright and glassy, boxy and climate controlled. Racino funds have increased purses by a healthy margin, attracting bigger fields of horses and inviting newcomers to join the sport. Management would like to set the tone for revitalized horse racing in Louisiana. New families are breaking into horse ownership, and Thoroughbred farms have sprung up beside country roads.

As Evangeline Downs settles into its new location, chalks up new stats on the 1-mile dirt track, and anticipates building an inner turf track, the state's other three Thoroughbred venues are undoubtedly taking notes. As of 2004, slots of one form or another were approved at all the Louisiana racetracks.

Our travels have taught us to be philosophical toward changes in the sport, including the use of casino revenue to underwrite a part of racing's expenses. Although the long-term benefits of marrying gaming to racing have yet to shake out, the new ED has accelerated the pace of such sporting in the South.

FAIR GROUNDS RACE COURSE (NEW ORLEANS)

Note to readers: At the time this book goes to press, most of New Orleans is still recovering from Hurricane Katrina, the worst natural disaster to strike the United States in at least a century. Fair Grounds Race Course suffered flooding, but it hopes to reopen in time for the 2006–2007 racing season.

One hundred fifty years ago, New Orleans was the third largest city in America. It attracted businessmen from the North and the East eager to expand their empires; more than a few were affluent horsemen. Racing caught fire, and New Orleans became the horse racing capital of the young republic. Among the Crescent City's renowned racetracks were the Union Course and the Metairie, whose ovals were considered among the best in America. Horses from Kentucky, Tennessee, and Virginia shipped down the Ohio and Mississippi rivers to race before large crowds. At Metairie, the stands were carpeted for the comfort of the ladies, and chefs from the city brought their fanciest foods. At one meet, the final prize was a $2,000 silver tea service.

Bird's eye view, Fair Grounds paddock, 2004

Ashado, Fair Grounds Oaks winner 2004

The long tradition of successful racing in New Orleans marches on with Fair Grounds Race Course, which stands on the agricultural grounds where the legendary Union Course was laid out in 1853. A decade later it took its present name. The track survived the Civil War, and in the late 1880s, a jockeys' school opened. In 1893, the course celebrated its first one hundred–day meet. A century later, it survived a devastating grandstand fire. In 2005, it was piecing life back together after hurricane Katrina.

Our first visit to the Big Easy followed the crush of Mardi Gras but came in time for the biggest shows of the year here, the early March running of the $300,000 Fair Grounds Oaks (G2) for three-year-old fillies and the $600,000 Louisiana Derby (G2) for all three-year-olds. Fair Grounds, rebuilt after a grandstand fire in 1993, emerged as a sleek six-story facility with a beautifully landscaped paddock and walking ring and plenty of tempered glass to shield spectators from the tropical sun and that predictable cloudburst. Modern cupolas topped the new roof.

On Oaks day, we watched the races from the clubhouse, downing iced vodkas and oysters on the half shell. We went to the paddock and then made our bets. At the end of the races, we returned to the city, worked our way across the French Quarter, and wrapped up the night with Mr. O'Brien.

Louisiana Derby Day was crowded, noisy, and fun. With no place to sit, it was like a good cocktail party where chairs don't matter. When the big race neared, we discovered we were of two minds about which of the eleven would be the better horse. It became personal, a split between Wimbledon and Pollard's Vision. Circling the paddock before the post parade, Wimbledon looked restless—he'd broken his maiden only a month ago at Santa Anita. His trainer was Bob Baffert, but his jockey, Javier Santiago, had been in the United States for only a month. Yet Pollard's Vision was named for Seabiscuit's Red Pollard, which we thought counted for something. He had opened 2004 with a place and a win at Gulfstream, proving he liked humidity and could easily win today.

Fabulous finish line view

When the field of eleven broke from the gate, Wimbledon dropped toward the back of the pack. Pollard's Vision stayed up, steadily moving forward ahead of Borrego and into the lead by mid-stretch. Heading for the wire, though, Borrego pulled ahead—until Wimbledon sailed wide to the front and left our other favorite to finish third. Wimbledon's time on the fast track for the 1 ⅟₁₆ mile was 1:42.71. We left Gentilly Boulevard and Fair Grounds Race Course with 50 percent of us happy, 50 percent wishing for an instant rematch.

HARRAH'S LOUISIANA DOWNS (BOSSIER CITY)

Harrah's closed escrow on Louisiana Downs in December 2002. With an eye on the calendar, workers immediately began remodeling the track Eddie DeBartolo the elder had built in 1974. Bright colors, new lights, new walls and floors, and new dining spaces and offices transformed the racing side. A flashy temporary casino rose up where the grandstand commons had stood. By opening day of the 2003 summer meet, Harrah's Louisiana Downs looked totally new. With ninety-three Thoroughbred racing days (in 2005), the season runs from late April to early October, closing with a short quarter horse meet. Harrah's Casino—which doesn't close—adjoins the racetrack through a food court and dining pavilion.

Racing here has been relatively robust since 1980, when old Louisiana Downs jumped into the big leagues with the Super Derby. The $500,000 Grade 2 race was a huge pot at the time, and competition from top three-year-olds

SNAPSHOT - FAIR GROUNDS RACE COURSE

Description: Not far from the Mississippi River, where it bends toward the French Quarter, are the grounds of one of the oldest venues in the nation. Though the original 400 acres were down to 145, before Katrina, the track flourished. A 7-furlong turf course was encompassed by a 1-mile dirt course that boasted the longest homestretch in the nation, 1,346 feet. When planning your trip, contact the track for current news on dates, times, and prices.

Season: Late November to late March

Address: 1751 Gentilly Boulevard, New Orleans, LA 70119

Phone: 504-944-5515/(fax) 504-944-2511

Web site: http://www.fairgroundsracecourse.com

Nearest airport: Louis Armstrong International Airport (MSY)

Getting there: On the banks of the Mississippi River in downtown New Orleans, off I-610, at Paris Avenue and Gentilly Boulevard

Admission: Grandstand: $1; clubhouse: $4

Parking: Free; valet: extra charge

Fine dining: Black Gold Dining, reservations suggested, dress code in place

Casual fare: Food courts located throughout the stands

Spirits: Conveniently placed throughout the facility

Extras: The racetrack hosted a special Mardi Gras card during the city celebrations, when some fans predictably arrived in masquerade; Jazz Fest, in late April, featured live music on race days

has kept it lively ever since. The Super Derby's first winner, Temperance Hill, had taken the Belmont Stakes (G1) four months earlier and was eventually voted the nation's champion three-year-old. The winner in 2003 was Ten Most Wanted, under jockey Pat Day.

Here at Louisiana Downs, the upland south is countryside at its prettiest. No cityscape competes for attention, no freeway suggests excitement just up the road. Across the infield, the landscape holds nothing but trees. Thundershowers are as predictable as the steamy bayou sunshine that follows,

Harrah's Louisiana Downs

and together they grow lush grass. From our table in the third-floor Harrah's Club, we overlook white fences and railings, flowers blooming around the paddock, a copper horse

A WORLD OF JOCKEYS

In 1854, the New Orleans Jockey Club organized the Great State Post Stake at Metairie at a two-heat, 4-mile distance. An entry fee of $5,000 per state was levied, and each starter was guaranteed $1,000 unless distanced (fallen too far behind to regain a competitive spot). The winner would pocket the rest. Kentucky, Mississippi, Alabama, and Louisiana accepted the challenge. The states' Thoroughbreds, respectively, were Lexington, Lecomte, Highlander, and Arrow. Running on a muddy track, Lexington came in first. His total time for the 8-mile race was recorded as 16:12.75. Lecomte, previously undefeated, took second. Arrow, distanced in the first heat, was withdrawn.

Among the jockeys was Abe Hawkins, a Louisiana slave. One week later, he again rode Lecomte in a rematch with Lexington, at the identical distance. Hawkins and Lecomte claimed the victory in an astounding time of 15:04.75. In the next decade, as a free man, Hawkins rode at Saratoga. He won

Jockey Marlon St. Julien

the Travers Stakes in 1866 and was by then "the most celebrated jockey in America."

Hawkins's feats were followed years later by those of young Isaac Murphy, a black Kentuckian who took reins in hand at age fourteen and went on to win 628 of his 1,412 starts, including three Kentucky Derbies. More than a hundred years later, his 44 percent career win total still stands as an all-time record. Murphy's sensitive handling of horses was called occult; today, some might refer to him as a horse whisperer. Oliver Lewis, another black jockey, won the inaugural Kentucky Derby, in 1875, on Aristides.

Until the twentieth century, many of the professional jockeys riding Thoroughbreds in America were black. They were gradually pushed from the starting gate by changing economics within the sport, shifting (and discriminating) social attitudes, and, in many cases, their separation from the equestrian way of life. In 2000, Marlon St. Julien became the first black jockey in seventy-one years to ride in the Kentucky Derby. "The Saint" had won the first race at Lone Star Park when it opened in 1997, and the next year he took the track's Jockey of the Year title, with seventy-eight wins and $1.7 million in purses. Since then, he has continued winning races in the Midwest.

Today's top-shelf jockeys come from virtually everywhere—the United States, Canada, Ireland, and especially Latin America. Collectively they illustrate the sport's international and ethnically diverse character. If nationalism and racial and ethnic pride are finally celebrated as strong threads in the fabric of Thoroughbred racing, then the sport has taken gigantic strides into the future.

Warming up before the race at Harrah's Louisiana Downs

weather vane atop the cabana, and jockeys in their carnival-colored silks.

Half-listening to the fourth race, we noted a change in announcers to Rodney Dangerfield, with his unmistakable "I get no respect" voice. The people at the next table, whom we had recognized from the clubhouse at Lone Star Park in Texas, stopped laughing and gave us the story. Track announcer Frank Mirahmadi (who also announces at Fair Grounds) likes to slip into voice impressions. His notoriety won him a part in the movie *Seabiscuit* as the Santa Anita track announcer.

We watched as race eight brought in our winners. A $30,000 claimer for fillies and mares, it paid on our quinella and our exacta box. Totally elated, there was nothing to do but order a round of champagne and invite the Lone Star contingent to join us. When they pointed out that the winning jockey, Gerard Melancon, was also the meet's leading rider, we decided to collect an autograph. After race ten, with Melancon's signature scrawled across our program, we pulled the road map from the glove box and headed toward the interstate.

SnapShot - Harrah's Louisiana Downs

Description: The fluffy white clouds drifting across the rolling horizon are reflected back in the acres of glass that cover the front of the sprawling grandstand. The new casino hums with life. The 1-mile track encompasses a 7-furlong turf course. There are two chutes on the main course, and the homestretch is 940 feet long.

Season: Late April through early October

Address: 8000 East Texas Street, Bossier City, LA 71111

Phone: 318-742-5555/(fax) 318-741-2591

Web site: http://www.harrahs.com/our_casino/lad

Nearest airport: Shreveport Regional Airport (SHV)

Getting there: Louisiana Downs is in Bossier City, just east of Shreveport, off of I-20. From I-20, take exit 26 (Bossier City) and follow signs to the track.

Fine dining: Harrah's Club, reservations recommended, dress code; The Steakhouse and Grill

Casual fare: Fat Tuesday's, Louisiana Bread Company, Pepper Rose Too, The Buffet

Spirits: The Inside Rail, other concessions throughout the facility

Extras: On-site gaming and entertainment; call or check the Web site for upcoming events

SOUTH TRAVEL SECTION

BELOW, YOU LL FIND A MILEAGE CHART LISTING THE DISTANCES BETWEEN THE REGIONAL RACETRACKS AND ALL THE CITIES DISCUSSED IN THE FOLLOWING TRAVEL SECTION. **T**HE CITY OR CITIES CLOSEST TO A TRACK ARE INDICATED BY AN **X**.

COAST TO COAST	Hot Springs, Ark.	Lafayette, La.	Miami, Fla.	New Orleans, La.	Shreveport, La.	Tampa, Fla.
Calder Race Course (Fla.)	1225 miles	965 miles	20 miles	855 miles	1170 miles	**X** 265 miles
Delta Downs Racetrack and Casino (La.)	440 miles	100 miles	1070 miles	**X** 230 miles	250 miles	865 miles
Evangeline Downs Racetrack and Casino (La.)	380 miles	**X** 20 miles	990 miles	150 miles	190 miles	785 miles
Fair Grounds Race Course (La.)	530 miles	135 miles	860 miles	**X** * miles	340 miles	655 miles
Gulfstream Park (Fla.)	1225 miles	965 miles	**X** 20 miles	850 miles	1170 miles	270 miles
Harrah's Louisiana Downs (La.)	195 miles	220 miles	1190 miles	350 miles	**X** * miles	985 miles
Oaklawn Park (Ark.)	**X** * miles	405 miles	1245 miles	535 miles	190 miles	1040 miles
Tampa Bay Downs (Fla.)	1040 miles	780 miles	295 miles	670 miles	985 miles	**X** 15 miles

*The racetrack is located inside or within 10 miles of the city limits.

MUST SEE / MUST DO

ARKANSAS

HOT SPRINGS

Hot Springs is home to the oldest national park in the U.S. system, established in 1832 to protect the forty-seven mineral springs in the area from early commercialism. The park encompasses the historic city district, including **Bathhouse Row** and many of the city's grand hotels and Victorian buildings, and covers some 6,000 natural acres, mountainous and forested, with trails, picnic tables, and campground areas. As Bathhouse Row comprises the greatest number of historic bathhouses in the country, it's no surprise that Hot Springs National Park's **visitor center** can be found in the old **Fordyce Bathhouse** (369 Central Avenue; 501-624-2701; http://www.nps.gov/hosp), which was built in 1915. Stop by for information on the town and park and for a tour of the building; stay for a film on the history of the Hot Springs bathing experience. Like Saratoga Springs in New York, the town attracted the wealthy seeking bet-

William Jefferson Clinton Presidential Library

ter health, and a magnificent Victorian resort town emerged to accommodate them. Although all the thermal springs are protected as purified drinking water, you, too, can get a sip of the healing waters from **Noble Fountain**, on Reserve Avenue near the red-brick promenade leading into the park.

Those who want to *do* rather than *see* can "take the waters" at **Buckstaff Bath House** (509 Central Avenue; 501-623-2308; http://www.buckstaffbaths .com), also run by the park service. This opulent downtown bathhouse, with stained glass windows, mosaic tile work, and marble floors, has been in operation since 1912. All linens and supplies are furnished. Options include heat therapy, massage, loofah treatment, manicures and pedicures, and more. Bathing suits are optional, and genders are discreetly separated by floor.

On the visual side of life, the city is a mini-mecca of fine art galleries. Stop in at the **Hot Springs Convention & Visitors Bureau** (134 Convention Boulevard; 501-321-2835/800-772-2489) for tourist brochures and travel information; the Web site is http://www.hot springs.org. For a visit of a very different sort, check out http://www.hot springsar.com/info/clinton. It will take you on "A Tour of President Clinton's Hot Springs," which includes his boyhood homes, his schools, and his

Bathhouse Row, downtown Hot Springs

favorite burger and barbeque joints! Serious political buffs might take the hour's drive to Little Rock and visit the recently opened **Clinton Library** (1200 President Clinton Avenue; 501-374-4242; http://www.clintonlibrary.gov).

FLORIDA

MIAMI

Gulfstream Park in Hallandale Beach is only twenty miles north of Miami, one of the world's hottest metropolitan centers. Miami Beach is America's Riviera. Its beach playgrounds and exclusive hotel swimming pools are the catwalk for supermodels, celebrities, paparazzi, and the leisure classes. An international center of filmmaking, television production, and fashion photography, the city is a cultural hub for artists, theatrical performers, and musicians. It is also the heart of the vibrant, sultry Latin American scene. A tropical paradise because of its nearly perfect weather, Miami offers an abundance of fishing, water sports, golf, and other recreational opportunities.

Choose your pleasure: **Art Basel Miami Beach** (301 W 41st Street; 305-358-5885; http://www.artbaselmiami beach.com), the acclaimed world class art exhibition; the **Miami International Film Festival** (305-237-3456; http://www.miamifilmfestival.com); architecturally rich **Coral Gables** (south

of downtown Miami); stylish **Coconut Grove** (http://www.ci.miami.fl.us/Coconut Grove); the **Historical Museum of Southern Florida** (101 West Flagler Street; 305-375-1492; http://www.histori cal-museum.org); and the **Miami Art Museum** (101 West Flagler Street; 305.375.3000; http://www.miamiartmu seum.org). For the children, visit the **Miami Museum of Science and Planetarium** (3280 South Miami Avenue; 305-646-4200; http://www. miamisci.org), **Miami Seaquarium** (4400 Rickenbacker Causeway; 305-361-5705; http://www.miamiseaquarium.com, **Monkey Jungle** (14805 Southwest 216th Street; 305-235-1611; http://www.mon keyjungle.com), and **Parrot Jungle Island** (1111 Patriot Jungle Trail; 305-258-6453; http://parrotisland.com). Investigate other temptations at http://www.timeout.com/miami; http://www.southbeach-usa.com; http://www.cityguide.travel-guides.com (select World City Guide: North America, Miami); http://www.kasbah. com (select A City: Miami).

The shopper with designer tastes and indestructible plastic can invest locally at several fine merchandise centers, including South Beach's **Lincoln Road** for one-of-a-kind boutiques; or at the **Village at Merrick Park** in Coral Gables, 358 Avenue San Lorenzo, Coral Gables (305-529-0200), which offers Gucci, Nordstrom, and Neiman-Marcus

Ocean Drive at sunset

South Beach digs

haute-couture garb; or at the Shops at **Bal Harbour**, 9700 Collins Avenue, Bal Harbour (305-866-0311).

Pro Player Stadium, 2267 NW Dan Marino Boulevard, home of the Florida Marlins and Miami Dolphins, is just around the corner from Calder Race Course; check the Miami Herald or the stadium Web site (http://www.proplay erstadium.com) for events and times, or call 305-623-6100 for the sports schedule. If you have an extra day for nature, visit **Everglades National Park** (we counted sixteen alligators on our road trip) near Miami (http://www.nps.gov/ ever) by hopping onto the Florida Turnpike (Route 821) south until it ends, merging with US 1 at Florida City. Turn right at the first traffic light onto Palm Drive (State Road 9336/SW 344th Street), and follow the signs to the park. If you prefer crowds, take the kids to Disney World in Orlando. Call 888-782-9722 for help with reservations.

TAMPA

Tampa is the third largest city in Florida. Its name means "sticks of fire" in Seminole, and it began as an Indian ground near a river, now called the Hillsborough, which meanders into the tropical waters of Tampa Bay and out into the Gulf of Mexico. The Cuban cigar industry began in Ybor City, now Tampa's nocturnal, energetic Latin district. By the 1920s, real estate had awakened to build some of Tampa's most charming neighborhoods. The modern downtown skyline includes several museums, the performing arts center, and the Florida Aquarium. Sports happen at Raymond James Stadium, home of the Super Bowl XXXVII champions, the Tampa Buccaneers, and the St. Pete Times Forum (formerly the Ice [hockey] Palace), home of Tampa Bay Lightning. Garrison Seaport Center sends cruise ships to the Caribbean and Mexico, and its adjacent Garrison Channelside includes a large shopping and dining district.

By day, explore the museums in downtown Tampa or the museum, specialty shops, and cigar stores in Ybor City. Or head to the Gulf Coast by way of the Courtney Campbell Causeway to Clearwater Beach and Belleair Beach and up to the historic sponge-fishing village of **Tarpon Springs**, where a little lunch at the Santorini Greek Grill on the Anclote River waterfront, 698 Dodecanese Boulevard (727-945-9400), would be appropriate in this Greek-heritage seacoast village.

Along with football and hockey, noted above, sports fans traveling in season may want to catch the major league Tampa Bay Devil Rays, who play ball at Tropicana Field, One Tropicana Drive, St. Petersburg (888-326-7297, for game times and ticket info).

For anglers and mermaids, the best headquarters for deep-sea fishing, sailing, cruising, and shelling are at Clearwater Beach. Book a half- or full-day outing with Daisy Mae Fishing Company (727-442-1502; http://www. daisymaefishing.com) or board the **Mar-Chelle II** (727-442-3770), and slather on

The Santorini Greek Grill

the sunblock for a memorable high seas adventure on the Gulf of Mexico.

LOUISIANA

LAFAYETTE

Just down I-49 from Evangeline Downs stands historic Lafayette, which dates to Revolutionary War times. This is the heart of bayou country, offering endless opportunities for unique Cajun tourism.

Acadian Village, Lafayette's original museum of authentic Acadian houses, takes you off the beaten path, into the bayou, and through the cultural history found only in southern Louisiana. Spaniards, French Canadians, Caribbeans, and Africans, whose traditions have blended over the centuries into the folk culture known as Acadian, settled the area. In the village, festivals throughout the year feature Bluegrass and Cajun music, crafts, and Creole and Cajun foods. Call 337-981-2364 or check the Web site (http://www.acadianvillage.org) for dates and events.

Lafayette Natural History Museum & Planetarium (433 Jefferson Street; 337-291-5544; http://www.lnhm.org) offers several different programs and exhibitions throughout the year on astronomy and natural history. Some are targeted for

Festival International de Louisiane

the youngsters in the family. Admission for adults is $8; for senior citizens, $6; for children ages five to sixteen, $5; for ages four and under, free. The museum is open every day except Monday.

Summertime in Lafayette means Friday night block parties downtown (through early June), art walks once a month on Saturday evenings, and plenty of other reasons to get out and stroll this university city. The city and its residents celebrate their rich heritage with several festivals, including the **Festival International de Louisiane** (337.232.8086; http://www.festivalinternational.com) in April, which celebrates the region's French heritage.

Take a swamp cruise, enjoy grand plantation architecture, sample spicy seafood platters, and dance the night away at one of the city's newest clubs. Their Web site (http://www.lafayettetravel.com) lists activities and offers tour planning and other cultural links.

NEW ORLEANS

Note to readers: The French Quarter, the Garden District, and St. Charles Avenue escaped the floodwaters of Hurricane Katrina in 2005, but no one knows how much of the city will survive. We have chosen, however, to retain the description of New Orleans written prior to the hurricane as a portrait of a place and as a tribute to this culturally rich and historically unique U.S. city and its residents.

Iron grillwork edges high balconies, masses of flowers cluster on doorsteps, and there is always the hint of subtropical dampness in the New Orleans air. You'll find an abundance of spicy Creole cuisine, smooth bourbons and sugary Hurricanes, and jazz that wails on until the dawn. Clear your calendar, come for the horse racing, and linger as long as you can. This amazing, exotic, multicultural metropolis that hugs the Mississippi is slow and southern, vital and vibrant.

New Orleans's famous wrought iron balconies

You won't need a French dictionary, just bring your joie de vivre and *laissez les bon temps rouler* (Let the good times roll.).

New Orleans was nicknamed the Crescent City for its birthplace in a cradle of the mighty Mississippi. From early days when French and Spanish traders and smugglers plied its waters, to the present, the river has remained the city's central aorta. To orient yourself and watch the river in relative solitude, visit **Audubon Park and Gardens** (504-581-4629; http://www.auduboninstitute.com). Designed by Frederic Law Olmsted, it is four hundred landscaped acres of natural southern flora, fountains, formal gardens, a zoo, a horseback riding station, a planetarium, and a golf course. The park takes in nearly a mile of riverfront and extends northeast into the city. Its address and easiest entrance is 6500 Magazine Street; you can also take the *John James Audubon* **riverboat** (504-586-8777) from Canal Street, downtown.

The Louisiana Purchase was the world's biggest and most significant real estate deal. The original sale document is displayed in the **Historic New Orleans Collection**, in one of ten treasure-filled galleries (533 Royal Street; 504-523-4662; http://www.hnoc.org). The gem of the collection is the 1889 Williams Residence, home of General and Mrs. L. K. Williams, a philanthropic, mid-twentieth-century couple dedicated to preserving the French Quarter. They filled their home with early eighteenth-century furnishings and other rare collectibles. Take a docent-led tour ($4, Tuesdays through Saturdays) of the home and galleries.

The early French Quarter included parade grounds, where soldiers of three nations and the Confederacy have drilled. Named in honor of Andrew Jackson, **Jackson Square** in the Quarter, between Decatur and Chartres streets, has become a gathering spot for the city's artists, who display and sell their work here. Facing the square is the classical St. Louis Cathedral, built in 1794. The centerpiece of the square, the statue of Andrew Jackson, was installed in 1856. Even if you don't normally visit cemeteries on vacation, you should made a visit to **Metairie Cemetery** (5100 Pontchartrain Boulevard). The legendary Metairie race track, built in 1838, closed during Reconstruction and later became a graveyard. In a city built below sea level, residents stay drier with above the ground monuments—some of them beautifully moving, others outrageously ornate. This may be your one chance to drive on a horse racing track, as the original oval is one of the routes through the cemetery.

Voodoo Bar

Jackson Square, St. Louis Cathedral

Stroll the city's art district, along Royal Street, especially between the 300 and 700 blocks. Worth a special tour is **Windsor Fine Art** (221 Royal Street; 504-586-0202; http://www.windsorfineart .com), whose three floors include works by classic European masters as Rembrandt, Chagall, and Dali and by contemporary artists and sculptors. Open daily.

Finally, venture into the city's eclectic shops. Antiques, art, and outrageous designs make The Big Easy a resource for rare mementos. In the French Quarter, enjoy the art galleries and clothing shops, which line Royal and Magazine streets, between Audubon Park and Canal Street. The **Shops at Canal Place** is an upscale shopping center with cinemas, a health club, and cafés

along the river (504-522-9200). The **Riverwalk Marketplace** (1 Poydras Street; 504-522-1555; http://www.river walkmarketplace) offers a half-mile of shopping, dining, and entertainment.

SHREVEPORT

The grandeur of an earlier era is ever present, with many sites designated National Historic Landmarks. Stroll the city and the waterfront. Downtown is filled with ambitious public buildings, majestic churches, and artistic murals decorating the sides of buildings. Visit the **Spring Street Museum** (318-424-0964) to see artifacts of the city's past, or tour the complex of authentic cotton plantations and historic homes and structures on the campus of Louisiana State University–Shreveport's **Pioneer Heritage Center** (318-797-5332) that reveal life before the Civil War.

Interested in other forms of transportation besides the four-legged variety? Pay a visit to **Ark-La-Tex Antique and Classical Vehicle Museum** (601 Spring Street; 318-222-0227; http://www.carmu seum.org). This 1920s auto dealer showroom was converted to gallery space for vintage vehicles and is on the Historic Register. Changing exhibits feature antique and classic fire engines, motorcycles, trucks, cars, and scale model cars; trains; life-size historic sets; period costumes; and related antique items. The building itself has ornate woodwork trim created in the showroom's rear work space. This nonprofit museum has a gift shop, and there are tours available for large groups.

Metairie Cemetery, site of the original racetrack

Shreveport renaissance

WHERE TO STAY

ARKANSAS

HOT SPRINGS

The Majestic Hotel
101 Park Avenue
501-321-9664
Hot Springs, AR 71901
http://www.themajestichotel.com
$79–$148
The Majestic, located in the heart of the city, was built in 1882 and recently renovated. It has been stylishly upgraded with a modern flair while preserving the architectural flavor that characterized grand resort lodging a century ago. On-premises dining features the Grady Manning dining room and Grady's Grill, Steakhouse, and Wine Bar. The resort offers spa services and includes a large, circular, heated swimming pool, and golf and tennis packages are offered through Hot Springs Country Club.

The Park Hotel
211 Fountain Street
501-624-5353/800-895-7275
http://www.thehistoricpark.com
$60–$125; pets extra
This historic hotel blends Spanish revival and art deco elements, earning it a spot on the National Register of Historic Places. Located right downtown, it's a short walk to the city's Bathhouse Row. Dining at the hotel's Acapulco's Restaurant on the patio means fresh southwestern cuisine; do happy hour at the Patio Bar and plan to meet the Oaklawn crowd.

FLORIDA

MIAMI

Delano Hotel South Beach
1685 Collins Avenue
Miami Beach, FL 33139
305-672-2000/800-606-6090
Seasonal packages from $315
Named for our thirty-second president, this hotel in the heart of South Beach is the choice of the chic and the famous. Guests can enjoy the hotel's spa, gym, restaurants, and bar.

Don Shula's Golf Club Hotel
7601 Miami Lakes Drive
Hialeah, FL 33014
800-24-SHULA
http://hotel.donshulahotel.com
Peak-season two-night packages from $309
Golfers can bring the clubs and check in for an 18-hole championship course at this sprawling hotel complex between Miami and Fort Lauderdale.

Doubletree Surfcomber Hotel
1717 Collins Avenue
Miami Beach, FL 33139

305-532-7715
http://www.doubletree.com
Winter rates from $229
This hotel is located on the oceanfront in the historic Art Deco District of South Beach.

The Fontainebleau Resort
4441 Collins Avenue
Miami Beach, FL 33140
305-538-2000
http://www.fontainebleau.com
$289–$489; suites higher
This hotel is classy MiMO (1950s Miami Modern). With its children's water park and other activities, it is a great place to stay with the family. Adults can enjoy the spa and gym—or the nightclub.

The Loews Miami Beach Hotel
1601 Collins Avenue
Miami Beach, FL 33139
305-604-1601
http://www.loewshotels.com/hotels/miamibeach
$289 and up
Enjoy a stay on the water at this fine hotel, which offers elegant, spacious rooms. There are six restaurants and lounges within the hotel.

TAMPA

Belleview Biltmore Resort, Golf Club, and Spa
25 Belleview Boulevard
Clearwater, FL 33756
727-373-3000/800-237-8947
Specials from $109
In Clearwater, on the Gulf Coast, nothing rivals this hotel for its century-old standard of tradition and elegance, with all the amenities.

Grand Hyatt Tampa Bay
2900 Bayport Drive
Tampa, FL 33607
813-874-1234/800-233-1234
Special packages from $169
Overlook the water from your room at the Grand Hyatt, and take its boardwalk path and spot the shorebirds in the nature preserve.

Hilton Clearwater Beach Resort
400 Mandalay Avenue
Clearwater Beach, FL 33767
727-461-3222/877-461-3222
Typically $152–$224
You can play volleyball on the beach, swat tennis balls day or night, golf, rent jet skis or a parasail, or just wade for miles in the water here.

Tampa (formerly Radisson) Riverwalk Hotel
200 N Ashley Drive
Tampa, FL 33602
813-223-2222/800-282-6817
$159 and up
Stay downtown and discover the walkable city.

LOUISIANA

LAFAYETTE

Bois des Chênes Inn
338 N. Sterling Street
Lafayette, LA 70501
337-233-7816
http://www.boisdeschenes.com
$100–$150
This historic 1820 Acadian plantation house has been beautifully restored and furnished with antiques. It has received numerous awards and is on the Historic Houses register. Five private suites. With advance planning, it's possible to accompany the scientist-owner on birding and swamp tours. Amenities include a complimentary bottle of wine; complimentary breakfast.

Hilton Lafayette
1521 West Pinhook Road
Lafayette, LA 70503
337-235-6111/800-HILTONS
http://www.Lafayette.Hilton.com
$79 and up
The Hilton Lafayette offers standard rooms (choose a king-size bed or two doubles) and spacious suites, with French provincial décor, views of the river, and spa packages. Other amenities include a shoe shine stand, a gift shop, daily morning paper, meeting rooms, and hotel dining and lounge entertainment.

NEW ORLEANS

Loew's New Orleans
300 Poydras Street
New Orleans, LA 70130
504-595-3300/800-23-LOEWS
http://www.loewshotels.com
$139–$399
From the gorgeous lobby to the exceptionally spacious rooms, Loew's has restored an historic building at the riverfront in a blend of colonial French and Creole flavors. We loved our grand room. Located in the exciting arts district, not far from the French Quarter, room views capture the French Quarter, the river, or the city. It offers a fitness center, several spas, a pool, and an attentive staff.

The Ritz-Carlton
921 Canal Street
New Orleans, LA 70112
504-524-1331
http://www.ritzcarlton.com
$245 and up
Sublime, that's the word here. This Ritz is charmingly southern and has a gorgeous garden courtyard, where you can shut out the world—but here on Canal Street, you can have it back in a minute. Big feather beds, down pillows, plush marble bathrooms, and full spa indulgences await you.

Wyndham New Orleans at Canal Place
100 Rue Iberville
New Orleans, LA 70130
504-566-7006
http://www.wyndham.com

$135–$579

Don't be dismayed by the corporate exterior; inside, delightful French ambiance rules. The lobby is elegant, decorated in rich florals and period French furnishings befitting a hotel in the French Quarter. Surrounded by some of the city's most exciting spots, the rooms have great views of the Mississippi and the city. Unwind or rev up with a Hurricane in the Green Bar or lobby lounge, or do laps at the pool. River 127, the hotel's continental-but-spicy restaurant opens at 6:30 a.m. for breakfast.

SHREVEPORT

Holiday Inn Financial Plaza
5555 Financial Plaza
Shreveport, LA 71129
318-688-3000/1-800-465-4329
http://www.holiday-inn.com/shreveport-fin
Rooms and suites from $68–$160
With indoor and outdoor heated pools and an exercise center and sauna to choose from, guests can relax and stay fit at the same time. Just off the lobby are the Market Restaurant, serving southern and Cajun cuisine at breakfast, lunch, dinner, and the Sunday brunch buffet; La Carrousel Lounge in the atrium.

The Remington Suite
220 Travis Street
Shreveport, LA 71101
318-425-5000/800-444-6750
http://www.remingtonsuite.com
$75–$175
In the heart of Shreveport, yet light years from the casino scene, you'll find the Remington, a small, luxury hotel of twenty-two suite accommodations, indoor heated pool, and fitness center. Suites vary in floor plan; all are individually and richly decorated and include wet bars, Jacuzzi baths, fresh flowers, and breakfast in bed. The Remington has its own restaurant. Additionally, guests receive complimentary membership in three of the city's most prestigious and semiprivate restaurants.

WHERE TO WINE & DINE

ARKANSAS

HOT SPRINGS

Belle Arti Ristorante
719 Central Avenue
501-624-7474
http://www.belle-arti.8m.com
$9–$36
Dining in this ornate Victorian building in the heart of Hot Springs sweeps you back in time for a twentieth-century experience. From the caprese to the grilled filet mignon in cognac cream sauce with green peppercorns to the Black Forest gateau cake, all was delicious. Plus, we finally "got it" regarding crème brulée.

Chef Paul's
4310 Central Avenue
Temperance Hill Square
501-520-4187
http://www.cpauls.com
$12–$40

The highlight of our southern travel dining, Chef Paul's, is a rare experience. Lunch and dinner are served in an opulent, intimate European setting, where every detail of the menu and presentation are quietly scrutinized. Dishes are inspired by continental, French, and Mediterranean cuisines. Angus beef arrives from Omaha, lamb from down under, seafood and shellfish are flown in daily. Many entrées and dessert ingredients are seasonally inspired. The extensive wine book includes a mini-course in understanding varietals, with regional notes on California wines.

FLORIDA

MIAMI

Ay Mamá Inés
11481 SW 40th Street
Miami, FL 33165
305-228-7778
Entrées from $16
No one should leave south Florida without sampling a good Cuban restaurant, and we recommend this legendary one in western Miami. There's plenty of time: it opens at 9 a.m. and doesn't stop serving until 11 p.m.

The Delano's Blue Door Restaurant
1685 Collins Avenue
Miami Beach, FL 33139
305-674-6400
Entrées from $16
Serving total elegance; we also recommend Delano's for Sunday brunch.

Sushi Rock SoBe
1351 Collins Avenue
South Beach, FL 33139
305-532-2133
$6.95–$24.95
If you enjoy a "nightclubby," nice 'n' loud, rock 'n' roll atmosphere, you should try this sushi café.

Tantra
1445 Pennsylvania Avenue
Miami, FL 33139
305-672-4765
Seasonal menus and variable prices
Enjoy this sensual Middle Eastern dining experience, one unlike any we've known, where entrées are among the most exotic and intriguing foods we've had.

Tequila Blue
736 Ocean Drive
Miami, FL 33139
305-695-1974
Drinks and entrées $4 and up
As the name implies, this restaurant, located in the Colony Hotel, offers plenty of specialty tequilas as well as fresh, homestyle Mexican dishes.

TAMPA

Armani's
6200 W. Courtney Campbell Causeway
Tampa, FL 33607
813-281-9165
Entrées from $27.00
For sophisticated, gourmet Italian dining, elevator up to the 14th floor of the Grand Hyatt, and wear business casual, with jacket.

Ashley Street Grille
200 N. Ashley Drive
Tampa, FL 33602
813-223-2222
Entrées from $14
Choose your table at this award-winning waterfront grill.

Bern's Steak House
1208 Howard Avenue
Tampa, FL 33605
813-251-2421
Steaks from $27
Meat lovers—as well as lovers of foie gras, caviar, and oysters—are in good hands in this exceptional atmosphere. Expensive but worthy.

The Gardens
217 Central Avenue
St. Petersburg, FL 33701
727-896-3800
$8–$14
Kick back with dinner and live jazz (music on the weekend) at an under-the-stars lounge beneath a signature banyan tree in the heart of historic downtown St. Petersburg.

Ybor City's Columbia Restaurant
2117 East 7th Avenue
Tampa, FL 33605
813-248-4961
$9.95 and up
Quaff a Cuban Manhattan and feast on sizzling Cuban and Spanish dishes at this lush, Latin-flavored restaurant.

LOUISIANA

LAFAYETTE

Antlers Restaurant & Bar
555 Jefferson St.
Lafayette, LA 70501
337-234-8877
http://www.antlers.com
$6.95–$13.95
Located in the heart of the city, Antlers is the oldest bar in town. A personable waitstaff serves up spicy Cajun plates and fresh, grilled seafood. Open late for live music on Friday nights. After dinner, stroll the historic city streets.

Prejean's

3480 I-49
North Lafayette, LA 70507
337-896-3247
http://www.prejeans.com
Entrées from $7.99

It's 9:00 p.m. on Thursday night, July 3, and this place is still packed. A Cajun band finishes its last set under the watchful eye of the huge 14-foot stuffed alligator that acts as the centerpiece as you enter the restaurant. Smaller alligator motifs, and an incredible stained glass riverboat, glow in the soft light. The interior is interesting, not fancy, but the authentic Cajun food has won prizes for two decades. Good wine to boot.

NEW ORLEANS

The Court of Two Sisters

631 Royal Street
New Orleans, LA 70130
504-522-7261
http://www.courtoftwosisters.com
$18 and up; brunch $25

In the Crescent City, every day can be Sunday at the Two Sisters jazz brunch in the French Quarter, from 9:00 to 3:00 daily. The aristocratic Creole siblings, born in the mid-nineteenth century, clothed society women from their notions shop on this Rue Royale site, which dates to the early 1700s. Enjoy this luscious, old-world setting with its award-winning courtyard dining. Pile your plate with duck à l'orange, seafood mousse, Cajun pasta, bananas foster, and bread pudding with whiskey sauce. The dinner menu features Creole.

Dickie Brennan's Steak House

716 Iberville Street
New Orleans, LA 70130
504-522-2467
http://www.dickiebrennanssteakhouse.com
$14.95 and up to market prices for lobster

Mr. B. studied cooking under Paul Prudhomme, and then in Italy, Mexico, and Paris, and has received too many dining awards to list. His steakhouse is dark and clubby, with rich wooden columns and beams. Our blackened prime rib entrée, with mushroom sauce and creamy mashed potatoes, was five-star; and the frozen lemon soufflé—awesome.

Mulate's

201 Julia Street
New Orleans, LA 70130
504-522-1492/800-854-9149
http://www.mulates.com
Entrées from $15.99

With or without dinner, dancing is too much fun. This authentic Cajun nightspot features dancing to live music, with fiddles, accordion, guitar, drums, and, of course, the washboard.

Olivier's

204 Decatur Street
New Orleans, LA 70130
504-525-7734
$14.95–$18.95

It's illegal to visit New Orleans—without sampling the exotic spices and flavors that make Creole cooking unique. Start with dinner here—where one family has raised five generations of chefs. We had the family favorite, Creole rabbit with an unforgettable oyster sage dressing. The shrimp scampi, sautéed in garlic with a lemony butter parmesan cheese sauce, was irresistibly rich.

Pat O'Brien's
718 St. Peter Street
New Orleans, LA 70116
504-525-4823
http://www.patobriens.com
Entrées from $8; $5 cover charge after 9 p.m.
Birthplace of the Hurricane. Legend says that in the 1940s, O'Brien was forced to unload his rum stock so he poured it into hurricane lamps, added passion fruit juice and sugar, and gave it away to sailors. Stop in for a nightcap. The setting is a two hundred-year-old theater building, with a beautifully restored carriage entrance. O'Brien's is actually three separate bars and a courtyard restaurant with fountains, a pianist, and prime river views.

Preservation Hall
726 St. Peter Street
New Orleans, LA 70116
504-522-2841
http://www.preservationhall.com
$8 admission
Dixieland is spoken here, 8:00 p.m. until midnight. Created as a sanctuary to protect and honor New Orleans jazz music in 1961, musicians play for half-hour sets. Requests (Dixieland only) are $5. All ages welcome.

SHREVEPORT

Chianti Restaurant
6535 Line Avenue
Shreveport, LA 71106
318-868-8866
$13.95–$27.95
We were thirsty, so we chose this restaurant by name and what a treat! Chianti is an elegant, romantic little Italian spot with candlelight dining and a piano bar. It features its own fresh pasta, along with seafood, veal, and other classical entrées. The fettucini alfredo was fab. The pollo alla Milanese, a breaded chicken breast sautéed in lemon butter and served with pepperoncini, garlic, and pasta, was nicely piquant and delicious.

Superior's Steak House
855 Pierremont Street, Suite 120 (in Towne Oak Square)
Shreveport, LA 71106
318-219-74123
http://www.superiorssteakhouse.com
$21.95 and up
Superior's is a dark, masculine, continental-style seafood and steak house, with piano and cigar bars. Enjoy its fine selection of premium wines with one of numerous entrées. Start with quail and grits or fried oysters, and move on to the main event, but save a little room for a bite of chocolate molten soufflé.

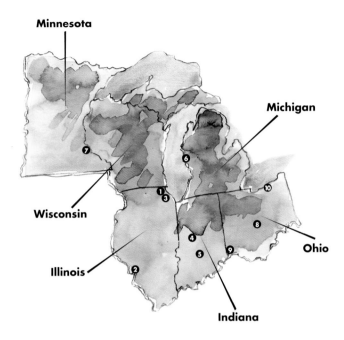

MIDWEST MAP LEGEND

Illinois
1 Arlington Park
(Arlington Heights)

2 Fairmount Park
(Collinsville)

3 Hawthorne Race Course
(Cicero)

Indiana
4 Hoosier Park
(Anderson)

5 Indiana Downs
(Shelbyville)

Michigan
6 Great Lakes Downs
(Muskegon)

Minnesota
7 Canterbury Park
(Shakopee)

Ohio
8 Beulah Park
(Grove City)

9 River Downs
(Cincinnati)

10 Thistledown
(North Randall)

THE MIDWEST

"estward the course of empire takes its way," wrote George Berkeley in 1736. His verse celebrated the young republic's potential. But the "west" in the Irishman's poem, which *was* the American West, was the wilderness beyond Pennsylvania and Virginia. When it became the Northwest Territory, land-hungry settlers spilled in, bringing cattle and horses among their worldly goods. A patchwork of small farms and towns sprang up, later to become Michigan, Illinois, and the handful of other states that compose today's Midwest.

Wherever a wealthy country gentleman built his new estate, horse breeding followed. By the 1840s, several cities in the "west" were prosperous, and jockey clubs had organized. Two decades earlier, Saratoga, Cincinnati, Detroit, Chicago, and St. Louis had boasted racing worthy of great regional matches, and had gotten them. Washington Park, opened in 1884 near Chicago, became the Midwest's most legendary track. The beautiful course crowned the Midwest circuit, easily rivaling eastern racing. In 1893, when Chicago hosted the World's Fair, it was also the scene of America's richest horse racing.

More than a century later, the midwestern racetracks are generally in good health. Elegant Arlington Park, near Chicago, leads the team.

ILLINOIS

ARLINGTON PARK (ARLINGTON HEIGHTS)

At the height of the Roaring Twenties, in 1926, Arlington Park broke ground on a flat, thousand-acre site in Arlington Heights, Illinois, northwest of Chicago. Some eighty years later, despite trial by national depression, a second world war, and a devastating grandstand fire, Arlington Park ranks as one of the nation's premier destinations for aficionados of the sport of kings.

Arlington's history has held great moments. In the 1950s, the new Arlington Classic became the world's richest race; jockey Eddie Arcaro chalked up his three thousandth win at the track; and the parking lot was expanded to hold fifteen thousand cars. In the 1960s, Dr. Fager ran the mile in 1:32.20, under an enormous weight of 134 pounds, setting a world record not broken until 1998. The next decade witnessed the introduction of both night and Sunday racing. Secretariat, racing in his only contest here, won the 1973 Arlington Invitational by 9 lengths. The

1980s brought the Arlington Million (G1), then the only million-dollar race, won in 1981 by the great John Henry, with Bill Shoemaker aboard. A team of new owners assumed Arlington's helm in 1983, including businessman Richard "Mr. D." Duchossois, and in 1984 John Henry repeated his Million feat before a crowd of forty thousand.

Then, the following summer, something in the clubhouse kitchen caught fire, and before the inferno could be contained, everything had been reduced to cinders—the grandstand, the offices, the records, the history. Duchossois bought out his partners after the fire, and in a feat that would later earn the Arlington team an Eclipse Award of merit, crews worked around the clock to prepare the track for the fifth running of the Arlington Million, scheduled just 25 days after the fire. More than 35,000 fans filled temporary bleachers and tents to witness the "Miracle Million" of 1985, won by England's Teleprompter. By the time Arlington opened its new facility in 1989, Thoroughbred racing in America had lost a bit of its luster. Not so for the new Arlington Park, where

Arlington Million 2004 on the turf

Arlington Park north entrance

the passion for live Thoroughbred racing continued unabated.

On our visit, media director Dan Leary met us in the morning and hosted a thoroughly interesting tour, beginning in the seven hundred thousand square foot grandstand, taking us through the electronic media studio and eventually escorting us up the palatial central stairway to the clubhouse. At the far end, a curved outdoor terrace overlooks the track, and inside, a succession of elegant dining rooms are charming in soft country-estate colors, lovely floral accents, and garden-party themes. The grounds are as beautiful as the interiors. The green-trimmed buildings and white rail fences, rolling lawns, and rooftop cupolas give this park a horse-country feeling.

Down beside the grandstand, the Corona people were putting on a little tropical party, with beer and limes on ice and a Jimmy Buffett–style band playing rock with a twist of calypso tossed in. The Park, as they call it, was a shady oasis, alive with little kids buzzing around like windup walking toys and a crowd of revelers sporting short-sleeved shirts in island motifs, khaki shorts, and more

SNAPSHOT - ARLINGTON PARK

Description: Arlington Park, twenty-eight miles northwest of Chicago, was founded in 1926 but devastated by fire in 1985. It rose from the ashes as an airy and spacious five-story structure. On every floor, window walls and wide balconies give spectators an unobstructed view of the paddock grounds and saddling area on the west side of the building, and the wide oval racetrack on the east. A 1 ⅛-mile dirt track encompasses a 1-mile turf course. The homestretch measures 1,049 feet.

Season: Early May or June to late September or October. The biggest race, the Arlington Million (G1), run on the turf, comes around every August.

Address: 2200 West Euclid Avenue, Arlington Heights, IL 60006

Phone: 3847-385-7500/(fax) 847-385-7251

Web site: http://www.arlingtonpark.com

Nearest airport: O'Hare International Airport (ORD)

Getting there: Located twenty-eight miles northwest of downtown Chicago. Accessible from I-90 and I-94. Arlington Park is accessible by rail from the city. But if you arrive by air, another option is to rent a car and drive to Arlington Heights, spending the night at the nearby Sheraton Northwest Chicago, as many of the horsemen and women do (3400 W. Euclid Avenue, Arlington Heights, IL; 847-394-2000; http://www.sheraton.com). It offers a free shuttle to the races.

Admission: $6; seniors (fifty-five and over): $3 on Wednesdays; children seventeen and younger: free when accompanied by a paying adult; reserved box seats: $3–$6

Parking: Free; preferred: $5; valet: $10

Fine dining: The Million Room, reservations recommended; groups can reserve the International Room, the Governor's Room, and the Marquee on the Green, all with elaborately catered buffets and menu selections; business smart dress codes upheld; call 847-385-7410 to discuss arrangements

Casual fare: Hearth Grill, Mr. D's, The Park, Cobey's Food Court, Paddock Pub, Silk's Deli

Spirits: Silk's Lounge, the Paddock Pub, Cobey's Bar, additional beverage stations located throughout

Extras: Arlington Park invites you to learn more about Thoroughbred Racing. Tours of the backstretch, starting gate, announcer's booth, and others may be arranged. Call or e-mail for details. Sundays are family days, with kid-friendly activities and animals.

The Red Hat Ladies do lunch at the races.

than a few skimpy tank tops and contoured jeans. As we quickly learned, the race fans and Thoroughbred owners who call Arlington Park their home track are varied and legion. A typical summer weekend finds the race park pleasantly full. On Father's Day, twenty-seven thousand spectators could easily turn out, and on Arlington Million (G1) Day, we might bump elbows with another thirty thousand hopeful winners. We chatted for a bit with the young bugler, Bonnie Brown, who had been selected to play the call to post.

Up on an outdoor clubhouse terrace, we came upon a bevy of lovely women having a rather fine time. All of them were coiffed in fancy red hats, enjoying lunch in the sunshine and sipping iced tea and other icy drinks garnished with fruit and little red straws. Our natural inquisitiveness took over, and soon we had joined them with flutes of brut. This fun-loving group of fifty-somethings and up belong to a chapter of the Red Hat Ladies. Each of them has taken a vow to embrace life at every turn. On this day, that meant 'ciphering to beat the odds; tomorrow they could be off on a Chicago harbor dinner cruise.

FAIRMOUNT PARK (COLLINSVILLE)

Summers can be hot here, on the eastern bluffs of the Mississippi River. The white grandstand with its red roof shimmers in the early heat. Morning training hours are just wrapping up; hoofbeats are muted in the dust that pulses around the horses' feet. St. Louis lies to the west, across the river, its golden arch reflecting the sunlight.

Seven burst from the Fairmount gate.

Fairmount winner Bathhouse Bet, April 27, 2004

Fairmount Park was the result of a collaboration between two Kentucky horsemen, Colonels E. R. Bradley and Matt Winn. Bradley, owner of four Kentucky Derby winners (Behave Yourself, Bubbling Over, Burgoo King, and Broker's Tip), founded Idle Hour Farm in Lexington, Kentucky (now known as Darby Dan Farm). Winn, who rescued Churchill Downs from financial ruin in 1902, promoted the Kentucky Derby (G1) into the premier sporting event it is today. Together, Bradley and Winn envisioned a mini version of Churchill Downs that would bring horse racing to the edge of the Mississippi.

Fairmount Park opened in September 1925 to an enthusiastic crowd. Only a few years later, the Depression came roaring in, but the track's pioneering spirit held fast. In 1947, when Fairmount flipped the switch on the lights that surrounded the 1-mile oval, it became the world's first 1-mile racetrack to provide nighttime racing—a bold move when the country was recovering from wartime restrictions and blackouts. The spectacle of night racing attracted people from as far away as Europe and Australia, and racing flourished here, with both harness horses and Thoroughbreds competing. A second track, Cahokia Downs, opened nearby in 1954.

Then fortunes began to turn again, and in 1979 Cahokia was shuttered. A dozen years later, an innocuous-looking boat set sail on the Mississippi and delivered an enormous wallop to horse racing: the first Mississippi riverboat gambling cruise. Within two years, more boats were plying the river, siphoning gaming money away from Fairmount. In 1994, casino gambling was also legal-

SNAPSHOT - FAIRMOUNT PARK

Description: On the Illinois side of the Mississippi River stands Matt Winn's smaller version of historic Churchill Downs. The white entry gate with its red peak welcomes you; new landscaping and upgrades make it a pleasant place to enjoy evening horse racing. The 1-mile track with two chutes has a 1,050-foot homestretch.

Season: Late March to mid-September

Address: 9301 Collinsville Road, Collinsville, IL 62234

Phone: 618-345-4303/(fax) 618-344-8218

Web site: http://www.fairmountpark.com

Nearest airport: Lambert-St. Louis International Airport (STL)

Getting there: Collinsville, Illinois, an old town populated by families of German heritage (once famous for its horseradish), is on the Mississippi River just across the water from St. Louis. Fairmount Park is one-half mile southwest of the I-55/70 and I-255 junction.

Admission: $2.50

Parking: Free; preferred: $2.00

Fine dining: Top of the Turf, Bar Two in grandstand area

Casual fare: Sunday Brunch at the Top of the Turf, First Turn Cafe, Secretariat Room

Spirits: Top of the Turf; beer, wine, and cocktails available in several areas

Extras: Armed Forces Night Special gives free admission and food to active armed forces members and their families.

ized in Missouri, and the floodgates opened. Five years later, harness racing at Fairmount was suspended.

Fairmount remains determined to survive. Here on the banks of the river, the track quietly goes about the business of racing. Like the swallows returning to the clay bluffs, the Thoroughbreds return to Fairmount every spring for another summer contest along the Mississippi.

HAWTHORNE RACE COURSE (CICERO)

Hawthorne Race Course, built originally in 1891, is today an inner-city track, sharing a block with recently closed Sportsman's Park. Smokestacks and factory façades fill the background; the history is steeped in Chicago lore. Purchased by Thomas Carey in 1909, Hawthorne suffered through a prohibition against gambling that shuttered the track for more than a decade. In 1922, it reopened, and a few years later, the

Hawthorne Gold Cup was added to the roster, as Carey wanted see a Gold Cup race in the Midwest that matched the caliber of those held on the coasts. Hawthorne enjoyed a surge in popularity, attracting notable horses such as Kelso, Dr. Fager, Equipoise, Round Table, and Black Tie Affair (Ireland). Today, the Hawthorne Gold Cup carries a hefty $750,000 purse and a Grade 2 rating. Run at 1 ¼ miles, it consistently attracts top horses competing for the purse and the solid gold trophy—presented by Thomas F. Carey III, grandson of the first Thomas Carey.

Sportsman's Park and Hawthorne Race Course merged in 2002, following the closing of the former. The merger added the prestigious Illinois Derby (G2) to the track roster. That year, champion War Emblem captured the Illinois Derby on his way to winning two-thirds of the American Triple

Pounding around the turn at Hawthorne

Airtime at Hawthorne

Crown. In 2004, the one-eyed colt Pollard's Vision earned his first graded stakes win in this event, powering away from the field. Named after Seabiscuit's famous rider, "Red" Pollard, who was also blind in one eye, the son of Carson City earned himself a trip to Kentucky based on his performance. (He finished a disappointing seventeenth in the Kentucky Derby.)

Hawthorne Race Course has survived its share of tough times. The Depression hit the track hard, as did World War II. In 1978, an arson fire leveled the old grandstands. Neighboring Sportsman's Park held the remainder of the Hawthorne meet, including the Gold Cup. New stands were erected at the track in only twenty-two months.

Hawthorne is a workingman's track, the backbone of racing. The constant city clamor of traffic and jets seems muted here in this 119-acre oasis in the middle of Chicago. With a few exceptions, Hawthorne has been an escape from everyday existence for Chicagoans since 1891. In the barn area, the rhythms of life continue almost unchanged as they have for the past century. Horses circle the barns to cool down, grooms pitch muck into buckets and fluff up bedding, bandages are applied to legs, blankets are smoothed on over sleek haunches. Many of the horses here now are the offspring of famous names that raced here earlier. The setting is scarcely altered. In a world of constant change and chaos, it's a reassuring sight.

SNAPSHOT - HAWTHORNE RACE COURSE

Description: Tucked onto 119 acres in the Chicago suburb of Cicero, Hawthorne Race Course stands out, eye-catching because it is so green. Tall brick walls flank the parking lot, and the front opens into a glass-covered stand overlooking the track. Elegant touches abound: high ceilings, potted plants, chandeliers. A restaurant lets patrons peer down onto the track as they dine. The infield has a sizable pond. Hawthorne's main track is a 1-mile oval with one chute and a 1,320-foot-long homestretch. There is a 7-furlong turf course as well.

Season: Hawthorne has two seasons, a spring meet and a fall meet. Its most prominent race, the $500,000 Illinois Derby (G2), runs in April.

Address: 3501 South Laramie Avenue, Cicero, IL 60804

Phone: 708-780-3700/(fax) 708-780-3677

Web site: http://www.hawthorneracecourse.com

Nearest airport: Chicago's Midway Airport (MDW)

Getting there: Hawthorne is in the southwest outskirts of Chicago, in Cicero, Illinois, accessible from Interstate 55 (Stevenson Expressway). Call or check the Web site for specific directions. Public transportation by bus or by train is also available.

Admission: $2; clubhouse: $4

Parking: Free; preferred and valet: extra charge

Fine dining: V.I.P. Room

Casual fare: The Derby Room, Gold Cup Dining Room, Grandstand Food Court, concessions located throughout the stands

Spirits: Bars located throughout

Extras: Handicapping seminar, fund-raising packages, seasonal promotions

INDIANA

HOOSIER PARK (ANDERSON)

Hoosier Park opened its doors in 1994 but has already taken some hits, with riverboat gambling and the recent opening of Indiana Downs cutting into the pie. It splits its live meets between standardbreds and Thoroughbreds, with the occasional quarter horse race thrown in for good measure. The track offers some twenty stakes races during the meet, most carrying guaranteed purses of $40,000. Headliners for three-year-olds include the Indiana Breeders' Cup Oaks (G3) and the Indiana Derby (G2), making the first weekend in October a substantial racing competition. The park's clubhouse sports fresh soft colors, with a creative menu featuring Asian flavors along with the traditional surf and turf plates and the weekend buffet spread. The Top of the Park party suite is crisply decorated with green-and-white-striped

Ex-NBA center Manute Bol and Keenan Steward

walls bordered by a racehorse motif. The polished wood bar at the front encourages patrons to gather at the windows to watch the horses cross the finish line.

We're at the park on the last Friday night in August. The enclosed grand-

Summer flowers at Hoosier Park

stand seats have filled up, and the grand-stand floor is packed with couples of every age, groups of young men in golf shirts and Bermuda shorts or black jeans and cowboy hats, and kids restlessly eyeing the snow cone carts. The track announcer is barely audible over the din. To get things going, we zoom in on race four, a claimer for fillies and mares who haven't won this year. A box is the smart way to go, we decide, and ante up a ten-spot on the one, five, six, and ten. As we stand in the rain for the 6-furlong race, our anticipation grows feverish as two of our horses move into position and another jostles for the rail. With a furlong to go, our final number surges forward and into the herd crowding the front. As they cross the wire, we're screaming happily—a trifecta win!

Hoosier Park hosted the World's Tallest Jockey on October 18, 2003. After his eleven-year stint with the NBA, Sudan-born seven-foot-seven Manute Bol launched a brief career as a jockey to raise political awareness and funds to help his war-torn homeland. On race night, it didn't matter that arthritic knees kept him off his horse; the house was packed, and track officials sent Manute straight to the winner's circle.

INDIANA DOWNS (SHELBYVILLE)

Sitting just off the interstate, surrounded by acres of cornfields, Indiana Downs is new and energetic. Wisps of trees and shrubs, not much taller than the cornstalks in the distance, line the driveway into the parking lots. In time, their proportions will help balance the setting, dominated by the rectangular white racetrack structure. Romanesque-style turrets capped in red distinguish the ultracontemporary facility, with exterior red spiral staircases winding up to the corporate suites and administrative offices. The architecture is creative, and it works. The glass-enclosed grandstand and clubhouse combined seat close to three thousand spectators. The jockeys have bright, roomy quarters—seven thousand square feet—constructed in record time to coincide with the

Indiana Downs

SNAPSHOT - HOOSIER PARK

Description: Hoosier Park has a 7-furlong dirt track with a 1,255-foot-long homestretch. There is no turf course here.

Season: Early September to late November. The Breeders' Cup Oaks (G3) and the Indiana Derby (G2) run in October, carrying rewards of $400,000 and $500,000, respectively.

Address: 4500 Dan Patch Circle, Anderson, IN 46013

Phone: 765-642-7223/(fax) 765-644-0467

Web site: http://www.hoosierpark.com

Nearest airport: Indianapolis International Airport (IND)

Getting there: Located northeast of Indianapolis in Anderson

Admission: $2; clubhouse: extra charge

Parking: free; valet: extra charge

Fine dining: The tiered Homestretch Restaurant, reservations required

Casual fare: Trackside Terrace, concessions located throughout the grandstands

Spirits: Hall of Fame Bar, other offerings throughout

Extras: Bobblehead nights, holiday theme promotions, T-shirts, and more

Newest on the circuit

inaugural Thoroughbred meet in April 2003. They're located behind the grandstand, with separate spaces for male and female riders.

Less than an hour from Hoosier Park, Indiana Downs joins the Midwest's mid-level racing circuit, which also includes Hawthorne and Fair-

mount parks in Illinois, the three Ohio Thoroughbred tracks (River Downs, Thistledown, and Beulah Park), and Ellis Park and Kentucky Downs in Kentucky. Entering its second year of operation in 2004, the independently owned and operated Shelbyville racetrack ambitiously offers meets for Thoroughbreds, quarter horses, and standardbreds (harness racing), the short quarter horse meet filling slots on Fridays during Thoroughbred season. Daily purses were just over $100,000, with several stakes races for Indiana-bred or -sired horses.

During 2004, the new track continued to experiment with the formula for success. The forty-eight-day meet began

WOMEN AT THE REINS

As recently as 1968, Thoroughbred horse racing was still off-limits to female riders. A year later, the earth shook, so to speak, or maybe it was Mother Nature nudging for equality on the equine. In 1969, Diane Crump became the first woman to ride in a Thoroughbred race and the first to ride in the Kentucky Derby. Her two historic races "opened the gate" for other female jockeys.

Julie Krone, who retired in 2005, is the top female jockey in the United States, by wins and earnings. Her pro career began in 1981, at age seventeen, with her first win on Lord Farkle at Tampa Bay Downs. Ten years later, she was the first woman to ride in a Triple Crown race, the Belmont Stakes, on Subordinated Debt, and in 1993, she became the first to win a Triple Crown race, capturing the Belmont on Colonial Affairs. She was inducted into the Thoroughbred Racing Hall of Fame in 2000, the first female jockey to be so honored.

Others who have made racing history include Robyn Smyth, the first woman to win a major stakes race. Greta Kuntzweiler, Rolanda

Retired jockey Rhonda Collins

Simpson, and Kris Prather are also pioneering jockeys who were nominated for, or have won, Eclipse, Darley, and other prestigious racing awards. Jockey Rhonda Collins, a 5'7" rider who grew up in Hawaii, rode in her first race at Churchill Downs in 1993 and continued to ride and win on the eastern and midwestern circuits. She won the first Hoosier Park Female Jockey contest in 2001 and announced her retirement in 2004. Not to vanish from the racing industry, however: Rhonda's new career, as a reporter for Television Games Network (TVG) has taken her out of the saddle, but her experienced eye still tracks the jockey in it.

with five days of racing per week. The track dropped Tuesday racing in favor of Sundays to attract weekend players. Head count and on-track handle were higher than in the previous year, although entries and the number of daily races had fallen slightly. Track officials expect an increase in available stalls to lure more Thoroughbred horsemen to ship in. Average daily wagering, seemingly part of a national trend, was down by 8 percent. The 2004 Indiana Downs meet ended with several new records. Rodney Prescott took the lead rider award, and Gary Patrick was honored as winning trainer.

MICHIGAN

Great Lakes Downs (Muskegon)

In the state that gave us Henry Ford and the Motor City, it seems fitting that the racetrack at Great Lakes Downs has a turn named for a freeway. The oval's backstretch parallels I-96, a ribbon of

Michigan's only Thoroughbred racetrack

asphalt that links Muskegon, on the shores of Lake Michigan, to Detroit, in the southeast corner of the state. So the track's northwest turn—the far turn in races of 5 furlongs or more—is known as the I-96 turn.

Great Lakes Downs (GLD) is a small, regional racing facility, transformed in 1999 from a harness track. Magna Entertainment Corporation bought GLD in 2000, converting the racing to Thoroughbreds. The stables now include 118 all-new horse stalls and new grooms' quarters. The jockeys have new state-of-the-art spa and health equipment.

SnapShot - Indiana Downs

Description: The traveler can see a massive white building rising up on the horizon, its bright red roof glinting in the early morning sunlight. Indiana Downs is the newcomer to the Midwest circuit, its new stands having been erected for a cool $35 million. It also operates two OTB facilities off the premises. Indiana Downs has a 1-mile dirt track and a 7-furlong turf course.

Season: Mid-April to the end of June. Following its inaugural meet for standardbreds in late 2002, Indiana Downs launched the Thoroughbred and quarter horse meet and now runs two live seasons into the summer.

Address: 4200 North Michigan Road, Shelbyville, IN 46176

Phone: 317-421-0000/(fax) 317-421-0100

Web site: http://www.indianadowns.com

Nearest airport: Indianapolis International Airport (IND)

Getting there: Located twenty miles southeast of Indianapolis, IN, off I-74 at Fairland Road and N. Michigan Road

Admission: Free

Parking: Free

Fine dining: Silks & Sulkies Dining Room

Casual fare: Dog 'n Suds, other concessions located throughout the grandstands

Spirits: The Paddock View Bar

Extras: Starting Gate Gift Shop, Family Pavilion with children's play area, showroom and exhibition pavilion north of the grandstand

When racing is at its summertime height, the infield at Great Lakes Downs belongs to the resident Canada geese and a hearty flock of blackbirds. The birds and waterfowl come and go, like the thundershowers that rumbled in and out on our evening visit in June. We had dinner in Derby's, the second-floor clubhouse restaurant. We regularly dashed out to the dark, rainy paddock to check the horses and then went to the betting windows. We took an early exacta and won big on the fifth race, a 6 ½-furlong claiming race for maidens and fillies.

When Detroit Racecourse ended live Thoroughbred contests in 1998, the scene shifted north, making Great Lakes Downs the last Thoroughbred blast in a state favoring harness racing. But Magna Entertainment hopes to pursue a bigger racetrack vision: an expansive horse racing/entertainment complex just west of Detroit. If it happens, Michigan could thunder loudly back into the horse racing world.

MINNESOTA

CANTERBURY PARK (SHAKOPEE)

Central Minnesota celebrated its first decade of organized horse racing at Canterbury Park under the ownership and management of the Canterbury Park Holding Corporation (CPHC) in 2004. The race park opened as Canterbury Downs in 1985, but it foundered until CPHC rode to its rescue. It has since settled in as the northernmost loop on a wide midwestern racing circuit. As the home of the unique Claiming Crown series, Canterbury also attracts a national network of horsemen and players.

Sitting in Shakopee, half an hour southwest of Minneapolis/St. Paul, Canterbury Park is a midsize track, edged by woodlands of pine, spruce, and fir. This is one of the friendliest racetracks we know; horsemen (that includes horsewomen, of course) are

Waiting for the leg up

Bringing the crowd to its feet

supported throughout the facility. The big open barns have wide connecting hallways as well as individual exterior doors on the stalls, and there are nice dorms for the jockeys and the grooms. The track kitchen offers good fare, and in the upper Turf Club level, Canterbury gives horsemen complimentary seating throughout the meet. The grandstand includes open-air and enclosed stadium seating. Dining and simulcast areas have been recently remodeled and expanded, and though not yet (in 2005) approved for slot machines, the Canterbury Card Club opened in 2000, a casino environment right next to the track. The house offers free poker lessons and funnels part of the "take" into the racing side.

Both Thoroughbreds and quarter horses compete on the menu during the long summer season, which features

SnapShot - Great Lakes Downs

Description: In 2000, as one of its first U.S. racetrack acquisitions, Magna Entertainment Corporation (MEC) upgraded many areas of the facility. Then, in 2004, MEC transferred ownership to Richmond Racing Company LLC, which will lease it back to MEC, freeing the giant MEC group to apply for a new license to build a gaming and racing facility near Detroit. Great Lakes Downs has a 5-furlong dirt track with two chutes. The homestretch measures a mere 580 feet from last turn to wire.

Season: Mid-May to late October
Address: 800 Harvey St., Muskegon, MI 49444
Phone: 231-799-2400/(fax) 231-798-3120
Web site: http://www.greatlakesdowns.com
Nearest airport: Muskegon County Airport (MKG)
Getting there: Located northwest of Grand Rapids, on the shore of Lake Michigan. From I-96, take East Ellis Road and go west. Turn north onto Harvey Street.
Admission: Free
Parking: Free
Fine dining: Derby's Restaurant and Lounge
Casual fare: Concessions stands located in the grandstand
Spirits: Derby's Lounge, concessions in the grandstand area
Extras: Karaoke nights' Ladies Night, Horseman's Ball, drink specials

Alternative horsepower at Canterbury

more than fifty stakes races and, in 2004, total purses of $1.8 million. The two biggest draws are the $100,000 Lady Canterbury Breeders' Cup Stakes in June and the mid-July Claiming Crown. The Thoroughbred Owners and Breeders Association and the National Horsemen's Benevolent and Protective Association developed the Claiming Crown to shine a spotlight on the importance of claiming horses, the most fundamental and thriving aspect of the sport. Ten thousand fans or more show up each year to enjoy this unique racing competition.

Canterbury Park officials have good reason to feel upbeat about the success of their business plan and the future of the state's only pari-mutuel racetrack. In mid-2003, *Fortune* analysts rated the race park in the top 20 percent of America's one hundred fastest-growing small companies.

OHIO

BEULAH PARK (GROVE CITY)

Ohio's oldest race track, Beulah Park, sitting in the agricultural heartland of central Ohio, has been conducting Thoroughbred racing since 1923 at a handsome fieldstone facility surrounded by a parklike grove of tall oak trees. Architectural details such as stone-pillared fences and landscaped walking paths meandering through the trees create a classic country theme reminiscent of Saratoga Race Course. After developer and home-builder Charles Ruma purchased Beulah in 1986, he added a

SNAPSHOT - CANTERBURY PARK

Description: The name tells all. A journey to Canterbury, its low castle spires spearing a northern sky dappled with cumulus clouds, is a pilgrimage of sorts to claim a crown. But the glass-fronted castle overlooks a racetrack, not a moat, and the jousting fields sport jockeys and racehorses going to the post. The main track is 1 mile in circumference. It surrounds a 7-furlong turf course. The main track has chutes at 1 ¼ miles and at 6 ½ and 3 ½ furlongs.

Season: Mid-May to early September. The crown in the park's Canterbury tale is the Claiming Crown, a significant competition held biannually in mid-July.

Address: 1100 Canterbury Road, Shakopee, MN 55379

Phone: 952-445-7223/800-340-6361/(fax) 952-496-6480

Web site: http://www.canterburypark.com

Nearest airport: Minneapolis/St. Paul International Airport (MSP)

Getting there: It's located about a half hour southwest of Minneapolis and St. Paul. Free shuttle from the Mall of America on selected dates; call or check the Web site for more information.

Admission: $4; children seventeen and under: free

Parking: Free

Fine dining: The Park Restaurant

Casual fare: Pizza & Pasta, St. Paul Snack Stand, Colombo Yogurt, Fiestavilla, Famous Dave's, The Sandwich Shop, State Fair Pronto Pups, Homestretch, Finish Line Deli

Spirits: Liene's Tap & Miller Gardens, The Horseshoe Bar, Paddock Lounge, Ascot Lounge, Chip's Bar

Extras: Boat shows, snowmobiling contests, craft and antique shows, many others

grand outdoor plaza, a paddock, and a walking ring, furthering the historic "Spa of the Midwest" ambiance. Two peak-roofed fieldstone kiosks capped with horse weather vanes flank the park entrance, while on the grounds, the grandstand, clubhouse, and backside barns have been improved. The older buildings are well maintained.

Beulah Park's Thoroughbred meet begins in the fall, with afternoon racing five days a week. In December, a holiday break shuts everything down; the winter/spring meet picks up in January, with regular racing until the first Saturday in May. Derby weekend concludes the track's racing activities for the season. In the summertime, big name entertainment comes to the infield for concerts.

Beulah Park encompasses all the complexities and ironies of Thoroughbred racing in the twenty-first century. With its classic style and southern traditions, it has developed a reputation for quality matches. Come early October, it hosts the heavily watched

Late autumn racing, Beulah Park

$100,000 Best of Ohio Endurance Championship. The 2003 field was big—twelve horses broke from the gate for the 1¼-mile competition. As odds-on favorite Devil Time rounded the first turn, his rider, William Troilo, feared that the horse was too far back to recover. Devil Time kept struggling to find his place as others began slipping behind. Then, at the far turn, he revved it up and took off, surging past his competitors to win the race by an incredible 16 ½ lengths, the widest winning margin since the race began in 1986.

For years, Beulah Park looked forward to an annual Breeders' Cup–sponsored competition and enjoyed its solid

Walking ring at Beulah Park

standing in the industry. With the arrival of the all-too-familiar economic challenges, however, the track's standing has dipped. Out-of-state riverboats and other gaming facilities have taken some of the gambling dollars that had previously enriched the racetrack. A number of other tracks on the Midwest circuit have installed slots or video lottery terminals (VLTs). As those tracks lure back the dollars that have leaked away, they also offer increased purses that in turn draw better racing competitions. If it could win the approval of the Ohio legislature, Beulah Park would join them, and the downslide could begin to turn around.

Beulah Park has been at the forefront of other wagering approaches. It was the first Ohio track, in partnership with River Downs, to develop an online wagering system. The economic boon from the new program, which includes live videos, day charts, replays, and other options, has climbed from an annual $3.5 million in 2000 to approximately $120 million in 2004. In February 2004, it hit an all-time high of more than $2.5 million in a single day's all-source wager-

ing. As the tenacious racetrack works to regain the momentum it knew before one-arm bandits ran elsewhere with the cash, it continues to deliver strong field cards and good, mid-level competitions.

RIVER DOWNS (CINCINNATI)

River Downs sits in a gorgeous spot facing the Ohio River. Across the river, the hills of Kentucky rise gently above a lush line of mature trees, their branches spreading wide and hiding the water. The vintage grandstand was built in 1925, when this was Coney Island Racetrack. The grandstand was remodeled in the 1970s, but the building's original feel was preserved. Its steel support beams have been sandblasted and painted a creamy white. The open-air roof, rising high overhead, gives the light interior an airy, spacious feeling. The River Downs paddock is one of the prettiest in North America. A small statue of a groom, shaded by young trees, stands in the center of a thick green mound of grass. Red salvia, stunning and profuse, encircles the entire paddock. Between the horse stalls off to the side, big hang-

SNAPSHOT - BEULAH PARK

Description: Welcome to the "Saratoga of the Midwest." From the low stone grandstands to the pretty walking ring with mature trees in the saddling paddock, this little course is still evocative of The Spa. Beulah Park has a 1-mile dirt track with a 1,100-foot homestretch. The turf course measures slightly less than 6 furlongs.

Season: The Beulah Park meet runs from September to May, ending on Kentucky Derby weekend, with a two-week holiday break in December. It is viewed as one long season, though it is often designated as fall and winter/spring seasons.

Address: 3664 Grant Avenue, Grove City, OH 43123

Phone: 614-871-9600/(fax) 614-871-0433

Web site: http://www.beulahpark.com

Nearest airport: Port Columbus International Airport (CMH)

Getting there: Beulah Park is located south of Columbus in Grove City, OH

Admission: $2

Parking: $1

Fine dining: Upper Club

Casual fare: Top of the Stretch Deli, concessions located throughout the stands

Spirits: Upper Club, Top of the Stretch, Starting Gate Lounge

Extras: Live music in the lounge on Saturday nights, T-shirt and cap days, seasonal contests and events

ing baskets drip with red geraniums and white petunias, healthy and full.

River Downs, placed to enjoy both the Kentucky and Midwest circuits, regularly stages memorable horse racing. Seabiscuit ran here twice, in 1936, finishing third in two handicaps. One of the most exciting River Downs meets was in 1976, when seventeen-year-old Steve Cauthen rode a record 109 winners at the Cincinnati track. "The Kid" ended the 1976 season as North America's Eclipse Award–winning apprentice jockey. Two years later, he swung a foot up on Affirmed to win the Triple Crown, the youngest rider to do so.

Labor Day weekend brings the meet's finale. River Downs wraps up the season with amusements for everyone. The 2003 River Downs Queen, Jennifer Zinser, a former Miss Kentucky, is fitted with her crown. At the far side of the grandstand, John Deere tractors are on display. Elsewhere, a rock band fills the air with a loud, fast tempo.

Our fashionably dressed party convenes for Sunday brunch with margaritas

View across the track, River Downs

and betting strategy at the Turf Terrace Restaurant, the two-story clubhouse overlooking the racetrack. The interior walls have cherry wainscoting, parquet floors, and mauve-and-pink accents. Outside, the sky alternates from pale gray and misty one minute to sunny and bright the next. Every time the rain stops, the crowd pours onto the apron to enjoy summer's last hurrah.

Jockeying for position, first turn

Today, after her win in race eight, jockey Rhonda Collins, covered with mud from the fast ride, gave her goggles to an elated fan, bent down to talk with a wide-eyed little boy, chatted with us for a few minutes, and then hurried to clean up and drive two and a half hours north to Hoosier Park, where she would race that evening. Race 14 was the last one of the evening here, and the best for our trio of high rollers. Our trifecta boxed Johnny Two Dot, Stormy Waters, and jockey Jeff Johnston, the meet's leading rider. The mathematician in our group put dollars on Johnny Two Dot to win and Take Back Cat to place. We also placed $2 on the eight horse. The ten-horse field brought mixed results. Our exacta box snared only the winner. The race was saved, however, by the mathematician, who had spotted both the winner and the placer, gleefully quadrupling his bet. He had pocketed every win of our day. Now that we had him figured out, the question was where to find an off-track betting (OTB) spot so we could make him play all night.

THISTLEDOWN (NORTH RANDALL)

Thoroughbred racing in the Buckeye state was reborn in the 1920s, when Ohio approved pari-mutuel betting. Thistledown, just southeast of downtown Cleveland, opened in the summer of 1925. The Depression a few years later hit the northern Ohio track hard. Fire destroyed the grandstand and clubhouse in 1944, prompting the new architecture to feature brick.

Magna Entertainment purchased the racetrack in 1999 and brought in a grab bag of goodies. A radical overhaul updated the interior and made major improvements to jockeys' quarters, barns, and stables. The new paddock and apron area are huge, with more space the for fans to get closer to the horses. Picnic tables, outdoor televisions, voucher windows, and concessions give families room to play. Inside, nine hundred monitors fill the grandstand. New simulcast theaters have been added, and on the fourth floor, the Starting Gate museum offers a video library for checking past performances, space for handicapping semi-

SNAPSHOT - RIVER DOWNS

Description: Climbing into the grandstand and looking out across the infield, you can immediately guess how River Downs earned its name. Today, a row of old and stately trees lines the river bank, hiding the Ohio River as it ripples onward to the Mississippi. A 1-mile track with two chutes and a 1,117-foot homestretch encircles a 7-furlong turf course.

Season: Mid-April to early September. The meet ends with the $100,000 Pepsi Bassinet Stakes and the $200,000 Miller Lite Cradle Stakes

Address: 6301 Kellogg Avenue, Cincinnati, OH 45230

Phone: 513-232-8000/(fax) 513-232-1269

Web site: http://www.riverdowns.com

Nearest airport: Cincinnati /Northern Kentucky International Airport (CVG)

Getting there: River Downs is located in Cincinnati, on the eastern edge of town, off I-275 and Route 52

Admission: Free

Parking: $1

Fine dining: Turf Terrace Club

Casual fare: Concessions located throughout the grandstands

Spirits: Turf Terrace Club; other concessions throughout the grandstand

Extras: Special events all summer; Labor Day weekend brings out the lovely River Downs queen, celebrity guests, live music, and relay events with prizes for the winners.

Shane Sellers warming up, 2003 Ohio Derby

nars, and displays of historical moments in Thoroughbred racing.

Opening weekend in early April means fifteen thousand fans are likely to pour into the stands. As the season gets underway and enthusiasm builds, the first Saturday in May welcomes another big throng. To enjoy the weather, have a julep or two and await the Louisville track's simulcast. Mid-June brings the 1 ⅛-mile Ohio Derby (G2). In 1963, Thistledown secured the Ohio Derby (previously run at now-defunct Randall Park), and gave it a permanent home. It is Ohio's oldest and most lucrative race, carrying a $350,000-guaranteed purse in 2005.

Welcoming spectators to the most important race in the state means the Federal-style red brick building, with its white pillars and railings, is decked in bunting. Above the roof, colorful silk banners on tall poles flutter against the summer sky. The day is guaranteed to bring surprises and probably make some history. In 1996, for example, future Horse of the Year and Racing Hall of Famer Skip Away won the Ohio

Thistledown racetrack

Capacity crowd awaiting the Ohio Derby

Derby. In 2003, trainer Kenny McPeek almost skipped the Derby to be on hand for racing elsewhere. Happily, he made the right decision, as he and owners R. David and Marylyn Randal watched their Wild and Wicked win by 3 ¼ lengths. At Thistledown, live racing is scheduled from Thursday through Sunday; and during the rest of the year, simulcasting keeps the track open until midnight daily. On Sundays, during the 187-day meet, an elaborate brunch is presented on the sixth level of the clubhouse. Silks Dining Terraces and the Silks Bistro are beautiful settings for a day of racing and relaxation. In the Silks, one can also support the domestic

wine industry by enjoying a nice selection of reds and whites from California and Washington State.

Stakes races from $20,000 to $350,000 fill the Thistledown calendar. In the summer, the track hosts a big-name concert series, a Bluesfest, and a chili cook-off. Thistledown's biggest card weekend comes with the Labor Day holiday, when the track may average fifteen races per day. On the preholiday Saturday, three-year-old fillies compete in the Ohio Debutante; on Sunday, two-year-olds go 6 furlongs in the Loyalty Stakes; and on Monday, the Governor's Buckeye Stakes invites three-year-olds and older to run the 1 ¼ mile for $75,000.

Thistledown may be the only track in recent memory where a jockey wedding has been performed in the winner's circle by the track chaplain. At the call to post in October 2001, the bride, jockey Rhonda Swan, entered the circle with her father. Wearing designer-made wedding silks, she and groom-jockey Scott Speith, also dressed in formal silks, exchanged vows.

SNAPSHOT - THISTLEDOWN

Description: Thistledown is an old and new sort of place. Started in 1925, the track has gone about the business of racing while Cleveland sprawled out around it. A red brick facility, recent upgrades include the Diamond Vision infield display board, a new saddling paddock, and new jockey quarters. Thistledown has a 1-mile dirt track with two chutes. The homestretch measures 978 feet from last turn to wire.

Season: Early April to late December. It hosts Ohio's biggest race, the Ohio Derby (G2), in mid-June.

Address: 21501 Emery Road, North Randall, OH 44128

Phone: 216-662-8600/(fax) 216-662-5339

Web site: http://www.thistledown.com

Nearest airport: Cleveland Hopkins International Airport (CLE)

Getting there: Ten miles southeast of Cleveland, off I-271 and exit 27A. Go west on Emery Road. Check the Web site for specific directions.

Admission: Free

Parking: Free; preferred parking: extra charge

Fine dining: Silk's Dining Terrace and Silks Bistro, reservations recommended

Casual fare: Concessions located throughout the stands

Spirits: Silks Lounge; beer, wine, and well drinks available throughout

Extras: Starting Gate museum, stable tours by reservation, summer concert series, chili cook-off, Labatt promotions, Win a Thoroughbred contest

MIDWEST TRAVEL SECTION

BELOW, YOU'LL FIND A MILEAGE CHART LISTING THE DISTANCES BETWEEN THE REGIONAL RACETRACKS AND ALL THE CITIES DISCUSSED IN THE FOLLOWING TRAVEL SECTION. THE CITY OR CITIES CLOSEST TO A TRACK ARE INDICATED BY AN X.

COAST TO COAST	Chicago, Ill.	Cincinnati, Ohio	Cleveland, Ohio	Columbus, Ohio	Evansville, Ind.	Grand Rapids, Mich.	Indianapolis, Ind.	Minneapolis/St. Paul, Minn.
Arlington Park (Ill.)	X 30 miles	330 miles	370 miles	385 miles	395 miles	210 miles	215 miles	385 miles
Beulah Park (Ohio)	355 miles	95 miles	155 miles	X * miles	315 miles	320 miles	175 miles	770 miles
Canterbury Park (Minn.)	430 miles	725 miles	770 miles	785 miles	765 miles	605 miles	610 miles	X 25 miles
Fairmount Park (Ill.)	285 miles	340 miles	550 miles	410 miles	X 165 miles	435 miles	235 miles	610 miles
Great Lakes Downs (Mich.)	180 miles	410 miles	335 miles	355 miles	470 miles	X 35 miles	295 miles	585 miles
Hawthorne Race Course (Ill.)	X * miles	300 miles	350 miles	360 miles	375 miles	185 miles	185 miles	410 miles
Hoosier Park (Ind.)	210 miles	145 miles	320 miles	160 miles	265 miles	260 miles	X 45 miles	620 miles
Indiana Downs (Ind.)	210 miles	90 miles	325 miles	185 miles	225 miles	310 miles	X 25 miles	620 miles
River Downs (Ohio)	305 miles	X 15 miles	255 miles	115 miles	220 miles	395 miles	120 miles	715 miles
Thistledown (Ohio)	350 miles	245 miles	X * miles	140 miles	465 miles	305 miles	315 miles	760 miles

*The racetrack is located inside or within 10 miles of the city limits.

MUST SEE / MUST DO

ILLINOIS

CHICAGO

Chicago is energetic, historically rooted, and multicultural with a touch of edginess. Its world-class museums and public institutions, inspiring architecture, major universities, corporate identity, and an innovative theater and jazz scene coexist on nearly thirty miles of Lake Michigan waterfront.

If the city is new to you, visiting a few essential landmarks will reveal some of what makes Chicago the destination of millions. On your own, discovering its great neighborhoods and unique character, we hope, will simply enhance its reputation. The lay of the land—we're talking the central city, also called The Loop, referring to the elevated train system that circles the area, and the waterfront—is easy to figure out. Driving isn't intimidating, but the hunt for a parking spot can be a hassle. Walking or taking cabs is recommended. **The Art Institute of Chicago** anchors and orients our itinerary, which serves up a mere nibble of incomparable Chicago.

The art institute (111 S. Michigan Ave.; 312-443-3600; http://www.artic.edu), founded in 1879, exhibits nearly five thousand years of human creativity, including a vast Asian collection, medieval art and armor, European and American period rooms, and modern

One-horsepower touring

and postmodern American and European art. Wealthy patrons' early generosity helped the art institute establish its acclaimed impressionist and postimpressionist collections. The building's interior neoclassical spaces are handsome. Visit the café and restaurant at the far northwest wing for refreshments; check the Web site for current admission prices and hours.

Leaving the art institute, head north on Michigan Avenue to sample the **Magnificent Mile**, so named for its numerous buildings—businesses, hotels, churches, outdoor cafés, and myriad shops and department stores—of rich architectural styles that have given Chicago its grand character. Among the highlights are the **Wrigley** (yes, the product is gum) **Building** with its four-sided clock tower at 400–410 N. Michigan; and the **Terra Museum of American Art**, at 664 N. Michigan, with works by Georgia O'Keeffe, John Singer Sargent, Mary Cassatt, and James Whistler. **Chicago Place**, 700 N. Michigan Ave., houses **Saks Fifth Avenue**, numerous specialty shops, and a food court. At 875 N. Michigan,

Lake Michigan shoreline

the **John Hancock Center** has a public observatory on the 94th floor (admission: $9.75 adults; $7.50 seniors; $6 children 5 to 12). Finally, the castlelike **Water Tower and Pumping Station** at 806 N. Michigan, two buildings that survived the 1871 Great Fire of Chicago, now house a photography gallery and a theater.

One of the city's most famous public art works is three blocks west of the art institute, on Dearborn Street. Here, at **First National Plaza**, the huge mosaic mural, *Four Seasons*, by Marc Chagall, rises fourteen feet high and is seventy feet long. The two-level plaza, with fountains, trees, and benches, is anchored by the soaring, tapered BankOne skyscraper. Stop, sit, and enjoy the city's ambience. For more of the city's best shopping, go east one block to State Street, and north to 111 N. State, to **Marshall Field's** celebrated department store, built between 1892 and 1907 as the largest retail store in the world. Today, it fills an entire city block.

Directly east of the art institute, across Columbus Drive, **Grant Park** is part of a greenbelt that extends along the beautiful Lake Michigan shoreline. The park includes open space, formal gardens, and tree-lined promenades, with the majestic multitiered **Memorial Buckingham Fountain** shooting water twenty feet high from 134 jets, as its centerpiece. Including quieter **Lincoln Park** to the north, this is the city's waterfront playground, with arts and crafts festivals, exhibits, political events, and street musicians setting up camp here. At the south end of the park are two other city institutions, the vast **John. G. Shedd Aquarium**, fed by the waters of Lake Michigan, and **The Field Museum**, one of the world's top natural history museums.

If you have more than a weekend for exploring the Windy City, spend time in the gallery district, take in the nightlife at Old Town, walk the shore at Lincoln Park, and explore the mansion neighborhoods of the Gold Coast.

INDIANA

EVANSVILLE

After a day at the races in Henderson, Kentucky, at Ellis Park Race Track, cross the river to Evansville for lodging, wining and dining, and some sightseeing. The third largest city in Indiana, Evansville flourished in the nineteenth century, as evidenced by several public buildings designed in high Victorian, Gothic, neoclassical revival, eclectic, and beaux-arts styles. The city offers a handsome riverfront skyline with walking paths, city parks, museums, and other cultural sites to enjoy.

Stop by the **Visitors Center** (401 SE Riverside Drive; 800-433-3025; http://www.evansvillecvb.org), which is housed in a Japanese-style pagoda built in 1912, and load up on brochures and maps. You may also want to visit the **Mesker Park Zoo & Botanic Garden** (2421 Bement Avenue; 812-435-6143) and the **Evansville Museum of Arts, History & Science** (411 SE Riverside Drive; 812-425-2406; http://www.emuseum.org). If you prefer to spend your time outdoors, drive out to **Burdette Park & Aquatic Center** (5301 Nurrenbern Road; 812-435-5602; http://www.evansvillegov.org). The park stretches over 150 acres and offers hiking trails, a lake for fishing, a miniature

Evansville at night

golf course, swimming pools, and river rides. Check out the Visitors Center Web site for other activities in town.

INDIANAPOLIS

Nearly everything is downtown: the state library; the convention center; a tempting, multilevel shopping mall; military and historical sights; and an array of sports arenas. Start with **Monument Circle**, at Market and Meridian streets, featuring **Soldiers and Sailors Monument**, a towering Civil War memorial with fountains, and a lower-level museum. South of the monument, at Washington, Illinois, and Meridian, is Circle Centre, a complete shopping complex, with several restaurants.

Walk west along Washington to the **White River**, where a promenade follows the water and takes you to the **NCAA Hall of Champions** (http://www.2ncaa .org), celebrating the student athlete. Next door is the **Indiana State Museum** (650 W. Washington; 317-232-1637), also part of the **White River State Park**. Between them flows the canal, extending from 10th Street to the White River. Along the landscaped **Canal Walk** at Walnut and Senate streets is the memori-

Benjamin Harrison Home

al for the *USS Indianapolis*, the WWII American battleship sunk by Japanese torpedoes on July 30, 1945.

Don't think of leaving the city without becoming reacquainted with our twenty-third president, Benjamin Harrison. A twenty-one-year-old Benjamin moved to the city in 1854 to practice law and later bought a sixteen-room Italianate Victorian home. The **Benjamin Harrison Home** (1230 N. Delaware Street; 317-631-1888; http://www.presidentbenjaminharri son.org) is an amazing place, open daily. Harrison had a telegraph installed in the library to tally election results, and the master bedroom holds his Whitney Home Gymnasium, with weights and pulleys discreetly hidden behind Victorian drapes. Check out the presidential Wedgewood china designed by his wife, Caroline, a gorgeous pattern of bold American corn motifs hand painted in gold on an indigo background— because no plant is more symbolic of America, she said.

Downtown athletic arenas include the **Indiana Convention Center** and **RCA Dome** (100 S. Capitol Avenue; 317-262-3389; http://www.iccrd.com), if you're

Indiana State House dome

NCAA's Hall of Champions

looking for Colts football. Across the street is **Victory Park**, for minor league baseball (501 West Maryland Street; 317-269-3542). The NBA Pacers and WNBA Fever, as well as the American Football League's Firebirds, play (and live concerts are staged) at **Conseco Fieldhouse** (One Conseco Court, 125 S. Pennsylvania Avenue; 317-917-2500; http://www.consecofieldhouse.com).

Indianapolis is also home to the three biggest one-day auto races in the world. The Indy 500, first run in 1911, is held on the last Sunday (Memorial weekend) in May, west of the city at the **Indianapolis Motor Speedway**. The Grand Prix follows in June, and the Brickyard 400 NASCAR teams pick it up at the speedway in August. On the grounds, at 4790 W. 16th Street, Indianapolis, are the Visitors Center and **Hall of Fame Museum** (317-492-6747). Find ticket information, maps, and other details at http://www.indy500.com; http://www.usgpindy.com; and http://www.Indianapolismotorspeedway.com. Or call 317-492-6700.

MICHIGAN

GRAND RAPIDS

Two blocks west of the Amway Plaza Hotel, on the west bank of the Grand River, is the **Gerald R. Ford Museum** (303 Pearl Street NW; 616-254-0400; http://www.ford.utexas.edu), where the life of the thirty-eighth president is on display in ten galleries. Holographic tours include the White House, the 1976 Republican National Convention, and a day behind the desk at the Oval office. Exhibits include the space shuttle program and other highlights of the Ford family's life. Don't miss the burglary tools (Ford didn't use them) in the Watergate gallery. Admission is $5 for adults, $4 for seniors, and free for children under fifteen. It's open daily, 9:00–5:00.

Stroll the **Grand River's Riverwalk** starting at the **Van Andel Museum Center** (272 Pearl Street NW; 616-456-3977;http://www.grmuseum.org/vamc/museum.shtml), and enjoy watching the surge of water over the rapids that gave

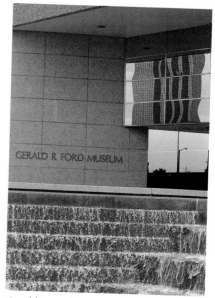

Gerald R. Ford Museum

the city its name. The museum has a multimedia exhibit on the city's past, including historic furniture styles and ornate wood carvings. Admission for adults is $7.00, seniors $6.00, and children ages three to seventeen $2.50 The museum is open 9:00 a.m. to 5:00 p.m. daily except for Sundays (noon to 5:00 p.m.).

The country's largest horse sculpture, fashioned after Leonardo da Vinci's drawings, can be found in the **Frederick Meijer Gardens and Sculpture Park** (1000 East Beltline Road NE; 616-957-1580/888-957-1580; http://www.meijergardens.org). Weighing fifteen tons and standing twenty-five feet high, it joins works by Rodin, Arnaldo Pomodoro, Henry Moore, and others. A two-story tropical conservatory includes a waterfall and the world's largest collection of carnivorous plants; and in spring, thousands of tropical butterflies emerge. It has nature trails and walkways on 125 acres. Admission is $10 adults, $8 seniors and students, $6 children 5–13, $3 children 3–4. It is open daily, but call for seasonal hours.

MINNESOTA

SHAKOPEE AND MINNEAPOLIS/ ST. PAUL

From mid-August into September, Shakopee hosts a weekend **Renaissance Festival** (http://www.renaissancefest

Minneapolis skyline

.com; 952-445-7361). Pack your peasant or nobility best and join the sixteenth-century crowd; among other pleasures at the three hundred-plus booths, you can buy new chain mail if yours has rusted a bit. Less than two miles north of Canterbury Park, on the river, is historic **Murphy's Landing** (http://www.three riversparks.org), a nineteenth-century living history village. NASCAR races take place at nearby **Raceway Park** (http://www.shakopee.org; 952-445-2257).

On your way north to Minneapolis, twelve miles northeast of Shakopee, outside Bloomington, you'll find the great **Mall of America**, with nearly five miles of storefronts and endless entertainment sites (http://www.mallofamerica.com; 925-883-8800). The Web site links you to local eateries and motels.

In case you're skipping the big mall, in the heart of downtown Minneapolis is the smaller, classier **Nicollet Mall**, between 6th and 7th streets, and the **IDS Center** made famous by the *Mary Tyler Moore Show* in the 1970s. On your way to the shops, stop and say hello to her new bronze statue.

Or, remembering the poet Henry Wadsworth Longfellow and the *Song of Hiawatha*, check out the "laughing waters" of **Minnehaha Regional Park** (612-370-4939), a little south of downtown, overlooking the Mississippi River.

If it's summer, it's national sports time. Take in a Twins game at **Hubert H. Humphrey Metrodome**, also home to the Vikings football team. For information, visit http://www.min neapolis.org, click on Things to do, and drop down to Professional Sports information for dates, tickets, and other details.

Both Minneapolis and Saint Paul are filled with great museums, theaters, parks, lakes and other venues. Call 612-339-7571 or 800-999-5589 and order a copy of *MplsStPaul* magazine (http://www.mspm.com).

OHIO

CINCINNATI

Start downtown at Fountain Square, which is surrounded by good shops, hotels, and nearby cultural sites, including the **Aronoff Center for the Arts**, the **Contemporary Arts Center**, and the **Taft Museum**. Just west of downtown are the sports complexes. Catch the Reds at **Great American Ball Park** or the Cincinnati Bengals at **Paul Brown Stadium**. Or take a riverboat cruise. Visit http://www.cincinnatimagazine.com for many more possibilities.

Overlooking Cincinnati, Eden Park is home to a number of cultural spots, including the **William Howard Taft Birthplace** and the **Cincinnati Art Museum** (Eden Park Drive, Walnut Hills; 513-721-ARTS; http://www.cincinnati artmuseum.org). Fringing Eden Park is the charming **Mount Adams** historic district, a neighborhood of little galleries, boutique shops, and vintage Victorian homes. Views of the city and the river from Eden Park are spectacular; we could have spent a lazy day watching the world in miniature as cars and riverboats passed below us. A small lake, exotic landscaping, gardens, and numerous sculptures fill the park.

When railroads were king, **Union Terminal** in Cincinnati was one of the country's handsomest. Built in 1933 as an example of art deco architecture at its finest, it still serves as the city's Amtrak station. The interior space is now home to several fine museums, including the **Museum of Natural History and Science**, the **Cinergy Children's Museum**, the city's **Historical Society** library, the **Cincinnati History Museum**, and an Omnimax theater. It houses a great gift shop and offers plenty of inexpensive parking. Entrance into the building is free, but admission to museums varies. For more information, you can contact Cincinnati Museum Center at Union Terminal (1301 Western Avenue; 513-287-7000/800-733-2077; http://www.cin cymuseum.org). It is open Monday through Saturday, 10:00–5:00; Sunday, 1:00–6:00.

CLEVELAND

Come for the ponies, stay for the music; that's our mantra for Cleveland. The city's newest draw is the **Rock & Roll Hall of Fame** (One Key Plaza; 216-781-ROCK; http://www.rockhall.com), an I. M. Pei designed ultramodern mountain of peaks and angles and curves. Thousands of artifacts, from instruments and costumes to posters and props, are exhibited, along with interactive stations of music and rock star biographies. Members of the liquor industry sponsor Wednesday-night free outdoor summer concerts on Key Plaza at the museum,

Eden Park overlooking Cincinnati

Cleveland

The Cleveland Orchestra

with discounts on museum admission during the evening.

The story of industrial America is told in the names on downtown's nineteenth-century warehouses and factories in this National Historic Register neighborhood on the bluff overlooking Lake Erie to the north and the Cuyahoga River to the west. Now being restored as an inviting, exciting section of the city, loft living, dining, and nightlife are the new barons. Stop in at the **Historic Warehouse District Development Corporation** (Offices at 614 Superior Avenue, Suite 617; 216-344-3937; http://www.warehousedistrict.org) to have questions answered. Explore the area, especially West Sixth, St. Clair, and Superior, and have an afternoon drink at an outside café.

Cleveland has two internationally acclaimed gems: the **Cleveland Museum of Art** (University Circle, 11150 East Boulevard; 216-421-7350/1-888-CMA-0033; http://www.clevelandart.org) and the **Cleveland Orchestra**, the most recorded orchestra in the world. It performs at Severance Hall, 11001 Euclid Avenue. Call 216-231-7300 or visit http://www.clevelandorchestra.com for further details.

COLUMBUS

Ever wonder how Christopher Columbus's ships looked? Take a tour of a replica, the *Columbus Santa Maria*, in **Battelle Riverfront Park** (614-645-8760). The fifteenth-century wooden ship stopped first at what is now the Dominican Republic, where organized horse racing in the Western Hemisphere got an early start.

Just outside Columbus, near Peebles, you'll find the **Serpent Mound State Park** (3850 State Road; 937-587-2796/800-752-2757; http://www.serpentmoundspark.com). The Serpent Mound is one of the finest examples of a serpent effigy in the United States, its meaning still something of a mystery. There are other mound sites in the Midwest, but none like this one. In a land still considered young by European standards, this timeless wonder will leave you feeling humbled. It's ninety minutes southeast of Columbus, and worth the drive. The head points to the summer solstice; the coils point toward the winter solstice and the equinox sunrise. This undulating serpent is nearly a quarter of a mile long and measures two to six feet high. An egglike object appears to be positioned in front of gaping jaws. He's been here since before the birth of Christ. The park is open daily from 10:00–5:00, except for Thanksgiving, Christmas, and New Year's Day. Parking starts at $8.

Columbus, on the Scioto River

WHERE TO STAY

ILLINOIS

CHICAGO

Loews House of Blues Hotel
333 N. Dearborn St.
Chicago, IL 60610
312-245-0333
http://www.hob.com
$139–$1,200
Loews House of Blues Hotel, located in the Marina City Complex next to the legendary House of Blues Club, combines fun and high-service blues and rock ambiance with unpretentious luxury. This unique, unconventional Chicago hotel, established in 1998, was designed using Gothic, Moroccan, Indian, and American Folk Art motifs reflecting the musical roots of its namesake nightspot. Smith & Wollensky Steakhouse and BIN 36 Wine Bar and Restaurant round out the complex.

The Peninsula Chicago
108 East Superior at Rush Street
Chicago, IL 60611
312-337-2888/866-288-8889
http://www.peninsula.com
$445 and up
In the heart of the city, the Peninsula is an oasis of amenities wrapped in chic. Its soft colors and bold architectural lines create an elegant backdrop for a fine city weekend. The 14,000 square foot Peninsula Spa and Fitness Center, on the top two floors, offers a full range of spa and fitness treatments. Its bold, Grecian flavors may transport you to the Aegean. Fine hotel dining awaits you in any of the several restaurants or cafés on the premises, with selections ranging from afternoon tea to light Asian dinners to gourmet seafood specialties. Request a view room oriented toward Michigan Avenue or the water.

INDIANA

EVANSVILLE

The Executive Inn Evansville
600 Walnut Street
Evansville, IN 47708
877-424-0888/812-424-8000
http://www.executiveinnevansville.com
$71–$160
In downtown Evansville, twenty minutes from Ellis Park, the Executive Inn adjoins the Evansville Convention Centre. Hotel amenities include Jacuzzi rooms and suites and an in-house chef-run restaurant serving fine lobster and seafood dinners on weekends. An indoor pool and exercise room are just waiting for you. Enjoy drinks in the lobby bar or do penance in the Time Out Lounge.

INDIANAPOLIS

The Canterbury Hotel
123 S. Illinois Street
Indianapolis, IN 46225
317-634-3000/800-538-8186

http://www.canterburyhotel.com
$175–$1599 (for the Presidential suite)
A registered historic landmark, this elegant 1928 hotel in the city's heart is Indiana's only hotel with membership in the prestigious Preferred Hotels and Resorts Worldwide. Renovated and modernized, it presents sophisticated European elegance throughout. Rooms are luxurious, with either king- or queen-size beds, and there's a Presidential Suite to make your Thoroughbred vacation exceptional. The hotel is located behind Circle Centre Mall, and a private entrance takes you to the shops.

The Radisson Hotel City Centre
31 W. Ohio Street
Indianapolis, IN 46204
317-635-2000/800-333-3333
http://www.radisson.com
$99 and up
In a former life, the Radisson was a Hilton, and the interior retains that tasteful, cultivated feel. The large lobby leads to a comfortable bar and grill for unwinding after a day in the streets. Rooms are handsomely tailored, with great city views from the upper floors. The rooftop pool delivers a refreshing swim with a stunning view onto Soldiers and Sailors Monument below. This is an excellent location at Monument Circle.

MICHIGAN

GRAND RAPIDS

Amway Grand Plaza Hotel
187 Monroe Avenue NW
Grand Rapids, MI 49503
616-774-2000/800-695-8284
http://www.amwaygrand.com
$119–$250

The Amway Grand offers lovely, sophisticated guest rooms with all the frills we like, and an indoor pool. Off the grand lobby are gift and coffee shops. The east wing was the original Pantlind Hotel, in 1925 considered one of America's top ten hotels. It still has the gold leaf ceilings, majestic chandeliers, central pineapple fountain, and Duncan Phyfe furnishings that attracted the wealthiest travelers. Fine dining at the hotel includes The Grill at 1913, a steakhouse.

MINNESOTA

SHAKOPEE AND MINNEAPOLIS/ST. PAUL

Crowne Plaza (Northstar) Minneapolis
618 Second Avenue South
Minneapolis, MN 55402
612-338-2288
http://www.msp-northstar.crowneplaza.com
$161 and up; also check hotel specials
Tuck us in! We felt completely removed from the whole world in this serene spot of quiet, plush rooms. With all the tempting amenities right here, sightseeing came second.

The Grand Hotel Minneapolis
615 Second Avenue South
Minneapolis, MN 55402
866-The-Grand (866-843-4726)
http://www.grandhotelminneapolis.com
$129–$399
This good downtown guesthouse began as the Minneapolis Athletic Club and has undergone grand renovation. Recently it was likened to the style of TV's *West Wing* for its elegant, understated sophistication. Rooms and suites are individually styled and cozy. All have, among other amenities, Egyptian cotton linens and down-filled comforters, big marble bathrooms, and earth-friendly Aveda bath products. It offers a pool, sushi bar, and Martini BLU restaurant for fine dining. This is the city's only Preferred Hotel member.

OHIO

CINCINNATI

The Cincinnatian Hotel
601 Vine Street
Cincinnati, OH 45202
513-381-3000/800-942-9000
http://www.cincinnatianhotel.com
$138–$350, call for packages and other rates
Fully restored to its original French Second Empire style, the small luxury hotel features elegant guest rooms with dressing rooms, Roman tubs or dual-head showers, bathrobes, and turn-down service. Its contemporary Palace Restaurant offers a superb dining experience.

Hyatt Regency Cincinnati
151 West Fifth Street
Cincinnati, OH 45202
513 579 1234
http://cincinnati.hyatt.com
$85–$179
Like the Westin, this hotel is located by Fountain Square and convenient for those interested in shopping, attending the theater or a Cincinnati Reds ball game, or just going for a stroll in downtown.

The Westin Cincinnati
21 E. 5th Street
Cincinnati, OH 45202
513-621-7700
http://www.westin.com/cincinnati
$153–$295
Conveniently located, this fine hotel overlooks Fountain Square and is connected to Tower Place Mall and its many shops by a sky bridge. It is also within walking distance of The Aronoff Arts Center and the Great American Ball Park.

CLEVELAND

The Glidden House
1901 Ford Drive
Cleveland, OH 44106
800-759-8358
http://www.gliddenhouse.com

$159–$229
The Glidden House mansion and estate are on the campus of Case Western Reserve University, making the 1910 French Gothic inn a hop away from the Cleveland Art Museum and campus events and a short drive from the city. Thistledown is less than thirty minutes by car. With charming, spacious guest rooms and serene gardens beyond tall, multipaned windows, the inn is a one-of-a-kind lodging. The Stone Hearth Pub, with its wide arched fireplace, is a cozy spot for drinks. Part of the inn, Sergio's, featuring Brazilian dining, is one of the area's acclaimed restaurants.

Ritz-Carlton Cleveland
1515 W. Third Street
Cleveland, OH 44113
216-623-1300/800-241-3333
http://www.ritzcarlton.com/hotels/cleveland
$200–$279, call hotel for best specials
Overlooking the now healthy Cuyahoga River, the fourteen-story downtown Ritz-Carlton, located near the Public Square, is part of the Tower City shopping and business complex. It's a short walk to major sports complexes, including Jacobs Field, for Indians' baseball; Gund Arena, where basketball happens with the Cavaliers; and Cleveland Browns Stadium, for football. Rooms on the executive level are luxurious, with sweeping views, featherbeds, marble baths, and twice-a-day housekeeping. The Lobby Lounge offers afternoon tea and a full bar for more hearty socializing.

COLUMBUS

Crowne Plaza Hotel
33 East Nationwide Boulevard
Columbus, OH 43215
614-461-4100/800-700-2619
http://www.crowneplaza.com
Average $111–$120 (with AAA discount)
Enjoy the downtown location of this four-star address.

Harrison House
313 West Fifth Avenue
Columbus, OH 43201
614-421-2202/800-827-4203
From $119
Step back in time at this fine bed and breakfast located between downtown and the OSU campus, in Columbus's historic and trendy Victorian Village. In this area of elegantly restored homes, you can take a walk along the Olentangy River, stroll through Goodale Park (http://www.victorianvillage.org), or explore the campus.

WHERE TO WINE & DINE

ILLINOIS

CHICAGO

Everest
One Financial Plaza
440 S. LaSalle Street
Chicago, Illinois 60605
312-663-8920
http://everestrestaurant.com

Dinners from $36

Everest, high in the sky, with its posh European atmosphere and tables lining the long row of picture windows looking west, is a memorable French gourmet experience. Chef-owner Jean Joho, who opened the restaurant in 1986, has created a sumptuous menu that focuses on Alsatian cuisine. We recommend one of the caviar appetizers and the Maine lobster in Alsace Gewurztraminer butter.

House of Blues Club and Restaurant
329 N. Dearborn Street
Chicago, IL 60610
312-923-2000
http://www.hob.com
Dinners from $12.95

The original Negro spiritual and blues genres now share the stage with other musical styles. Begun in 1992 by Harvard University and Hollywood lights Dan Ackroyd, John Belushi, and River Phoenix, the club promotes innovative musicians. Dinners are classic to regional, with smart southern accents. Get tickets in advance. Come back for Sunday breakfast, and, as they say at the gospel choir brunch, "Praise the Lord and pass the biscuits."

INDIANA

EVANSVILLE

Milano's
500 Main Street at Fifth
Evansville, IN 47713
812-484-2222
$9–$15

Milano's is a relaxing little spot that features traditional Italian cooking. This is where you'll deliberate among such temptations as chicken parmigiana, hearty lasagna, or ravioli. The ambiance is a marriage of casual and upscale; come as you are. Closed Sundays.

INDIANAPOLIS

Dunaway's Palazzo Ossigeno
351 South East Street
Indianapolis, IN 46204
317-638-7663
http://www.dunaways.com
Dinners from $24

Just southeast of downtown, the former Oxygen Palace (once home to the Indiana Oxygen Company) is an exceptional dining experience. Owner Jeff Dunaway brings his unique creativity to the interiors and menu of this steakhouse with an Italian flair. It was the first restaurant in the city to offer a rooftop dining terrace, and its rambling interior spaces are configured for romantic dining or intimate "dinners in the kitchen with the chef." Art deco decor blends with the Tudor and Gothic bones of the original building. A thousand wines and ports and live entertainment are available. Located just southeast of downtown, we recommend taking a cab in the evening.

The Eagle's Nest
Hyatt Regency
One South Capitol Avenue
Indianapolis, IN 46204
317-231-7566/317-616-6170
http://www.hyatt.com
$22–$65

Glide around the downtown Indianapolis skyline while treating yourself to a magnificent culinary experience in this revolving rooftop restaurant. Specialties include classic steak and prime rib entrées, salmon, and seafood. We loved the Maryland crab cakes and lobster bisque. Our pasta primavera with blackened salmon was incredible. Service is excellent, and, of course, the twenty-third floor roost delivers a spectacular view. The restaurant is decorated with a whimsical sun, moon, and stars motif and fresh flowers. Reservations suggested, business casual dress.

MICHIGAN

GRAND RAPIDS

B.O.B.
20 Monroe NW
Grand Rapids, MI 49503
616-356-2000
http://www.thebob.com
Dinner from $7–$30
B.O.B. stands for Big Old Building. After dinner, enjoy comedy, live music, and the microbrewery.

Tre Cugini
100 Monroe Center
Grand Rapids, MI 49503
616-235-9339
http://www. trecugini.com
$14–$29
Housed in the 1874 Italianate Ledyard Building, this classic Italian restaurant features freshly made pastas, seafood, veal, and lamb, in a white tablecloth setting. No jeans, please.

MINNESOTA

MINNEAPOLIS/ST. PAUL

Cosmos (formerly Le Meridien)
(in Graves 601 Hotel)
601 1st Ave. N.
Minneapolis, MN 55403
612-312-1168
http://www.graves601hotel.com
Entrées $20–$30 and higher
Dress for the evening. We were sent here so our favorite Hollywood and country music stars could spy on us when they slip quietly in for dinner. Diverting from predictable Italian and steak entrées, we recommend the wild boar chop with sweet potatoes, and the poached lobster with foie gras, porcini, and artichokes. Well worth the culinary surprises dished up by Executive Chef Seth Bixby Daugherty.

Dakota Jazz Club & Restaurant
1010 Nicollet Mall
Minneapolis, MN 55403
612-332-1010
http:www.dakotacooks.com
$16–$30
Reserve a curvy booth on the first floor of this hip nightspot and enjoy an excellent

regional dinner before the topnotch music and noise heat up. Try the beef and root veggies in red wine, or, better yet, dare to do the dreamy walleye dumplings. For dessert, the chocolate pudding is a must.

Dangerfield Restaurant
1583 1st Ave. E.
Shakopee, MN 55379
952-445-2245
Sandwiches, salads, and steaks from $6.99
Enjoy regional possibilities such as a walleye salad; or try the London broil. They also have a new fajita selection. Casual and friendly.

OHIO

CINCINNATI

The Palace Restaurant
(in the Cincinnatian Hotel)
601 Vine Street
Cincinnati, OH 45202
513-381-6006 for reservations
http://www.palacecincinnati.com
$28–$40
Zagat calls the Palace one of the city's finest. Its creative, contemporary entrées offer pleasant surprises. Try the marinated Cervena venison chop, accompanied by a roasted chestnut tartlet and turnip and celery puree, with a fruity huckleberry sauce. Or do the tender beef short ribs with a cabernet reduction and horseradish whipped potatoes. Dessert must be the irresistible frozen mango guava soufflé drizzled with roasted pineapple sauce and served in a cocoanut-macadamia tuile.

Palomino
505 Vine Street
Cincinnati, OH 45202
513-381-1300
http://www.r-u-i.com/plo
$12–$40
Part of a Seattle-based restaurant chain, the Palomino looks onto Fountain Square, giving it one of the city's liveliest views. Handblown glass chandeliers, classical columns, and marble accents enhance the urban setting. Dinners feature fresh, brick-oven grilled chicken and seafood, along with pastas and big salads. It offers a full bar. End your dinner with the oven-roasted pear bread pudding, and return on Sunday for the all-day happy hour.

CLEVELAND

Blue Point Grill
700 West St. Clair Avenue
Cleveland, OH 44113
216-875-7827
$17–$70
In the historic Hoyt Building, the city's finest seafood restaurant offers an oyster sampler, sushi selections, and red curry sauce on the sea bass. Traditionalists can enjoy staples such as chicken, swordfish, and salmon. The modern aquatic theme jazzes up the lofty, high-ceilinged interior. Outdoor dining offers nice street views. Service and presentations are equally fine. Fashionistas should start at the sophisticated mahogany bar and enjoy the high-end crowd.

D'Vine
836 W. St. Clair Avenue
Cleveland, OH 44113
216-241-8463
http://www.dvinewinebar.com
$9–$14 (for tapas)
Sixteen flights of wine (samples of four wines grouped by type or region), domestic and international, starting at $11.00; or individual tastes from $5.50. Beers and a wonderful array of tapas are also offered.

Johnny's Downtown
1406 West 6th Street
Cleveland, OH 44113
216-623-0055
$21.95 and up
For excellent Italian and continental entrées, Johnny's is the place. There are actually three Johnny's in Cleveland, but this one is tops. The L. F. & S. Burgess Grocers Building, which houses the restaurant, was the first building in the Warehouse District to undergo restoration. Johnny's has won the *Cleveland Magazine* Silver Spoon Award for Best Fine Dining Restaurant, and since 1994, the Zagat restaurant guide has called it the city's number one restaurant. Executive chef Vid Lutz offers steaks, veal chops, pastas, and seafood on a rich, exceptional menu. Reservations are essential; seemingly everyone who's made it to the top is here, every night.

COLUMBUS

Brazenhead Irish Pub
1027 West Fifth Avenue
Columbus, OH 43212
614-737-3738
Most items under $10
Enjoy the Irish ambience in this old style pub and grill, also known as the Fifth Ave Pub. Stained glass windows, fireplaces, and antique photos adorn the walls here. More than thirty different beers in bottles and another dozen or so on tap will give you plenty to choose from.

"M" (a Mitchell's Steak House)
(in the Miranova office tower)
45 N. 3rd. Street
Columbus, OH 43215
614-621-2333
http://www.cameronmitchell.com
$19–$36
Four blocks from Indiana's statehouse is this architecturally fun restaurant on the Scioto River, a spot that wins awards for its menus, wines, service, and ambience. Enjoy its wonderful wide outdoor terrace. Dine on truffle chicken with mushroom bread pudding, and reserve your space in heaven. Dessert should be the ice cream sandwich, with peach and apple sorbet and crème fraîche. Wine tasting is on Wednesdays, 5:00–7:00 p.m.

Fountain Square, Cincinnati

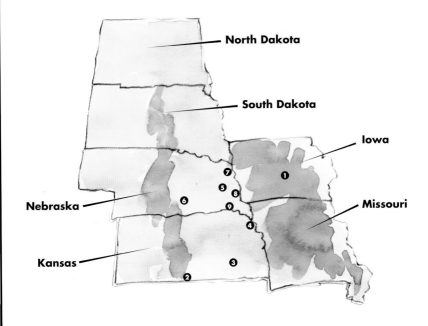

GREAT PLAINS MAP LEGEND

Iowa
❶ Prairie Meadows
(Altoona)

Kansas
❷ Anthony Downs
(Anthony)

❸ Eureka Downs
(Eureka)

❹ Woodlands Race Park
(Kansas City)

Nebraska
❺ Columbus Races
(Columbus)

❻ Fonner Park
(Grand Island)

❼ Horsemen's Atokad Downs
(South Sioux City)

❽ Horsemen's Park
(Omaha)

❾ State Fair Park
(Lincoln)

THE GREAT PLAINS

O n the wide, endless prairie, where the sky dips low to touch the fertile earth, the horse was the homesteader's beast of burden. Together, man and animal ripped long furrows in the soil and filled them with seed corn and wheat. Come summer, to celebrate the bounty of their toil, families climbed into the buggy and rattled off to the agricultural fair, life's biggest social event. As many still do, they packed the grandstand to revel in the sound of horses thundering around the oval.

By the late 1800s, dedicated racecourses appeared on the plains. As the sport became more prestigious, when a man acquired a registered blood horse, his social standing also rose a notch.

Riders—on the plains and across the West—honed their skills at fairs and small tracks alike, and the more talented moved on, as they still do, some to become top jockeys in other regions of the country.

One of the first racetracks built on the western prairie, Nebraska's Aksarben, opened in 1895, in Omaha. It also became a place to witness history. For more than a century, citizens gathered at Aksarben to hear great orators or to rally the soldiers before they marched off to war. From Des Moines to Sioux City, racetracks peppered the heartland. Like fireflies at dawn, many have vanished. Yet a handful press on, stubbornly protecting the regional racing circuit and the hopeful horseman's way of life.

IOWA

PRAIRIE MEADOWS (ALTOONA)

Prairie Meadows, established in 1989, is one of the newest racetracks to appear on the Thoroughbred scene. It endured financial difficulties until the county became the owner and leased it to the nonprofit Racing Association of Iowa. The central Iowa track has established a good reputation—especially among the quarter horse crowd, who love the fast, hard track—as a place where purses are decent and show every indication of growing. Yes, there's a casino behind the racetrack's generosity. Unlike most racinos, racing and gaming at Prairie Meadows essentially share the same space. The grandstand, for example, is full of slot machines. Casino revenues have made it possible for Iowa to attract far-reaching attention with its enticing purse structure.

Revived interest in horse breeding throughout Iowa has spiced up the racing pool as well.

With a 1-mile dirt track and essentially two meets, which accommodate Thoroughbreds beginning in mid-April and mixed racing later in the summer, Prairie Meadows commands the national spotlight for several days in early July as host of the Iowa Festival of Racing, with total purses topping $1 million dollars. Racing celebrities on hand for the 2004 event included trainers Steve Asmussen and Bob Baffert and such leading jockeys as Pat Day, Victor Espinoza, and Mark Guidry. The highlight of the series, which opens with the Iowa Oaks (G3) and Iowa Derby, was the $300,000 Cornhusker Breeders' Cup Handicap (G2), a 1 ⅛-mile race for three-year-olds and older. Among the Handicap's most competitive entrants was Grade 1 winner Perfect Drift. But after a heart-pounding stretch run,

Racing at Prairie Meadows

Roses in May came home a 1 ½-length winner.

As Prairie Meadows finds its niche in horse racing, and even considers adding a turf course to the facility, it faces challenges that many noncasino tracks would be happy to have to resolve. The nonprofit group operating the racetrack currently turns over a percentage of revenues to the Des Moines public schools and to other deserving groups and organizations. Now that table games, such as craps and blackjack, have been approved, track operators want permission to expand the casino and add a hotel. Anticipating future gambling revenues, other entities in the county and state are hungrily holding out their plates for a slice of the pie. Talk of riverboats arriving in Des Moines—with gaming, of course—has sparked plenty of closed-door meetings as Prairie Meadows and the city revisit what numbers would make for a good partnership, preferably one that would exclude competition from the boats.

KANSAS

ANTHONY DOWNS (ANTHONY)

Anthony Downs, in south-central Kansas, is not far from the Oklahoma line. Racing dates back to 1904 at this rural site, where the open-air grandstand has

On the way to the paddock

SNAPSHOT - PRAIRIE MEADOWS

Description: Prairie Meadows, in Polk County, near Des Moines, has been around since 1989. Slot machines were installed in 1995, and today Prairie Meadows hosts a robust mixed meet. For Thoroughbreds, the Cornhusker Breeders' Cup Handicap (G2) is the highlight of the meet. The main track is 1 mile, with two chutes. There is a separate 5/8-mile training track. There is no turf course.

Season: There are two consecutive meets here. The first is for Thoroughbreds and starts around the end of April and goes into the first week in July. The second meet is a mixed one for Thoroughbreds and quarter horses, which starts in July and runs until September.

Address: 1 Prairie Meadow Drive, Altoona, IA 50009

Phone: 515-967-1000/(fax) 515-967-1344

Web site: http://www.prairiemeadows.com

Nearest airport: Des Moines International Airport (DSM)

Getting there: Prairie Meadows, in Altoona, is off I-80 and U.S. Route 6, outside Des Moines.

Admission: Free

Parking: Free

Fine dining: Champions Restaurant

Casual fare: Paddock West, Hop's Horsemen's Lounge, The Homestretch, Daily Double Deli

Spirits: Hop's Horsemen's Lounge and elsewhere in the facility

Extras: Handicapping seminars, prerace breakfast buffets on Saturday mornings, Friday and Saturday evening dinner buffets. The casino attracts prime entertainment during the summer, including live concerts, dancing, salsa, and big band groups.

thick wooden bench seats and all but hugs the rail beside the racetrack. Everything about the facility speaks of an earlier era. Roots of racing go deep here; the track announcer has forty years on the job, and one of the owners is a woman in her eighties, who has raced here for decades, as many people have. The town of Anthony was established in 1878 as the seat of Harper County.

This small plains track puts on a six-day mixed meet of horses and greyhounds, over two three-day weekends in mid-July. To celebrate the track's centennial in 2004, race days included musical entertainment, a first-annual barbeque contest, a chuck wagon breakfast, a night of dancing, and stick-pony racing for the kids. Contact the racetrack via the Anthony Fair Association, Anthony Downs, 521 E. Sherman, P.O. Box 444, Anthony, Kansas 67003, 620-842-5989, http://www.ohmygosh.com.

Eureka Downs (Eureka)

Calling itself the horse racing capital of Kansas, Eureka Downs draws on historic precedent. Seat of Greenwood County,

Ready for some racing action

the town of Eureka sits beside the Fall River, in the vicinity of dozens of little creeks and three sizeable lakes. About sixty miles southwest of Wichita, the region boasts of its bluestem prairie grass, nutritious for grazing livestock.

Eureka, established in 1862, is one of the oldest towns in Kansas, and its original racetrack was built at the fairgrounds in the 1890s. In the mid-1960s, fire claimed the 1920s grandstand. The new building is metal, tan, with a brick-red roof. Watching the races, patrons look out to a 5-furlong bullring dirt track surrounding an infield pond. It's a small, simple place, neatly kept, where trucks and cars park on the grass.

A twenty-one-day mixed meet of Saturday-Sunday racing generally opens the first of May and concludes on the Fourth of July weekend. Fans of all ages, friendly and casual, may number in the low thousands. In 2004, Eureka Downs tallied decreases of nearly 25 percent in both wagering and purses. Total handle for the 2004 meet was just over $311,000 for a total of ninety-three races, mostly featuring quarter horses, with an average purse of $3,350. The racing is subsidized by casino dollars. Contact the racetrack at 210 N. Jefferson Street, Eureka, Kansas 67405, 316-583-5528, http://www.eurekadowns.com.

Woodlands Race Park (Kansas City)

Woodlands Race Park (The Woodlands) sits on a rise of open plain that's fast disappearing, its edges being chopped away by development. But for now, The Woodlands remains well named. Tall stands of deciduous trees follow the land's rolling contours to the edge of the horizon. Flocks of blackbirds swoop above the dry grasses, darkening the sky like a million peppercorns tossed high. Leaves cling uneasily to their branches. The chill that sets the autumn colors hasn't quite arrived, though gray skies warn of its coming.

We spent our weekend at The Woodlands with friends we made in late summer at Arlington Park. They took us into every nook and cranny of the race-track, from the stables to the Horsemen's Café. This was closing week-end for the yearly meet, a thirty-day pro-gram of mixed quarter horse and Thoroughbred racing that began in late September and finishes on November 1.

For many horsemen and women here, racing on the plains takes in Thoroughbred tracks in Kansas, Nebraska, Minnesota, Iowa, Oklahoma, and even Illinois. Whereas owners every-where transport their horses long dis-tances to compete for purse money, here on the edge of the West, the miles between tracks from state to state can be substantial. In comparison with purses at big, glamorous tracks, those at The Woodlands are modest, around $60,000 total per day. Yet competition for prize money can be just as vigorous.

Being close to the action allowed us to observe that most horse people here

The Woodlands clubhouse

have both hands on the process all of the time. They wear all the hats: owner, trainer, exerciser, groom, and stable hand. On race days, they bring the ani-mals to the paddock, saddle them, and parade them. After the race, they remove the tack, take the horses back to the stable to cool down, and bathe them. This is very different from the media view of a racing stable, where teams of experts oversee specific aspects of an ani-mal's care.

At the Woodlands' entrance, doors swing open onto a large lobby, where long escalators climb to the upper level, the boxes, the Turf Club, and the main simulcast space. The left side of the

The first horse out wants the rail.

Stretching out for the photo

building's north side, where the view looks to the paddock as well as to the track, and they are close to the stairs that exit to the paddock.

The Woodlands track was fast the weekend we were there. On Friday, it was cool and gray, and on closing day the mercury dropped and rain fell with cold determination. Big winter coats and scarves suddenly appeared. The Turf Club Restaurant filled quickly, as did the boxes. Camaraderie on the final day was high, with attendance at 4,200. In our group, wives, business pals, girlfriends, and kids showed up to watch "our horse," GoodBetterBest, run in race eight, the $30,000 Woodlands Handicap.

Before the race, we went into the paddock to see our horse, take pictures, scowl at the skies, and hope the rain would pick up, making the track sloppy, more to GoodBetterBest's liking. We put $10 to win on him and returned to the grandstand to watch. The four-year-old colt was slow out of the gate and never made up the lost ground. The winner's trophy went to Canyon De Oro, a Kentucky-bred.

lobby leads to the grandstand, with covered stadium seats—not extensive, but necessary, because autumn in Kansas is both gorgeous and unpredictable. Most race fans watch the contests from the upper level.

On the second level, the informal Turf Club Restaurant overlooks the finish line, and some tables are affixed with televisions. The west side of the floor holds simulcast areas, banks of pari-mutuel windows, two large bars, and a couple of deli counters. The rest of the floor holds box seating, where the owners and trainers—the lifeblood of the sport—camp out. They cluster at the

SNAPSHOT - WOODLANDS RACE PARK

Description: Thoroughbreds and quarter horses share this northwestern Kansas track on the outskirts of Kansas City. Narrowly spared by a devastating tornado a few years ago, the modern facility conducts racing (greyhounds, too, in the twin facility across the parking lot) during a one-month fall meet, on a 1-mile track with a 990-foot homestretch. There is no turf course.

Season: Late September to late October; features the Woodlands Handicap as the meet concludes

Address: 9700 Leavenworth Road, Kansas City, KS 66112

Phone: 800-695-7223/913-299-9797/(fax) 913-299-9804

Web site: http://www.woodlandskc.com

Nearest airport: Kansas City (Missouri) International Airport (MCI)

Getting there: From I-70, take exit 411B (I-435N), then merge onto KS 5 S/Leavenworth Road (exit 15A). Make a U-turn onto KS 5 N/Leavenworth Road and go ⅒-mile to The Woodlands.

Admission: Free

Parking: Free

Fine dining: The Turf Club Restaurant, open during live horse racing, $2 cover charge, reservations suggested

Casual fare: Woody's Specials

Spirits: Several bars on the clubhouse level; beer and wine beside the paddock

Extras: Truck raffle, collectible giveaways, Halloween events

NEBRASKA

COLUMBUS RACES (COLUMBUS)

Columbus, located northwest of Omaha in the elbow of the Loup and Platte rivers, came to life in 1942, and much like the racing at Fonner Park, its horse racing overlaps with the Platte County Fair, held here in the summer. The racing that follows the short Omaha meet starts in late July and ends in early September. That means the meet begins with summer at its hottest, when thunderstorms and even tornados can threaten the program.

Dual lightning strike at Columbus Races

The grounds here are nice, and the buildings are well maintained. For the horsemen and women who race here today, driving in and getting set for the meet brings with it an extended family

THE FIRST RULE OF MARRIAGE

David Sirucek is committed to the health of the horse racing industry. He's on the board of the Kansas Thoroughbred Association and attends endless state racing commission meetings. A big, beefy man in a white Stetson that shades his watchful blue eyes, he also takes credit for introducing his wife to the world of Thoroughbreds. Truth is, Lu Kizer, a tall, attractive blond, grew up around animals in Nebraska.

Dave Sirucek treats his winner.

The Sirucek-Kizer stable is small, but it's growing steadily through breeding, claiming, and buying horses. Each spring, the two trailer their mares to a Kentucky stud farm and then waits anxiously for a healthy new foal. In the meantime, there's work, racing, and in the best of seasons, prize money to haul to the bank. Dave's rule of handicapping: "I bet against the favorites. That's the long shot school, and it's the right way to go." Lu never wagers. "Hell, every nickel I have is already on the horses."

When Dave takes their horses to the Arlington meet, Lu takes other horses to races in Nebraska. But during the Woodlands meet, she's either at the track, at the grocery store, or at the stove, cooking for the crowds of horse people staying with them while their horses race. Despite their rigorous schedules, Dave and Lu will rarely turn down a cold beer or a good party. It's how they met, in 1993, in a line dance at a bar.

In 1996, as they were contemplating marriage, Dave watched as Cigar scored his sixteenth consecutive win in the Arlington Citation Challenge Invitational and fell in love with the horse. When Cigar was entered in the Woodward Handicap (G1) at Belmont Park that September, Dave and Lu decided they'd be there to watch. Just to complicate things, New York struck them as a good place for a honeymoon. So along with packing came the scramble to get blood tests and the marriage license. The day before the trip, while working at The Woodlands, they found the jockey's chaplain and repeated their marriage vows. The bride wore jeans, the groom his Stetson and boots.

At Belmont Park, Cigar won the Woodward by four lengths, and the newlyweds went home elated. When December rolled around, they celebrated Christmas morning by beginning a tradition Dave now calls their first rule of marriage. Every Christmas morning, regardless of the weather or wind chill, they saddle up and ride on their farm. And maybe there's a second rule: when they return to the Bluegrass for spring breeding, they always stop at the Kentucky Horse Park to visit the now-pensioned Cigar.

feeling. Owners and trainers know each other, buy each other drinks at the clubhouse bars, help each other out anyway they can, and wish each other success—until the animals break at the gate, that is.

With a healthy casino industry in the state, the horse racing industry is also looking up. Columbus's stakes values are on the rise, and the number of horses stabled at the track in 2004 increased over the previous year to the barns' capacity of eight hundred, with a waiting list. Columbus Races is at 822 15th Street, Columbus, Nebraska 68601, in Agricultural Park, 402-564-0133, http://www.columbusraces.com.

Leaping Plum wins again.

FONNER PARK (GRAND ISLAND)

Racing at Fonner Park has endured for more than half a century at the facility it built in 1954. When horse racing dried up at Aksarben in Omaha in 1995, the 5-furlong course at Fonner stepped forward as the state's new big track. Launching the Nebraska Thoroughbred racing year, Fonner opens almost as soon as the danger of blizzards has passed. It races into mid-May, with an approximately forty-day meet. The thirteen-week meet offers a $400,000 stakes program, highlighted by the $100,000 Bosselman-Gus Fonner Stakes. The minimum purse for 2004 was $4,000. The windfall reflects the success of gaming at Horsemen's Park, Omaha, owned and operated by Nebraska Horsemen. Fonner Park, a nonprofit enterprise, supports charitable activities throughout the region.

The 280-acre grounds are modest; the glass-enclosed grandstand has the flat roof so favored at midwestern tracks. When the meet is over, residents return for other midwestern events, such as livestock shows, fireworks and dancing on the Fourth of July, 4-H shows, and the Hall County Fair in August.

Fonner's roster of interesting characters and celebrities has included a

Charging for the wire at Fonner Park

horse or two. In an unrivaled winning streak, the Kentucky-bred gelding Leaping Plum won eight renewals of the Grasmick Handicap between 1995 and 2003. When Plum was twelve, beyond the legal age limit for racing, his owners got special permission from the state racing commission to race him. In his final start, in 2004 at age thirteen, he finished the Grasmick in fourth, after which his owners decided to retire him. During his racing career, Leaping Plum earned $371,584 and captured the hearts of thousands of fans. His farewell put Fonner Park in the national spotlight, and the track honors him now with the annual Leaping Plum Day.

Fonner Park is located just off Interstate 80 in Grand Island at 700 E. Stolley Park Rd. For more information, write to the park at P.O. Box 490, Grand Island, Nebraska 68802, or phone 308-382-4515. You can also visit the Web site, http://www.fonnerpark.com.

HORSEMEN'S ATOKAD DOWNS (SOUTH SIOUX CITY)

In the northeastern corner of the state stands a nice little track built in the 1960s, now essentially engulfed by the casino beside it. Horsemen's Atokad Downs, located in Dakota County, near the Iowa border, missed three years of live racing in the late 1990s but since then has hosted a one-weekend, three-day meet. Its ⅝-mile oval

Victory, Randall Robinson

sports two chutes. With seating for five thousand spectators, Horsemen's usually fills a sixteen-race card, for Thoroughbreds and quarter horses, toward the end of September.

Horsemen's Atokad Downs has no legal relationship to the Omaha casino, Horsemen's Park, and does not pull in the dollars the latter does. Far from the other state tracks, with limited competitions and a brief meet schedule, this is a meet many owners have difficulty scheduling. Some in the industry also point toward the state line, claiming that the track's frail status is not helped by Sioux City (Iowa) folks who "won't cross the river." Even so, the meet offers $65,000 each day in total purses, with the Robert E. Lee Classic awarding $20,000—modest by name-track standards, but regionally adequate.

A few weeks after Atokad horsemen vacate, the facility reopens for the Breeders' Cup World Championships simulcast. Since 2003, Atokad has stirred up in-house excitement on BC day by offering coffee and donuts, BC T-shirts for early birds, a breakfast buffet, and handicapping contests with attractive purses. Ambitious management at the South Sioux City site looks ahead to filling more racing days and making the racetrack grounds into a concert scene. Renovations and improvements to the buildings have drawn positive comments. Horsemen's Atokad Downs, 1524 Atokad Drive, can be reached at 402-494-5722, P.O. Box 796, South Sioux City, Nebraska 68776. For more information, contact the Nebraska Racing Commission at http://www.horseracing.state.ne.us.

HORSEMEN'S PARK (OMAHA)

Horsemen's Park in Omaha—not to be confused with Horsemen's Atokad Downs in South Sioux City—is in truth a flashy casino, "a great simulcast facility,"

Nebraska jockey colony in the early 1950s

which includes a ⅜-mile dirt track for its annual weekend horse racing meet, four days of live racing that arrives on a Thursday in mid-July, as soon as Lincoln racing falls silent. At Horsemen's, the competitors gallop into a setting complete with musicians, bands, cold drinks, hot snacks, tents filled with amusements, and a general festival atmosphere. The gesture to live racing, which starts quickly and intensifies into one long party, keeps the casino license well oiled. Most important for the Nebraska horse industry, the successful Omaha casino subsidizes racing elsewhere in the Cornhusker state. Contact them at 402-731-2900 or at http://www.horsemens

park.com. The facility address is 6303 Q Street, Omaha, Nebraska 68117.

STATE FAIR PARK (LINCOLN)

After visiting Fonner Park, we're flying east, figuratively speaking, to Lincoln and then to Omaha along the route that took Americans west in the 1800s. I-80 is really more than one hundred years old, starting out as the Overland Trail, carved out by pioneers, settlers, and gold seekers.

In mid-May, Nebraska's capital takes up Thoroughbred racing at the Lincoln fairgrounds. The meet covers four-day weekends lasting into the second week of July, with both night and afternoon racing around the ⅜-mile track. The grandstand is boxy and open, with covered seating in the upper levels of the stadium that overlook the large infield lake. The glassed-in clubhouse seats 2,500 at both tiered seating and dining tables. Total attendance in summer 2004 was 59,000. The state fair racing office can be reached at http://www.statefair.org or by calling 402-471-4155. Write to them at P.O. Box 81223, Lincoln, Nebraska 68501.

State Fair Park

GREAT PLAINS TRAVEL SECTION

BELOW, YOU'LL FIND A MILEAGE CHART LISTING THE DISTANCES BETWEEN THE REGIONAL RACETRACKS AND ALL THE CITIES DISCUSSED IN THE FOLLOWING TRAVEL SECTION. THE CITY OR CITIES CLOSEST TO A TRACK ARE INDICATED BY AN X.

COAST TO COAST	Des Moines, Iowa	Grand Island, Neb.	Kansas City, Mo.	Lincoln, Neb.	Omaha, Neb.
Anthony Downs (Kans.)	455 miles	340 miles	**X** 260 miles	340 miles	430 miles
Columbus Races (Neb.)	210 miles	**X** 65 miles	270 miles	85 miles	90 miles
Eureka Downs (Kans.)	354 miles	335 miles	**X** 150 miles	275 miles	330 miles
Fonner Park (Neb.)	280 miles	**X** ✽ miles	285 miles	95 miles	125 miles
Horsemen's Atokad Downs (Neb.)	200 miles	245 miles	275 miles	150 miles	**X** 95 miles
Horsemen's Park (Neb.)	140 miles	150 miles	185 miles	55 miles	**X** ✽ miles
Prairie Meadows (Iowa)	**X** ✽ miles	295 miles	205 miles	200 miles	145 miles
State Fair Park (Neb.)	190 miles	100 miles	195 miles	**X** ✽ miles	60 miles
Woodlands Race Park (Kans.)	205 miles	290 miles	**X** 20 miles	190 miles	185 miles

✽ *The racetrack is located inside or within 10 miles of the city limits.*

MUST SEE / MUST DO

IOWA

DES MOINES

Terrace Hill (2300 Grand Avenue; 515-281-3604; http://www.terracehill.org) has been the governor's home for a number of years, after being donated to the state of Iowa in 1971 by heirs of Frederick Hubbell, one of the city's first millionaires, who bought it in 1884. The eighteen thousand square foot Victorian mansion, overlooking the Raccoon River valley, was designed by Chicago architect William Boyington, who also designed Chicago's Water Tower, one of the few buildings to have survived the Great Chicago fire of 1871. Terrace Hill, with sweeping views of the city and the state capitol, is open for tours March through December, 10:00 a.m. to 1:30 p.m. The governor and his family live privately on the third floor.

A permanent collection that features contemporary art from the nineteenth century to the present, the **Des Moines Art Center** (4700 Grand Avenue; 515-277-4405; http://www.desmoinesartcenter.org) holds Edward Hopper's famous *Automat* and Henri Matisse's *Woman in White*; works by Georgia O'Keeffe, Francis Bacon, Mark Rothko, and John Currin; and many other avant-garde, postimpressionist, and minimalist works.

MISSOURI

KANSAS CITY

An ebony starlit night on the plains has serious competition from the sparkling lights of the hilly city on the river. Saturday night in Kansas City carries a magical feeling. Wide landscaped boulevards sweep you around town, past landmark buildings illuminated to spotlight their architectural features. Spacious parks and arboretums fill the city, and of the city's impressive 160 fountains, some

Terrace Hill

Kansas City nightfall

29 (at last count) sculptured water fountains are bubbling and lovely under the lights. Check http://www.kcfountains. org for locations and history.

Kansas City is made up of wonderful neighborhoods—the convention center downtown; Crown Center, at Grand and Pershing; Country Club Plaza, between Broadway and Madison; with 47th running through its heart. Flowing briskly through the neighborhood is **Brush Creek**, the perfect spot for sightseeing or relaxing at a sidewalk bar or café. Nightlife in Westport is fairly young—a noisy, colorful bar scene. On a lofty rise above the city, the famous **Nelson-Atkins Museum of Art** stands at 4525 Oak Street, with other art institutions near it. The **University of Missouri-Kansas City** is here, and of course, all the sweaty fun that goes along with professional teams including the Jazz, the Chiefs, and the Royals. Use http:// www.kcstar.com/sports for finding the game you want and the tickets you need.

On the city's west end, at **West Bottoms**, are the remaining livestock yards of the industry that put Kansas City on the map and created its first baronial class. For a peek at some of those baronial homes and stunning city views, drive up 51st Street to the Jacob Loose Memorial Park neighborhood.

Modeled after sister city Seville, Spain, **Country Club Plaza** (4775 Central; 816-753-0100) is fourteen square blocks of high-end shopping, fine arts, dining, and outdoor enjoyment. The streets are lined with shops with leaded-glass windows and red-tiled roofs that cap inviting doorways, planters and pots of seasonal flowers, and water fountains on the corners.

Developed by the Hall family of Hallmark greeting cards, **Crown Center** (2450 Grand Avenue; 816-274-8444) includes two hotels (the Westin and the Hyatt Regency), fine dining, theaters, and shopping services. It is a magical place at Christmastime, when its outdoor skating rink, the Ice Terrace, is bedecked in holiday splendor and all the lights are on. Featuring one of the largest Christmas trees in the nation, the decorations at the eighty-five-acre center are magnificent.

To learn more about everything that Kansas City can offer, check out http://www.visitkc.com (order a city tour guide there); http://www.palmers guide.com/plaza, for good maps and shopping guides; and http://www.arts links.org for the aesthetic world.

Arrowhead Stadium, Kansas City

NEBRASKA

GRAND ISLAND

In Grand Island, examples of all phases of life on the prairie have been assembled at the **Stuhr Museum of the Prairie Pioneer**, on more than two hundred acres, four minutes north of I-80 at US 281 and US 34, at 3133 West Route 34. Phone 308-385-5316 for seasonal hours and information. The park, with beautiful headquarters, includes an entire sixty-building railroad town, which holds the boyhood home of actor and Grand Island native Henry Fonda. It also exhibits Indian artifacts, and in the summer it displays hundreds of antique automobiles and farm machinery. For other sightseeing suggestions, check out the visitors bureau's Web site, http://www.visitgrandisland.com, or call 800-658-3178.

LINCOLN

If all you really want to do is watch football, make Lincoln, an hour southwest of Omaha, your destination in the fall. The **University of Nebraska**, chartered in 1869, is home to the Cornhuskers, a superb football team, whose every home game move is analyzed by more than seventy thousand live fans, loyally dressed in red. Get tickets at http://www.unl.edu or phone 402-472-3111 or 800-8BIGRED. Lincoln is also the state capital. Called the **Tower of the Plains**, Lincoln's capitol is a four hundred-foot masterpiece designed by New York architect Bertram Goodhue, who also designed West Point. A bronze sculpture of a man sowing grain tops the building; brilliant mosaic murals depicting the state's Indian and pioneer heritage enliven the interior dome. Go to http://www.capitol.org or http://www.ci.lincoln.ne.us for more information.

OMAHA

Omaha, a little more than two hours from Grand Island, is a clean, vibrant city. Although it already had great civic appeal, to celebrate its 150th anniversary in 2004, it launched a $2 billion renovation. Culturally, Omaha is home to the **Joslyn Art Museum** and the **Durham Western Heritage Museum**, two nationally recognized repositories of western art and artifacts. Two blocks south of the Central Park Mall is the city's historic **Old Market Square District**, an area of early Italianate city buildings built for food processing. Tour the **Anheuser-Busch Beer Depot** in this neighborhood, now home to shops and cafés. In September, the city hosts one of the West's premier rodeos, the **River City Roundup**. For all your cravings, check http://www.visitomaha.com or call 866-YES-OMAHA for information and literature.

Old Marketway Passage, Omaha

WHERE TO STAY

IOWA

DES MOINES

The Suites of 800 Locust Street
800 Locust Street
Des Moines, IA 50309
515-288-5800
http://www.800locust.com
$175–$365
In the heart of the city, the Suites has an old world flavor married to all the modern amenities and friendly service we expect. Rooms range from those with fireplaces, window seats, and an atrium to suites. It offers a fitness center and spa services and is four blocks to nightlife.

MISSOURI

KANSAS CITY

Hotel Phillips
106 West 12th Street
Kansas City, MO 64105
816-221-7000/800-433-1426
http://www.hotelphillips.com
$94–$244, call hotel for room configurations and best rates
The Hotel Phillips is an elegant art deco boutique hotel right downtown, close to the Kansas City Convention Center and convenient to theaters, parks, and shopping. Rooms, offering complete guest services, feature European-style beds and bedding. Built in 1931, the hotel is on the National Register of Historic Places, a AAA four-diamond property, and the city's only Preferred Hotels and Resorts member. A $20 million renovation in 2001 has given it high tech mobility; enjoy drinks at the vintage bar. Dinners at Phillips ChopHouse are also highly rated.

Marriott Kansas City Downtown
200 West 12th Street
Kansas City, MO 64105
816-421-6800
http://www.marriott.com
$79–$220
We hope to repeat our sensory experience in our ninth-floor room with its bay window overlooking the convention center street scene. Farther off, in the misty moonlight, loom the soaring blue towers at Bartle Hall that mark the city's western gateway. The room's English floral bedclothes and comfy love seat in red, cream, and green plaid struck just the right note. The hotel has courteous service and a nice pool.

NEBRASKA

COLUMBUS

Traditions Inn Bed and Breakfast
2905 14th Street
Columbus, NE 68601

308-382-4210
http://www.traditionsinn.com
$59–$109 (ask about seasonal packages)
This historic 1890s former private residence, the Dickinson House, has the restaurant and pub, while the adjoining Dutch Colonial-style Maxwell House offers three private guest rooms and one suite. Rooms include period furnishings, private entrances, plush robes, a jacuzzi, whirlpool baths, and a fireplace. Breakfast included.

GRAND ISLAND

Holiday Inn Grand Island I-80
7838 S Hwy 281
Grand Island, NE 68803
308-384-7770
http://www.ichotelsgroup.com/h/d/6c/1/en/hd/grine
$99.95–$110.95
The hotel is located ten miles from Fonner Park, just off Interstate 80, beside the Platte River, and eight miles east of downtown Grand Island. Enjoy a refreshing swim in the indoor pool.

LINCOLN

Embassy Suites Hotel Lincoln
1040 P Street
Lincoln, NE 68508
402-474-1111/800-362-2779
http://www.embassysuites.com
$129–$159, based on availability
Stay right in downtown Lincoln in this sparkling spot with its nine-story-high atrium, waterfalls, and glass-walled elevator. Request an upper floor with views down onto and beyond the city and the UNL campus. From here, you can explore the city and the shops in the MarketPlace. The hotel has an indoor pool, and dining is offered in the hotel's casual, friendly sports bar restaurant, which earns high marks. It is one mile to the awesome state capital.

OMAHA

Hilton Garden Inn
1005 Dodge Street
Omaha, NE 68102
402-341-4400
http://www.hiltongardeninnomaha.com
$80–$159
While in Omaha, stay at the newest city hotel, in the heart of the matter, within walking distance to Old Market shopping and the Qwest Convention Center. The hotel has a nice open-air pavilion restaurant, a lounge, and an indoor heated pool at your toe tips. All the expected perks are yours.

SOUTH SIOUX CITY

Marina Inn and Conference Center
4th and B Street
South Sioux City, NE 68776
402-494-4000
$59–119
Right in the heart of the city, overlooking the Missouri River, is this fine 181-room hotel, with all the wished-for amenities and an indoor pool. Kahill's restaurant, on the premises, overlooks the water. Take advantage of the paved and lighted Riverwalk or relax in the shade of the garden terrace. Complimentary airport shuttle for all high-flying travelers.

WHERE TO WINE & DINE

IOWA

DES MOINES

801 Steak and Chop House and the Embassy Club
801 Grand Avenue, Suite 200
Des Moines, IA 50309
515-288-6000
http://www.800SteakandChop.com
$20.95–$44.95
Some of the city's finest dining is found at the hotel's 801 Steak and Chop House and the Embassy Club on an upper floor of the Suites of 800 Locust Street, with its spectacular views.

The Royal Mile
210 4th Street
Des Moines, IA 50309
515-280-3771
$10.95–$$21.95
Enjoy the brews in this traditional English pub, which has twenty-six beers on tap and a selection of eighty others. The dinner menu—bangers and mash, fish and chips, and more—will even please British diners.

Splash Seafood Bar and Grill
303 Locust Street
Des Moines, IA 50309
515-244-5684
$19.95–$49.95
It has won four stars from Des Moines dining guides, acclaim from residents, and has earned *Wine Spectator* awards regularly since 2001, all for its delicious, fresh-daily menu and wine selections. Seafood is flown in from major fishing ports from Seattle to the Keys and served creatively with delicious island resort themes. Whimsical decor prevails; request an atrium table, and don't let the eleven-foot mounted mako shark scare you.

MISSOURI

KANSAS CITY

Fiorella's Jack Stack Barbecue
101 W. 22nd Street, Suite 300 (Wyandotte Street)
Kansas City, MO 64108
816-472-7427
http://jackstackbbq.com
$8.95–$26.95
You can't be in the beef capital without doing a serious barbecue dinner. We've never had it this perfect. This newest Jack Stack is rustic and casual, with natural beams, bricks, and stone. We started at the bar, which was pleasantly noisy and very friendly. At our table we enjoyed succulent lamb rib chops and pork ribs. The grilling secret is hickory wood embers in traditional brick ovens. For the nonhops lover, the wine list is well varied. After several samples, we settled down with an Australian Shiraz to go with the lamb.

The Phoenix Piano Bar and Grill
302 W. 8th Street
Kansas City, MO 64112
816-472-0001
http://www.phoenixjazz.net/
$12.95–$21.95
You've got to have some jazz in the town that took it international. Clubs are located throughout the city, so catch the mood downtown at the Phoenix, over drinks at the bar or dinner at a table. Try the amazing blackened salmon entrée. Go online at http://www.experiencekc.com for information about the Jazz Museum and other clubs, and make a full night of it.

12th Street Lounge
Marriott Kansas City Downtown
200 West 12th Street
Kansas City, MO 64105
816-421-6800
http://www.marriott.com
Appetizers from $4.95
For spinning the night away, the Marriott has its cozy, contemporary 12th Street Lounge, an energetic niche with live music and snappily dressed couples showing off on the dance floor.

The Wyandotte Café
7833 State Avenue
Kansas City, KS 66112
913-788-7851
Breakfast from $3.99
Horse people aren't famous for all night partying; you're much more likely to see them at breakfast, either in the racetrack café or somewhere nearby that serves manly portions of pancakes, omelets, and hash browns. Only ten minutes from the track, the Wyandotte Café, with its retro 1950s red, black, and white interior and its hot rod, jitterbug, Elvis, and Marilyn themes, often serves the Woodlands crowd. It's open twenty-four hours.

NEBRASKA

COLUMBUS

Traditions Inn
2905 14th Street
Columbus, NE 68601
308-382-4210
http://www.traditionsinn.com
$8.50–$29.95
This historic 1890s former private residence, the Dickinson House, includes the Tea Room, the Parlor, and the Fireside Room, for high tea and either cozy or formal dining. Plan your trip right and get in on the gourmet wine tasting dinners or mystery theater night, also with dinner.

GRAND ISLAND

The Library Restaurant & Lounge
2530 Saint Patrick Ave.
Grand Island, NE 68803
308-381-1115

$9.99–$15.99

Just north of Conestoga Mall (at Hwy. 281 and 13th Street), the ever-popular Library features steak, naturally, and cuts their beef right on the premises. The Library opened in the 1970s, and the old bookshelves that lined the walls are still there, still filled. Diners do read on the premises, but you won't need a library card because the books stay here.

LINCOLN

Vincenzo's (in Haymarket)
808 P Street
Lincoln, NE 68508
402-435-3889
$9 and up

In Lincoln's historic Haymarket District, this dressy dinner spot probably serves the finest traditional Italian entrées in the city. One of the most popular dishes is the chicken Soto, a sautéed chicken breast with melted mozzarella and a rich, spicy tomato sauce. Before dinner, enjoy the neighborhood's galleries, shops, outdoor cafés, and bars.

OMAHA

The Passport Restaurant
1101 Jackson Street
Omaha, NE 68102
402-344-3200
http://www.passport-restaurant.com
$21.95 and up

In Omaha, walk from the Hilton Garden Inn five blocks to the Passport, in Old Market, where the motto is "Don't serve the customer, pamper him." Or her. The menu is both heartland and international, with delectable seafood and steaks and culturally exotic flavors in dishes such as the Spanish paella and chicken Taipei. The Passport's bold columns, glossy floors, and high draped ceilings create a handsome space with creative nautical hints. It offers live music throughout the evening.

SOUTH SIOUX CITY

Kahill's Steak, Fish, and Chophouse
(at Marina Inn and Conference Center)
4th and B Street
South Sioux City, NE 68776
402-494-5025
$11.95–$32.95 (market price for lobster)

Kahill's, overlooking the Missouri River, features a warm, contemporary setting for its wide range of entrées, including halibut, lamb chops, top sirloin, and other classics. Sunday brunch is $10.95 for adults, with champagne-pouring after 12:00 p.m. Reservations suggested on weekends and Sundays.

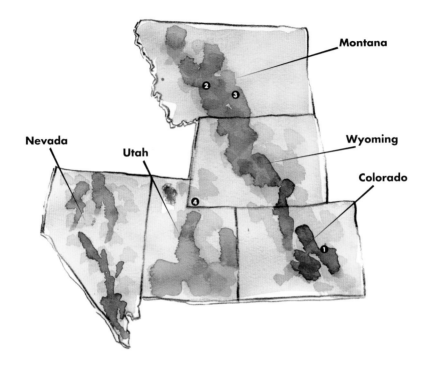

WEST MAP LEGEND

Colorado
❶ Arapahoe Park
(Aurora)

Montana
❷ Montana ExpoPark
(Great Falls)

❸ Yellowstone Downs
(Billings)

Wyoming
❹ Wyoming Downs
(Evanston)

THE WEST

*I*n the majestic western landscapes of white-capped mountain ranges, red earth canyons, and verdant river valleys, the prized horse has long been the small, muscular, fast-sprinting quarter horse. Considered the first breed native to America, the quarter horse developed early among Virginia horsemen; the first official quarter horse race took place there in the late 1600s. As Americans moved west, so did the horse. Given the quarter horse's characteristic easygoing nature and good herding ability, cowboys and ranchers throughout the West and the Southwest depended on the fast, sturdy breed for driving huge herds of livestock across vast grazing lands.

Western racing, too, featured the quarter horse—along with the Appaloosa and the paint—whether speed was tested on the state fair track or across an open pasture. But the appearance of Thoroughbreds at western races was inevitable, both for the sheer sport of competition and because Thoroughbred racing was more lucrative and more prevalent elsewhere in the United States. Today, the combination of Thoroughbred and quarter horse competitions is as much a part of the West as the Stetson, the silver belt buckle, the seasoned Wranglers, and the dusty-toed boots.

COLORADO

ARAPAHOE PARK (AURORA)

Metropolitan Denver sprawls eastward, into the prairie. Out here, about fifteen miles southeast of the heart of Denver, a sign announces: Aurora, Colorado. Founded in 1891, during the height of the silver-mining boom, Aurora is Colorado's third largest city, a center for technical and manufacturing businesses. Small farms stand out between subdivisions, and stars are bright in the nighttime sky. At Aurora's eastern edge, the prairie creeps back in, reclaiming the landscape. Here, on the rim of the vast plain, where the horizon is delineated by the sky, lies Arapahoe Park.

Arapahoe Park was built in 1982, closed in 1983, and reopened nearly a decade later to replace Centennial Park, which had closed in 1985, in Littleton. Roadblocks to Arapahoe's success included casino competition and the track's remote location. There is no easy way to get here, no major interstate

Judging the competitors

dumping people off at the front door. From Aurora you continue east, as if you were going to Kansas.

The track's isolation has hindered its public visibility, literally and figuratively. Arapahoe is currently Colorado's only horse racing track. (Greyhound racing, at several dog tracks in the state, seems to appeal more to the public.) Arapahoe, which offers modest purses for live racing, survives on its simulcast revenue.

The track owner, Wembley U.S.A., has announced plans to develop some of the surrounding land to attract more people, and the corporation has applied for video slots. Approval now hangs on the

All even at the Arapahoe start

vote of the people. With the right mix of enticements, those who drive out here will discover that Arapahoe is a hidden gem. The facility is clean and bright, the lawns neat and trim, and the vast open spaces that surround the buildings offer a calming respite from urban cityscapes.

Stretching for the wire, Montana State Fair

MONTANA

MONTANA EXPOPARK (GREAT FALLS)

Racing at Montana's two longest meets—Montana ExpoPark in Great Falls and Yellowstone Downs in Billings—typifies classic racing in the West, where quarter horses dominate the meets and riders hold other industry jobs such as horseshoeing. In 2005, Montana racing opened at the state fair in July, at ExpoPark, for a ten-day meet. The racetrack at ExpoPark takes up a small section of the 130-acre state fairgrounds property on the west side of the Missouri River, near downtown. Well in advance, reserved season dining is snapped up, at $150 for a table for four. The grandstand gets crowded, too, with beer and cold drinks flowing. Here

as elsewhere in the state, the purses are small but growing, recently ranging from $2,500 to $20,000 and sometimes higher. A typical ten-race card at any of the tracks will see mixed breeds appearing back to back throughout the afternoon, wild three hundred–yard dashes followed by 5-furlong and 1-mile races.

All year long, ExpoPark hosts activities of all sorts, reflecting not only the Old West but the modern West as well. The state fair, craft fairs, trade shows, agricultural events, and livestock shows and sales fill the pavilions. The state's Pro Rodeo circuit, a heavily attended competition, holds the finals here. Even in winter, when the plains are one long blanket of snow, the indoor arena is open for horseback riding and jumping. Address: 400 Third Street NW, Great Falls, MT 59404; phone: 406-453-

SNAPSHOT - ARAPAHOE PARK

Description: A 1-mile dirt track with two chutes and a 1,029-foot homestretch is the stage for a mixed program of Thoroughbreds and quarter horses.
Season: Early June to late August
Address: 26000 East Quincy Avenue, Aurora, CO 80016
Phone: 303-690-2400/(fax) 303-690-6730
Web site: http://www.wembleyco.com
Nearest airport: Denver International Airport (DEN)
Getting there: East of Denver. From I-70, get on East 470 Tollway (exit number 289). Head toward Colorado Springs/Fort Collins. After approximately seven miles, exit at East Quincy Avenue (exit 13). Turn left (east) onto East Quincy Avenue. Track is approximately two miles ahead.
Admission: Free; general admission on live-racing weekends: $3.00
Parking: Free
Fine dining: Turf Club, Clubhouse
Casual fare: Concessions located throughout the stands
Spirits: Drinks available in dining areas and at numerous bar stations
Extras: Outdoor pavilion for picnics and special events, banquet facilities available for groups, live entertainment on special days, gift shop

0080/(fax) 406-453-0080; Web site: http://www.mtexpopark.com.

YELLOWSTONE DOWNS (BILLINGS)

The racing here at MetraPark, in Billings, follows on the heels of MontanaFair, a large regional agricultural fair staged on the Metra grounds. As the host of Montana's longest horse racing meet, Yellowstone Downs wraps it up for horsemen and race fans alike with its late August through late September program. Leaves are tipped in warm autumn colors, set in by cooler days. This time of the year, Yellowstone Downs takes its chances with the weather. Rainstorms may occasionally cancel the races, which also cancels the purses, as by state regulation lost race days cannot be made up. Like the skies overhead, the racing scene at this south-central Montana venue is anything but static. Recently, DreamWorks Pictures showed up to borrow Speak in Code, a bay gelding stabled here, for a small role in their movie *Dreamer* (2005). Address: 308 Sixth Avenue N., P.O. Box 1138 Billings, MT 59103; phone: 406-256-2449/406-869-5251 (during race season)/(fax) 406-633-2503; general Web site for MetraPark: http://www.metrapark.com.

The state has three other, very brief, meets: the Western Montana Fair and Races in Missoula, for six days in mid-August (406-421-3247; http://www.westernmontanafair.com); the Northwest Montana Fair in Kalispell, for two weekends in August (406-758-5810; http://www.nwmtfair.com); and the Eastern Montana Fair in Miles City, a three-day meet that runs in conjunction with the exciting, annual Bucking Horse Sale (406-232-9554). The State Board of Horse Racing has recently suggested that Montana's five active racetracks consolidate into a single, longer annual meet in Billings. The fundamental issue for everyone concerned is how best to both sustain the sport and increase the purses. Montana racing is hobbling along for the moment, but none of the tracks is thriving. Without *some* new plan, few would argue, Montana racing may limp along to its final halt.

WYOMING

WYOMING DOWNS (EVANSTON)

Cruising through Wyoming in the summer? Perhaps on I-80 en route to Cheyenne for the world's largest rodeo, or heading north to Jackson Hole or south from Yellowstone? If you checked yes even once, you just got lucky. Wyoming Downs, ten miles north of Evanston, in southwest Wyoming, is easily within freeway reach.

Celebratory group at Yellowstone Downs

Tight finish, Wyoming Downs

Owned by the Phoenix Leisure Corporation, Wyoming Downs is barely twenty years old. Under the flat roof, the open-air grandstand can seat 2,500 people during its nineteen-day summer meet, which ends before the rapid onset of fall. Across the 7-furlong oval, the Rocky Mountain foothills ramble along the horizon. Sun shadows chase each other, purple and gold, across the rolling vista. The infield is a veritable refuge for wildlife, the pond inhabited by ducks and geese.

Quarter horses compete in derbies and futurities running the spectrum of prize money from $1,000 to $100,000 for the Silver Dollar Futurity. Wyoming Downs's purses for Thoroughbreds are modest; the biggest prizes up for grabs are a pair of $5,000 races. Most of the Thoroughbreds compete in claiming races, with claiming prices as low as $1,600 and winning purses around $1,000. Still, the track has attracted its share of big names in the Thoroughbred

SNAPSHOT - WYOMING DOWNS

Description: The open-air grandstand seats 2,500. The track is 7 furlongs.
Season: Late June to late August, Saturdays and Sundays
Address: 10180 Highway 89 North, Evanston, WY 82931; send correspondence to P.O. Box 1607, Evanston, WY 82931
Phone: 307-789-0511/866-681-7223/(fax) 307-789-4614 (race season)
Web site: http://www. wyomingdowns.com
Nearest airport: Evanston, WY (EVW); Salt Lake City, UT (SLC)
Getting there: On Highway 89 approximately ten miles north of Evanston
Admission: General, lower-level apron (open-bleacher seating): $5; reserved seating, covered upper grandstand: $7; reserved seating, covered lower grandstand: $8
Fine dining: Clockers Corner, reservations advised
Casual fare: fast food concessions stands on both levels of the grandstand
Spirits: bars on both level of the grandstand
Extras: Military day, U.S. flag giveaway, fireworks, handicapping contests with cash prizes, charity drives

Close company against the Rockies' foothills

world. In 1989, legendary rider William "The Shoe" Shoemaker made a stop here as part of his farewell tour. Trainer Jeff Mullins, who saddled 2004 and 2005 Kentucky Derby entrants Castledale (Ireland) and Buzzards Bay, got his start here. Indeed, Wyoming Downs is the perfect starting point for a new face in the industry, a training ground of sorts. The meet runs for two months of Saturday and Sunday racing, and the track packs as much action and attraction into those dates as it possibly can. As a result, attendance is decent throughout the meet, with horsemen, gamblers, and families traveling from the four points to enjoy a bit of fun at the races.

WILLIE SHOEMAKER

When the news came across the wires that Bill Shoemaker had died in his sleep, I just grabbed my coat and took a walk in the early fall sunshine. For me, Shoemaker (1931–2003) represented the best of racing's golden age. Back then "The Shoe" rode larger than life and coast to coast. My god, he rode old Silky Sullivan and Gallant Man and Round Table. He rode Damascus and Ack Ack and my all-time favorite, John Henry. He shattered the world record for victories in a single season at the ripe old age of twenty-one.

Shoemaker's farewell tour at Wyoming Downs

Then the "good old boy" with magic hands and quiet countenance turned it up a notch. There's Willie flashing across the finish line at Churchill Downs under a brilliant hand ride in the 1955 Kentucky Derby. There's Willie bullying his way along the inside rail aboard Bad N Big in the Longacres Mile. Old Willie boy (as my granny used to call him) rode enough winners that if you put them end to end, he would have ridden three times around the circumference of the earth and still crossed the finish line by five o'clock.

The Shoe was king of cool, an icy-veined, diminutive sphinx who didn't move his horse until it was "time," and then he found a tiny sliver of light on the rail and blew by the chalk horse at the wire. He had the softest hands that the sport of kings will ever know, and somehow he got his mounts to run with the wind and not through the wind, as if he aligned himself with the forces of nature like other jockeys adjust their stirrups. Shoemaker beat his rivals with finesse and timing. He pummeled them with patience, stalked the pace horse like a ghost that wouldn't go away, and found the wire a tick before the devil knew he was home free.

Even now, I see him lean across time and space and ask for it all and, as the body of horse and rider become one, make straightaway for some inner rail and a sliver of just-appearing light, and some distant wire where we go when Always is. —Larry Lee Palmer

WEST TRAVEL SECTION

BELOW, YOU'LL FIND A MILEAGE CHART LISTING THE DISTANCE BETWEEN THE REGIONAL RACETRACKS AND ALL THE CITIES DISCUSSED IN THE FOLLOWING TRAVEL SECTION. THE CITY OR CITIES CLOSEST TO A TRACK ARE INDICATED BY AN X.

COAST TO COAST	Denver, Colo.	Evanston, Wyo.	Great Falls, Mont.
Arapahoe Park (Colo.)	X 25 miles	470 miles	790 miles
Montana Expo Park (Mont.)	775 miles	610 miles	X * miles
Western Montana Fair and Races (Mont.)	900 miles	565 miles	X 205 miles
Wyoming Downs (Wyo.)	460 miles	X * miles	620 miles
Yellowstone Downs (Mont.)	550 miles	600 miles	X 220 miles

*The racetrack is located inside or within 10 miles of the city limits.

MUST SEE / MUST DO

COLORADO

DENVER

Denver, commonly known as the Mile High City, sits on the high plains just east of the foothills of the Rockies. To the west is a dramatic skyline. To the east, the heat shimmers away to the flat horizon. It's a city of history and youth, of graceful aging and urban sprawl. Originally founded in 1858, Denver started its brawling life as part of the Kansas Territory. Four years later, after the creation of the Colorado Territory, Denver was incorporated as a city. From its dusty, tumultuous birth, Denver has grown into one of the largest cities in the country and a great tourist destination.

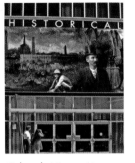

Colorado History Museum

For visitors wanting to learn more about Denver's history, the city has several museums, including the **Colorado History Museum** (1300 Broadway; 303-866-3670; http://www.coloradohistory.org), the **Denver Museum of Nature and Science** (2001 Colorado Boulevard; 303-322-7009; http://www.denverartmuseum.org), the **Black American West Museum & Heritage Center** (3091 California Street; 303-292-2566; http://www.blackamericanwest.org), and the **Museo de las Americas** (861 Santa Fe Drive; 303-571-

4401; http://www.museo.org). Younger visitors will enjoy the **Children's Museum of Denver** (2121 Children's Museum Drive; 303-433-7444; http://www.mychildsmuseum.org) and the **Denver Museum of Miniatures, Dolls & Toys** (1880 Gaylord Street; 303-322-1053; http://www.dmmdt.com).

Denver also boasts the largest city park system in the nation (call 303-964-2512 for information), 650 miles of paved bicycle paths, and ninety-five golf courses. There are also the **Denver Botanic Gardens** (1005 York Street; 720-865-3500; http://www.botanicgardens.org), the **Denver Zoo** (2300 Steele Street; 303-376-4800; http://www.denverzoo.org), and the **Downtown Aquarium** (700 Water Street; 303-561-4450; http://www.downtownaquariumdenver.com). If shopping and strolling through the big city streets are what you like, Denver has the tenth largest downtown in the United States, the heart of which is a mile-long pedestrian walkway lined with shops and outdoor cafés, the **16th Street Mall** (303-534-6161; http://www.denver.org). Denverites are passionate about sports; seven national teams, from baseball to soccer teams, call the city their home base. Hearkening to Denver's early roots as cattle and horse country, the rodeo is big as well. Explore http://www.denver.org to find your favorite indulgences.

MONTANA

GREAT FALLS

"The grandest sight I ever beheld," Meriwether Lewis said of the place at the

Denver skyline

Black Eagle Dam, Great Falls

Missouri River where the water drops four hundred feet, roaring down over five spectacular waterfalls. It was June 13, 1805, and he was standing at the Great Falls, a place "truly magnificent and sublimely grand," even to an explorer who had seen more than his share of the extraordinary West. Today, hydroelectric dams tame the falls, yet the wild, rocky spectacle of the upper Missouri remains. Great Falls offers other rare opportunities to immerse yourself in the spirit of the West. Explore the **Missouri River and its trails** (for suggestions, see http://www.thetrail.org and http://www.fs.fed.us/r1/lewisclark), and catch up on Lewis and Clark's Corps of Discovery history. They were the first American explorers here. An interpretive park at the river's edge, **Lewis and Clark National Historic Trail Interpretive Center** (4201 Giant Springs Road, Great Falls; 406-727-8733; http://www.fs.fed.us/r1/lewisclark/lcic), presents natural exhibits and describes the challenges of the Lewis and Clark Expedition through this part of the state.

In 1898, Charles M. Russell arrived in Montana. At the age of sixteen, he was already an artist, wild about everything to do with the West. He painted and sculpted scenes and characters that portrayed the West with detailed realism. His cowboy and western art brought him national acclaim and continues to fetch huge sums. He settled in Great Falls, where you can enjoy the world's largest collection of his works at

the **C. M. Russell Museum**, which includes his log studio and home at 400 13th Street, North Great Falls, 406-727-878. Check the Web site at http://www.cmrussell.org.

WYOMING

EVANSTON

The town of Evanston, which got its start as a railroad camp in 1868, still hints of the Old West, with flat-fronted brick buildings on the main street that sport old ads for merchandise, their paint fading. For the community of eleven thousand, immersion in the horse industry extends well beyond the driveway into Wyoming Downs. Every weekend during the summer, the Uinta County fairgrounds (122 Bear River Drive) is the site of that ubiquitous Western event, **the rodeo** (307-789-4785; http://www.uintacountyfair.com).

Other events include the August **Roundhouse Festival** (at the Roundhouse & Railyards Machine Shop; 307-783-6320), celebrating the town's railroad heritage. You can tour the historic roundhouse (a service facility for locomotives) and railway yards, see a model train show, and listen to stories of the old days. For picnicking, bicycling, hiking, fishing, or bison watching, there is **Bear River State Park** (307-789-6540; http://wyoparks.state.wy.us), located within the city limits. For more information about local activities, go to http://www.evanstonwy.org.

Flaming Gorge National Recreation Area

After leaving the racetrack on our driving tour from California into the West, our next stop was **Rock Springs**, about forty-five minutes east of Evanston, on I-80. Studying our map, we realized we were a long way (but might never be closer than now) from some legendary places we hadn't yet seen. There was nothing to do but establish our base camp hotel and drive on. One day took us south, into **Flaming Gorge National Recreation Area**, a spectacular tract of mountains, canyons, meadows, and forests sprawled across Wyoming and Utah and shaped by the Green River, which eventually hooks up with the Colorado.

South of Jackson, Wyoming

Flaming Gorge Dam, in Utah, controls the upper Green River, turning that section of it into a deep reservoir. The visitor's center, adjacent to the roaring Flaming Gorge dam, offers educational panoramas showing native wildlife, how the dam operates, and other exhibits that we're told change regularly. A vending machine sells packaged drinks and snacks. We drove there on U.S. 191 south from Rock Springs and returned via US 530, traveling north to Green River, Wyoming. A couple of very small towns skirt the state line at Wyoming and Utah, but start out with a full tank of gas and drinking water. The highways in and out are long and winding, and weather can be unpredictable. If you have time, stay a day or two for camping, fishing, and swimming. There are some lodges for those who prefer fresh sheets to sleeping bags, but reserve in advance. Study maps ahead of time, and check the area out in detail at these Web sites: http://www.go-utah.com/Flaming Gorge-National-Recreation-Area; and http://www.utah.com/nationalsites/fla ming_gorge.htm.

On another day, we drove north from Rock Springs to resort **Jackson**, Wyoming, which sits just beside the southern foot of Grand Teton National Park. The town of Jackson is safely described as upscale rustic. Its hideaway vacation mansions and ranch properties shelter many a wealthy American in summer, and in winter, world-class skiing draws the international pros to the region's four major area ski resorts. Downtown, wide plank-board sidewalks lead to numerous familiar high-end shops, many merchandising various western themes. Frequent cultural arts events and political activism are a defining part of community life here. Throughout the compact shopping and business district, good restaurants and cafés abound, along with fine art galleries, sporting goods shops, and plenty of motels and hotels. For all things related to the town of Jackson, look online at http://www.jacksonholenet.com/ or http://www.jacksonhole-skiing.com/ski_resorts.

The **Grand Teton National Park** (http://www.nps.gov/grte) is quite simply magnificent. In addition to the gorgeous scenery, there is something for everyone here: biking, bird watching, hiking, fishing, rafting—the list goes on and on. Enjoy your stay in a lodge or cabin or pitch a tent for a few nights.

WHERE TO STAY

COLORADO

DENVER

The Brown Palace Hotel
321 17th Street
Denver, CO 80202
303-297-3111/800-321-2599
http://www.brownpalace.com
From $199
Located in the heart of downtown Denver, this landmark hotel—with its Tiffany stained-glass ceiling crowning a nine-story lobby—has earned the distinction of being rated four stars. Since 1892, The Brown Palace Hotel has welcomed travelers into the unusual triangular building that it occupies. The 241 guest suites, 33 executive staterooms, and 3 presidential suites have been updated and are meticulously maintained, offering a comfortable, interesting stay. Royalty, presidents, and rock stars have slept within these walls. The Brown Palace Hotel has the added attraction of offering several dining options as well as "ghost tours" in October. According to the hotel staff, "Some guests have never checked out"!

The Grand Hyatt Denver
1750 Welton Street
Denver, CO 80202
303-295-1234/(fax) 303-292-2472
http://GrandDenver.Hyatt.com
Rooms from $94
Starting with its gorgeous, gleaming marble-and-maple lobby, the Grand Hyatt is an exceptional treat for Denver visitors. Located just two blocks from the 16th Street Mall, the hotel's rooms are spotless and comfy, with marble baths and luxurious little personal products to sample. Stay on an upper floor to enjoy views of Denver under the lights at night. There's a presidential suite, fitness center, swimming pool, and 1876, the hotel's fine dining restaurant.

MONTANA

GREAT FALLS

La Quinta Inn and Suites
600 River Drive South
Great Falls, MT 59405
406-761-2600
http:/www/lq.com
$129–159
This hotel has a three-diamond rating from AAA. Here the rooms have river views, and the River's Edge Trail starts just beyond the hotel.

WYOMING

EVANSTON

High Country Inn
1936 Harrison Drive
Evanston, WY 82930

307-789-8980/888-621-3220
$45–$66
Located in the inn is Wyoming Downs's Off-Track Betting and Sports Bar, a lodging sponsor for the track, which simulcasts horse races from around the country. All of its rooms have been recently renovated.

Holiday Inn
1675 Sunset Drive
Rock Springs, WY 82901
http://www.ichotelsgroup.com/h/d/hi/hd/RKSWY
307-382-9200/800-HOLIDAY
$99–$156
If you're traveling to Flaming Gorge National Recreation Area or Jackson, you can make Rock Springs your point of departure. With its indoor pool and Jacuzzi, happy hour setup, and complimentary continental breakfast, the Holiday Inn, convenient to the freeway and downtown alike, offers guests a friendly atmosphere.

WHERE TO WINE & DINE

COLORADO

DENVER

Bistro Vendôme
1424-H Larimer Square
Denver, CO 80202
http://www.bistrovendome.com
303-825-3232
$31–$50
Acclaimed owner-chef Eric Roeder believes in simple sophistication and has earned raves from *Zagat* and *Wine Spectator* for his attention to the details of fine dining. Vendôme feels like Paris, imported, and features hearty plates of classical French fare, but with a lighter touch. With more than sixty French wines stocked in the cellar—and a sampler tasting available—dinner promises to be superb.

Palace Arms
(at the Brown Palace Hotel)
321 17th Street
Denver, CO 80202
303-297-3111/800-321-2599
Entrées $35 and up
Treat yourself to wining and dining in the style of The Brown Palace Hotel. This fine restaurant in the heart of the hotel offers a menu to die for. Start your meal with a salad of seasonal greens; then savor the perfection of the crispy East Coast striped bass. Make sure you save room as you still have an entire dessert menu to browse!

MONTANA

GREAT FALLS

The Cattlemen's Cut Supper Club
369 Vaughn Frontage Road South
Great Falls, MT 59404
406-452-0702
$10.95–$34.95

Established in 1988, Cattlemen's is a Great Falls institution, although diners must look elsewhere for dancing. Make reservations and mingle with a cowboy or two at this supper club, which features steaks and pasta dishes, with full bar service. Open for lunch as well.

WYOMING

ROCK SPRINGS

Log Inn Supper Club
529 B Street (1-80, ext 99)
Rock Springs, WY 82901
307-362-7166
$12.50–$32.00 (market price for lobster)
Out on the interstate just east of Rock Springs, this restaurant with its big, cozy dining room accommodates large crowds who want "real" food. We noticed that some patrons recognized everyone in the house but us. The steaks are good, portions are generous, and a separate bar area also welcomes travelers dining alone.

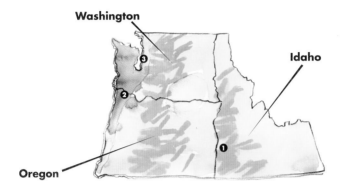

Washington

Idaho

Oregon

Pacific Northwest Map Legend

Idaho
❶ Les Bois Park
(Boise)

Oregon
❷ Portland Meadows
(Portland)

Washington
❸ Emerald Downs
(Auburn)

THE PACIFIC NORTHWEST

Welcome to
LES BOIS
PARK

*I*n 1811, a member of the Astor fur-trading company wrote that Indians in the Dalles area of the Columbia River gathered every year to race their horses and gamble. This may be the first written observation of racing in the Pacific Northwest, a huge region that did not become Oregon Territory until 1848. By then, homesteaders near present-day Tacoma were celebrating the Fourth of July with horse racing and other fun events. As communities grew, hamlets from Oregon to Montana and into Canada measured off their main streets for match racing. Agricultural fairs welcomed horse racing, too, and local meets became week-long regional competitions that traveled from Portland to Great Falls. Across the region, young jockeys—riding at the county fairs—were learning their trade. The best would eagerly move on to bigger towns, better horses, greater thrills.

Most of the organized racing activity in the Pacific Northwest centered in western Washington and Oregon, while western Montana's abundant grasslands made it the region's primary breeding center. The early sport often matched trotters, but by the turn of the century, Thoroughbreds were becoming the steed of choice. Seattle formed its jockey club in 1873, and in 1889, when the chestnut colt Spokane won the Kentucky Derby, the Montana-bred horse drew national attention to the Pacific Northwest. In 1889, the year the Derby first offered the $2 ticket, Spokane paid $34.80, a nice return even by modern standards.

IDAHO

LES BOIS PARK (BOISE)

Southwestern Idaho's Les Bois Park sits on the grounds of the Western Idaho Fair, which opens each fall after the end of Les Bois's Thoroughbred season. Less than five miles northwest of downtown Boise, the racetrack is "just down the river a ways," according to a local fisherman we asked. Built in 1969, the track opened in 1970 with a split meet in the spring and fall. The regular live race meet was canceled in 2005, with summer's live racing confined to three days during the Western Idaho Fair. In 2004 and earlier years, Les Bois hosted a forty-five-day, mixed-race season from early May to mid-August.

While not visible from the grandstand, the Boise River is marked by tall stands of cottonwood trees lining the banks. (*Les Bois* means "the trees.") Les Bois's grandstand and

Gary Stevens

Turf Club seating offer picturesque views of the hills leading into Boise National Forest. By our visit in mid-summer, the grasses covering the rolling hills had dried to dusty brown, and windows in the new houses reflected the sun like golden mirrors.

Average attendance at Les Bois has typically been around two thousand people per night—with grandstand seating capacity at three thousand. On our visit, we watched countless friends and neighbors greet each other with smiles and waves. The locals are just as friendly with visitors. The younger crowd loves Wednesday and Saturday nights, when drink specials, music, and dancing energize the racing scene.

Additional entertainment comes in the form of a children's play area, horseshoe pits, and sprint boats. These miniature boats, each piloted by a full-size driver, race around a narrow channeled course in the infield lake between races.

In past regular meets, in addition to the weekly purses, Les Bois offered a stakes race or stakes trial each weekend during the summer. The main event of the season, the Idaho Cup Weekend, included the Futurity and Derby stakes for Idaho-bred Thoroughbreds. Combined purses of more than $300,000 in prize money were up for grabs over the two days of stakes races.

It's fair to call Les Bois Park a bit remote even from racing competitions on the Pacific Northwest circuit, and its operational status has lately fluctuated nervously. Yet it enjoys recognition as the launching ground for jockey Gary Stevens, a Boise native and son of a successful Idaho racing family. One of America's top-echelon riders, Stevens was inducted into the Racing Hall

Les Bois Park

of Fame in 1997. His achievements include three Kentucky Derby (G1) victories. Winner of the prestigious Eclipse Award in 1998, the boy from Boise claimed his first career win at Les Bois Park in 1979 on Little Star.

OREGON

PORTLAND MEADOWS (PORTLAND)

Celebrating nearly sixty years of horse racing, Portland Meadows has been an Oregon institution since 1946. The track opened, literally, under the brightest of lights, making history on September 14, 1946, as the first track in the nation to offer evening post times. The grandstand had been wired for lights by General Electric, a news-making innovation at the time. Portland Meadows also has the distinction of having the highest number of female riders in the United States. Many of them are strong competitors in the saddle, taking top honors here and going on to exercise and train at bigger stables.

Down the backstretch; Mt. Hood looms

Portland Meadows is located in the Delta Park area just north of downtown, on the north side of the Willamette River and just south of the Columbia River, which separates Oregon and Washington. It sprawls out over one hundred gorgeous acres with pleasant views of Mt. Hood to the southeast, and the hills surrounding

SNAPSHOT - LES BOIS PARK

Description: Les Bois Park, in western Idaho, holds mixed-breed, summer horse racing on the high desert (although no meet was held in 2005 except for the county fair races). This is Out West, it's casual, and it doesn't draw from—or feed—a tight circuit of racetracks. The horsemen's big weekend has been the Idaho Cup, with race purses totaling more than $300,000. The track offers ongoing simulcasts. The track is 6 furlongs, with a 220-yard stretch. There is no turf course.

Season: Until 2005, live racing was held at the Western Idaho Fairgrounds from early May through mid-August. Check the track Web site for updated information.

Address: 5610 Glenwood Road, Boise, ID 83714

Phone: 208-376-3991/(fax) 208-378-4032

Web site: http://www.lesboispark.org, though the site is minimally useful

Nearest airport: Boise Airport (BOI), three miles from downtown

Getting there: Five miles north of Boise, on the Western Idaho Fairgrounds

Admission: Nominal fee

Parking: Free

Fine dining: The Turf Club

Casual fare: The club house; summer barbecue available on the patio

Spirits: Turf Club, clubhouse, and at park concessions

Extras: Dancing and entertainment with night racing, kids' activities

Stretch run at Portland Meadows

the majestic Columbia River Gorge can be enjoyed on clear days.

With its recent cosmetic enhancements, Portland Meadows has a clean new look and feel. The enclosed paddock—practical in a slightly maritime climate—is white and bright, and a new carpet of grass on the apron softens the scene in front of the grandstand. The grandstand seats two thousand, with another six-hundred-plus seats available in the Club House and

SNAPSHOT - PORTLAND MEADOWS

Description: The facility has seating capacity for 2,600. The Portland Meadows dirt track is a 1-mile sand oval, with 6-furlong and ¼-mile chutes. Portland Meadows does not have a turf course.

Season: Generally mid-October through April, approximately eighty days. It offers good, midlevel competition during its fall/winter meet; the $40,000 Portland Meadows Mile purse is the biggest.

Address: Portland Meadows, 1001 North Schmeer Road, Portland, OR 97217

Phone: 503-285-9144/800-944-3127

Web site: http://www.portlandmeadows.com

Nearest airport: Boise Airport (BOI), three miles from downtown

Getting there: Off I-5, just north of the Willamette River, exit east on N. Schmeer Road

Admission: Grandstand: free; clubhouse: $4 per table; Turf Club: free if you dine there, $2.50 if not dining.

Parking: Free

Fine dining: The Turf Club Restaurant

Casual fare: Simulcast Café, Finish Line Café, Clubhouse Café, various concessions

Spirits: Paddock Bar, Simulcast Café, Finish Line Café, Clubhouse Café, Turf Club Bar

Extras: Gift shop, nine-hole infield golf course open in the off-season in the Turf Club on the second and third floors.

Owners and regular fans alike tend to congregate at the Paddock Bar. The bar sits adjacent to the indoor paddock and is tended by "Johnny No-Sweat." Johnny has manned the bar here for more than thirty years; he's an institution, a regular go-to source for statistics, information, and general speculation around the track.

Portland is now an MEC-owned track, which the Oregon racing community hopes will lead to an economic injection on several levels. Live racing takes place on Fridays, Saturdays, Sundays, and Monday afternoons throughout the October-to-April season, offering twenty-nine Thoroughbred stakes. The biggest are the West Oregon Futurity and the Portland Meadows Mile, which is run on the final day of the meet. Twenty-one stakes races for quarter horses are also offered at the track. The facility offers simulcast programs throughout the year.

WASHINGTON

EMERALD DOWNS (AUBURN)

Emerald Downs, spanning 167 acres in one of the last rural areas of central Puget Sound, is truly a jewel. On clear days, Mt. Rainier dominates the skyline to the south, providing a magnificent backdrop for the brightly colored silks racing around the track. With the Auburn hills in the distance and open fields brushing the racetrack on every side, a day at the races is a day in the countryside.

We love Emerald Downs. We were here on opening day in 1995, celebrating the return of Thoroughbred racing to Washington, absent since grand old Longacres had fallen dark three years earlier. We're here so often, a bunk in the grooms' quarters would come in handy. The racing season is nice and long, beginning in mid-April and wrapping up six months later, with

Labor Day 2003, Emerald Downs

Final race at historical Longacres Park, September 21, 1992

respectable handicaps and stake races every month throughout the meet. Important ones include the $75,000 Budweiser Emerald Downs Handicap in June, the $100,000 Mt. Rainier Breeders' Cup in July, and the $250,000 Longacres Mile (G3) in August. The Mile, a tradition carried over from the old Longacres track, has been run since 1935, and many outstanding runners have won it.

The Emerald Downs season ends on an exciting note. Closing weekend, in mid-October, features Washington Cup Day, a stellar afternoon of stakes races open only to Washington-bred horses and featuring the $100,000 Joe Gottstein Futurity for two-year-olds. (Gottstein founded Longacres Park in 1933 and initiated the Longacres Mile; he was inducted into the Washington Thoroughbred Racing Hall of Fame in 2003.) This celebration packs in the racing fans and carries all of the aura and noisy intensity of a regional Breeders' Cup meet, with talented Washington-breds vying for state championship titles.

From the covered grandstand seating at track level to the enclosed

SNAPSHOT - EMERALD DOWNS

Description: A contemporary Emerald Downs has taken over where Longacres Race Track left off. The track is a 1-mile oval, 80 feet wide in the backstretch, 90 feet wide in the homestretch, with 6½-furlong and 1¼-mile chutes. There is no turf course.

Season: Mid-April through mid-October, approximately ninety-two days

Address: 2300 Emerald Downs Drive, Auburn, WA 98001; send correspondence to Emerald Downs, PO Box 617, Auburn, WA 98071.

Phone: 253-288-7000/888-931-8400

Web site: http://www.emdowns.com

Nearest airport: Seattle-Tacoma International Airport (SEA), fifteen miles

Getting there: From Seattle, take I-5 south twenty-five miles to Hwy 18. Exit, go east three miles and enter Hwy 167 N. Exit a half-mile ahead, following signs to racetrack.

Admission: $4; reserved seats in the clubhouse: $6; boxes: $24 for four seats, or $36 for six seats

Parking: Free; preferred: $4; valet: $7

Fine dining: Rainier Restaurant, the Turf Club

Casual fare: Winner's Food Court, Paddock Grille, Track Side Deli, Classics Food Court, Snacks at the Track, Park Concession, Espresso Stands

Spirits: Emerald Lounge, Rainier Lounge, Champions Sports Bar, Blinkers Bar, Clubhouse Bar, Suites Bars

Extras: The Gift Horse souvenir shop, at entry level, with a fine selection of books for the horse lover and a family fun area with kids' activities; Irish Day; Fireworks; Chinook Pass Cigar Lounge

Emerald paddock from fourth floor viewing

upper floors with the clubhouse, Turf Club, and private suites, the race park can accommodate nearly twenty thousand people. This is a bright, spacious, modern facility. Done in silver, burgundy, and teal, with large pots of brilliant flowers ablaze at the entrance, it feels like a new civic sports complex, where exciting contests are about to take place.

The upper levels are reserved for private parties in several different rooms and suites, all with tree house views of the grounds and majestic Mount Rainier. The Turf Club is generally open to members only, though it is available to others occasionally.

The adjacent Turf Club Bar and the Chinook Pass Cigar Lounge—a retreat for true racing traditionalists—make ideal places for a victory celebration. Down at the rail, this racetrack offers an opportunity for race fans to get behind the scenes. If you arrive early enough, the Quarter-Chute Café at the north end of the complex is open to the public, though it's actually the horsemen's kitchen. Guests can come in, have breakfast near the barns, and talk with (we would never eavesdrop on) owners, jockeys, and trainers. With advance reservations, fans can also arrange for a behind-the-scenes tour of the stables and shed rows.

In our early days here, we scuffed our own boots a bit on the backside; in fact, Michael joined a partnership that purchased Game On Ice, a three-year-old in Doc's Racing Stables. The colt was favored for his first race ever. Dressed in our Winner's Circle finery, our party turned out to cheer. It was nerve-racking. He was boxed in from the start, could not break free, and finished a disappointing fifth. A few weeks later, we put him in his second race, a $25,000 claimer, thinking no one would touch him. He was favored, and there we were at the rail when he won! And there we were to say farewell when he was claimed. As Michael recalls philosophically, "Everyone was quite bipolar—happy and depressed at the same time."

SIR BARTON CHALKBUSTERS

In addition to wagers on long shots that often net us some spare change, we like to run a few private contests at Emerald Downs. Our oldest tradition happens on opening and closing days, when we bring a party of close friends. We set our betting limit at $2 per person, per race, and we keep precise records. At the end of the day, the loser—the decision might come down to dimes—takes us all to dinner. Sir Michael will not forget the mere 20¢ loss that cost him $900 as the host of a small victory party at Seattle's sumptuous El Gaucho steakhouse. Our other favorite contest is Chalkbusters, in which we bet on the horse to come in last, and the stakes, if you will, are increased to buying dinner with endless glasses of champagne.

PACIFIC NORTHWEST TRAVEL

BELOW, YOU'LL FIND A MILEAGE CHART LISTING THE DISTANCES BETWEEN THE REGIONAL RACETRACKS AND ALL THE CITIES DISCUSSED IN THE FOLLOWING TRAVEL SECTION. THE CITY OR CITIES CLOSEST TO A TRACK ARE INDICATED BY AN **X**.

	Boise, Idaho	Portland, Ore.	Seattle, Wash.
Emerald Downs Race Track (Wash.)	510 miles	155 miles	**X** 25 miles
Les Bois Park (Idaho)	**X** ∗ miles	425 miles	500 miles
Portland Meadows (Ore.)	430 miles	**X** ∗ miles	170 miles

∗The racetrack is located inside or within 10 miles of the city limits.

MUST SEE / MUST DO

IDAHO

BOISE

For centuries, Idaho was the undisturbed homeland of several Indian groups. In 1805, Meriwether Lewis and William Clark, the first white men to explore the territory that became our forty-third state, made their transcontinental Expedition of Discovery. Fur trappers, traders, and missionaries came next, followed by miners. Gold was unearthed in 1852, and Boise City sprang up as a supply center. Today, Boise residents cherish the scenic Boise River, which makes the capital city a high desert oasis amid the landscape of barren hills and sprawling farms. Among its early settlers, the Basques continue their rich traditions, especially in the city's Basque Block, which houses a museum, restaurants, and shops.

Boise's **Public Market**, held on North 8th Street, runs Saturdays from mid-April through October. This farmers' showcase is an amazing jumble of growers, craftspeople, and vendors. Along with wonderfully fresh, organically grown produce, the market sells specialty jams and jellies, fresh flowers, paintings, and glassworks. Hungry?

Saint Chapelle Winery

Enjoy crepes made right before your eyes, taste local wines, and sample individual pies.

During the warmer days of the Les Bois race meet, dare to recapture your youth by renting an inner tube at **Barber Park** (located about six miles from downtown on Eckert Road between Warm Springs and Boise Avenues; http://www.cityofboise.org/BoiseRiver) and floating down the river into the city, where shuttle buses will return you to your car for a $2 fee.

For a look at life on Idaho's mining frontier, visit **Silver City** (open May through September), an authentic ghost town seventy-nine miles southwest of Boise, off Highway 78. This mining town dates back to 1864 and boasts more than seventy historic buildings. Food, drinks, a museum, and tours are available.

It would be a crime to leave southwestern Idaho without a taste of its booming wine industry. Pick up a deli lunch and visit some of the dozen or so vineyards and wineries in the Caldwell area, just twenty miles west of Boise. For specific vineyard and tour information and directions, visit http://www.idahowine.org. For all other Boise travel and entertainment information, visit http://www.boise.org/.

Downtown Boise with Porsche parade

OREGON

PORTLAND

From its roots as an 1840s trading center, Portland has grown thoughtfully, even cautiously, protecting and balancing the city's natural resources with urban needs. Much of Portland's charm lies in its unexpected blend of business and cultural attractions. It has beautiful natural spaces, such as the sprawling green retreat of Tom McCall Waterfront Park at the edge of the Willamette River; the elm-shaded paths and benches in the South Park Blocks; and the five thousand acres of natural wilderness of Forest Park, which is inside the city limits. Fountains, gardens, and public art tucked into unexpected spaces also demonstrate how creatively a city can enhance its visual dimension.

No finer example of this creativity exists than the city's acclaimed **Pearl District**, an enclave of art galleries, lofts, and studios that took over and revitalized the old warehouse district (a hidden pearl, thus the name), loosely demarked (at present) by Naito Parkway, NW Broadway, West Burnside, and the 405 freeway. Some call it the

Oregon Historical Society

new Soho. Treat yourself to its **First Thursday Gallery Walk** evening event(http://www.firstthursday .org; monthly), which includes open houses at seven studios and galleries. Great restaurants, cafés, bookstores, outdoor musical events, and a nearly year-round farmers' market add to the Pearl's exuberant mix of street activities.

For shopping, visit **Pioneer Place**, a four-block retail center on SW Morrison between 3rd and 5th avenues, downtown (503-228-5800). Upscale shops include Tiffany & Co. and Saks, with nearly one hundred other boutiques or franchises. Then head south to SW Park Avenue to explore two of Portland's oldest and best-loved cultural institutions: the Oregon Historical Society and the Portland Museum of Art.

Changing exhibits from the collections of the **Oregon Historical Society**, 1200 SW Park Avenue (503-222-1741, twenty-four-hour events line 503-306-5198; http://www.ohs.org; closed Mondays), present the wonderful diversity of regional and state history. Lectures, seminars, and even the society's holiday parties offer other opportunities to sharpen your understanding of Pacific Northwest subjects. Just west across the park is the oldest art museum in the Pacific Northwest, **The Portland Art Museum**, located at 1219 SW Park

Downtown Portland looking east

Avenue (503-226-2811; http://www .portlandartmuseum.org; closed on Mondays). Founded in 1892, the museum has collections that include representative works ranging from pre-Columbian to contemporary American art and sculpture, with ongoing exhibits.

Portland, which is surrounded by rivers, volcanic mountains, and forests, is less than two hours from the Pacific Ocean, whose sandy beaches and commercial fishing villages are worthy of a day trip. Northeast of the city lies the cavernous and spectacular **Columbia River Gorge** and **Multnomah Falls**, the second highest falls in the country, cascading some 620 feet. Check http://www.trips.stateoforegon. com/multnomah_falls/ for details.

WASHINGTON

SEATTLE

Carved from the dense evergreen forests that hug the shores of Puget Sound, Seattle is an international port city with a rich history in lumber, fishing, and trade. Its boom eras—a shipping industry that exploded during the Yukon Gold Rush, the rise of the aerospace industry, and the birth of a software giant—have helped define the city as cosmopolitan, energetic, and sturdy. It's easy to navigate, and there is a lot to do. Fly in early or stay over after the races, and make your Seattle racing vacation one for the books. Despite Seattle's reputation for perpetual rain, it's more often cloudy than wet, and the weather is usually gorgeous in the summer and fall.

Ferry crossing Puget Sound

Seattle Center with Space Needle

A day in the city should begin with a walk through the seafood and produce stalls of **Pike Place Market** (206-682-7453), starting at its landmark entrance sign at Pike Place and Pike Street, where an information kiosk can help orient you. (Parking is easiest at the market garage at 1531 Western Avenue.) Established in 1907, the internationally celebrated market—now nine acres of fresh produce, fish, meats, gifts, crafts, cafés, street musicians, and services—has remained a venue selling directly to the consumer.

End your tour of the market by climbing down the Pike Street Hill to Alaskan Way, which hugs the waterfront, and let your senses catch all the sounds and smells of life and commerce along the piers and shops on **Elliott Bay**. Stop for refreshments at one of the harbor-view restaurants overlooking the water. Here you can board a **Washington State Ferry** (http://www.wsdot.wa.gov/ferries) crossing the sound to Bainbridge Island, for a thirty-five-minute ride with terrific views of this northwest water wonderland. When you dock on Bainbridge, it's an easy walk to nice shopping and dining options.

Back on the mainland, take the waterfront trolley to nearby historic **Pioneer Square**. The oldest part of the city, it's a vibrant historic district bound by Alaskan Way, Jackson Street, Fourth Avenue, and Yesler Way. An ambient area of preserved brick buildings and shaded benches for resting and people watching, it's a little mecca of bookstores, antique shops, and galleries. At night, Pioneer Square pulsates with energy from its dozens of bars, nightclubs, and restaurants.

From Pioneer Square, it's a mere slide into first. Sports fans won't want to miss **Safeco Field**, home of the Seattle Mariners, at 1250 First Avenue (206-628-0888). It was recently voted one of the best parks in baseball. The new **Seahawks Stadium** (206-381-7816) is just next door, and the Seattle Supersonics (206-281-5800) plays at **Key Arena** at the Seattle Center on top of the hill.

For your aesthetic fix, don't miss the **Seattle Art Museum** (100 University Street; 206-654-3100; http://www.seattleartmuseum.org), which displays impressive permanent collections of Asian, African, Northwest Coast Native American, modern, and European art. Its ongoing lectures and art film series offer further stimulating experiences. The **Frye Art Museum**, on First Hill (704 Terry Avenue; 206-622-9250; http://www.fryeart.org), specializes in international and representational art of the nineteenth century forward, with contemporary art as well. Its Gallery Café is a charming spot for a light meal. Admission to the Frye is always free.

Head east out of the city to Woodinville, an essential destination for tasting some of Washington's best varietal wines. Several fine wineries and a brewery are within easy distance of each other. Get a map at http://woodinvillewinecountry.com, and call wineries to confirm tasting hours. Start at **Chateau Ste. Michelle**, 14111 NE 145th Street (425-415-3300), one of the state's oldest and largest wineries. Go next to **Columbia Winery**, 14030 NE 145th Street (425-488-2776), established in 1962. There are more than a dozen others in the area. If your taste runs instead—or also—to hops, the **Redhook Ale Brewery**, 14300 NE 145th Street (Woodinville; 425-483-3232), with its enticing Forecasters Pub, should put the final frothy head on your field trip.

WHERE TO STAY

IDAHO

BOISE

Doubletree Hotel Boise Riverside
2900 Chinden Boulevard
Boise, ID 83714
208-343-1871/800-222-8733
http://www.boiseriverside.doubletree.com
$90–$170
A gorgeous spot along the river, the Doubletree Riverside is a lush retreat from the city. Mature trees, landscaping, and a cool river breeze create a welcome respite from the summer heat. The hotel features the Riverside Grill for casual all-day dining, with breakfast and lunch buffets. The lounge, Club Max, offers drinks and entertainment nightly.

Grove Hotel
245 S Capitol Boulevard
Boise, ID 83702
208-333-8000/888-961-5000
http://www.grovehotelboise.com
$99–$159

To enjoy the action in the heart of the city, we recommend the Grove Hotel, adjacent to the Bank of America Centre, a multipurpose convention center and sports arena. Boise's only AAA four-diamond property, the Grove offers an elegant nouveau-European style. It boasts four unique restaurants: Emilio's, with sophisticated ambiance and regional cuisine; the Zone Bar & Grill for casual fare; The Bar, with an extensive martini and cocktail list; and Satori Sushi.

OREGON

PORTLAND

Benson Hotel
309 SW Broadway
Portland, OR 97205
503-228-2000
http://www.bensonhotel.com
$140–$170

Built in 1912, the Benson Hotel, on the National Register of Historic Places, is gorgeous. The rich walnut woodwork, crystal chandeliers, and Italian marble staircase provide old-world elegance without being stuffy. Spacious rooms overlook the hustle and bustle of downtown. The Benson is home to Portland's El Gaucho Steakhouse, as well as the London Grill and a jazz club in the lobby lounge.

Hotel Vintage Plaza
422 SW Broadway
Portland, OR 97205
800-263-2305
http://www.vintageplaza.com
$149–$189

The hotel offers exquisite lodging options, from its above-the-fray starlight rooms, garden spa rooms, and townhouse suites to its pleasingly appointed "regular" deluxe rooms with their rich, bold decor and Oregon wine-country motifs. In the heart of the city, the Vintage is just blocks from many of the region's landmarks. The Vintage's cozy and rustic Italian Pazzo Ristorante makes a great spot for drinks and dinner, complete with an authentic wood-burning pizza oven.

WASHINGTON

SEATTLE

The Alexis Hotel
1007 First Avenue
Seattle, WA 98104
866-356-8894
http://www.alexishotel.com
$165–$279

More than a century old, this charming boutique hotel, located downtown, is on the National Register of Historic Places. Its public spaces and guest rooms feature wonderful northwest art and seasonal art exhibitions.

Fairmont Olympic Hotel
411 University Street
Seattle, WA 98101
206-621-1700
http://www.fairmont.com
$319–$359
With its stellar rating, you can't go wrong at the Fairmont, which sits in the heart of the city, surrounded by art galleries, museums, shops, and bookstores, barely half a mile from the waterfront and sports complexes. From its majestic lobby, grand double staircases lead to 450 spacious suites and guest rooms. Off the lobby are its two widely acclaimed restaurants, The Georgian and Shucker's Oyster Bar.

The Sheraton Seattle Hotel and Towers
1400 Sixth Avenue
Seattle, WA 98101
206-621-9000
http://www.sheraton.com
$169–$379
The Sheraton, too, suits our discriminating taste, with its wraparound views, sumptuous rooms, lavish baths, and workout and spa facilities. Join the regular crowd for a drink in the contemporary Gallery Lounge. The Seattle Convention Center (aka Washington State Convention and Trade Center) is a jump away at 800 Convention Place (206-694-8000), so cruise through its public spaces and enjoy the art exhibitions, free musical performances, and a Galleria shop or two. The convention center's Web site (http://wsctc.com) is a thoroughly useful window guide to what's happening in the city.

WHERE TO WINE & DINE

IDAHO

BOISE

Bardenay
610 Grove Street
Boise, ID 83702
208-426-0538
http://www.bardenay.com
$6.95–$18.95
Don't leave Boise without stopping at Bardenay, in the Basque Block, probably Boise's most popular nightspot. Named for the sailor's term for cocktail, Bardenay serves a full menu of inventive bar food and cocktails. On our visit, the crowd spilled merrily out onto the sidewalk, overflowing even the outdoor seating area. Bardenay is one of very few restaurant-distilleries in the nation. Along with the home-brewed alcohol, fresh-squeezed juices fill fruit drinks.

The Cazba
211 North 8th Street
Boise, ID 83702
208-381-0222
http://www.cazba.com
$8.95–$27.95
If your palate craves a spicy entrée, you can find fabulous Greek and Eastern Mediterranean cuisine at The Cazba. The large menu includes gyros, shish kabobs, and wraps, all served in generous portions. The charmingly appointed restaurant offers indoor seating as well as a large street-side dining area.

OREGON

PORTLAND

Jake's Famous Crawfish
401 SW 12th Avenue
Portland, OR 97205
503-226-1419
$7.95–$31.95
Jake's Famous Crawfish has been a Portland landmark for more than 110 years and is housed in one of the restored buildings we keep raving about, where ceilings soar, regional art climbs the walls, and vintage architectural details create an inviting ambience. Jake's earns high marks among the nation's leading fresh seafood restaurants, with its amazingly extensive menu.

Portland City Grill
111 SW Fifth Avenue
Portland, OR 97204
503-450-0030
http://www.portlandcitygrill.com
$7.95–$89.95
We're happy to quote the Portland City Grill, which boasts "the best view in town," with its roost on the thirtieth floor of the Unico US Bankcorp Tower. The perfect lookout for your geographic orientation, it's open late every night and offers great steaks, seafood, a sushi/sashimi menu, and extensive drink selections. Catch happy hour any day of the week, live piano in the bar, and a friendly clientele.

WASHINGTON

SEATTLE

El Gaucho Steak House
2505 First Avenue
Seattle, WA 98121
206-728-1337
http://www.elgaucho.com
$14.95–$115
Widely known for its top-quality steaks and famed cigar lounge, dark, sexy El Gaucho will satisfy even the hungriest guest. In addition to its prime aged beef, the menu includes seafood, poultry, and lamb entrées. Live music seven days a week, dancing on Friday and Saturday nights, and a full bar make this arguably Seattle's best dining spot.

Waterfront Seafood Grill
2801 Alaskan Way
Pier 70
Seattle, WA 98121
206-956-9171
http://www.waterfrontpier70.com
$14.95–$90
Anchoring the quiet end of Pier 70 on the waterfront, the Waterfront Grill has fabulous sparkling nighttime views of Puget Sound. Its floor-to-ceiling windows offer a 270-degree view of Elliot Bay, Magnolia Bluff, and the Space Needle. During warmer months, ask for a table on the patio. The Waterfront features gourmand everything, from creative appetizers to luscious desserts.

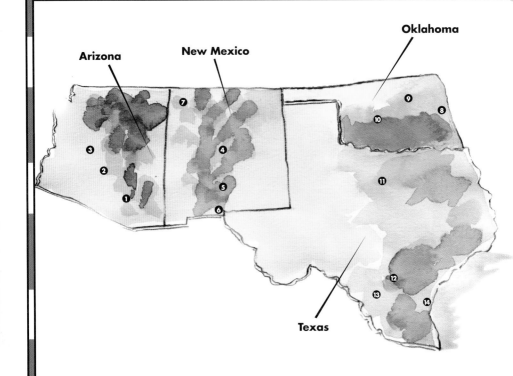

SOUTHWEST MAP LEGEND

Arizona
1 Rillito Downs Park
(Tucson)

2 Turf Paradise
(Phoenix)

3 Yavapai Downs
(Prescott)

New Mexico
4 The Downs at Albuquerque
(Albuquerque)

5 Ruidoso Downs
(Ruidoso)

6 Sunland Park Racetrack
and Casino
(Sunland Park)

7 SunRay Park
(Farmington)

Oklahoma
8 Blue Ribbon Downs
(Sallisaw)

9 Fair Meadows
(Tulsa)

10 Remington Park
(Oklahoma City)

Texas
11 Lone Star Park
(Grand Prairie)

12 Manor Downs
(Austin)

13 Retama Park
(Selma)

14 Sam Houston Race Park
(Houston)

THE SOUTHWEST

I t's a place where sprawling, open range is corralled by rocky river washes and rugged coppery canyons. Summers can be dry. On good days, billowy white clouds drift lazily across the piercing blue sky, and longhorn cattle roam freely. That is, until the cowboy rides up on his quarter horse. The fast, quick mount, introduced into colonial Virginia, was especially bred to endure a long seasonal drive to fresh grazing land and to respond rapidly to control the powerful surge of a herd. So, of course, when the rancher is ready for a little friendly recreation or public competition, his reputation is in part determined by his mount. From southeastern New Mexico to northern Arizona, the county fair circuit has served as his main performance ring.

In the early twentieth century, lured by big money in Thoroughbred competitions, forward-thinking quarter-horse owners expanded into the more lucrative breed. Then came the 1930s, and gambling was spurned in many corners; outlaw racing quietly kept the horses running. In Texas, a few small bush tracks went "under the radar" until the 1980s, when gambling on horse racing was legalized once more. Racing in the Southwest today embraces both Thoroughbreds and sprinters. Notable figures who started their careers in New Mexico, such as former quarter horse trainer D. Wayne Lukas, jockey Mike Smith, and the Asmussen family, who established El Primero Training Center in Laredo, have expanded their reputations well beyond cattle and sagebrush country.

ARIZONA

THE ARIZONA COUNTY FAIRS

Any weekend of the year, from Coconino to Cochise counties, if you go looking for a horse race in Arizona, you can bet your boots you'll find one. There are only three commercial Thoroughbred racetracks in this "land of little rain," as writer Mary Austin called it, and they cover nearly the entire calendar. Toss in the fifteen county fairs that have been hosting races since the late 1800s—with one town racing as early as 1866—and somewhere, you have a date.

The fairground tracks are dirt and the meets are short—usually four days each—cycling from February into October. Counties lacking their own fairgrounds with racetrack facilities hold meets at Rillito Downs Park, Turf Paradise, or Yavapai Downs. All fifteen counties in the state participate, which says much about the long intertwining of horses and people throughout Arizona. The here-and-gone weekend fair meets rope in hundreds of people who may get to see live horse racing only once a year. Attendance at commercial tracks helps perpetuate the Arizona horse industry at the local level. In 2003, 164,000 spectators attended Arizona fair racing, and $18 million total handle changed hands. To match up a weekend of county fair racing before or after your spa getaway, visit http://www.raccom.state.az.us.

RILLITO DOWNS PARK (TUCSON)

In 1943, after two years of operation, the original Tucson racetrack, Hacienda Moltacque, was replaced by what would become Rillito Park, a private horse ranch and training track in the sand beside the Rillito River. Quarter horses were the steed of choice; later, the menu expanded to include Thoroughbreds and occasionally Arabians. Famed trainer Bob Baffert won his first Thoroughbred

Close-up action

race here in 1979 with Flipper Star. Modern Rillito Downs Park, surrounded on all sides now by city, hosts Arizona's first meet of the year, running from January 1 to the first week in March. Horses charge around the ⅝-mile dirt track on Saturdays and Sundays, at 4502 North First Avenue at River Road (520-293-5011). Winter in southern Arizona is usually sparkling clear and delightful. Sip a margarita or gnaw a spicy burrito as the horses run

Impatient for a win

under a sky dappled with clouds sailing over the foothills of the Santa Catalinas. Next thing you know, you're betting the superfecta and counting on real estate money.

TURF PARADISE (PHOENIX)

The camels sprint from the starting line, their riders bent low over their undulating backs. Overhead, palm trees sway in the breeze, the edges of the green oasis stretch toward the sharp-edged mountains. No, we aren't in the Middle East; we're in northwest Phoenix. Thoroughbreds and quarter horses dominate the meet here, but some think they're upstaged during the annual camel and ostrich races.

The race park, which celebrated its fiftieth anniversary in 2005, opened in 1955 on 1,400 acres of desert land and was held by one owner for twenty-five years. Then it changed hands periodically until Jerry Simms bought it in 2000. Most areas of the facility have recently been upgraded, remodeled, or built new, making Turf Paradise a handsome, tropical oasis for a weekend racing getaway. The 2003 season marked its best year in decades, with live attendance jumping 4 percent and handle (wagering) rising 5

Another sunny day, Turf Paradise

Kentucky Derby day, Turf Paradise

percent over the previous year. By the end of the 2004–2005 meet, nearly a million fans had wagered $300 million at the track.

With the Frixenet chilling on ice, Turf Paradise's 167-day live race meet begins in September and circles around until the following May. Racing takes place five days a week; the track is dark on Tuesdays and Wednesdays. The ten featured Thoroughbred stakes held in the fall are mostly at the $40,000 purse level and are followed by the bigger events of winter and spring. February showcases the Turf Paradise Derby, Turf Paradise Handicap, and Arizona Oaks, each offering a $75,000 purse for 2006.

Turf Paradise is on the track to success with its innovative ways. In the summer of 2003, an equine swimming pool was built in the stable area. Holding 140,000 gallons of water, the thirty-by-sixty foot warm water pool offers therapy for six horses at a time, in water twelve feet deep at its deepest end. With the pool's gentle exercise methods, racing officials noted immediate improvements in equine health, which also helped increase field sizes at the track.

YAVAPAI DOWNS (PRESCOTT)

Two hours north of Phoenix, Prescott Downs is neither gone nor forgotten—nor racing horses these days. Here at this 5,400-foot elevation, where ponderosa pine–clad mountains rim the valley and narrow creeks crisscross the land, Thoroughbred racing may have shifted permanently to the jurisdiction of the Yavapai County Fair Association, which has managed it off and on since the 1950s. In 2002, the nonprofit Yavapai Fair opened its contemporary tan-and-brown grandstand and 1-mile dirt racetrack facility—with its new

SNAPSHOT - TURF PARADISE

Description: Billed as Arizona's premier racetrack, Turf Paradise is establishing its reputation as a track to watch, with horses, jockeys, and trainers also enjoying notable successes in California and across the West. The thoroughly remodeled facility looks great, and its amenities are first class. The track is a 1-mile dirt course with a 7-furlong inner turf course. The main stretch is 999 feet.

Season: Late September to mid-May

Address: 1501 W. Bell Road, Phoenix, AZ 85023

Phone: 602-942-1101/(fax) 602-942-8659

Web site: http://www.turfparadise.com

Nearest airport: Phoenix Sky Harbor International Airport (PHX); Tucson International (TIA)

Getting there: Fourteen miles northwest of downtown Phoenix, approximately one mile from Interstate 17

Admission: $2; clubhouse: $4

Parking: Free; valet: extra charge

Fine dining: Clubhouse and Turf Club, offering American and southwestern cuisine. Admission is $5 per person.

Casual fare: The Sandwich Shop, other concessions inside and out

Spirits: Silks Room Bar, other concessions throughout

Extras: Camel and ostrich racing, family fun days, handicapping seminars, concerts

Eye on the prize

name—in Prescott Valley, not far from "old" Prescott Downs. With accommodations for ten thousand people, Yavapai Downs begins its meet on Memorial Day weekend and doesn't let up until Labor Day. During the rest of the year, the new track is a training facil-

ity, and the grounds are used for trade shows, festivals, and many other community events. Racing happens at 10501 Highway 89A, Prescott Valley (928-775-8000; http://www.yavapai downsatpv.com). Rodeo and motorbike events, along with other activities, carry on at Prescott Downs.

NEW MEXICO

THE DOWNS AT ALBUQUERQUE (ALBUQUERQUE)

Watching the races from a table in the glass-walled clubhouse or standing down beside the rail, should your gaze drift toward the horizon there's no mistaking the geography of the place. Beyond the track to the east are the sandstone Sandia (Spanish for "watermelon") Mountains, rosy pink and dotted, seedlike, with cactus climbing the jagged slopes. The New Mexico state fairgrounds have stood on this spot since the 1880s; horse racing arrived in the 1930s, making this the

RACING TO CLASS AT UA

In the course of our travels, we've talked to hundreds of racetrack employees. Time and again, they've said they got into the business because they loved going to the races or being around horses. Retired jockeys or agents regularly move into professional positions at the tracks. Others make a horizontal leap from other industries, such as banking, marketing, or sales. We met only two people who said that after graduating from high school they chose a college where they could formally study the racetrack business. It was virtually impossible to do so until the mid-1970s.

More than thirty years ago, a handful of racing people got together in Tucson and helped develop the University of Arizona's (UA) Race Track Industry Program (RTIP). It is one of the few college-level degree programs in which students can pursue a Bachelor of Science degree with the option of a specialty in racetrack or animal management. Veterinary and equine science programs, of course, have been curriculum staples at colleges and universities—some of them highly prestigious research institutions—for more than a century. Unlike those, the University of Arizona's racing program focuses on other aspects of the industry, such as facility management, marketing, and racing law; or farm management, equine breeding, training, and sales. Since its inception, the school has also hosted an annual industry symposium for professionals in the field, which looks at current and long-range industry issues, a symposium the students organize and manage. The program also offers them opportunities to accept internships at racetracks throughout North America and overseas. For more information on the UA racetrack curriculum or the annual symposium, visit the Web site at http://www.ua-rtip.org.

oldest racetrack in New Mexico. When the casino operation was established in 1999, the Downs, like the state's other three tracks, jumped back into competitive horse racing. The addition of more dates for 2005 helped boost revenues further.

The Downs at Albuquerque claims some of the state's richest racing days, with a meet that opens in early April and wraps up in June. It's the only state racetrack running a live meet on Kentucky Derby (G1) day, and in our experience, if you can't be in Louisville, a live meet anywhere is the second best option. Reflecting its roots as the home of the summer agricultural fair, Albuquerque holds a second meet in the fall, concurrent with the New Mexico State Fair, a big regional event with rodeos, carnivals, music, southwestern food, and exhibits. The seventeen-day fair meet, held in September, draws a lighter crowd; in recent years, typical of the national norm, fairgoers

The view east from the track

have been conservative with their voucher money.

New Mexico is one of the few states where casinos now operate at the racetracks as well as independently. The state viewed the expansion as critical to the health of the horse industry, and it has been. Since 1998, when legislation allowed the tracks up to three hundred slots each, all four state tracks

The Downs

have felt the financial upswing. At the Downs, to spice things up further, a unique card called the Lineage was created a few years back. This day is exclusively for New Mexico–bred horses. The carrot for bettors is its Pick-9 wager, which pays $250,000 to the lucky gambler who can spot nine consecutive winners that day.

RUIDOSO DOWNS (RUIDOSO)

The races at Ruidoso Downs, east of Ruidoso on I-70 (1461 Hwy. 70 West), are the town's biggest attraction. The sixty-day summer meet leans in favor of the quarter horse and draws big crowds of horsemen and race fans from around

Ruidoso quarter horses sprint for the finish.

the state, and well beyond. That is especially the case for the Zia Festival and Labor Day weekend, when the biggest quarter horse race in the country wraps up the meet with the $2 million All-American Futurity. For more information, visit http://ruidosodownsracing.com or call 505-378-4431.

SUNLAND PARK RACETRACK AND CASINO (SUNLAND PARK)

Throughout the Southwest, racing favors the quarter horse. However, it's been several decades now since the Thoroughbred first galloped onto the regional track, and the scales are finding their balance. Sunland Park, in southern New Mexico, is barely a hop over the line from El Paso, Texas. But Sunland got its three-decades-plus lead over racing in the Lone Star State because New Mexico gave an earlier thumbs-up to pari-mutuel wagering. Sunland Park, opened in 1959, is essentially a suburban El Paso casino, where the slots feed the horses. They do so mighty well, with several important races featured during the eighty-day meet, from late November into early April.

SNAPSHOT - THE DOWNS AT ALBUQUERQUE

Description: This no-frills facility is boxy and comfortable. A recent multimillion dollar renovation to the barns expanded its capacity for stabling horses racing on the circuit.
Season: Early April into June; September
Address: 201 California Street NE, Albuquerque, NM 87108; send correspondence to P.O. Box 8510, Albuquerque, NM 87198
Phone: 505-266-5555
Web site: http://www.abqdowns.com
Nearest airport: Albuquerque International Sunport (ABQ)
Getting there: On the state fairgrounds
Admission: Free
Parking: Nominal fee
Fine dining: The Jockey Club
Casual fare: Concessions throughout the facility
Spirits: Jockey Club and several fully stocked bars
Extras: Cash-prize drawings every week; special buffets and menus during the live meet; other seasonal promotions

Sunland at night

Sunland Park is a big contemporary space that blends architectural hints of the old West and old Mexico. The domed exterior is stuccoed in reddish sunset shades. Inside, the racing areas are spacious. The Turf Club offers a view of El Paso and the mountains. One casino level, too, overlooks the track, always an encouraging feature. The Sunland meet features thirty substantial stakes races. Most anticipated are two big races for three-year-olds in late March, scheduled a few weeks ahead of the Kentucky Derby. Colts have a shot at the 1⅛th-mile $500,000 WinStar Derby, and fillies race 1¹⁄₁₆th miles for $250,000 in the WinStar Sunland Park Oaks. These two races are the biggest events in the history of Thoroughbred racing in New Mexico, and they attract contestants mainly from the Southwest. The year 2003 was nationally exciting for Sunland Park. That year, WinStar Derby winner Excessivepleasure went on to capture

SNAPSHOT - SUNLAND PARK RACETRACK AND CASINO

Description: Sunland Park is a big contemporary space that blends architectural hints of the old West and old Mexico. Track is a 1-mile oval, with 1¼-mile and 6½-furlong chutes.
Season: Late November into early April
Address: 1200 Futurity Drive, Sunland Park, NM 88063
Phone: 505-874-5200
Web site: http://www.sunland-park.com
Nearest airport: El Paso International (ELP), twenty minutes away
Getting there: Ten minutes west of downtown El Paso, just off I-10
Admission: Free
Parking: Free
Fine dining: Riley's Restaurant, Ventana's
Casual fare: Jackpot Grill, Horseman's Lounge, Tecate Cantina
Spirits: Lounges and bars throughout casino
Extras: Handicapping seminars; bobblehead, t-shirt, and poster giveaways; car shows, concerts

the Iowa and Indiana (G3) Derbies, and WinStar Oaks winner Island Fashion later took the Delaware Oaks (G3) and Alabama Stakes (G1). Total purses for the meet run toward $20 million annually, with the daily average hitting $250,000.

SUNRAY PARK
(FARMINGTON)

The Four Corners region of northwest New Mexico marks the turf, so to speak, of the Sunshine State's newest racetrack, SunRay Park. SunRay sits in the San Juan River Basin, five miles east of Farmington, one of three small towns—Aztec and Bloomfield are the other two—that populate the valley. Though the region is largely rural, balloon festivals, rodeos, open and juried art and trade shows, Indian cultural performances, the Connie Mack world series (baseball), and bike races mark the seasons like stones encircling a fire. For horseplayers, August kicks off the best part of the year.

One-fourth mile to go

SunRay Gaming, the casino group that leases SunRay Park from San Juan County, runs a split meet from early July through Labor Day and again from late September into early November. Race days are Friday, Saturday, Sunday, and Monday, beginning in the afternoon. Quarter horses are featured in 60 percent of the races, Thoroughbreds in 40, and nearly half of all horses competing here are New Mexico–breds. Races include stakes, allowance, handicap, claiming, and futurities contests, with stakes purses paying as much as $60,000. The park is located at 39 Road 5568, Farmington. For more information, visit http://www.sunraygaming.com, or call 505-566-1200.

OKLAHOMA

BLUE RIBBON DOWNS (SALLISAW)

Long before white settlers arrived, Oklahoma was Indian territory—and

Pressing for a win

still is for members of the Five Nations, as well as many smaller tribes. So it is no surprise that one of the state's three active racetracks is now owned by Native Americans. (A fourth, Will Rogers Downs in Claremore, may resurrect live racing in 2006.) In a recent acquisition, a subsidiary of the Choctaw Nation purchased Blue Ribbon Downs just hours before a foreclosure auction. The group owns other gaming spots in Oklahoma, but this is its first foray into the business of horse racing. Restoring the racetrack to health is likely to be an interesting ride. For a variety of reasons, eyes everywhere are watching.

The pride of this eastern Oklahoma racetrack is its quarter horse contests. Blue Ribbon is the oldest of the state's three current horse tracks and the first in the region to introduce pari-mutuel racing. (In 1983, the year before mutuels were approved, this Sallisaw site hosted the richest nonmutuel day of racing anywhere.) Electronic gaming machines were slated for installation in late 2005.

Blue Ribbon Downs offers spring and fall meets. Both meets are mixed but predominantly feature quarter horses from early March to early May and Thoroughbreds from August to the end of October. As they do at some other racetracks, jockeys here generally wear the track's plain-colored silks. New ownership has brought upgrades to the dirt course as well as to the horse barns, with tentative plans to expand in other directions.

FAIR MEADOWS (TULSA)

The top of the Oklahoma racing triangle is here in Tulsa, at Fair Meadows. Part of the state fair grounds now called Expo Square, Fair Meadows has a mixed quarter horse and Thoroughbred summertime meet and is a small, friendly, casual spot. The 6-furlong dirt track, with its tight, challenging turns, alternately showcases fast cars and high-octane horses. After cars race in the fall and winter, Fair Meadows reconditions the surface for horses. The track runs thirty-three evenings of mixed racing from mid-June to late July. Spectators get their

---

SNAPSHOT - BLUE RIBBON DOWNS

Description: The Turf Club offers climate-controlled seating and great views of the track. Down at the track, the open-air grandstand is covered and has a large interior simulcast area. Behind that, also covered, is a nice gazebo area overlooking the saddling ring. The track has a 7-furlong dirt course.

Season: Early March to early May, predominantly quarter horses; August to end of October, Thoroughbreds

Address: 3700 West Cherokee, Sallisaw, OK 74955; send correspondence to P.O. Box 489, Sallisaw, OK 74955

Phone: 918-775-7771/(fax) 918-775-5805

Web site: http://www.blueribbondowns.net

Nearest airport: Sallisaw Municipal Airport (JSV); Fort Smith Municipal Airport (FSM)

Getting there: Twenty miles west of Fort Smith, Arkansas; 101 miles southeast of Tulsa, Oklahoma

Admission: Grandstand: $2.00; Turf Club: $3.50

Parking: Free

Fine dining: Turf Club Restaurant, with a menu that ranges from big burgers to T-bone steaks

Casual fare: Fast-food concessions throughout the facility

Spirits: Turf Club Restaurant and other grandstand and casino bars

Extras: Groups can hold private events in upper-level rooms.

Teamwork, *Randall Robinson*

the Web site at http://www.fairmead
ows.com, or call the racing office at 918-
743-7223. Expo Square's street address is
4609 E. 21st Street, Tulsa. The main
Expo office number is 918-744-1113.

money's worth, with twelve races a
night—five for quarter horses, five for
Thoroughbreds, and one each for
Appaloosas and paints. The racing
office handles more than four hundred
entries per day, which makes for large
fields, averaging ten or more horses per
race. Thoroughbreds race for purses
that range from $11,000 to $40,000,
good amounts for racing at this level.

General admission puts you in the
bleachers of the big, open grandstand,
or you can claim a table in the Winning
Colors restaurant on the main floor
and watch from there. With the big
simulcast facility next door, the body
count for live racing has dropped somewhat, but on weekends, especially for a
quarter horse futurity, there will be
1,200 or more on hand.

Horse racing at Expo Square is
one piece of a varied entertainment
draw that dates to 1903 when this was
called the Tulsa Free County Fair. Over
the years, the grounds and facilities
have expanded to include a handsome
brick pavilion built in the 1930s. Expo
Center was added in the 1960s. For
horsemen and livestock dealers, new
barns out beyond the track rise tall and
buff colored, with peaked red roofs
and high windows for natural lighting.
The facilities include 1,200 stalls and
are considered some of the best livestock facilities in the country.

For directions and detailed information about the meet and parking, visit

REMINGTON PARK (OKLAHOMA CITY)

Remington Park is the newest addition
to the Oklahoma racing circuit. The
facility was built in the mid-1980s, at a
cost of nearly $100 million. Its name was
inspired by the acclaimed Old West
painter, sculptor, and fiction writer
Frederic Remington (1861–1909).
Though born in the East, he spent years
on the western plains, capturing dynamic scenes on canvas and sculpting small
statues of the American Indian, the cowboy, the horse, and the soldier.
Remington Park pays its highest tribute
to its namesake artist, and to several others, in its Equine Art Gallery

From the penthouse suites down to
the grandstand, Remington Park is a
handsome, sophisticated environment.
On the upper levels, private suites are
decorated in styles from casual to formal. Throughout the building, big walls
of windows on every level give spectators a wide-open view of the track, the
paddock gardens, and the surrounding
grounds. When night racing arrived in
2001, Remington, operated by Magna
Entertainment Corporation (MEC),
became an exciting new destination for
evening entertainment. Now the
Oklahoma City track races exclusively at
night. In November 2004, voters
approved slot machines here, and the
new Remington Park Casino is scheduled to open in late 2005.

Remington Park's Thoroughbred
meet starts in early August and runs
through late November. One of its two
biggest races is the Edward J. DeBartolo
Memorial Breeders' Cup race, usually
held on Labor Day weekend, a 1⅛-miler
for three-year-olds and older with a

Remington Park's inaugural race, September 1, 1988

$125,000 prize attached. The other race, also for three-year-olds, is the Oklahoma Derby (G3), held near Thanksgiving, for $150,000. Midsize races during the meet typically carry purses of $40,000. Among the jockeys and horse people at Remington are regional winners who've often just ridden in from the Lone Star meet. Headliners include jockey Cliff Berry, who took second place (for wins) in the 2004 Grand Prairie meet; in 2004 he also claimed lead rider status at Remington for the eighth straight year.

SNAPSHOT - REMINGTON PARK

Description: The totally climate-controlled facility is ultra-modern, featuring walls of glass overlooking the track from all spectator levels. A 1-mile dirt track with two chutes encircles a 7-furlong turf course. The homestretch measures 990 feet from the last turn to the wire.

Season: Thoroughbreds run from late July/early August to late November. A mixed meet of quarter horses is held in the spring.

Address: One Remington Place, Oklahoma City, OK 73111

Phone: 405-424-1000/(fax) 405-425-3297

Web site: http://www.remingtonpark.com

Nearest airport: Will Rogers World Airport (OKC)

Getting there: Near the junction of I-44 and I-35, just northeast of downtown Oklahoma City

Admission: $3.50; seniors (sixty-two plus): $1.50; 17 and under: free

Parking: Free

Fine dining: The Silks Restaurant; Eclipse Restaurant; penthouse suites may be rented for groups of fifteen to forty, appropriate dress required

Casual fare: A variety of choices throughout the facility

Spirits: Player's Lounge (nonsmoking), other concessions throughout

Extras: Thursday night appetizer and drink specials; college-night Fridays, with $1 admission, $2 beers, and live music

TEXAS

LONE STAR PARK (GRAND PRAIRIE)

The far-flung prairie is a prolific habitat of seed grasses and tiny, delicate-looking wildflowers, both subtle and beautiful. One would not likely call this fragile ecosystem " majestic." What is magnificent, however, is the modern Thoroughbred coliseum that stands tall upon this tender sweep of ground. Lone Star Park, with its deep, rich earth tones and indigenous building materials, proudly showcases its Spanish southwest heritage. The wide main entrance is flanked by dramatic arched windows rising several stories; a balcony with a commanding view of the paddock and gardens stretches over the entrance. Above the balcony, a grand oval window in a baroque frame is crowned by the bust of a horse and encircled by standards flying Old Glory,

the Texas state flag, and the flag of Lone Star Park. A solitary five-pointed star caps the window. Finishing the roofline is a dark domed cupola with a slender white spire.

At a time of huge transition in the racing world, when the sport is underwritten by gaming at some tracks but hobbling along at others, youthful, magnificent Lone Star Park is doing well. The fifth major sports facility to join the Dallas–Fort Worth Metroplex group, Lone Star has become the most lucrative destination on the young Texas Thoroughbred racing circuit. Attendance and total on-track handle have grown steadily since it opened in 1997. The park has a crowd capacity of 20,000, with a 1,200-seat simulcast facility—although Texas does not allow slots or VLTs. On a big race weekend, Lone Star hosts a national roster of Thoroughbreds and top name horse people. Local trainer Steve Asmussen,

Grand spot on the prairie

Full field and a large crowd at Lone Star

with his stable of Thoroughbreds and quarter horses nearby in Arlington, Texas, helps assure that out-of-state champions work hard for their victories. As of 2004, Asmussen had received six Trainer of the Year awards at Lone Star and that year broke North America's all-time record for trainers, by number of wins.

The world was watching Lone Star's full lineup on October 30, 2004, when the 22nd annual Breeders' Cup World Championships came to town for the first time. Expecting some fifty thousand

people, Lone Star added thousands of seats and hired hundreds of extra workers to make the day run smoothly. For the first time in its eight-year history, Lone Star hosted a split meet, reopening on October 1 with several big stakes programs moved into the fall. Lone Star Million day features the Lone Star Park Handicap (G3), the Texas Mile (G3), and the Lone Star Derby (G3), each a $300,000-guaranteed race.

At the clubhouse entrance, patrons encounter a sculpture of Texas-owned Alysheba and jockey Chris McCarron. The duo won the 1987 Kentucky Derby (G1) and Preakness (G1) stakes; Alysheba also took the Breeders' Cup Classic (G1) and Eclipse Horse of the Year title in 1988. Inside the Lone Star gates, spectators meet up with southwest art deco interiors. Top-of-the-roost suites are dark and sedate and corporate looking. As is the custom with grand racetracks in the modern era, the hallways leading to the private rooms serve as veritable art galleries displaying fine equestrian paint-

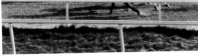

SNAPSHOT - LONE STAR PARK

Description: Spanish southwest architecture never looked better than at Lone Star Park, which sets the pace for Thoroughbred racing in Texas. A 1-mile dirt oval with one chute encompasses a 7-furlong turf course. The homestretch measures 930 feet.

Season: Early April to mid-July, with a short fall meet added in 2004.

Address: 1000 Lone Star Parkway, Grand Prairie, TX 75050

Phone: 972-263-7223/(fax) 972-237-1155

Web site: http://www.lonestarpark.com

Nearest airport: Dallas-Fort Worth International Airport (DFW)

Getting there: Located fifteen minutes west of downtown Dallas. From I-30 west, exit Belt Line Road north.

Admission: $3

Parking: $2; valet: $7

Fine dining: Penthouse suites, Silks Dining in the Clubhouse, Jockey Club

Casual fare: Mustard's All American Hot Dogs, Cilantro's Tex Mex Cantina, Pepper's Burgers, BBQ stand, and numerous small concessions

Spirits: Readily available throughout the facility

Extras: Regular handicapping seminars; weekend big name musical entertainment; July Fourth fireworks festival; two gift shops; family amusement areas; Heineken, Miller Lite, and Budweiser promotions; and more. Lone Star also annually hosts the Texas Summer Yearling Thoroughbred sales at its adjacent Fasig-Tipton Pavilion.

Near the paddock

dirt track, and the jockey scales inside a tile-roofed gazebo capped by the Lone Star racehorse weathervane.

MANOR DOWNS (AUSTIN)

Manor Downs (say MAY-ner), sitting on the eastern edge of Austin, is a rural hill country racetrack. It's in a quasirural section of Travis County, breezy with prairie wildflowers that grow rampant through the surrounding fields. Manor Downs, which opened in the mid-1970s and introduced pari-mutuel wagering in 1990, is the oldest pari-mutuel racetrack in Texas.

ings and sculptures. The grandstand is proportionately smaller than those at many other racetracks we've visited; this configuration may help explain the success story here, where more square footage is dedicated to high-end players. An enclosed grandstand includes outside stadium and reserved seating.

Escorted by PR man Darren Rogers, we rambled over the property; past the west end of the grandstand and clubhouse building; across umbrella-covered terraces where billowy canopies shield the sun; past the Vegas-like Post Time Pavilion simulcast facility with its lush exterior gardens; to the family park area, complete with picnic spots and big toys. Magnolia trees and concrete benches line the walkways near the paddock, where a bold black racehorse and rider sculpture stands. Ornamental grasses and variegated greenery edge a shallow pool nearby. From the saddling paddock, jockeys and horses pass through a glass-enclosed tunnel to the racetrack. As the bugler sounds the call to post, a typical weekend afternoon finds eight thousand or more spectators gleefully awaiting the start of the race.

In the Silks Restaurant, where we threw down our entertainment dollar, we wined on mimosas and dined on a savory fifteen-course, two-buffet-table spread. From our linen-covered table, we had a great aerial view of the infield lakes, the turf course encircled by the

For years, Manor was the center of the Texas quarter horse world, but Thoroughbreds now compete here, too. Manor Downs's eighteen-day live meet spans late February to late May, with mixed Thoroughbred and quarter horse racing staged every weekend. In 2004, the meet's three Thoroughbred stakes races offered purses from $5,000 to $10,000. The track's two biggest purse days are the Longhorn Futurity, Invitational, and Derby; and the Manor Downs Futurity, awarding a total of nearly $400,000 in prize money.

On a warm summer day, Manor Downs is quiet. Bettors sit at picnic tables or stand beneath the TVs, watching hopefully. Across the parking lot stands the Turf Club, built in the 1950s as a private residence. When Manor Downs passed into the hands of its present majority owner in the mid-1970s, the house served as her home.

Manor Turf Club

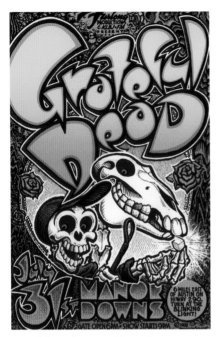

Grateful Dead concert, Manor Downs

Frances Carr Tapp, tanned and trim, with thick auburn hair, is one of very few women ever to own and operate a racetrack. A professional entertainment promoter, Tapp traveled on tour with the Grateful Dead. When they stopped touring, Tapp settled in Austin, the "live music capital of the country."

Tapp and her husband bought the Manor Downs property, which already had its grandstand setup, and turned it into the site of musical and western events. Long a social activist, Tapp readily engages in the lively politics of horse racing regulations.

Manor Downs's most significant political moment occurred on July 4, 1986. Farm Aid II, a live concert benefit staged to draw attention to the plight of the American small farmer, was nearly in place and ready to roll at another Austin venue. Just days before the performers, including cofounders Willie Nelson, Neil Young, and John Mellencamp, were set to go, the event was halted over liability licensing. Tapp, who had her own license ready, called Nelson's manager and the concert had found its home. Suddenly, 9211 Hill Lane became a blur of activity. A helicopter pad was poured; stages, wiring, lighting, generators, portable restrooms, water, first aid, and food facilities were set up; and space was organized for parking and camping. The event raised thousands of dollars that directly benefited the family farm movement.

SNAPSHOT - MANOR DOWNS

Description: Manor Downs is the smallest of the four Thoroughbred tracks in Texas. Manor races quarter horses, Thoroughbreds, paints, and Appaloosas. In 2002, the facility laid an all-new track, a 7½-furlong oval with a 6-furlong chute, enabling it to add Thoroughbred racing (at distances up to 1¼ miles) to its slate of offerings. There is no turf racing.
Season: Early March to mid-May; weekend racing. Simulcast players take over the rest of the year.
Address: 9211 Hill Lane, Manor, TX 78653
Phone: 512-272-5581/(fax) 512-278-1892
Web site: http://www.manordowns.com
Nearest airport: Austin Bergstrom International Airport (AUS)
Getting there: Ten miles east of Austin, off Highway 290 East
Admission: $2; seniors and students: $1; seating: extra charge
Parking: Free; preferred parking: extra charge
Fine dining: Turf Club
Casual fare: Concessions located throughout the stands
Spirits: Turf Club and concessions stands
Extras: Reduced admission ($1.00) for all military personnel with ID

RETAMA PARK (SELMA)

The southwestern Texas prairie is awash in a low-growing scrubby bush, whose small yellow flowers brighten its stalks in the springtime, adding to the riot of colorful wildflowers for which Texas is famous. This is the broom bush of the genus Retama. Just like the hardy Retama that surrounds it, Retama Park has weathered adversity. Opened in 1995, the track has overcome bankruptcy and a change of ownership to demonstrate the viability of horse racing in southern Texas. Horsemen at Retama represent stables from Florida to California. When the live meet ends in mid-October, Retama reverts to a year-round training facility.

Retama Park is located in Selma, Texas, a small burg sixteen miles northeast of San Antonio. Settled in 1847, Selma flourished as many Polish and German families settled here. In the early 1900s, as San Antonio exploded, Selma began declining. A century later, Selma's population is inching upward again, and its new-housing market shows signs of vigor. Retama Park has been a positive factor in the town's economic health.

Fifty-Cent Day at Retama

The new park features a classically designed grandstand, with sweeping lines and a southwestern flavor. Attractive archways lead to interior sections, the tans and reds of the building blending with the Texas soil. Stucco exterior walls bring to mind the Spanish-style missions found throughout the Southwest. Attractive ornamental streetlights and white fences punctuate the exterior, where the oasislike landscaping is well tended.

On a day of premier races, be they Thoroughbred, quarter horse, or Arabian contests, six thousand or more fans will relax in the air-conditioned comfort of the enclosed stands or clus-

SNAPSHOT - RETAMA PARK

Description: The sandstone-colored stands, with their solid square towers and arched windows, seem to have been built from the very earth beneath them. Retama's five-story grandstand towers over the 1-mile oval, the sweeping turns following the 7-furlong inner turf course. The homestretch measures 990 feet from last turn to wire.

Season: A mixed meet for quarter horses, Thoroughbreds, and Arabians begins in early August and closes in mid-October.

Address: 1 Retama Parkway, Selma, TX 78154

Phone: 210-651-7000/(fax) 210-651-7099

Web site: http://www.retamapark.com

Nearest airport: San Antonio International Airport (SAT)

Getting there: Northeastern San Antonio, off I-35

Admission: $2.50; seniors (sixty-two and over): $1.50; children fifteen and under: free; active duty and retired military members: free

Parking: $2.00; valet: extra charge

Fine dining: Terrace Dining Room, Turf and Field Club

Casual fare: Food courts located in the stands

Spirits: The Race Book and Sports Bar

Extras: Special admission days, musical performances, fireworks display

ter in the warm Texas sunshine, cold beers and chili dogs in hand, to enjoy the thunder and dust of the competitors racing around the oval.

SAM HOUSTON RACE PARK (HOUSTON)

Encircled by pines, Sam Houston Race Park is twelve years old and sparkling— bold and contemporary in a youthful, energetic way. The main building is large and white, topped with square white cupolas on a green metal-paneled roof and trimmed out in barn-red columns and crossbeams. And what a gorgeous summer evening Houston delivered on our last visit there: apricot skies and a ripe mango sunset framed by clouds of lavender and peach. It was the last Friday in June, official opening of the 2003 racing season.

We picked up race cards and programs and rode the escalator to the second-floor Jockey Club. One of Sam Houston's race handicappers, front and center, with the long sweep of windows and the track behind him, was wrapping up his fan education talk before the races got underway. The race program contained a four-page wagering guide (one of the best we've seen for beginners). The media guide explained basic differences between quarter horses and Thoroughbreds; the former bred for sprinting, with their muscular bodies, the latter more slender and linear, capable of greater endurance. Racing distances are regulated to accommodate these characteristics of the breeds.

Before laying down our cash, we restrained ourselves somewhat at the endless, delectable buffet, where beautifully arranged platters awaited the roomful of diners. A handsome, dark, mirrored bar ran nearly the length of the clubhouse restaurant. Our table, overlooking the ⅛-mile pole, had a small TV we never needed.

As we got to the betting, we also practiced our credo—Go to the paddock, look at the horses—and perfected the three-stop, long-stride loop: first loop to spot the winner in the paddock; second loop to invest at the pari-mutuel window;

Sam Houston Race Park

SHRP main entrance

in bright geometric patterns hung from the ceiling, casting this cavernous space in a festive mood. The jeans and boots crowd seemed to be primarily mid-twenties to early midlife, mostly beer drinkers, animated and friendly. Up on the sedately hushed third floor, we discovered the private suites and lounge area.

The main floor was noisy, packed with people patronizing the food concessions and watering holes while others filled the paddock and grandstand. When the evening races ended, Texas honky-tonk artist Jerry Jeff Walker ("Woman in Texas" and "Mr. Bojangles") began his concert, performing on a silver and neon-lit stage beside the grandstand. Hundreds of people gathered outside, the kids all dancing.

One last bite of dessert and we happy first-timers at Sam Houston Race Park were ready to call it a night. A member of our party who had lived for a year in London pronounced the evening a success. "I wondered why they all went to Ascot," she remarked. "Now I know."

and third loop, back to the clubhouse for a fresh drink, in time to watch the race. Between courses of wagering, wining, and dining, we explored. From the Jockey Club restaurant we went through several standing areas, past the shoeshine man, several bars and buffets, and a large section of blue stadium seating overlooking the track. Here and downstairs, banners

SNAPSHOT - SAM HOUSTON RACE PARK

Description: Sam Houston Race Park, on the northwest outskirts of Houston, is a handsome, contemporary facility with a western feeling. The dirt track is 1 mile; the turf track is ⅞ of a mile.

Season: From July through December, with racing generally from Thursdays through Sundays; night racing on Fridays. Quarter horses are the featured runners in a meet that begins in July and continues into early November. Thoroughbreds then take to the track from mid-November through December.

Address: 7575 N. Sam Houston Parkway West, Houston, TX 77064

Phone: 281-807-8700/800-807-RACE/(fax) 281-807-8754

Web site: http://www.shrp.com

Nearest airport: Houston Intercontinental Airport (IAH); Houston Hobby Airport (HOU)

Getting there: In the northwest suburban Houston area, on Beltway 8 between I-290 and I-45

Admission: Adults: $3; seniors: $1; after 9:00 p.m. on concert Fridays: $5; children under twelve: free

Parking: $3; valet: $6

Fine dining: The Jockey Club, Winner's Circle Restaurant

Casual fare: Numerous and varied concessions on all floors of the facility

Spirits: Concessions are conveniently located throughout the facility and on the apron.

Extras: Handicapping seminars; summer fireworks; musical events on Friday evenings featuring such top country entertainers as Jerry Jeff Walker, the Bellamy Brothers, Cory Morrow, and John Anderson; gift shop on main floor at north end of grandstand

SOUTHWEST TRAVEL SECTION

BELOW, YOU'LL FIND A MILEAGE CHART LISTING THE DISTANCES BETWEEN THE REGIONAL RACETRACKS AND ALL THE CITIES DISCUSSED IN THE FOLLOWING TRAVEL SECTION. THE CITY OR CITIES CLOSEST TO A TRACK ARE INDICATED BY AN X.

COAST TO COAST	Albuquerque, N.M.	Austin, Tex.	Dallas, Tex.	Farmington, N.M.	Houston, Tex.	Oklahoma City, Okla.	Phoenix, Ariz.	Prescott, Ariz.	Ruidoso, N.M.	Sallisaw, Okla.	San Antonio, Tex.	Santa Fe, N.M.	Tucson, Ariz.
Blue Ribbon Downs (Okla.)	700 miles	445 miles	250 miles	880 miles	490 miles	160 miles	1165 miles	1115 miles	735 miles	X *	525 miles	690 miles	1200 miles
The Downs at Albuquerque (N.M.)	X *	810 miles	640 miles	185 miles	880 miles	545 miles	470 miles	415 miles	185 miles	700 miles	820 miles	65 miles	505 miles
Fair Meadows (Okla.)	655 miles	495 miles	260 miles	835 miles	500 miles	105 miles	1120 miles	1065 miles	690 miles	X 90 miles	575 miles	645 miles	1155 miles
Lone Star Park (Tex.)	640 miles	205 miles	X 15 miles	820 miles	250 miles	210 miles	1055 miles	1055 miles	580 miles	265 miles	285 miles	635 miles	940 miles
Manor Downs (Tex.)	810 miles	X 20 miles	195 miles	990 miles	150 miles	390 miles	1065 miles	1105 miles	765 miles	450 miles	95 miles	805 miles	950 miles
Retama Park (Tex.)	820 miles	65 miles	260 miles	1005 miles	190 miles	450 miles	985 miles	1085 miles	685 miles	515 miles	X 20 miles	885 miles	870 miles
Remington Park (Okla.)	550 miles	395 miles	210 miles	730 miles	450 miles	X *	1015 miles	960 miles	585 miles	160 miles	470 miles	545 miles	1050 miles
Rillito Downs Park (Ariz.)	510 miles	945 miles	960 miles	445 miles	1070 miles	1045 miles	110 miles	215 miles	395 miles	1215 miles	875 miles	575 miles	X *
Ruidoso Downs (N.M.)	210 miles	755 miles	580 miles	395 miles	880 miles	580 miles	515 miles	580 miles	X *	695 miles	685 miles	275 miles	400 miles
Sam Houston Race Park (Tex.)	880 miles	160 miles	235 miles	1055 miles	X 20 miles	445 miles	1180 miles	1275 miles	880 miles	485 miles	195 miles	870 miles	1065 miles
Sunland Park Racetrack and Casino (N.M.)	260 miles	625 miles	645 miles	445 miles	755 miles	805 miles	425 miles	525 miles	145 miles	960 miles	560 miles	325 miles	310 miles
SunRay Park (N.M.)	175 miles	1060 miles	820 miles	X *	1055 miles	720 miles	455 miles	400 miles	360 miles	875 miles	995 miles	205 miles	460 miles
Turf Paradise (Ariz.)	450 miles	1065 miles	1085 miles	435 miles	1195 miles	1010 miles	X 20 miles	100 miles	520 miles	1150 miles	1000 miles	515 miles	135 miles
Yavapai Downs (Ariz.)	415 miles	1145 miles	1055 miles	395 miles	1275 miles	1010 miles	X 95 miles	X 10 miles	575 miles	1115 miles	1080 miles	475 miles	210 miles

*The racetrack is located inside or within 10 miles of the city limits.

MUST SEE / MUST DO

ARIZONA
PHOENIX

From the rocky, saguaro-studded foothills of the Sonoran Desert to the pine forests and red earth chasms of the Grand Canyon, Arizona is a land of stark, spectacular natural beauty. In every direction, the earth and sky put on fine natural shows of shadow and light, shape, texture. National forests and wilderness areas cover much of Arizona; a quarter of the state is Indian reservation land. Because of the inviting climate from October to early May, Arizona is the sportsperson's paradise.

Phoenix and its surrounding towns are teeming with museums and art galleries. In Phoenix, visit the internationally renowned **Heard Museum** (2301 North Central Avenue; 602-252-8848; http://www.heard.org), where ten galleries house a phenomenal Native American collection. Younger party members will enjoy the **Arizona Science Center** (600 E. Washington Street; 602-716-2000; http://www.azscience.org), with its planetarium and hundreds of hands-on exhibits.

In Scottsdale, stroll through downtown and its art galleries on Thursday nights during the **Scottsdale Artwalk** (480-945-8475). For art on a grander scale, there is **Taliesin West** (12621 N. Frank Lloyd Wright Boulevard; 480-860-2700; http://www.frank lloydwright.org), a Frank Lloyd Wright masterpiece.

PRESCOTT

Prescott, a well-preserved, handsome Victorian frontier town, was founded in 1863 and became the capital of Arizona Territory until political powerhouses wrestled the honor back to Tucson and ultimately on to Phoenix. Prescott has several museums and outdoor recreational spots. Stop by the **Phippen Art Museum** (4701 Hwy 89 North; 928-778-1385; http://www.phippenartmuseum .org) for art of the American West and the **Smoki Museum** (147 N Arizona Street; 928-445-120; http://www.smo kimusuem.org) for a look at Native American culture. Hikers, bikers, and equestrians can enjoy the many trails around Prescott (http://visitprescott.com/outdoor.html). The 9.2-miles (round-trip) **Prescott Peavine Trail** just outside town can be traversed by all three groups. If you have the time, take a trip to **Sedona** (an hour northeast of Prescott) or the **Grand Canyon** (two hours north).

Four Seasons' relaxation, Scottsdale

Grand Canyon's north rim

TUCSON

Ride the tram into **Sabino Canyon** in the Coronado National Forest (520-749-2861; http://www.sabinocanyon.com). West of the city, visit the wondrous **Arizona Sonora Desert Museum** (520-883-2702; http://www.desertmuseum .org) to explore desert habitat in all its complexity. You can also take a walk on the dusty streets of the real West at the **Old Tucson Studios** (201 S. Kinney Road; 520-883-0100; http://www.oldtuc son.com). Many Hollywood stars have done so. Then head for the Mexican border. Plan to park your car on the U.S. side of **Nogales** (http://www .nogaleschamber.com), and walk through the border checkpoints for an afternoon of bargain hunting in Mexico. If your lifestyle permits, travel down to Tombstone and Bisbee. Wherever you go, you'll find turquoise, silver, leather, Indian pottery, beadwork, copper items, rugs, weavings, and original artwork.

Navajo necklace

OKLAHOMA

OKLAHOMA CITY

Vast and semi-arid, Oklahoma was sparsely settled, by Indians and a few others, when the U.S. government opened it to white settlement in the 1890s. The land rushes led to statehood. Oil was discovered early in the twentieth century, bringing prosperity to a triangle of cities. Oklahoma today supports the nation's largest Native American population and is one of the best places for immersion in the authentic cowboy and western culture. **The National Cowboy & Western Heritage Museum** (1700 N.E. 63rd Street; 405-478-2250; http://www.

End of the Trail, *James*

nationalcowboymuseum.org) is among the finest regional museums in the country. It includes more than 200,000 square feet of exhibit space devoted to art masters of the American West, including Charles Russell, Frederic Remington, and James Earle Fraser, whose monumental, 18-foot sculpture *End of the Trail* dominates one alcove. Other highlights feature a re-created western town, a firearms gallery, and Native American exhibits.

Oklahoma City rode from the Old West into the twentieth century not on horses but on steel rails. Four railroad companies rolled through the city, operating from a section now known as **Bricktown** (http://bricktownokc.com), for its series of brick buildings. Renovated in recent decades, this is a great place for sightseeing, shopping, and dining. Take a ride on the canal, and enjoy the mosaic murals depicting Bricktown's early days, including its rich African American culture. Prominent blues and jazz clubs enlivened many a night here.

Even in late November, when Remington Park shuts off the lights, all is not lost for the horseman. Come January, Oklahoma City's **Heritage Place** (2829 S. MacArthur Boulevard; 405-682-4551; http://www. h e r i t a g e p l a c e . c o m) becomes a big midwinter event, serious and social. Horse buyers, consignors, and spectators from around the country converge here several times a year for meetings and sales. Heritage Place includes a 4½-acre indoor auditorium that seats one thousand, a club, a restaurant, and cocktail stations at every turn. The auction grounds include an outdoor arena with stadium seating.

SALLISAW

Twenty miles east of Blue Ribbon Downs, just across the Oklahoma state line on the Arkansas River, lies **Fort Smith National Historic Site**, in downtown Fort Smith (301 Parker Avenue; 479-783-3961; http://www.nps.gov/fosm). The present fort, built in 1838, was used as a supply center during the Civil War and then as a seat of justice for the adjacent Indian Territory. Take a tour of the buildings and barracks. Then head northeast to the **Belle Grove Historic District**, with its stately homes in various architectural styles. Have dinner at the restored **Sparks House** at 201 N. 14th Street (501-785-2292), with its original 1850s woodwork and chandeliers.

NEW MEXICO

ALBUQUERQUE

In rugged and sparsely populated New Mexico, the ancient earth itself is a spectacle. Everywhere, the brilliant palette and textures of nature are sharply focused under strong, clear light. At daybreak and dusk, the sky may be aflame in fiery pinks, corals, purples, oranges, golds, and yellows. Twilight often brings a canopy of clearest indigo. Those who have made this land their home—Indians, Hispanics, colonial

Albuquerque International Balloon Fiesta

Mexicans, and territorial settlers—have gathered earth, stone, and pine and sculpted them into adobe shelters. Archetypal cliff homes and pueblos survive as architectural blueprints for modern builders.

On the shady banks of the Rio Grande lies Albuquerque, the state's largest (half a million residents) city. Stop by the **visitors center** (20 First Plaza, East Convention Center; 800-284-2282; http:/www.itsatrip.org/abqinfo) in downtown, then take the **Plaza to Plaza** self-guided tour, a 1.3-mile walk through 250 years of local life from downtown to **Old Town** (http://www.albuquerqueoldtown). The city originated in the Old Town area in 1706 as a Spanish farming settlement. You can enjoy the historical attractions as well as the many galleries and shops. Central Avenue, part of old **Route 66**, is still ablaze with its 1950s neon signs, tiny motels, and thriving cafés.

Although we recommend an odyssey by automobile through New Mexico, you may prefer to see this enchanted land by hot air balloon. Learn about the early days of ballooning at the **Anderson-Abruzzo Albuquerque International Balloon Museum** (9201 Balloon Museum Drive; 505-768-6020; http://www.cabq.gov/balloon), then embark on a breathtaking ride with one of the city's **hot air ballooning companies** (for information, http://www.abqcvb.org).

FARMINGTON

This is high elevation Navajo country, with its Anasazi and Chacoan ruins hidden among the cliffs. Farms dot the valleys and mesas, irrigated by the San Juan and La Plata rivers, tributaries of the Colorado. Hillsides are covered in tall piñon pines overlooking rocky canyons and sandy arroyos.

Aztec Ruins National Monument

Here in Farmington (http://www.farmingtonnm.org), Navajo arts and artifacts await you. The juried art show, the **Totah Festival** (800-448-1240) on Labor Day weekend, when the SunRay Park meet ends, is well worth catching. Fifteen minutes away, near Aztec, with its unusual southwestern-Victorian Main Street, is the misnamed **Aztec Ruins** (505-334-6174; http://www.nps.gov/azru). These prehistoric Anasazi lands hold archaeological treasures.

Thirty miles west of Farmington, you'll find **Shiprock Pinnacle**, the famous 1,700-foot-high basaltic outcropping, in the town of Shiprock. Another thirty miles west is the **Four Corners**, where Arizona, Colorado, Utah, and New Mexico meet. You may well find other tourists here, willing to snap a picture of you in a contortionist's posture, with hands and feet straddling the four state boundaries.

RUIDOSO

High in the White Mountains, the Ruidoso ("Noisy") River tumbles through this charming little resort town of the same name. Ruidoso's main street, Mecham Drive, is lined with brightly painted storefronts that hold art galleries, shops, cafés, and restaurants. One historic remnant, **Dowlin's Mill** (641 Sudderth; 505-257-2811; http://www.historicoldmill.com), beside the river, is still operating, selling specialty flours, gifts, and books in the

shop. The **Ruidoso Downs Race Horse Hall of Fame** is to be found in the **Hubbard Museum of the American West** (841 Hwy 70; 505-378-4142; http://www.hubbardmuseum.org), which houses the ten thousand horse items of a wealthy eastern horsewoman who began collecting as a child.

Spring, summer, and fall in Ruidoso mean hiking, horseback riding, biking, and trout fishing on the trails and in the creeks of this pine-forest enclave, standing at eleven thousand feet. Golf courses are abundant. In the winter, Ruidoso bustles with skiers filling the tourist cabins and flying down the slopes of Sierra Blanca. Lands of the Mescalero Apache reservation adjoin Ruidoso; **Ski Apache** (505-336-4356), which the reservation operates, is another popular spot. For more, visit http://ruidosonow.com.

SANTA FE

Cradled by the juniper-studded Sangre de Cristo Range of the Rocky Mountains, Santa Fe, in north-central New Mexico, is said to be the oldest continuous settlement in America. Early Pueblo Indians built a cluster of adobe dwellings here, beside the river. The Santa Fe River bisects downtown Santa Fe, capital of New Mexico. The storied central plaza and many of the city's fine museums cluster on the north side. Everywhere are buildings in every possible hue of adobe, with their exposed

The oldest dwelling in America, Santa Fe

pine beams and brightly painted wood trim. Surrounding homes and shops, tiny informal gardens of bright flowers and vines creep up thick textured mud walls, while cottonwoods, junipers, and sycamores offer casual canopies of shade overhead. A stop at the **Palace of the Governors** (505-476-5100; http://www.palaceofthegovernors.org) or the **Institute of American Indian Arts Museum** (http://www.iaian cad.org/museum), both on Palace Avenue near the plaza, is essential. Don't miss the **Georgia O'Keeffe Museum** (217 Johnson Street; 505-946-1000; http://www.okeeffemuseum.org). Revered as one of America's premier abstract expressionists, the very private and sharp-minded O'Keeffe discovered the beauty of natural New Mexico in the 1930s.

Loretto Chapel, Santa Fe

Head next to **Canyon Road**. Once an old Indian trail leading into the foothills, it is now one of Santa Fe's primary addresses for galleries, cafés, and restaurants. Its wares epitomize the artistic, eclectic creativity that gives Santa Fe

Zilker Botanical Garden

much of its modern mystique. In the daytime, continue along on the Upper Canyon Road to the **Audubon Society** (1800 Upper Canyon Road; 505-983-4609; http://www.audubon.org), where you can hike and bird-watch along the scenic foothill trails.

TEXAS

AUSTIN

Plan your Texas trip in early April to catch Thoroughbreds at both Sam Houston and Manor Downs, and then focus on the annual **Texas Hill Country Food and Wine Festival** (http://www.texaswineandfood.org). Sponsored in part by *Saveur* magazine, the four days feature a lineup of celebrity chefs, wine and beer makers, food writers, and international food figures hosting gourmet events throughout the city. Enjoy a winery luncheon or a champagne breakfast, a seminar on tequila and mescal, cigar tastings, a session for how to prepare a proper cowboy breakfast, visits to area vineyards, and a Saturday night celebration at KLRU, home of *Austin City Limits*.

Water, water, everywhere, and finally we're wading in at Barton Springs Pool in **Zilker Metropolitan Park** (2201 Barton Springs Road; 512-867-3080). Pack a takeout cowpoke lunch (ribs, slaw, potato salad, ice-cold beer, pecan pie, and lots of napkins) and choose your H_2O. The damming of Barton Creek created the 1,000–foot long, spring-fed public pool, with its natural gravel bottom and year-round temperature of 68 degrees. The Barton Creek greenbelt meanders for eight miles, past cliff walls and shady groves of virgin stands of trees. Enjoy touring the ponds at **Zilker Botanical Garden**.

The huge twenty-six-mile-long **Lake Austin**, one of a series forming the chain of Highland Lakes, is swimmable at several spots. Our favorite swimming access, Walsh Boat Landing, lies just north of **Oyster Landing Marina** (3825 Lake Austin Boulevard; 512-480-9003), where we ritually stop for a glass and wings or a salad. Definitely do the mango margaritas at the **Hula Hut**, and sample an authentic, old world–style pizza at the **Boatyard Grill**.

DALLAS

With the city's bold architecture sparkling under dramatic lighting, downtown Dallas presents a breathtaking nighttime skyline. When you get to town, stop by the **Dallas Visitor's Center**, 100 S. Houston Street, near Dealey Plaza. A tour of downtown might start at **Pioneer Park**, located between Griffin and Ackard on Young. It's next to the **Dallas Convention Center** (http://www.dallasconventioncenter.com) and across the street from world-class architect I. M. Pei's **City Hall**. A few blocks east at Ervay and Main stands the exclusive Neiman-Marcus department store, founded in 1907 by Dallas merchants Herbert Marcus, Al Neiman, and Carrie Neiman Marcus.

A walking tour of Dallas isn't complete without stopping to consider the national tragedy of November 22, 1963—the assassination of President John F. Kennedy. Go west on Main to Market, where you'll find the simple JFK memorial and the **Conspiracy Museum** (110 S Market Street; 214-741-3040), or continue on to Dealey Plaza, where the president's motorcade turned to go north on Elm, under the Texas School Book Depository. If you're so inclined, visit the **Sixth Floor Museum** at 411 Elm Street (http://www.jfk.org), where details of

Big Tex, Dallas Fair Park

Fountain Place

the assassination are presented and the life of JFK is celebrated.

We also recommend the entertainment and art district **Deep Ellum** (http://www.deepellumtx.com) for nightlife, blues, jazz, rock, dancing, microbreweries, espresso, and more. The refurbished warehouse district, especially along Elm, Main, and Commerce streets between downtown and Fair Park, includes such legendary spots as Blind Lemon, Blue Cat Blues, the Copper Tank Brewery, The Bone, Red (for that martini bar), and Sons of Hermann Hall (for country music). For a bit of shopping, try **Dallas Market Center**, 2100 Stemmons Freeway, the world's largest wholesale and retail merchandise center.

Another fun destination is the **Dallas Fair Park** (http://www.fairparkdallas.com), on nearly three hundred acres just two miles east of downtown. It hosts the State Fair of Texas, which

Dallas skyline

draws three million visitors every fall, many who come to ride the world's largest Ferris wheel. The city-run park's art deco pavilions house nine museums and other attractions, including **Science Place** (214-428-5555; http://www.sci enceplace.org); the **Cotton Bowl Stadium**; the **Natural History Museum** (214-421-3466; http://www.dallasdino.org); an aquarium; and an IMAX theater.

Only the **Dallas Cowboys** (http://www.dallascowboys.com) have snagged the distinction of being called America's Football team. The preseason games at Texas Stadium, in nearby Irving, get underway in early September, so if you're here for fall racing at Lone Star Park, you're in luck.

HOUSTON

Bayou Bend (713-639-7750), at 1 Wescott in River Oaks, is a museum and former home of early city philanthropist Ima Hogg. She became a preserver of Americana, furnishing her home with fine period items. Lush gardens and grounds give you a good taste of an original River Oaks estate.

In the district southwest of downtown you'll find the **Museum of Fine Arts** (1001 Bissonnet; 713-639-7300; http://www.mfah.org). This is the largest museum in the Southwest, holding impressionist and postimpressionist works and many other pieces by Texan and American artists. Nearby, the **Menil Collection** (http://www.menil.org) emphasizes surrealist and other works. Founded and funded by John and Dominique de Menil, it is housed in a contemporary all-metal space designed by Renzo Piano, itself a work of art (1515 Sul Ross Drive; 713-525-9400). The de Menils also gave the city the nearby **Rothko Chapel** (1409 Sul Ross Drive; 713-524-9839; http://www.rothkochapel.org), designed by Philip Johnson, which houses abstract expres-

Houston from Buffalo Bayou

sionist works by Mark Rothko. Check on exhibit schedules, lectures, and other information regarding the Houston art scene at http://www.houston-guide.com and http://www.museumdistrict.org.

You may also want to visit **The Johnson Space Center** (http://www.nasa.gov/centers/johnson), where you can pet a live moon rock, and **Hermann Park**, an oasis in the city, complete with a zoo and botanical gardens.

Almost any day is good for sports in Bayou City, and the arenas are all in the vicinity of downtown. The Astros play baseball at **Minute Maid Stadium**. Nearby is the new **Toyota Center** for bas-

The Menil Collection

ketball (NBA Rockets, WNBA Comets) and hockey, starring the Aeros. The new Houston Texans (formed in 1999 as the 32nd NFL franchise in the nation) are always ready for live NFL football at the big, new **Reliant Stadium**, with its innovative retractable roof. Get information on current games, tickets, and times and find phone numbers at http://www.hchsa.org or check individual team Web sites.

Several great neighborhoods are worth exploring for shopping. The upscale shops at **River Oaks Shopping Center**, the predictable but energetic **Galleria**, **Rice Village**, and the bohemian and alternative **Montrose** district rank among the best. For trendy western wear, check out **Pinto Ranch** and Boot Town.

SAN ANTONIO

You can't go to San Antonio and pass up seeing the **Riverwalk** in downtown (http://www.thesanantonioriverwalk .com). Lush with thousands of trees and shrubs, flowers festooning every bank, this vista can be enjoyed on foot or from a boat (800-417-4139/210-244-5700; http://www. riosanantonio.com). Then

The Alamo

check out the **San Antonio Zoo and Aquarium** (3903 Saint Mary's Street; 201-734-7184; http://www.sazooaq .org). With more than 3,800 animals in residence, this zoo is one of the largest in North America. The zoo has globally recognized conservation programs for birds and animals such as whooping cranes, snow leopards, and black and white rhinos.

No visit to San Antonio would be complete without a stop at the **Alamo** (210-225-1391; http://www.thealamo .org). The city grew around it, so this world-famous landmark is now in the city instead of in the middle of the prairie. Explore the site of one of the most famous battlegrounds in American history, where for thirteen days, a small band of Texans, including Davy Crockett and Jim Bowie, held off the centralist army of General Antonio Lopez de Santa Anna. Despite the eventual overpowering of this courageous band, the Alamo has been romanticized across America as the symbol of liberty and freedom.

Riverwalk, San Antonio

WHERE TO STAY

ARIZONA

PHOENIX

Four Seasons Resort Scottsdale at Troon North
10600 East Crescent Moon Drive
Scottsdale, AZ 85262
480-515-5700
http://www.fourseasons.com/scottsdale
$295–$575
With 210 subtle, earth-toned rooms clustered in twenty-five casitas, this hotel delivers an exquisite Sonoran Desert getaway at Pinnacle Peak, including golfing at Troon North. Guest rooms offer panoramic desert or resort views and gas fireplaces, and the hotel has a lagoon-style swimming pool and complete spa and fitness services. Options include patio fireplaces and private plunge pools.

PRESCOTT

Hassayampa Inn
122 E. Gurley Street
Prescott, AZ 86301
928-778-9434/800-322-1927
http://www.hassayampainn.com
$119–$249
The 1927 Hassayampa Inn is Prescott's oldest and grandest hotel, with restored art deco touches from the soaring, decorative ceiling beams to the fine dinnerware in the hotel dining room. The hotel offers sixty-eight comfortable rooms and is perfectly located in downtown Prescott, surrounded by museums, bistros, shopping, and great sightseeing.

TUCSON

Westward Look Resort
245 E. Ina Rd.
Tucson, AZ 85704
800-722-2500
http://www.westwardlook.com
Off-season from $89; seasonal from $289
Set in the dramatic Santa Catalina foothills of Tucson, the gorgeous resort fills 650 acres where guests can enjoy luxurious spa pampering along with golf, horseback riding, and hiking. Dining on the premises is sumptuous. The hotel has preserved the land's natural beauty, and the grounds are almost a wildlife sanctuary.

NEW MEXICO

ALBUQUERQUE

Hyatt Regency Albuquerque
330 Tijeras Avenue Northwest
Albuquerque, NM 87102
505-842-1234/800-233-1234
http://www.hyatt.com
$140 and up
This four-diamond corporate hotel is two blocks from historic Route 66. Rooms are

tastefully decorated in soft colors, and guest services include massage and fitness packages. Bolo's Saloon, in the fountain courtyard, is a pretty spot; lounging beside the third floor outdoor pool, with views of the city, is delightful.

RUIDOSO

Shadow Mountain Lodge
107 Main Road
Ruidoso, NM 88345
505-257-4886/800-441-4331
http://www.smlruidoso.com
$99–$129
A getaway designed for adult couples, the luxury lodge features warm woodsy guest rooms with fieldstone-fronted fireplaces, kitchenettes, and a hot tub and a gazebo set among the aspen and pines. The neatly landscaped grounds of this parklike alpine retreat are awash in colorful flowerbeds.

SANTA FE

Inn and Spa at Loretto
211 Old Santa Fe Trail
Santa Fe, NM 87501
505-988-5531/800-727-5531
http://www.hotelloretto.com
$229–$459
The inn sits beside the Santa Fe River at the end of historic Santa Fe Trail and is ideal for travelers who believe in strolling through the city. Guest rooms are adorned with hand-carved furnishings and southwestern art themes. Enjoy the outdoor pool and live entertainment in the cocktail lounge, and try the SpaTerre for relaxation and healing therapies.

La Fonda Hotel
100 East San Francisco Street
Santa Fe, NM 87501
505-982-5511/800-523-5002
http://www.lafondasantafe.com
$219–$529
Historic La Fonda, once one of the famous Harvey Houses along the railroad route, stands on the city's main plaza. Artists have always congregated here in the bar—so put on your boots and silver and see who's in town. Guests in the Terraza suites enjoy complimentary breakfasts and a private rooftop. La Fonda also has an outdoor pool and nightly live entertainment.

OKLAHOMA

OKLAHOMA CITY

Renaissance Oklahoma City Convention Center Hotel
10 North Broadway
Oklahoma City, OK 73102
405-228-8000
http://marriott.com/property/propertypage/OKCBR
$139 and up
Staying at the Renaissance assures you'll be close to all heart-of-the-city temptations and the nightlife-oriented Canal District. The hotel delivers great service and sophisticated amenities and features an indoor pool and spa, with the Water's Edge Lounge just where we hoped it would be. Caffeina's and the Falling Water Grill, both in the hotel, stand ready to handle all your appetite needs.

SALLISAW

Best Western Blue Ribbon Inn Sallisaw
706 S. Kerr Boulevard
Sallisaw, OK 74955
918-776-0567
http://www.bestwestern.com
From $62
A sponsor of Blue Ribbon Downs, this hotel is only three miles from the track, just off I-40. Nearby attractions include Robert S. Kerr Reservoir, eight miles south of Sallisaw, with observation decks for swimming or viewing watercraft navigating this lock on the Arkansas River, and Tenkiller State Park, for scuba diving and boating.

TEXAS

AUSTIN

The Driskill Hotel
604 Brazos Street
Austin, TX 78701
512-474-5911/800-252-9367
http://www.driskillhotel.com
$195–$380
Cattle baron Jesse Driskill built this Romanesque boutique hotel in the 1880s to rival the grand hotels in the East. Located in the heart of the city's nightlife district, the six-story Driskill offers modestly sized Victorian guest rooms and a friendly, efficient staff.

DALLAS

Adolphus Hotel
1321 Commerce Street
Dallas, TX 75202
214-742-8200/800-221-9083
http://www.hoteladolphus.com
From $225–$1,250
For traditional old-money hotel ambience downtown in the financial district, we recommend the elegant Adolphus Hotel.

The Mansion on Turtle Creek
2821 Turtle Creek Boulevard
Dallas, TX 75219
214-559-2100
http://www.mansiononturtlecreek.com
Rooms from $400–$2,400
Built in the 1920s by a Dallas cotton king, who spared no Italianate detail, the mansion is the flagship property of Rosewood Hotels and Resorts. Antique-filled rooms feature bold fabrics, original art, floral arrangements, and unusual objects. Rooms offer private balconies overlooking lush gardens and the outdoor pool.

EL PASO

Camino Real El Paso
101 South El Paso Street
El Paso, TX 79901
915-534-3000/800-769-4300
http://www.caminoreal.com/elpaso
$159 and up

The classy Camino Real El Paso, ten miles from Sunland Park, is downtown in the city's revitalized historic district, near the convention center. We love a lobby with crystal chandeliers, a grand staircase, and lavish use of sensuous Italian marble. The look everywhere is pure elegance.

HOUSTON

The Houstonian Hotel Club and Spa
111 N. Post Oak Lane (west of I-610)
Houston, TX 77024
713-680-2626/800-231-2759
http://www.houstonian.com
$149–$1,500
Located on the western edge of Memorial Park, the Houstonian is a large, luxurious oasis, with three swimming pools and eighteen shady acres of gardens to help you survive the city's sultry summer. Rooms are sumptuous, with marble baths and floor-to-ceiling windows overlooking the gardens. Enjoy spa services and other amenities, such as Town Car service for shopping.

Westin Galleria Houston
5060 W. Alabama
Houston, TX 77056
713-960-8100
http://www.westin.com/galleria
$299–$309
The Westin's rooms and suites, furnished in soft wood tones with soothing pastels and trademark Heavenly Beds, are very comfortable, and the hotel elevator stops at the adjoining air-conditioned mall. The Daily Grill, serving American cuisine, is open for breakfast, lunch, and dinner.

SAN ANTONIO

Marriott Plaza San Antonio Hotel
555 South Alamo
San Antonio, TX 78205
210-229-1000/800-727-3239
http://www.plazasa.com
$179–$239
Billed as a resort in downtown San Antonio, this 252-room hotel has whatever you need. It features a whirlpool and heated pool, lighted tennis courts, and a fitness center, all within walking distance of the Riverwalk.

Radisson San Antonio Downtown Market Square
502 West Durango
San Antonio, TX 78207
210-224-7155/800-333-3333
http://www.radisson.com/sanantoniotx
$79–$169
Located in the Market Square in the heart of downtown San Antonio, this hotel will keep you comfortable and close to the attractions. Its 250 rooms offer voice mail, data ports, and express check in/check out. Request a room with a balcony facing the city's dramatic skyline.

WHERE TO WINE & DINE

ARIZONA

PHOENIX

Wright's
(in the Arizona Biltmore Resort and Spa)
2400 Missouri Avenue
Phoenix, AZ 85016
602-954-2507/602-955-6600
http://www.arizonabiltmore.com/dining/wrights.asp
$21–$32
Dine at the lush Arizona Biltmore with the spirit of legendary architect Frank Lloyd Wright pervading the evening. Wright's interpretations of desert light and line define this majestic resort hotel. Enjoy contemporary American cuisine in the garden patio, or dine in a private wine cellar. After dinner, tour the hotel, with its gilt ceilings, bold regional art, and gardens.

PRESCOTT

The Peacock Dining Room
(in the Hassayampa Inn)
122 E. Gurley Street
Prescott, AZ 86301
928-778-9434
http://hassayampainn.com/dining.htm
$14–$28; market price on Australian lobster
The Peacock Room's extensive menu features the classics, from pasta to steaks, duck, chicken, and seafood, along with creative reinterpretations. Start the morning with lemon soufflé pancakes, and kick back at the end of the day with live jazz in the bar, Wednesday through Saturday evenings.

TUCSON

The Arizona Inn
2200 East Elm Street
Tucson, AZ 85719
520-325-1541/800-933-1093
http://www.arizonainn.com
Entrées from $29
The Arizona Inn epitomizes elegant southwestern dining in a tastefully appointed 1930s-era setting. We love the main dining room's commanding fireplace and cathedral ceiling, and the garden patio terrace is pure paradise. The dinner menu features classic and continental cuisine.

NEW MEXICO

ALBUQUERQUE

El Pinto Restaurant
10500 4th Street NW
Albuquerque, NM 87411
505-898-1771/(fax) 505-897-8147
www.elpinto.com

Entreés from $8.79
The third-generation owners of El Pinto, northwest of the city in the Rio Grande valley, continue serving their grandmother's traditional Spanish recipes. Dine in the shade of the cottonwoods on one of the restaurant's delightful old-world-ambience courtyard patios, and savor the flavors of authentic Mexican dishes.

66 Diner
1405 Central Avenue, NE
Albuquerque, NM
505-247-1421
http://www.66diner.com
$4–$7
Get your kicks and taste of nostalgia at this 1950s-style diner located on old Route 66. The burgers, onion rings, soda fountain, and jukebox are all here. Order the trademark Route 66 Pileup and a chocolate malt and listen to a few tunes by the Beach Boys and Elvis.

FARMINGTON

Clancy's Pub
2703 E. 20th Street
Farmington, NM 87402
505-325-8176
Inexpensive
Stop for lunch or dinner and treat yourself to an icy imported beer. Clancy's offers everything from soup and sandwiches to sushi and steaks. Monday night specials include the half-price "build your own burger" bar.

Señor Pepper's
144 W. Navajo
Farmington, NM 87402
505-327-8176
$4.95–$8.95
Farm-fresh ingredients make the regional dishes in this colorful atmosphere delicious. Check out the comedy performances on weekend evenings.

RUIDOSO

Wendell's Steak and Seafood Restaurant
Inn of the Mountain Gods
287 Carrizo Canyon Road
Mescalero, NM 88340
505-257-5141/800-545-9011
http://www.innofthemountaingods.com
Entreés from $22
Steak, seafood, and southwestern dishes are all served up at this casino resort, a few miles up the road from Ruidoso, with awesome views of Lake Mescalero and the White mountains. Dine on the outdoor patio and then retire to Wendell's Piano Lounge for drinks and nightly music. Dinner reservations recommended.

SANTA FE

Coyote Café
132 West Water Street
Santa Fe, NM 87501
505-983-1615
http://www.coyotecafe.com/santafe.htm

$18–$42
The decor is an aesthetic experience, with adobe walls in pastel colors displaying bold southwestern artwork. Start with a Brazilian daiquiri from the café's signature cocktail collection. When we dined here, the evening's magnum opus was the pepper pepita-crusted pork tenderloin, accompanied by chorizo spoon bread and roasted tomatoes. Enjoy a nightcap in the rooftop cantina.

The Pink Adobe Restaurant and the Dragon Room Bar
406 Old Santa Fe Trail
Santa Fe, NM 87501
505-983-7712
http://www.thepinkadobe.com
$14.50–$21.50
Start or end the evening at the Pink Adobe's legendary Dragon Room Bar, consistently rated first in Santa Fe, one of the top one hundred bars in the country. The three hundred-year-old pink adobe building stands opposite the San Miguel Mission. The Dragon Bar opened in 1977 with an enclosed patio and the roof engineered to accommodate the trees already there.

OKLAHOMA

OKLAHOMA CITY

Jazmoz Bourbon Street Cafe
(in Bricktown)
100 East California
Oklahoma City, OK 73104
405-232-6666
Entreés under $30
Anytime there's a mingling of bourbon and jazz, we try to arrive early. With its extensive bar fare, Jazmoz pours all the drinks you've heard of and serves up a nice menu of steaks, seafood, pastas, and numerous Cajun temptations. Tempt fate with the tasty Voodoo pork chops, and enjoy an evening of great music.

SALLISAW

The Ole South Pancake House
1405 S. Kerr Boulevard
Sallisaw, OK 74955
918-775-3766
Moderately priced
Serving generous platters of good southern-style fare, the Ole South welcomes hungry diners 24 hours a day, seven days a week.

TEXAS

AUSTIN

Eddie V's Edgewater Grille
301 E. Fifth Street
Austin, TX 78701
512-472-1860
$20–$50
Downtown at this palate-pleasing, upscale seafood house, we did a double order of the grilled oyster appetizer served with a spicy Thai sauce and called it a superb

entrée. You might try the macadamia nut–encrusted butterfish with cocoanut curry or have steak. Live music at the piano and in the full bar lounge.

DALLAS

Avanti Restaurant at Fountain Place
1445 Ross Avenue
Dallas, TX 75201
214-965-0055
http://www.avantirestaurants.com
$9–$24
After a tour of the Conspiracy Museum, walk a few blocks and talk it over at the Avanti Restaurant, located in Fountain Place. The food is delicious, and the beautiful I. M. Pei and Partners–designed water park is both magical and soothing.

The French Room at the Adolphus Hotel
1321 Commerce Street
Dallas, TX 75202
214-742-8200
$44–$72
The New York Times lauds this romantic spot, with its soaring ceilings, French murals, crystal chandeliers, and other exquisite touches. Specialties on the menu include rack of lamb with eggplant potato cakes and Kobe beef shortribs with basil gnocchi, easily paired with a French red from the extensive wine list, which also offers an opportunity to sample hard-to-find sparklings and champagnes.

The Mansion on Turtle Creek Restaurant
2821 Turtle Creek Boulevard
Dallas, TX 75219
214-559-2100
Entrées $26–$90
Dinner at the Mansion is a must. The dinner menu, under the direction of Chef Dean Fearing since 1985, features southwestern cuisine with interesting touches. Entrées include braised duck enchiladas and lobster tacos. Surely this is your only opportunity to dine in a silver vault. And of course, there's a cigar bar. Jackets and ties, please; no denim or tennis shoes.

EL PASO

Dome Bar and Dome Restaurant
Camino Real El Paso
101 South El Paso Street
El Paso, TX 79901
915-534-3000/800-769-4300
$7.95–$23.95
We know now why *GQ* rated the Dome Bar in the lobby of Camino Real El Paso, with its centerpiece Tiffany dome, as one of the world's top twelve bars. The Dome Restaurant, with its elegant, soaring windows, is a rare setting indeed. An added feature: the hotel's dance club is open late on weekends.

HOUSTON

Goode Company Barbeque
5109 Kirby Drive
Houston, TX 77098
713-522-2530
http://www.goodecompany.com

$7.50–$10.25
This address is the original 1977 location; three others attest to its popularity. You'll find a fabulous menu of barbequed meats, seafood, and burgers. The building is rustic and small but has a large outdoor spot filled with tables. Across the parking lot is the Goode Company Barbeque Hall of Fame, carrying an amazing assortment of Goode merchandise with southwestern motifs.

La Carafe
813 Congress at Travis
Houston, TX 77002
713-229-9399
$3.00/glass to $180/bottle
Choose a nightcap from one of thirty wines by the glass at La Carafe, where the jukebox delivers the music and the vintage bar is lit by candlelight.

River Oaks Grill
2630 Westheimer at Kirby
Houston, TX 77098
713-520-1738
http://www.riveroaksgrill.com
Entrées from $21–$35
The sophisticated, clubby interior here, dark and brassy, fits with the piano bar and a menu filled with temptations. A bottle of champagne and the seafood sampler led to our delicious entrée, a snapper filet with crumbled tortilla coating and stuffed with blackened crabmeat. Dinners are served from 5:30 p.m., but the bar opens an hour earlier.

SAN ANTONIO

Bourbon St. Café
2267 NW Military Drive
San Antonio, TX 78216
210-979-8666
Most entrées under $20
For the best in Creole, Cajun, seafood, or steak, check out this popular spot. The Bourbon St. Café specializes in creative and tasty dishes, and the tender juicy steaks will have you coming back for more.

Tomatillos Café y Cantina
3210 Broadway
San Antonio, TX 78209
210-824-3005
Entrées from $4 to $14
If you love southwestern cuisine, then a visit to Tomatillos is a must. Featuring large portions and "the best margaritas in San Antonio," Tomatillos is reputedly the best Tex-Mex in the city.

The Tower Restaurant
Hemisfair Park
San Antonio, TX 78209
210-223-3101
Entrées from $16 to $30
Located in the Tower of the Americas, the tallest freestanding building (750 feet) in America. At 550 feet above the ground, diners savor the sparkling city views as they enjoy aged sirloin steaks and grilled salmon fillets with lobster sauce. A slice of turtle cheesecake finishes off this amazing meal. Reservations are suggested. The tower features observation rooms and decks as well as the restaurant.

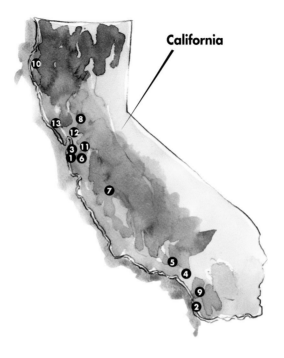

CALIFORNIA MAP LEGEND

California Tracks

❶ Bay Meadows Race Track
(San Mateo)

❷ Del Mar Thoroughbred Club
(Del Mar)

❸ Golden Gate Fields
(Berkley)

❹ Hollywood Park
(Ingelwood)

❺ Santa Anita Park
(Arcadia)

California State Fairs

❻ Alameda County Fair
(Pleasanton)

❼ The Big Fresno Fair
(Fresno)

❽ Cal Expo
(Sacremento)

❾ Fairplex Park
(Pomona)

❿ Humboldt County Fair
(Ferndale)

⓫ San Joaquin Fair
(Stockton)

❶ San Mateo County Fair
(at Bay Medows Race Track)

⓬ Solano County Fair
(Vallejo)

⓭ Sonoma County Fair
(Santa Rosa)

CALIFORNIA

old—and the rush was on! From 1848 into the mid-1850s, miners and entrepreneurs spilled into northern California, transforming the state forever. In mind-boggling numbers they came, riding or leading every caliber of horse into this new Promised Land. Soon, in San Francisco and Sacramento, newly wealthy, enterprising Easterners were pitting their finest racing stock against each other—on the racecourses they joined forces to build. They brought organized Thoroughbred racing to the Pacific Coast and influenced the sport's development nationally. San Francisco became the early horse racing epicenter of California. Among the bright lights were George Hearst, Leland Stanford, James Ben Ali Haggin, Theodore Winters, and perhaps most memorable today, A. J. "Lucky" Baldwin, owner of the vast Rancho Santa Anita, which he developed into Santa Anita Race Track.

Before Baldwin's era, horse racing in Southern California followed the Spanish tradition of the grand *caballero* in his silver-studded leathers, proudly astride a fine steed. (Accounts of early Los Angeles racing include one that says in the 1840s, members of the aristocratic Pico and Carrillo families wagered their entire fortunes on a 4-mile match race between a native-bred and a newly imported blood horse.) Following the Baldwin era, state anti-vice law closed most of California's racetracks—until mid-Depression-era thinking revisited gambling as a source of needed revenues. The mid-1930s brought three elegant new racetracks to the Southland. With expanded water resources feeding strong growth in the Los Angeles region, the state's power base shifted from north to south, too. The Los Angeles economy flourished during the twentieth century, and horse racing followed the big money.

CALIFORNIA TRACKS

BAY MEADOWS RACE TRACK (SAN MATEO)

Breaking the wire, Bay Meadows

Bay Meadows, twenty miles south of San Francisco, opened in 1934, providing fresh competition for Tanforan Racetrack, which stood nearby in the San Bruno hills. Although California had made it illegal to bet on horses in the early 1900s, Tanforan had intermittently run exhibition meetings during the dark years between 1909 and 1934. Bay Meadows owner William P. Kyne, who had lobbied hard for the return of racetrack betting, brought his years of experience as Tanforan's general manager to the new track.

The facility's earth-toned horizontal lines are complemented by a mix of vertical components bordering the wide portico that leads to the Turf Club. Tall terra-cotta pillars are banked by clay pots of bushy green palms, while slender silver poles soar skyward, flying the racetrack's logo banners. The effect, as one approaches the entrance, is fresh and creative.

When Bill Kyne launched Bay Meadows, he helped innovate and modernize the sport of horse racing. In its inaugural year, he installed the country's first totalizer board, followed by the first photo-finish camera. In 1939, he added the first fully enclosed starting gate in the United States. Kyne also created the daily double wager. When a Los Angeles horse was flown north to compete in the Burlingame Handicap in 1945, it marked the first use of air transport for shipping racehorses. In its modern era, Bay Meadows's most unique feature is its fully enclosed, climate-controlled paddock, with a separate outdoor walking and saddling ring that can be viewed from inside all levels of the facility.

Racing by the bay

The Bay Meadows stakes program, too, includes historical footnotes. The oldest stakes race on the West Coast, the Bay Meadows Handicap was inaugurated in 1934. Racing Hall of Famers Seabiscuit and jockey George Woolf won its fourth and fifth runnings. The inaugural Bay Meadows Derby, in 1954, went to the three-year-old colt Determine. Three weeks later, the colt went east to win the Kentucky Derby. Now hosting both a spring and a fall meet, the track offers a $2 million stakes program, including four Grade 3s and one Grade 2 race. The biggest purses of the meets are both run on the turf—the spring-run San Francisco Breeders' Cup Mile carries a prize of $200,000, and the Bay Meadows Breeders' Cup Handicap (G3) awards $125,000 for the 1 ⅛-mile competition.

If there is an endangered species list for racetracks, Bay Meadows is on it. It occupies prime land that has developers drooling. Owned by a land development group, it could be in danger of ending up in the history books. We hope change is not in the cards.

DEL MAR (DEL MAR)

Paradise, heaven, and nirvana—that's what people say when they reach for words to describe Del Mar. Lovely flower gardens and borders line every walkway, and tropical plants reach their peak of color for the forty-three-day summer meet. With the 1990s remodel, the premises are many times larger and modernized, but the classic Spanish architecture and details originated by Bing Crosby, with portico arches and rosette windows, have been retained. Images of Southern California's sun-splashed Spanish motifs, a nearly perfect climate, and visions of lazy afternoons on bougainvillea-drenched patios beside the sea fit Del Mar like a Hollywood movie backdrop. And why not? Those elements were the seedlings from which Del Mar grew and blossomed into the most romantically beautiful racetrack in the United States.

Bing Crosby and cofinancier Bill Quigley, with actor Pat O'Brien, were the principal founders of the racetrack. The inspiration followed Santa

SNAPSHOT - BAY MEADOWS RACE TRACK

Description: Bay Meadows is the oldest of California's Thoroughbred racetracks. The classic art deco lines of the San Mateo racetrack have been revisited in recent years and now intermingle with contemporary architectural elements. It has a 1-mile dirt track with a 7-furlong, 32 foot-wide turf course.

Season: In 2005, Bay Meadows launched an extended meet, with racing held in the winter/early spring, early summer, and fall, alternating its meets with racing at nearby Golden Gate Fields.

Address: 2600 South Delaware Street, San Mateo, CA 94403

Phone: 650-574-7223/(fax) 650-345-6826

Web site: http://www.baymeadows.com

Nearest airport: San Francisco International Airport (SFO)

Getting there: Located twenty miles south of San Francisco, in San Mateo

Fine dining: Turf Club, Jockey Club Restaurant; arrangements can also be made for the Kyne Room and the Director's Room

Casual fare: Hofbrau Carvery, Pick A Wiener, Sweet Treats, Apron BBQ, Clubhouse Snack Bar Grill, The Hot Dogger, Pizzeria

Spirits: Jockey Club Bar and other spots

Extras: Seasonal giveaways, racing contests, handicapping seminars, Friday night entertainment, and more

Entrance to Del Mar Turf Club

Anita's opening earlier in 1934, as Crosby watched the public's enthusiastic embrace of horse racing. He didn't have far to look for a building site. The Del Mar fairgrounds complex in north San Diego County had just opened, with plenty of land available for the world-class racetrack Crosby had envisioned.

On the track's opening day, July 3, 1937, Crosby greeted the guests at the gate in his yachting cap and boating attire, then slipped into a powder blue jacket, white slacks, and straw hat to welcome the crowd of fifteen thousand a bit later. Bing's own horse, High Strike, won the day's first race, and a few races later, actress Barbara Stanwyck presented the Inaugural Handicap trophy to E. E. "Buddy" Fogelson (later the husband of actress Greer Garson), owner of Grey Count. During the season, after the races ended on Saturday nights, private partying began upstairs

in the Turf Club, with Bing in charge, surrounded by his preferred guests. So many entertainers attended Del Mar that evenings, as one might imagine, became unforgettable parties, featuring spontaneous performances. Crosby sold out in 1946, but his association with Del Mar had secured the track's ongoing mystique. Movie stars and national figures kept coming—Liz Taylor, Dick Powell, David Jannsen, Edgar Hoover. "Where the Turf Meets the Surf," the phrase Bing coined for the Del Mar theme song, still opens the races every day.

Easily spotted from the road, Del Mar Thoroughbred Club sits in a wide, gentle slough between freeway and beach. The freeway here is I-5, south of Los Angeles and north of San Diego. The wetlands are part of the San Dieguito River, and the beach is the Pacific Ocean. Geography has spared the lowlands around the racetrack from development, and some surrounding hillsides remain natural. When we arrived, it was still early, so we toured the entire building, down to the nooks and crannies. El Palacio, the elegant pastel-and-Spanish Turf Club, was set for a buffet, with long-skirted tables holding appealing arrangements of fruit and flowers, as luscious looking as the luncheon platters.

Bing with buddies

Hanging baskets dripping with flowers outlined the outdoor patio. A heavenly spot, its wraparound views take in the arroyo and foothills, with the racetrack straight below.

Just inside the Palacio's main room, a round antique table held a fresh bird-of-paradise bouquet so stunning that I stopped when I saw it. The room's walls were done in soft seashell pink; on the far wall hung a grand oil painting of a Victorian horse racing scene, imposing in size, yet soft and impressionistic, the art of fantasy. On the dining tables, small glass vases filled with flowers repeated the colors in the oil painting.

On the sixth floor, an attractive bartender was happy to share her favorite memory of a day at the Del Mar races. It was Cigar's year—1996—and the horse was on a sixteen-race winning streak. But in the Pacific Classic (G1), in a history-making moment, Cigar finished second to long shot Dare And Go. "We had a bunch of people who bet the long shot," she recalled. "And the place went nuts!"

As the races started, we ordered Del Margaritas upstairs in the Terrace Restaurant overlooking the paddock, a lovely spot for watching people and horses below. Then, to be close to the action, we headed to the tiered Stretch Run Grill. As the name implies, we weren't directly in front of the finish line, but we were only yards from the track, with monitors nearby.

As the afternoon waned, we waited for the day's highlight: the $150,000 San Clemente Handicap (G2). After reading the *Daily Racing Form*, I concluded that jockey Julie Krone was set to win. She looked good, and it seemed like a good day for wagering. I bet her on Katdogawn in the 1-mile turf for fillies, with three crisp twenties that I had been saving for this race. At the top of the stretch, screaming all the way, we watched her pull forward and pound away, overtaking favorite Atlantic Ocean. There was no speeding away after the race, as we lined up to cash the voucher and collect quadruple my bet, for a tidy little dinner sum.

SnapShot - Del Mar

Description: Del Mar is an elegant, beautiful playground of horses and stars, with the stunning California coastline as their backdrop. A 1-mile dirt track encompasses a 1⅛ mile turf course. A diagonal chute through the infield makes it happen. The main track has two chutes, and the stretch measures 919 feet.

Season: A forty-three-day meet, from late July to mid-September

Address: 2260 Jimmy Durante Boulevard, Del Mar, CA 92014

Phone: 858-755-1141/(fax) 858-792-1477

Web site: http://www.dmtc.com

Nearest airport: San Diego International Airport (SAN)

Getting there: Located in the city of Del Mar, twenty miles north of San Diego and one hundred miles south of Los Angeles on Interstate 5

Admission: $5 and up; children under seventeen: free when accompanied by an adult

Parking: $5; valet: extra charge

Fine dining: Il Palacio Restaurant, for members; Clubhouse Terrace Restaurant

Casual fare: Stretch Run Grill, Café de Sol

Spirits: Available in all dining areas and throughout the facility

Extras: Del Mar is packed with special events all season long, from fancy hat contests to a microbrew festival. Small groups of musicians play on weekends, jockeys sign books and autographs, and commemorative giveaways accompany special race days.

GOLDEN GATE FIELDS (BERKELEY)

From the grandstand, you look across the track to the Berkeley hills, to stucco houses bleached by the sun, and to cars racing by on the I-80 freeway, bordered by a line of trees. On a perfectly sunny day, it could be the subject of the quintessential West Coast painting.

The most incredible feature of Golden Gate Fields is that it stands on the edge of the San Francisco Bay, overlooking bridges, sailboats, and islands. San Francisco, one of the most vibrant cities in the world, sits across the waves, a dozen miles away. It's an amazing location; we vow never to take it for granted.

Clerk of scales Paul Nicolo

Within the facility, the paddock is especially, as they say down the road in Silicon Valley, user friendly. It's long and narrow; green and white covered horse stalls line the trackside, and owners and jockeys meet to confab in the center of the walking ring. Running the length of the ring on the grandstand side is the public viewing area, a covered, three-tiered sweep of steps that accommodates a large crowd. The paddock design lets you feel you are right there alongside the eclectic clientele of horse owners who can be just as colorful and interesting as their Thoroughbreds. On our visit, hundreds packed into this space before the third race, crowding to get a glimpse of Merv Griffin, pioneering talk show host, performer, and powerful media executive, resort financier, vintner, and philanthropist. Happily for him, his three-year-old Skipaslew won the Golden Gate Derby (G3), and Mr. Griffin flew home with $55,000.

Every weekend the tracks hosts either an important handicap race with a purse of $75,000 to $150,000 (and often a nice bonus to a California-bred winner) or a graded stakes such as the Golden Gate Derby (G3). For the right winner, the Gold Gate Derby can be a prequalifier for the Kentucky Derby in early May.

THE OAK TREE RACING ASSOCIATION

Established in 1969 as a short autumn meet to fill the void between the close of Del Mar and the opening of the winter/spring Santa Anita meet, Oak Tree is an association of horsemen who have partnered with Santa Anita to offer a thirty-two-day meet at the facility each October. In fact, the existence of this meet has been instrumental in Santa Anita's three-time hosting of the Breeders' Cup Championships. The first time it did so, in 1986, the track drew nearly seventy thousand fans. Although Santa Anita hasn't seen a crowd like that in years, as racing enters the twenty-first century it appears that improved media coverage in general has lured people to the track to discover—or rediscover—the joys of the sport. In fall 2004, a record thirty-seven thousand were on hand during an October weekend for Oak Tree's most exclusive day of racing, the California Cup for state-bred runners, first held in 1988. Falling in the middle of the meet, its ten-race card also represents one of the final big stakes events before the Breeders' Cup championships two weeks later.

In 1983, Oak Tree hired Trevor Denman to call the races. The talented South African race announcer hasn't missed a year at the microphone since then and has no plans yet to skip town.

Merv Griffin wins the 2004 Golden Gate Derby.

As northern California's leading race venues, Golden Gate Fields and neighboring Bay Meadows attract some of the West's top horses, riders, and trainers.

Golden Gate Fields opened in 1941 but closed almost immediately when torrential rains destroyed the track area. Then World War II intervened. Up again by 1946, the lightning-fast track set the scene for several world speed records. In April 1949, Bill Shoemaker, then a seventeen-year-old apprentice jockey, won his first race here. The great gelding John Henry ran here in 1984 as a nine-year-old, overtook local favorite Silveyville in the Golden Gate Handicap (G3), set a new course record for 1 ⅜ miles on turf, and later became North America's

Horse of the Year for the second time. Ten years later, the track's first match race went off between filly Soviet Problem and her male competitor Lazor. They alternated for the lead in the 6-furlong battle until Soviet Problem pulled ahead to a 4 ½-length victory.

Golden Gate Fields is a great place to watch such feats live. Its three levels (grandstand, clubhouse, and Turf Club) accommodate fifteen thousand fans in any manner they like, with snack bars and watering holes at every turn and plenty of roomy smoke-free interior areas. The covered grandstand and clubhouse box seats wrap you in the fresh air that sweeps over the meandering infield ponds. The upper Turf Club level, with walls that hold an array of equine art, including framed Gucci and Hermès silk racing scarves, presents a sophisticated, contemporary interior of brass railings, teal blue carpets, and burgundy table linens. Just off the Turf Club lobby, the Bay View Lounge sports a classy bar and dining tables that follow the room's curved lines. The prime feature of the lounge is the window wall, with its 180-degree view of San Francisco Bay. It's hard to imagine that a day at the races can get much better than this.

SNAPSHOT - GOLDEN GATE FIELDS

Description: First opened in 1941, the track was purchased by Magna Entertainment Corporation in 1999; rumors of redevelopment on the 225-acre prime property abound. A 1-mile track encompasses a ⁹⁄₁₀-mile turf course. The homestretch measures an even 1,000 feet.

Season: A recently revamped schedule (2005) now includes fall, spring, and summer/fall meets.

Address: 1100 Eastshore Highway, Berkeley, CA 94710; send correspondence to P.O. Box 6027, Albany, CA 94706

Phone: 510-559-7300/(fax) 510-559-7467

Web site: http://www. goldengatefields.com

Nearest airport: Oakland International Airport (OAK), San Francisco International Airport (SFO)

Getting there: Located off I-80, overlooking the eastern shore of the San Francisco Bay; eleven miles east of San Francisco and eight miles north of Oakland

Fine dining: Turf Club Restaurant

Casual fare: Stretch Run Grill, Café de Sol

Spirits: Paddock Pub and elsewhere

Extras: Promotional giveaways include racing caps, T-shirts, calendars, and other seasonal gifts; handicapping contests; beverage specials and voucher prizes accompany selected races

HOLLYWOOD PARK (INGLEWOOD)

From the beginning in 1938, rich history, rich purses, and rich patrons have characterized the atmosphere at this still-glamorous racetrack founded by one of the biggest names in early film history, Jack Warner. He organized his pals in the entertainment industry as stockholders (including Al Jolson, Walt Disney, and Irene Dunne), and away they went. Some were already horsemen; many were merely dedicated gamblers; none could resist having a stylishly grand time at the races.

Swaps bronze, Hollywood Park

More than sixty-five years later, the story hasn't changed much. Ups and downs have hit the industry, and the live fan base has been siphoned off, as it has elsewhere, by state lotteries, off-track simulcast parlors, and Internet betting. Casinos have struck a few blows, and yet Hollywood Park (HP) was the first racetrack in the United States to build a card room on its premises. HP continues to present some of the richest racing anywhere. Among the Hollywood jet-setters who race their horses here are actor Kevin Costner, director Steven Spielberg, country singer George Strait, and media executive Merv Griffin.

Hollywood Park is a sprawling, classy, gorgeous place. Rambling red bougainvillea, scarlet salvia, and orange bird-of-paradise flourish. Palms, planted when Hollywood (the city) was also young, are now twenty feet around. The infield lake, bisected by the lush turf course, is a haven

RACING TO THE RESCUE

Some Thoroughbreds, like Smarty Jones, retire from the track and go on to a second, more lucrative career in the breeding shed. Geldings and horses running in the lower claiming ranks may appear on local fair and show circuits or end up in the backyard of a small-scale horse owner. The unlucky ones have a short life span once they pass through the stable gates; there are simply too many horses and not enough homes for them, so a percentage of retired Thoroughbreds are ultimately euthanized or sold for slaughter. It's a topic the industry addresses quietly, although concern for the welfare of retired horses is demonstrated throughout the sport, and many segments of the industry contribute to equine welfare.

In recent years, numerous groups dedicated to the care and well-being of the retired racehorse have popped up; the largest is the Thoroughbred Retirement Foundation (TRF), established in 1982, with various outreach, networking, and vocational programs underway in the East and Southeast. As part of the Kentucky Horse Park, near Lexington, a key feature of the new TRF Secretariat Center for Equine Adoption will be an Internet database linking potential owners with the right horses. Check into it at http://www.trfinc.org.

Annually, numerous awards are presented to members of the rescue effort in recognition of their service. Among them, the Thoroughbred Owners and Breeders Association in 2004 honored Kentuckians Herb and Ellen Moelis, who founded Thoroughbred Charities of America (http://www.thoroughbredcharities.org) in 1990. In California, the California Equine Retirement Foundation (CERF) was founded in 1986 by Grace Belcuore and, with help from Santa Anita and other sponsors, has provided a haven to 225 retired racehorses. Its ranch in Winchester, California, is open to the public. Check http://www.cerfhorses.org for its activities.

for pink and white flamingoes and other tropical shorebirds. Like other venues from a grander era of horse racing, HP can hold tens of thousands, and a "quiet" weekday still brings six thousand out to watch the ponies.

On just such a day, we rode the private elevator up to the exclusive Turf Club, where vigorous paintings of horses, rendered in rich colors and various artistic styles, lined the outer hallway. We sat outdoors on the Turf Terrace, at a table dressed in white linen. The space holds one thousand diners or more in a pretty setting with a great view of the track and the grounds. Quickly settling in, we scanned race one and noted that Tyler, one of our favorite Baze boys, was on horse five, Mypeppermintpattie, in the first race. We know him as the leading rider here, so it made sense to go check out the horse. The "Patty" looked good, and the odds were 12-1. It quickly came to pass that $50 got us $600.

Hollywood Park has witnessed many amazing moments in its history. Seabiscuit won the inaugural Hollywood Gold Cup in 1938, and in 1951, Citation

Pulling up in the final stretch

was crowned the world's first equine millionaire with his victory in that same race. Affirmed became the first $2-million horse in taking the 1979 Gold Cup (G1). In 1984, a redesigned Hollywood Park hosted the inaugural Breeders' Cup championship races. One of the most significant riding feats of all time took place here in 1999, when Laffit Pincay Jr. won his 8,834th race aboard Irish Nip, a victory that broke jockey Bill Shoemaker's twenty-nine-year-old record for lifetime wins.

Hollywood Park opens in late April, and the spring is peppered with Grade 2 and Grade 3 races. Late May welcomes the Shoemaker Breeders' Cup Mile (G1) to launch the big-time action. July brings the most legendary race on the bill, the $750,000 Hollywood Gold Cup (G1). With thirty-one graded stakes races—seven of them Grade 1 matches—on Hollywood's sixty-four-day bill, and stakes purses alone paying out $9.2 million during the season, the international Thoroughbred world pays attention when HP races.

We heard a TV announcer say unofficially that the Gold Cup is the first U.S.

Hollywood Park paddock, from the turf club

stop on the road to the Breeders' Cup World Thoroughbred Championships, a stellar one-day meet that rotates around the country each autumn. Gold Cup afternoon 2004 kicked off with an exciting win for Rock Hard Ten in the $400,000 Swaps Breeders' Cup Stakes (G2). In the sixty-fifth running of the Hollywood Gold Cup, Chilean-bred Total Impact fought his way past Olmodavor and heavily favored Even the Score to win by 1¼ lengths. The day also included the inaugural Laffit Pincay Jr. Award, honoring a dedicated member of the Thoroughbred industry. That year, retired jockey Pincay presented the award to seventy-seven-year-old Bob Benoit, who began in racing as a sports editor in 1951 and has been general manager of Hollywood Park since 1977. His reaction to the honor: "Indescribable," he said, the high point of his half-century-plus in racing.

SANTA ANITA PARK (ARCADIA)

Through the Front Runner restaurant's clear windows, diners look across a precisely combed racetrack to the San Gabriel Mountains, the spectacular

Santa Anita racing action on the dirt

SNAPSHOT - HOLLYWOOD PARK

Description: During remodeling a decade ago, the clubhouse was turned into a card-club casino—the first such facility at a racetrack in North America. In 1999, Churchill Downs Inc. took over the Hollywood Park reins to the tune of $140 million. A generous 1⅛ mile dirt track with one chute surrounds a 1-mile turf course. The homestretch measures 991 feet.

Season: Hollywood Park holds two meets. The first one is from late April to late July; the second one runs from early November to late December.

Address: 1050 South Prairie Avenue, Inglewood, CA 90306

Phone: 310-419-1500/(fax) 310-672-4664

Web site: http://www.hollywoodpark.com

Nearest airport: John Wayne International Airport (SNA), Los Angeles International Airport (LAX)

Getting there: Located in central Los Angeles, only three miles from the Los Angeles Airport

Admission: $7; Turf Club: $20

Parking: $3; valet: extra charge

Fine dining: Turf Club Restaurant, $20 admission fee (nonmembers), dress code, reservations required; Clubhouse Terrace Restaurant, dress code

Casual fare: Whittingham's Pub & Deli, Finish Line Café, Grandstand Food Court, Paddock Grill, others throughout facility

Spirits: Hollywood Bar, Longshots Sports Bar, Mel's Stute Bar, Jack Daniel's Bar, other beverage counters and kiosks located throughout the facility

Extras: Winning Colors Gift Shops (on two levels); Clubhouse Salon; personal Press Boxes; Track Kitchen with viewing platforms for morning workouts; commemorative racing gift giveaways; special seasonal promotions and live entertainment

northern backdrop to Santa Anita Park. On this morning, the sun courses along the southern sky, intensifying the green of the palm trees clustered throughout the park. High clouds dapple the mountain peaks and shadow the canyons' ribs. We're ordering brunch, looking at the day's racing program, and rolling up our sleeves for some first-class Thoroughbred racing. The long (200-foot) curvy bar on the next level is lined with people murmuring. Before long, it will be boisterous, with standing room only.

Yesterday, December 26, we caught the opening day of the meet. The holiday atmosphere hasn't faded, and the energy of the new meet gearing up makes this an exciting place to be.

A crowd at the paddock

Looking down on the track, where pageantry of the sport shines colorfully, we are glad to be among the players. The scene—first-tier horses and jockeys; the crowd; the mild temperature; and the park's southern Mediterranean ambience, with its arid, western California views—shared with friends is stimulating.

ERICA NORDEAN, ARTIST

The equestrian paintings that hang in the hallway of the Hollywood Park Turf Club are dynamic. In some, big, bold colors and curves capture the might and muscle of the horse. In others, controlled, cubist compositions suggest the pent-up anticipation of animals and jockeys moving onto the track just before a race. In still others, strong abstract impressionism renders the raw energy and speed of horses seemingly in midair, flying above the earth. The same versatile hand and eye is at work in all of them: that of artist Erica Nordean.

Pageantry, Erica Nordean

Erica recalls the first stirrings of her equine art career. "It's the same old story," she says. "Horse crazy as a kid, just a nut about horses." Like most youngsters, she also loved to draw and paint. The Washington State native became an exercise rider and then began a part-time career in real estate, which allowed her time to work with horses and to paint. She studied technique at Pratt Institute, but the disciplined study of equine musculature was an ever-present aspect of watching the animals closely as she worked with them.

Friends in the racing world encouraged her to circulate some of her paintings, so she took them to a small gallery in Kirkland, Washington. The gallery gave her a solo show. Then the Washington Breeders and Owners Association featured her art on the cover of their monthly publication, *The Washington Thoroughbred*. In her early thirties, she took a deep breath and said good-bye to steady income to concentrate full time on painting.

How does an artist continue to find fresh inspiration? "I go to the racetrack in the morning. I go out of my mind, I go through my mind," she replies, excitement welling in her voice. "I'm always looking for an angle I haven't seen before, always searching for it. I try to stay loose." Her favorite style, she says, "depends on the day. It might be graphic, or it might be loose and abstract."

Over the years, Nordean's concern for the treatment of animals has deepened. A percentage of her art commissions goes to support the Pegasus Foundation, a welfare and rescue organization based in Southern California, with worldwide affiliations. This, says the artist, is what matters most about her work.

Santa Anita infield concert

Santa Anita, a three-time host of the Breeders' Cup Championships (1993, 1996, and 2003), offered lucrative racing and prestigious stakes from the beginning. The track, which opened on Christmas Day, 1934, introduced the nation's richest prize of that era, the Santa Anita Handicap. Soon, the Arcadia venue established West Coast racing as the glamorous, upper-class activity it had always been in the East.

Formal racing made its start near this site on the outskirts of Los Angeles in 1907, when E. J. "Lucky" Baldwin opened a 1-mile racetrack on his vast estate, part of which is now the Los Angeles County Arboretum. Baldwin, who made his fortune in the gold rush, bought an enormous parcel of land in the San Gabriel Valley in 1875, which he developed into Rancho Santa Anita (named after one of his daughters). His legendary track operated for two years. It closed after Baldwin's death, when moralistic legislators halted sport gambling. When the passage of pari-mutuel legislation occurred in the early 1930s, dentist Charles H. Strub purchased part of Baldwin's estate and shepherded in Southern California's new era of racing.

Among the track's most recent enhancements is Sirona's, a huge bar and live concert stage overlooking the

SNAPSHOT - SANTA ANITA

Description: Having undergone a recent $45 million renovation, Santa Anita remains one of the all-time classiest racecourses in America. A unique, downhill-starting turf course is one of the trademarks here, with its main chute of 1¾ miles and a main stretch of 1,408 feet. The dirt track measures 1 mile, with two additional chutes. The homestretch measures 990 feet.

Season: Late December to mid-April; reopens in late September for its affiliation with the Oak Tree Association's thirty-two-day meet

Address: 285 West Huntington Drive, Arcadia, CA 91007

Phone: 626-574-7223/(fax) 626-446-1456

Web site: http://www.santaanita.com

Nearest airport: Los Angeles International Airport (LAX), Hollywood-Burbank Airport (BUR)

Getting there: Arcadia is about fourteen miles northeast of downtown Los Angeles.

Admission: $5; children seventeen and under: free with paying adult; clubhouse and reserved seating: extra charge

Parking: $3; valet: extra charge

Fine dining: Front Runner, overlooks the finish line, reservations suggested; Americana Room, located in the Turf Club; Chandelier Room and Turf Club Terrace, outside overlooking the track. All enforce a dress code.

Casual fare: Clocker's Corner, Terrace Food Court, concessions stands located throughout the facility

Spirits: Sirona's, at the paddock; Front Runner; Chandelier Room; other bars, counters, and kiosks throughout

Extras: Ongoing events from handicapping contests to concerts to art shows and giveaways. Open year-round for simulcast betting and mornings 5:00 to 10:00 for free observation of workouts. Enter through Gate 8.

paddock gardens and lined with simulcast screens. For race fans seeking a more traditional setting, the Chandelier Room, with glamorous French chandeliers and a fine equestrian art collection, offers an elegant spot for celebrating finish line firsts.

Every year, Santa Anita draws national attention as it chalks up great racing drama and showcases its heroes. Participants from across the nation and around the world—including the Whitneys, Frank Stronach (Why not? he owns the place), Dubai royalty, and a trail of other prominent owners—attend its winter/spring meet. One magnet is the $750,000-guaranteed Santa Anita Derby (G1), a major Kentucky Derby prep that's been won by nine three-year-olds who claimed the Churchill Downs trophy just weeks later.

Since 1999, Santa Anita has also competed against Gulfstream Park in the lucrative Sunshine Millions, pitting California- and Florida-bred contestants against each other at both tracks. The eight winter races are held in late January and offer combined purses of several million dollars. Graded stakes races are run several times a week here and offer some of the biggest money in the country. The Santa Anita Handicap (G1), for example, a race for four-year-olds and up, runs in early March, with a purse of $1 million.

Santa Anita is also forever linked with legendary horses and riders, such as Seabiscuit, the comeback runner who carried America's hopes in the 1930s, and gentleman jockey George Woolf. Woolf, one of the country's all-time great jockeys, is immortalized with the presti-

THE DERBY RESTAURANT

The day's last winner has crossed the wire at Santa Anita Park. Patrons stream into the warm California evening, palm trees rustling in the breeze. Haven't had your fill of the racing world yet? Then head around to nearby Derby Restaurant for a good steak dinner and a side order of racing history.

The Derby was known as Proctor's Chicken House in 1938, when jockey George "The Iceman" Woolf purchased it. That year, he had guided Seabiscuit to victory in a thrilling match race against War Admiral, one of the most emotional races ever held on American soil. Sadly, Woolf perished in a racing accident in 1946, and five years later his widow sold the restaurant to the Sterniolo family. Today, their son, Charles, owns and manages it, safeguarding an era and a legend, which he is always happy to share with diners.

Woolf and Seabiscuit memorabilia are everywhere. The main dining room is covered with photographs and artwork of horses from across the decades charging down the racetrack. Dominating the room is a painting of that 1938 match race between Seabiscuit and War Admiral. When the blockbuster 2003 movie *Seabiscuit* was in production (parts were filmed at Santa Anita), producers turned to this historical eatery for many of Woolf's racing possessions, such as his silks and his "lucky" saddle.

When people have a big win at the races, Sturniolo says he can count on them to show up here for dinner. The Derby is a favorite spot of fans and horsepeople alike, and it is packed after a day of racing at Santa Anita. This is the perfect place for spotting well-known owners, jockeys, and trainers. The upstairs apartment where the Woolfs lived is unused, though the private dining room on that floor caters to VIPs needing a quiet place to meet. The food is superb, the atmosphere unique.

The Derby Restaurant
233 East Huntington Drive
Arcadia, CA 91007
626-447-8174/626-477-2430
http://www.thederbyarcadia.com

gious George Woolf Memorial Jockey Award, established after his tragic death in a 1946 racing accident at Santa Anita. Life-size bronze casts of Woolf and Seabiscuit stand at the paddock entrance. Other top riders who plied their trade at the Arcadia track include Johnny Longden, with 6,032 career wins, and Bill Shoemaker, who took his first riding championship at Santa Anita in 1951 and repeated the feat for sixteen years straight. More recently, jockeys Laffit Pincay Jr., Kent Desormeaux, Alex Solis, Gary Stevens, Chris McCarron, and Mike Smith have ranked among the top riders here. Santa Anita's most successful trainers of late have included Bob Baffert and Bobby Frankel, each of whom has scooped up his share of racing awards over the years.

With the pastel art deco aesthetic of its architecture looking as soft and chic as ever and the racing continually first class, Santa Anita deserves its reputation as one of the country's all-time grand racing venues. Factoring in Del Mar and Hollywood Park along with Santa Anita, Southern California's golden triangle of racetracks sustains much of the state's horse racing economy.

CALIFORNIA COUNTY FAIRS

SAN JOAQUIN FAIR (STOCKTON)

And we're off to California's county fairs, nine in all, each putting its own stamp on the sport, with mixed breeds running and purses ranging from modest to large, in a setting where the grandstand may be a century old and landscaping around the tote board is modest but colorful. The fair loop itself is a mini-tour through the Garden of Eden as well as a jaunt up along the foggy north coast to Ferndale and south into Pomona, in eastern Los Angeles County. In June, fences beside

Call to post at San Joaquin County Fair

the highways hold ripening crops or bales of fresh-cut hay. From Sacramento to Fresno, rows of leafy grapes and orchards of apples, almonds, and cherries cover the Central Valley. By October, en route to Fresno, the grape crush fills the air with heavy fruity sweetness.

The racing circuit kicks off at San Joaquin Fair in Stockton in mid-June, and the horses don't cross the final wire until early October in Fresno. San Joaquin, first stop on the route, contributes nearly $14 million to the state's horse industry. The fair was established in the 1860s but closed for racing from 1909 until 1933, when the pari-mutuel ban was lifted. Fast forward to 2004: San Joaquin, along with several other tracks, wrapped up its meet with increases in attendance, fields, and all handle—and a boost in optimism. Address: 1658 South Airport Way, Stockton, CA 95206; phone: 209-466-5041/(fax) 209-466-5739; Web site: http://www.sanjoaquinfair.com.

ALAMEDA COUNTY FAIR (PLEASANTON)

From San Joaquin, the carousel circles around to the Alameda County Fair. It was built in Pleasanton in 1858, and the fairgrounds were the setting of some

The tote board tells the story, Solano County

feeling of a classic county fair. The grandstand is old and relatively small, and crowds have held steady for several years. The compact fairgrounds now sit at major freeway intersections, and preliminary revitalization plans for future use of the grounds are underway. Address: 900 Fairgrounds Drive, Vallejo CA 94589; phone: 707-551-2000; Web site: http://www.scfair.com.

SONOMA COUNTY FAIR (SANTA ROSA)

The Sonoma County Fair, in Santa Rosa, hosts another big fair on the county circuit, with a total meet handle usually running just under $40 million. Sonoma County's biggest race is the $100,000 Joseph T. Grace Handicap, a 1¹⁄₁₆-mile race for three-year-olds and older, established in the early 1970s. As with Pleasanton and Solano, a year-round simulcast facility operates on the grounds. The fairground's new ⅞-mile turf course opened in July 2005. Address: 1350 Bennett Valley Road, but send correspondence to P.O. Box 1536, Santa Rosa, CA 95402; phone: 707-545-4200/(fax) 707-573-9342; Web site: http://www.sonomacountyfair.com.

Warming up at the Alameda County Fair

early Hollywood horse racing movies. On opening day, fans pour onto the apron and climb into the large covered grandstand as the afternoon races begin. With its close proximity to Golden Gate Fields and Bay Meadows, the ten-day fair delivers good purses and features a number of jockeys familiar to the crowd, including Hall of Fame rider Russell Baze, Roberto Gonzalez, and David Flores. The race menu is enhanced by stakes purses totaling more than $320,000, awarded to Thoroughbreds, quarter horses, Appaloosas, and Arabians. The 2004 meet concluded with record-setting fair attendance and handle of nearly $36 million. Address: The Alameda County Fairgrounds, 4501 Pleasanton Avenue, Pleasanton, CA 94566; phone: 925-426-7600/(fax) 925-426-7599; Web site: http://www.alameda countyfair.com.

SOLANO COUNTY FAIR (VALLEJO)

When it opens in mid-July, the Solano County Fair, in Vallejo, delivers the true

Backside (detail), Randall Robinson

SAN MATEO COUNTY FAIR (SAN MATEO)

In late August, Bay Meadows reopens for its spin as the ten-day San Mateo County Fair meet. Summertime racing draws a casual crowd as well as an opportunity for other horsemen to get into the game. Bay Meadows stands alone on the fair circuit for not racing "emerging breeds" or mules. Prominent trainers stabled here include Jerry Hollendorfer and Jeff Bonde, who partner with northern California's top jockeys to claim a high percentage of wins. On our recent trip to the fair, the day's meet belonged to Russell Baze, who rode in six races and went to the winner's circle after four of them. Address: 2495 South Delaware Street, San Mateo, CA 94403; phone: 650-574-3247/(fax) 650-574-3985; Web site: http://www.sanmateo countyfair.com.

HUMBOLDT COUNTY FAIR (FERNDALE)

At Ferndale, in Humboldt County, the most northerly fair on the circuit runs

Busting through the gate

its meet concurrently with San Mateo's. The north coast has been racing for more than a century, often under cool, coastal clouds and heavy gray skies. The big industrial-red grandstand and covered stadium seats seem just right in this traditional agricultural and logging spot. Rows of red horse barns fill the back, and a forest of redwoods stretches beyond the ½-mile track. Ferndale is a charming Victorian town, where the gathering spot of horsemen and race fans for dinner after the races is The Palace Saloon, located on Main Street. Address: 1250 Fifth Street, Ferndale, CA 95536; phone: 707-786-9533; Web site: http://www.humboldt countyfair.org.

CAL EXPO (SACRAMENTO)

Nowhere is the fair-racing scene as big and as rich as it is in the state capital. The Sacramento County fairground, called Cal Expo, is home to a large grandstand befitting a region steeped

Sunrise (detail), Randall Robinson

RACING IN THE BLOOD

Jockey Russell Baze rides regularly at Bay Meadows. In 2001, he reached his 7,500th career win at the track, and the next year rang the 8,000 bell there. A household name on the Bay Area circuit, Baze came into an extended horse racing family, including uncles and cousins. His father rode, as did Baze's tiny grandmother, who raced on a small Pacific Northwest circuit. But none of his kinfolk—and only four other jockeys in history—have matched his winning records.

Since 1992, Baze has surpassed 400 wins every year, except for 2003, when injury sidelined him for eight weeks. In 1995, his record won him a special Eclipse Award, and in 1999 he was inducted into the Racing Hall of Fame. On June 2, 2005, Baze rode career winner number 9,000 at Golden Gate Fields, and he currently stands second to Laffit Pincay Jr. among all-time winning jockeys.

Fairplex paddock

in horse racing from the gold rush days. The fair pulls in a million people each year, and the grandstand is one of the few that includes a Turf Club, which serves a daily buffet during the meet.

Cal Expo took the bold step of opening its 2004 meet with one card of races beginning at noon and another one in early evening. Cal Expo also launched a new standardbred meet during the fall, with night harness racing Wednesdays through Saturdays.

Whether you catch Thoroughbreds at the fair or standardbreds in the fall, we recommend touring the capitol grounds and making a quick stop in Old Sacramento for a glass or two of *vino blanco* and a plate of calamari at the Rio City Café, 1110 Front Street, on the Sacramento River. As you walk the plank sidewalks here, try to imagine this quaint area in the 1850s, when it was the commercial hub of the city. Address: 1600 Exposition Boulevard, Sacramento, CA 95815; phone: 916-263-3000/877-225-3976; Web site: http://www.calexpo.com.

FAIRPLEX PARK (POMONA)

Fairplex Park, in Pomona, is a big place, and the grandstand is from an older era than that of Sacramento. Towering palms line its ⅝-mile bullring track, with its notoriously tight turns. Midweek attendance was moderate on our visit, but mules, quarter horses, and Thoroughbreds took to the track. There was also an invigorated performance by the Budweiser Clydesdales, an amazing team of 18-hand, one-ton workhorses with their handsome white-feathered legs.

Fairplex Park grandstand

Like Cal Expo, Fairplex hosts a lucrative meet and has enjoyed a run of increased attendance and handle at its seventeen-day meet. In 2004, twelve of the seventeen stakes purses increased by 20 percent, with the two top races, the Barretts Debutante and the Barretts Juvenile, for two-year-olds, both at $120,000. Jockey Martin Pedroza set a record with his fifty-one wins during the meet, at a success rate of 38 percent. Address: 1101 W. McKinley Avenue, Pomona, CA 91768, but send correspondence to P.O. Box 2250, Pomona, CA 91769; phone: 909-623-3111/(fax) 909-865-3602; Web site: http://www.fairplex.com/fp.

THE BIG FRESNO FAIR (FRESNO)

Our final day of county fair racing was among our most informative and enjoyable. Despite its emerging urban character, Fresno is very much an agricultural community, where interest in horse racing runs deep and big crowds fill the grandstand for all the races. The mixed

Winning by Ten (detail), Randall Robinson

Big Fresno Fair meet runs for eleven days in October and wraps up with the Bull Dog Stakes.

Press director Dan White answered our endless questions about racing here, and on the way to the parking lot at the end of the day, we even toured the cavernous electronics trailer where audio- and videotapes of the races are produced and simulcast signals are sent and received. Address: 1121 S. Chance Avenue, Fresno, CA 93702; phone: 559-650-3247/(fax) 559-650-3226; Web site: http://www.fresnofair.com.

DOC TO THE JOCKS

John Maffeo, medical director of Sequoia Community Health Centers in Fresno, and his partners have been volunteering their professional services to the Fresno Fair jockeys since 1999. They are there to assess matters and determine the treatment strategy if a rider is injured or doesn't feel right.

"Jockeys know their bodies very, very well," Dr. Maffeo comments. The key to getting them to seek medical attention, he says, is in the day-to-day continuity of having a familiar medical team available. Maffeo drops in at the jockeys' room or takes their calls on his cell phone. He mainly treats simple primary care needs and minor sports injuries.

Dr. Maffeo discusses an ailment.

For jockeys, chronic back flare-ups are common. Because of their exertions on the track, especially during the summer or when riding in a hot climate, they are also always at risk for dehydration. Clouds of dirt and even small rocks get kicked up during a race, so Maffeo may treat minor abrasions. In an agricultural area such as Fresno County, the presence of pollens and other allergens make allergies in general another common problem among the jockeys.

The track physician is the one who determines whether a jockey should be excused from a race. If so, he alerts the racing steward, who will line up another jockey, a substitute rider who's waiting eagerly for the sudden opportunity to jump on a horse.

CALIFORNIA TRAVEL SECTION

BELOW, YOU'LL FIND A MILEAGE CHART LISTING THE DISTANCES
BETWEEN THE REGIONAL RACETRACKS AND ALL THE CITIES
DISCUSSED IN THE FOLLOWING TRAVEL SECTION. **T**HE CITY OR
CITIES CLOSEST TO A TRACK ARE INDICATED BY AN **X**.

COAST TO COAST	Del Mar	Los Angeles	San Francisco
Alameda County Fair	450 miles	350 miles	**X** 40 miles
Bay Meadows Race Track	480 miles	380 miles	**X** 20 miles
The Big Fresno Fair	320 miles	220 miles	**X** 190 miles
Cal Expo	490 miles	390 miles	**X** 90 miles
Del Mar	**X** * miles	100 miles	485 miles
Fairplex Park	95 miles	**X** 30 miles	410 miles
Golden Gate Fields	480 miles	380 miles	**X** * miles
Hollywood Park	105 miles	**X** 15 miles	385 miles
Humboldt County Fair	735 miles	635 miles	**X** 260 miles
San Joaquin Fair	440 miles	340 miles	**X** 80 miles
San Mateo County Fair	480 miles	380 miles	**X** 20 miles
Santa Anita Park	110 miles	**X** 15 miles	390 miles
Solano County Fair	485 miles	385 miles	**X** 35 miles
Sonoma County Fair	530 miles	430 miles	**X** 55 miles

*The racetrack is located inside or within 10 miles of the city limits.

MUST SEE / MUST DO

DEL MAR

Jake's, Del Mar

Del Mar Thoroughbred Club nestles so near the beach that horses once exercised in the sand and swam in the ocean. When the last race is run, it's our turn. We aren't taking the freeway to dinner. All along the South Coast Highway, beachside communities deliver hip, neorustic, and high-style dining. With the surf crashing, a salty breeze blowing, and diamond-bright stars above—or even when the muffled fog rolls in—the ocean is a dark gift of nature by night.

Two blocks east of the ocean, Camino Del Mar (Highway 101) runs through the heart of Del Mar village, still an authentic old California coastal town—albeit one where real estate prices are now out of sight. Residents are fervent in their anti-McMansion stance and have preserved the scale and individuality of architecture that make downtown Del Mar fun to browse and relax in. Quaint it isn't; it's authentic and refreshing. Explore specialty shops from one end of town to the other, visit **Del Mar Plaza** (http://www.delmar plaza.com) on Camino Del Mar, and then hop down to the beach for some fresh salt air and tide pool exploration.

From Del Mar, drive north four miles on the Coast Highway, and check out cute **Cardiff-by-the-Sea** (http://www.

Del Mar beach

cardiffbythesea.org), a small town above the ocean with houses climbing into the hills. Developed by an Englishman, Cardiff is actually part of Encinitas but likes to be thought of as separate. It offers upscale shopping, plenty of beach space for surfing and swimming, and good dining on Restaurant Row.

Don't leave without a drive into La Jolla or San Diego. La Jolla, eight miles south of Del Mar, is home to the University of California, San Diego, and Scripps Institution of Oceanography. Long and lovely, **Scripps Beach** (La Jolla Shores Drive), with its dune buggy–driving lifeguards, is another utterly wonderful piece of paradise.

San Diego is a world apart. Rich in Spanish mission revival architecture and possessive of its early Spanish colonial and Mexican history, **Old Town San Diego** (San Diego Avenue and Twiggs Street) is a unique place to begin investigating the past. Shop downtown at multistoried Horton Plaza. Nearby, the **Gaslamp Quarter** (http://www.gas lamp.org) offers great little restaurants with sidewalk café–style dining. The waterfront shops and the grounds at **Marina Park** (750/850 State Street), anchored by the convention center, can easily fill a day. **Balboa Park** (1549 El Prado; 619-239-0512; http://balboa park.org) houses fifteen museums, acres of landscaped gardens, as well as the renowned **San Diego Zoo** (2920 Zoo Drive; 619-718-3000;

http://www.sandiegozoo.org). Check http://www.sandiego.org or http://www.sannet.gov for all the details on city attractions and events.

LOS ANGELES

Los Angeles, the fantasy and entertainment capital of the world, has many faces. Most intriguing to us is its intense, ultra-glamorous, and creative tempo. Here, the world's superstars live richly, sometimes beyond comprehension, residing in opulent spaces and flying to parties at luxurious and remote destinations. The average Angeleno, by contrast, is just trying to make a buck, to sit down at night to a little slice of the American dream. LA—synonymous with the California Dream—and its perimeter, is home to some eight million residents.

To get around LA, forget good walking shoes—the car's the thing. By the end of WWII, Los Angles, more than any U.S. city except Detroit, had embraced the automobile culture. As the city sprawled onto the beach and up into the San Gabriel Mountains, the automobile and the new freeway system wed happily—one of the few Hollywood marriages to last, for better or for worse. There is a transit system, but this isn't New York City. Do rent a car.

Our current favorite neighborhoods in L.A. are downtown, Beverly Hills, Marina del Rey, Santa Monica, and West Hollywood. So we started our

The new Walt Disney Concert Hall

adventure at the heart of the city, right downtown. City center has been reinvigorated with loft conversions, street-level cafés and shops below corporate towers, upscale dining and lodging spots, and exciting museums. On Grand Avenue, between Temple and First, are the **Mark Taper Forum** and the **Ahmanson Theater** (135 N. Grand Avenue; 213-628-2772; http://www.taperahman son.com) and the **Dorothy Chandler Pavilion** (213-972-8001; http://www.los angelesopera.com). Just down the block is the **Walt Disney Concert Hall** (111 South Grand Avenue; 323-850-2000; http://wdch.laphil.com/home.cfm), with its unique stainless steel exterior. Four blocks due east of Disney Hall, on Spring and First streets, is the **LA Times Building,** designed in the 1930s by Gordon B. Kaufmann, who also designed Santa Anita Park and the Hoover Dam.

Just northeast of modern downtown, on the other side of US 101, take a stroll down Olvera Street and through more than two centuries of history in the **El Pueblo de Los Angeles** area (http://www.cityofla.org/ELP/hisnfo .htm). The central plaza marks the spot where Los Angeles originated in the late 1700s as a Hispanic settlement. The **Avila Adobe**, now retrofitted, is the oldest surviving residence in the city and houses two museums offering up city history (10 Olvera Street; 213-680-2525; http://www.laokay.com/Adobes-Historic.htm). Stop at the **El Pueblo Visitors Center** on Olvera for a brochure on the historic buildings (tours available, 213-680-2381). Enjoy the world-famous **bazaar** on Olvera Street, a mélange of Mexican food, art, souvenirs, and bargains.

Head southwest from El Pueblo to Wilshire Boulevard, which extends all the way to Santa Monica on the ocean, passing through Beverly Hills. Going west on Wilshire you'll find numerous classic art deco structures, as well as two of the city's biggest cultural treasures: the **Los Angeles County Museum of Art** (LACMA), at 5905 Wilshire (323-857-6000; http://www.lacma.org), and **La Brea Tar Pits** next door (323-934-7243; http://www.tarpits.org). LACMA, founded in 1910, is the largest art museum west of Chicago, with a nearly universal art collection. La Brea Tar Pits feature the remains of LA's now extinct Ice Age animals, who wandered into a preshistoric "lake" of tar and met a slow, oozy death.

Continue along Wilshire to **Beverly Hills** (http://www.beverlyhills.org), one of the city's most prestigious neighborhoods, with a thriving business and retail district. The William Morris Agency, Merv Griffin Enterprises, and DreamWorks have their offices here. Shopping is equally high-end, especially in the golden triangle, a wedge of exclusive boutiques and designer shops lining Rodeo Drive and Wilshire and Santa Monica boulevards. Keep an eye out for residents such as Steve Martin, Cher, Eddie Murphy, and Bette Midler.

In Beverly Hills you can pick up **Sunset Boulevard**. In the 1920s, it was a dirt road leading from the studios up into the hills, where the movie people lived. As Hollywood grew, promoters began lining the strip with restaurants, nightclubs, hotels, and smaller movie houses. Movie stars flocked to Sunset Strip for after-hours dinner and recreation, and fans and tourists soon followed. Sunset Boulevard remains the hippest place in the city, where celebrities and underlings may be spied in their trendiest and most outrageous gear. The legendary nightclub **Ciro's** is now home to oft-televised stand-up comedians at the **Comedy Store** (8433 Sunset Boulevard, 323-656-6226). If it's sold out, trek over to the **Laugh Factory** (8001 Sunset Boulevard, 323-656-1336).

Griffith Observatory

Cruise northeastward on Sunset and eventually you'll reach Hollywood, birthplace of the film industry in the early twentieth century. With so many varied landscapes immediately nearby, Hollywood could be transformed into any setting from the Wild West to Mount Everest to 20,000 leagues under the sea. As one-reel nickel movies evolved into feature films, big studios sprang up along Prospect Avenue (renamed Hollywood Boulevard). From 1916 to 1946, the movie industry was the biggest employer in Southern California.

The 1950s brought recording studios and the birth of the rock star/movie star phenomenon. In 1958, the star-studded **Hollywood Walk of Fame** (http://www.seeing-stars.com) was created to honor influential members of the industry. Most of the big studios have moved elsewhere now, but the Kodak Theatre, opened in 2001 on Hollywood at Highland, hosts the movie industry's most prestigious awards event, the Academy Awards.

Dozens of historic landmarks line the streets of Hollywood. Visit the **Hollywood Heritage Museum** (2100 North Highland; 323-874-4005; http://www.hollywoodheritage.org), once the barn studio of prolific director Cecil B. DeMille, and **The Charlie Chaplin Studios** (1416 N. La Brea Avenue). If your interests run instead to exterior residential remodeling ideas, take notes while you're rolling along

Santa Monica Pier

Sunset over the Pacific

Mulholland Drive in the Hollywood Hills. The hills hold palatial residences that are home to countless wealthy movie stars and other Los Angeles figures. The Hollywood sign, erected in 1923, lurks above you.

Just north of Hollywood is **Griffith Park**. On a clear day, it is one of the best places in the city for getting the lay of the land. One of the largest municipal parks in the United States, it comprises 4,100 acres, which include wide meadows as well as narrow trails and bridle paths climbing to an elevation of 1,600 feet in the foothills of the rugged Santa Monica Mountains. The **ranger station** is located at 4400 Crystal Springs Road (http://www.ci.la.ca .us.com). You can also stop by the **Griffith Observatory** (2800 East Observatory Road; 323-664-1181; http://www.griffith obs.org), scheduled to reopen in May 2006 after renovation.

If you'd rather drive west than east on Sunset Boulevard when you leave Beverly Hills, you can visit the **Getty Center** (1200 Getty Center Drive; 310-440-7300; http://www.getty.edu). It's up in the hills, with incredible views, noteworthy architecture, and outdoor sculptures. Although the space is rambling—five pavilions hold the mainly European art collections—an intimacy is created in the use of lines and spaces, fountains and courtyards. Along with its world-class museum, the Getty comprises a complex of research, conservation, and educational arms.

By now you'll be ready to escape Los Angeles with its gridlock and auto fumes. Head straight west to the beaches and resort communities lining Santa Monica Bay. **Santa Monica** has art galleries, touristy California souvenir shops, and cafés and restaurants. The **Santa Monica Pier**, at the foot of Colorado Boulevard, marks the northern edge of the beach. UCLA's **Ocean Discovery Center** (http://www.odc .ucla.edu), at the pier, displays local marine life. Dining options, the events calendar, and more can be explored at http://www.santamonica.com.

Walk the pier south to **Venice**. On the boardwalk, you'll find plenty of sidewalk vendors and, if you're fortunate, some amazing street performers. There are a number of specialty food shops, art galleries, and small clothing shops for you to enjoy. Don't leave without taking a stroll along the bungalow-lined canals that evoke the town's European namesake. Before staging your LA exit, we also suggest stopping someplace for a cocktail and raising a glass or two to remarkable Southern California.

SAN FRANCISCO

At just forty-six square miles, San Francisco is among the smallest of world-class cities. Tightly confined by its peninsular geography, this hilly cos-

The Golden Gate Bridge

mopolis spills to the very edges of the sea—the Pacific Ocean on the west and San Francisco Bay to the north and east. From atop its higher peaks, you can feast on majestic views of the Golden Gate Bridge, ferries and sailing regattas skirting the bay's small islands, and the windswept Marin headlands in the distance. Or look east to the Bay Bridge stretching high above the water, connecting the city with the East Bay metropolis. Look down, and the city's iconic landmarks—the clock-faced Ferry Building on the Embarcadero, the soaring Transamerica pyramid, the Museum of Modern Art's striped cylindrical tower—stand out amid the clusters of skyscrapers, rows of pastel Victorian houses, narrow streets winding into secluded hills, and other distinctive enclaves worthy of exploration.

The discovery of gold in 1848 turned this remote seaport village into a mecca for adventurers, and wealth gen-

Transamerica Pyramid

erated through mining shaped the modern city. Cable car engineering made the hills navigable, and Nob Hill became legendary as the domain of the wealthy. Opulence, typified by the Palace Hotel, seemed to know no limits. After the 1906 earthquake and fires destroyed much of the city, San Francisco rebuilt in grand fashion, celebrating its resurrection in 1915 with the Panama-Pacific International Exposition. In 1989, when an earthquake twisted apart the Embarcadero freeway, the city seized the opportunity to demolish the bay shore eyesore. San Francisco's gorgeous waterfront vistas are back, and at the foot of Market Street, the city's most famous thoroughfare, the handsome Ferry Building again reigns supreme.

Start your sightseeing by picking up brochures, maps, and schedules at the city's **Visitor Information Center**, on the lower level of Halladie Plaza (900 Market Street, 415-391-2001 for current city events updates), beside the cable car turnaround at Powell and Market. The Powell Street cable car line (at Market; http://www .sfcablecar.com) runs up and down hill to the edge of Chinatown, where it splits into two lines, both proceeding down to the waterfront. On the lower level of the plaza as well is the Powell Street station of the Bay Area Rapid Transit (BART), the underground transit system. BART (http://www.bart .gov) travel is best for getting to the East Bay and back or for saving calf muscles along Market, but it does not penetrate other areas. Buses do, and a (Muni) terminal is also located here on the lower level. For trendy shopping at **Union Square**, board the Powell Street cable car or walk up Powell to Geary or Post streets, which frame the square.

Along **Market Street** are the Financial District, numerous exclusive shops and hotels, and the upscale San Francisco Shopping Centre. A few blocks farther south, and just west of Market, between Hyde and Van Ness, the **Civic Center** complex begins, which includes the new Main Library, City Hall (with its baroque gilt dome), the Opera House, and the Symphony Hall. Key players in the city's intertwined financial, political, and cultural circles stride along Market street impeccably clad in designer classics and the latest European fashions.

The **San Francisco Museum of Modern Art** (151 Third Street; 415-357-4000; http://www.sfmoma.org), in the heart of downtown, is one of the city's most dynamic architectural structures. Its central cylindrical skylight appears ringed in black and white. Four floors display permanent and visiting exhibitions. It includes an extensive bookstore and gift shop and has a good café. Across the street are the **Yerba Buena Gardens** (899 Howard Street; 415-543-1275; http://www.yerbabuenagardens.com) and the **Center for the Arts** (701 Mission Street; 415-978-2787), which adjoin **Moscone Convention Center** (747 Howard Street; 415-974-4000; http://www.mosconecenter.com).

Nowhere in the city is artistic creativity more concentrated than in the **Castro district**, a neighborhood at the south end of Market Street. San Francisco's affluent gay and lesbian community tends to concentrate here, where shopping is eclectic and dining and nightlife are abundant. Just beyond the Castro, where Market Street becomes Portola Avenue, is **Twin Peaks**, with superb views—when not socked in by the notorious fog.

Golden Gate Park (Fulton at 36th Avenue/Lincoln at 41st Avenue; 415-831-2700), stretching from the Haight

Alcatraz Island

Ashbury section of the city out to the ocean, is legendary for its Summer of Love folk and rock concerts in the 1960s. These days it's enjoyed by a diverse mix of residents and visitors, who picnic, play sports, attend outdoor concerts, and explore its numerous themed gardens. Museums in the park include the **California Academy of Sciences** (875 Howard Street; 415-321-8000; http://www.calacademy.org) and, for art, the new **de Young Museum** (50 Hagiwara Tea Garden Drive; 415-863-3330; http://www.thinker.org/deyoung), which has recently replaced its former self.

San Franciscans are passionately outspoken about most matters involving city life. This vital energy spills over to concern for protecting and enhancing the region's natural and built environments. Many of the city's best-loved landmarks, originally planned to solve municipal challenges, were so strikingly designed that they have become huge tourist destinations.

The **Golden Gate Bridge**, a perfect example of form married to function, spans the entrance to San Francisco Bay, connecting the city with Marin County. When it opened in 1937, the burnt orange bridge was the longest and tallest suspension bridge in the world, and it is still the third largest single-span bridge. Its six lanes carry traffic, while its pedestrian walkway is always bustling with tourists. Its hollow twin towers rise 746 feet above the water.

Niebaum-Coppola Winery, Napa Valley

Like the bridge, the famous zigzag section of **Lombard Street**, between Hyde and Leavenworth, was designed to solve a problem: the steep summit of Russian Hill. The solution was eight switchbacks added in the 1920s for cars. This short stretch is now one-way for vehicles descending it, but pedestrians can hike up or walk down its sidewalk at will. If you drive down Lombard, continue east another two or three blocks and then turn left (north) on Taylor Street and walk another seven blocks, you've reached Fisherman's Wharf, on the **Embarcadero**, the wide, palm-lined boulevard that curves around the San Francisco Bay waterfront. Check out the **San Francisco National Maritime Historic Park** at the Hyde Street Pier (900 Beach Street, 415-556-8177, http://www.nps.gov/safr/local/top .html), with its nautically oriented museum, then walk east, enjoying the artists' tables, fellow tourists, souvenir shops, seafood restaurants galore, and pungent wharf smells that recall an earlier time when fishing still dominated this storied spot. To learn of many other things worth doing here, check http://gocalifornia.about.com/cs/san francisco/a/sffishwharf.htm

Consider wrapping up your city tour by looking back on it—from **Alcatraz Island**, three miles out in the bay. "The Rock" was built as a military fort in 1859 and later became a military prison and then a federal penitentiary, which closed in 1963. Some of its buildings include the prison, historic officers' quarters, barracks, and a small morgue. Advance reservations for tours are often necessary and include ferry transportation from Pier 41. Call 415-705-5555, or go to http://www.nps.gov/alca for ticket information and tour schedules.

Back on the mainland, the **Palace of Fine Arts** (3301 Lyon Street; 415-567-6642) is adjacent to the **Exploratorium** and dates to the Panama-Pacific International Exposition, the 1915 world's fair celebration described earlier. Fair buildings were built on reclaimed bay land near the Marina District. The fine arts building, a gorgeous neoclassical rotunda designed by Bernard Maybeck, is the only survivor and was restored in the 1960s. Science exhibits fill the interior, which also has an auditorium that hosts an indie film festival each May. Near the Golden Gate Bridge, the Exploratorium sits on the eastern edge of the Presidio (3601 Lyon Street; 415-397-5673; http://www.palace offinearts.org; http://www.explorator ium.com).

The San Francisco sojourner besieged by too much time and money will appreciate our final suggestions for hitting the trail—outings to California's famed wine country and the spectacular Yosemite Valley in the Sierra Nevada mountain range. The Sonoma and Napa valleys are within ninety minutes of the city. More than two hundred **wineries**—many of them world class, producing only a few dozen cases per year—line Highway 29 and its quieter twin, the Silverado Trail, or dot the narrow crossroads connecting them.

Among our many favorite wineries are Niebaum-Coppola (Rutherford), Opus One (Oakville), Trefethen (Napa), B.R. Cohn (Glen Ellen), and Robert Mondavi (Oakville). Explore individual winery Web sites, among them: http://www.niebaum-coppola .com/site.php; http://www.opusone winery.com; http://www.trefethen.com; http://www.brcohn.com; http://www .robertmondaviwinery.com. Many have links to or recommendations for nearby lodging and fine dining, should you decide to linger. Save an hour to visit charming downtown St. Helena. If you visit Glen Ellen, in Sonoma County, stop at **Jack London State Historic Park**, in

Glen Ellen (4000 London Ranch Road; 707-938-5216; http://www.parks.sono ma.net/JLPark.html), for a tour of the writer's lair, the House of Happy Walls, and the ruins of his Wolf House.

From San Francisco, **Yosemite** is four and a half hours east. En route, you cross the wide Central Valley, heart of California's farm and ranch lands and its enormous agribusinesses. As the freeway (I-580) runs out, Highway 120 winds across cattle country and into the rocky foothills of the Sierra Nevada, through small gold rush towns that celebrate their heritage while juggling growth, tourism, and environmental issues. Climb higher and the world empties, forests thicken, and pines grow taller. At Big Oak Flat, the park's west entrance on Highway 120, pick up maps, postcards, books, granola bars, and water. For the next hour, you're up, down, and around, immersed in the rarest of scenery. Finally, you drop down into the awesome Yosemite Valley (http://www.nps.gov/yose, and http:// www.yosemitepark.com). The rest is up to you.

Yosemite

WHERE TO STAY

DEL MAR

L'Auberge Del Mar Resort and Spa
1540 Camino Del Mar
Del Mar, CA 92014
858-793-6493/800-245-9757
http://www.laubergedelmar.com
$300–$530 during racing season
Within a block of the beach, right in Del Mar village, and only a few blocks from the racetrack, L'Auberge tries to anticipate everything you might want, from select goodies waiting in your room prior to arrival to spa services. Dine at J. Taylor's on the premises; catch live jazz on the weekends; and luxuriate in private, delightful oceanside surroundings with a fireplace, patio, or balcony room.

LOS ANGELES

The Mosaic Hotel
125 South Spalding Drive
Beverly Hills, CA 90212
310-278-0303/800-463-4466
http://www.preferredhotels.com
$229 and up
The Mosaic, with forty-seven charming rooms and attentive guest services, is perfectly located for exploring the best of Beverly Hills, including the exclusive shops on Rodeo Drive and Wilshire Boulevard. Guest room decor emphasizes tranquility, with soothing prints of natural subjects on the walls, and plush bedding. With a view of the landscaped patio and pool area, the lounge makes a perfect retreat for rest and a drink before taking in the marvels of the city again.

The Regent Beverly Hills
9500 Wilshire Boulevard
Beverly Hills, CA 90212
310-275-5200/800-545-4000
http://www.regentbeverlyhills.com
$400 and up ($4,000 for a presidential suite)
Celebrities play or stay here—as we all should. Hotel expansion has created two distinct styles to the hotel, where lights such as Warren Beatty have taken up residence. The stunning lobby, dining room, bistro lounge, and bar are visually rich with warm woods, Murano chandeliers, and lush floral arrangements. Guest rooms can include private terraces, dining rooms, sunken tubs, and private screening rooms with satellite hookup. Full spa services are available. This is a perfect location for walking to Century City, deluxe shopping, and exclusive dining.

The Ritz-Carlton Marina del Rey
4375 Admiralty Way
Marina del Rey, CA 90292
310-823-1700/800-241-3333
http://www.ritzcarlton.com
$279 and up
A fishing pier, a public promenade, a park, and six thousand boat slips make Marina del Rey, nestled between Venice and Manhattan beaches, the most nautical of LA neighborhoods. One of our weekends coincided with the opening of the Santa Anita meet on December 26. At the entrance to the Ritz, we loved the majestic Christmas

tree, covered with dazzling lights and delicate golden balls. Rooms here are spacious and luxurious, with nice conversation areas for discussing the party itinerary over bubbly. The gleaming white marble baths come with haute little body products, and housekeeping is particularly attentive.

The Wyndham Bel Age
1020 N. San Vicente Boulevard
West Hollywood, CA 90069
310-854-1111/877-999-3223
http://www.wyndham.com
$143–$259
The plush muted-yet-distinctive architectural features and appointments in the Wyndham lobby create a sense of expectation upon arrival, as does the hotel's elegant and international clientele. Fine art lines the hallways and fills every room. Our suite was spacious, comfortable, and very quiet, though we were perfectly positioned for an enjoyable night on Sunset Boulevard. The hotel bar often stays crowded and animated until closing. In the morning, coffee and breakfast beside the Wyndham rooftop pool were an ideal way to start our day while studying the lush Beverly Hills to the northwest. Make reservations well in advance to avoid disappointment.

SAN FRANCISCO

Claremont Resort, Spa, and Tennis Club
41 Tunnel Road
Berkeley, CA 94105
510-843-3000/800-478-3101
http://www.claremontresort.com
$165 and up
A shimmering grand dame of a luxury resort sitting tall against the Berkeley hills, the Claremont has been a prestigious address for decades. One of the premier hotels of the early twentieth century, the Claremont has hosted celebrities, dignitaries, and scholars of all nations. With commanding views of the San Francisco bay area, it feels exquisitely isolated and yet is just a little southeast of the UC Berkeley campus. It offers tennis, spa packages, nightly entertainment, and special events, and it is within walking distance of numerous little shops and cafés.

The Clift Hotel
495 Geary Street
San Francisco, CA 94102
415-775-7500/800-652-5438
http://www.clifthotel.com
$325 and up
At the storied Clift, you can opt for a loft, a suite, or an apartment. As with other traditional hotels, rooms are not overly spacious, but their soothing tones, ornate mirrors, and goose-down bedding are luxurious. The hotel's Redwood Room serves perfect martinis; drinks are also available in the more casual "living room." The Clift is perfectly situated within the theater district near Union Square for fine entertainment and shopping. Exercise equipment and spa treatments are available upon request.

Intercontinental Mark Hopkins Hotel
One Nob Hill
999 California Street
San Francisco, CA 94108
415-392-3434
http://www.ichotelsgroup.com
$165–$3,500

Explore Nob Hill from the very top, where cable cars run in several directions. Established in 1926 on the site where the mansion of Central Pacific Railroad partner Mark Hopkins once stood, the hotel, with its regal entrance, commands unforgettable views of the city and bay. Its 380 rooms include luxurious suites with outdoor patios and every amenity one expects at such an address, along with twenty-four-hour room and meal service. Do not skip the nineteenth floor Top of the Mark restaurant for dinner. Test one of the bartender's one hundred specialty martinis.

Sheraton Palace Hotel
2 New Montgomery
San Francisco, CA 94105
415-512-1111
http://www.sfpalace.com or http://www.sheraton.com
$229–$599
Opened in the 1870s, the Palace Hotel was entirely rebuilt after the 1906 earthquake and fires. The elegant meeting rooms and ballrooms, and the exquisite Garden Court dining room—with its ornate chandeliers; marble columns; and immense, domed, stained glass ceiling—create a baronial, European-style atmosphere. Situated on Market Street and containing other popular dining spots and designer boutiques, it is convenient to numerous cultural institutions and the shops at Union Square. Guest rooms are perfectly sophisticated.

WHERE TO WINE & DINE

DEL MAR

Americana Restaurant
1454 Camino Del Mar
Del Mar, CA 92014
858-794-6838
http://www.americanarestaurant.com
$49.95 dinner for two
Despite the black-and-white tile floors and black-and-chrome barstools, the Americana is accented with old-world touches rather than 1950s nostalgia. On Tuesday nights, a guest bartender rolls in; on Wednesdays, wine prices are rolled back; and on Thursdays, the house is shaking or stirring half-price martinis. For dinner, when the white tablecloths and candles come out, we recommend starting with the ahi tuna tartare and progressing to the seared duck with couscous and dried fruits and fig sauce.

Del Mar Brigantine
3263 Camino Del Mar
Del Mar, CA 92014
858-481-1166
http://www.brigantine.com
$18–$34
Yes, we closed the bar here, but not without help. Innocently stopping in for a cocktail, we encountered a small party of Aussie turf writers who had been at the races, too. There went our winnings, but the evening was worth it. We treated us all to a round of incredibly perfect Cajun fried oysters, crab cakes, and oysters Rockefeller—with champagnes and neat bourbons, and then progressed to the heated outdoor deck for views of the ocean and our fabulous seafood dinners.

Jake's Del Mar
1660 Coast Boulevard
Del Mar, CA 92014
858-755-2002
http://www.jakesdelmar.com
$19 to market price for lobster

Drop down two blocks west of Camino Del Mar (Highway 101), and you're on the water. Designed by internationally known architect Ken Kellogg, Jake's features soaring ceilings, big windows, and ocean views. The menu features sensational fresh seafood and steaks, served with delicious and surprising fusion touches. Weekdays, enjoy happy hour with drinks and appetizers at the bar.

Milton's Delicatessen and Restaurant
(in Flower Hill Mall)
2660 Via De La Valle
Del Mar, CA 92014
858-792-2225
http://www.miltonsbaking.com
$7.95–$14.95

Management says the horse crowd has breakfast here; we know the jockeys won't touch most of the goodies on the menu, or even the enticements in the well-stocked deli cases. But with a soaring brick wall, light streaming in from big windows, great food, and camaraderie among strangers who skim the newspaper or the *DRF* at the next table, we give it a yes.

LOS ANGELES

Casa Escobar
14160 Palawan Way
Marina Del Rey, CA 90291
310-822-2199
http://www.casaescobar.htm
$5.95–$17.95

If you're staying in Marina del Rey, a short walk toward the ocean along Admiralty Way and you're here. Casa Escobar, established in the 1940s, may be the most creative of any Mexican restaurant we've ever known. Cozy little nooks, colorful walls and furniture, an endless menu of exotic tropical drinks, and great fresh Mex entrées make this a hit. A personal favorite, the chicken mole, was perfect. Having a good time is highly encouraged by the restaurant staff.

Mirabelle
8768 W. Sunset Boulevard
West Hollywood, CA 90069
310-659-6022
http://www.mirabelle.com
$18–$44

Serving nice and late (until 12:30 a.m.), Mirabelle is a friendly, noisy party just hoping you'll join in. Its eclectic interior features interesting patterns in wood and fabric, and there's a comfy lounge area and exterior patio. The menu runs toward the sea, with oysters, scallops, and crab, but excellent chicken and steaks are offered, too. You'll find great music, excellent service, and a wide array of fine wines.

Trilussa
9601 Brighton Way
Beverly Hills, CA 90210
310-859-0067

$7.95–$19.95
High-style Italian is what we have here, with excellent fusion plates and great service throughout dinner, taken at the bar. Filled with many perfect-looking people on this Saturday night, Trilussa was crowded, noisy, and energizing. The lobster ravioli was great.

SAN FRANCISCO

The Cliff House
1090 Point Lobos
San Francisco, CA 94121
415-386-3330
http://www.cliffhouse.com
$9.50–$28
Sitting virtually over the Pacific Ocean at Point Lobos, the 140-year-old Cliff House now encompasses the two-level Bistro, along with a new wing for Sutro's and the Zinc Bar. The sparkling, contemporary interiors overlook a 180-degree ocean view that takes in the Marin Headlands. The food here is good, though the location is the lure. Open for breakfast at 9:00 a.m. After your meal, hike down to Ocean Beach, just south of the restaurant, and enjoy the moods of sky and water up close.

The Garden Court
(at the Sheraton Palace)
2 New Montgomery (at Market)
San Francisco, CA 94105
415-512-1111
http://www.gardencourt-restaurant.com
$17–$30
Open for breakfast at 6:30 a.m., the Garden Court provides a grand yet intimate setting, whether it's for a memorable downtown dinner or the gourmet champagne brunch on weekends. The space is opulent, with marble floors and columns, tall potted ferns, dazzling chandeliers, and the celebrated domed glass ceiling. Entrées feature California and American cuisine. Solo musicians perform on weekends. Smart casual attire is suggested.

Ristorante Fior d'Italia
(in the San Remo Hotel)
2237 Mason Street
San Francisco, CA 94133
415-986-1886
http://www.fior.com
$9–$32
Billed as the oldest Italian restaurant in America, the Fior d'Italia became a landmark of the city's North Beach neighborhood, where many early Italian American residents were commercial fishermen. Although the original Union Street site closed in February 2005 following a fire, the owners expect to open at their new location (November 1, 2005) six blocks away in the charming old San Remo Hotel. Fior d'Italia's specialties will remain traditional Italian seafood dishes.

Ristorante Umbria
198 Second Street
San Francisco, CA
415-546-6985
http://www.ristoranteumbria.com
$5.25–$23.50
This intimate little Italian spot is contemporary and cozy, with extensive, interesting use of woods throughout. Rustic tile floors and decorative finishes recall the owners'

regional roots. Authentic Italian entrées are deliciously prepared, from the fresh *insalate* and home-baked *panini* to pizza, pasta, chicken, seafood, and, one of our favorites, *saltimbocca di pollo,* a poultry version of the veal classic. For lighter fare, the pizza Margherita is fresh and tasty. Located in the SoMa (for South of Market) district, Umbria is a handy spot if you're attending a Giants game at the SBC Park. Open for lunch and dinner, with outdoor seating.

Skates on the Bay
100 Seawall Drive (at the Berkeley Marina)
Berkeley, CA 94702
510-549-1900
http://www.sakatesonthebay.com
$16–$52
On the Berkeley side of the San Francisco Bay, Skates delivers fine dining with creative flair. It's a lively after-racing spot. Built on pilings over the water, Skates offers spectacular views across the bay. Specialties include fresh grilled seafood, Omaha steaks, and herb-roasted poultry. If you're game for an herbaceous cocktail, try the "green" bar menu—perhaps a grand thyme, made with gin, vodka, fresh thyme, and Grand Marnier; or a lavender cosmos martini.

John McCirrick, famed British bookmaker

CONCLUSION:
THE GRAND FINALE

*I*n our life-at-a-glance planner, all the big race days are circled in red. As horses test their mettle on ovals from Dallas to Dubai, from New York to Newmarket, from Los Angeles to Longchamp, we tear off the pages from January to September, noting the winners of all the major races. Come late October, speculation about who's truly the most powerful and swiftest reaches its most fevered pitch. The matter is resolved on a single autumn day, with the running of the Breeders' Cup World Thoroughbred Championships. These eight races, all Grade 1, define the most important day in international horse racing. Older races may be more steeped in history, pageantry, and tradition, but winning a Breeders' Cup (BC) race is the highest of honors. And, with a purse of $4 million, the Breeders' Cup Classic, a 1 ¼-mile contest on the dirt, is the richest race in America.

The Breeders' Cup races rotate annually among U.S. Thoroughbred racetracks, which welcome an audience that often exceeds fifty thousand spectators. (It was held at Woodbine in Canada in 1996.) Unlike a day spent waiting for a single, penultimate race, the Breeders' Cup is a roller coaster ride through eight different categories. Because the quality of competition is world class, the winning horses often receive coveted Eclipse Awards at the sport's year-end banquet. Often, Horse of the Year, the sport's highest individual honor, is decided by the outcome of the Breeder's Cup Classic.

The Breeders' Cup, brainchild of breeder and philanthropist John Gaines (1928–2005), premiered—and was televised—at Hollywood Park in 1984. The eight-race roster currently carries a combined $14 million in prizes. Some 80 percent of Breeders' Cup contestants are U.S.-bred, the others are primarily from Europe. Each race is limited to fourteen contestants. The races are: the Distaff (for fillies and mares), the Turf (for three-year-olds and up), the Juvenile (for two-year-olds), the Mile (for three-year-olds and up), the Filly and Mare Turf, the Juvenile Fillies, and the Sprint (for three-year-olds and up). The grand finale, the Breeders' Cup Classic, is a ten-furlong race currently worth $4 million, divided among the top five finishers. In the winner's circle, the winning owner receives a Breeders' Cup bronze-on-marble trophy, bearing the replica of an imposing Italian horse created by renaissance sculptor Giovanni de Bologna.

Months in advance, the Breeders' Cup team begins preparations on every aspect of the event, from the dining rooms to the paddock to the quarantine facility that houses the foreign horses. The racetrack, fervent about making its spotlight day the best in BC history, readies itself with the fluff-

and-spit-shine. A smart host city, too, recognizing the potential impact of a hundred thousand plus visitors, puts out the welcome mat, infusing the days leading up to the celebration with its best regional flavor.

On race day, a Saturday in late October or early November, celebrities (who may or may not own horses) hide out or willingly parade before the paparazzi lens. Media's biggest personalities arrive early, plug in, hype the excitement, and cover every aspect of the racing. Bantering sages such as Mike Battaglia and Kenny Mayne offer their perspectives, and British racing personality and bookie John "Muttonchops" McCrirrick is always on hand— sometimes wrapped snugly inside a buffalo robe and Davy Crockett cap, other times suitably duded-out in western boots, suede jacket, bolo, and, uh, a good-guy-white straw hat. While hand signaling his picks to the bookmakers back home, he's glad to toss betting tips to the tens of thousands of spectators assembled at the racetrack.

The Breeders' Cup is one of four days (the other three are the Triple Crown race days) during which regular patrons of the host track aren't guaranteed seats, unless they're card-carrying turf club members or own a private suite at the track. The event's admission policy, meant to be fair to all race fans, is based on a lottery system announced weeks in advance, with applications and seating processed by the BC itself. In 2004, the pageant, held for the first time at Lone Star Park in Texas, sold out in the first days of the lottery. Some attribute this to recent moments in racing that have captured new audiences. Two years' running of near-Triple Crown sweeps by Funny Cide and Smarty Jones, and the release of the beautifully rendered Seabiscuit movie in 2003, mesmerized even casual followers of the sport. Lone Star's marketing and publicity teams capitalized on Texan allure, too, romanticizing the western mystique, wide-open spaces, and bigness as goodness.

The 2005 contests were staged at Belmont Park, Long Island, which has hosted the event four times. As we pen this final chapter, Saint Liam is the 2005 winner of the BC Classic. His rider, jockey Jerry Bailey (five-time Classic winner), his trainer, Richard Dutrow Jr., and his owners, Suzanne and William Warren Jr., await the outcome of Eclipse voting, hoping Saint Liam wins the coveted Horse of the Year title. (Check http://ntra.com for the latest news on, as well as history of, the Breeders' Cup.) In each successive year, the promotional efforts of NTRA and Breeders' Cup have added up to an increasingly successful event for the sport.

No other sporting event rivals the tempo and excitement of Thoroughbred racing or is layered in so many dimensions. People and horses are united at every level of the sport, whether backside groom or front office executive, small-time owner or royal-family breeder. In our travels, we've scouted racetracks large and small, gorgeous and rickety, drinking in the scene from Del Mar to New York City and everywhere in between. We've caught the fast train to the Breeders' Cup several times. Buoyed by the mass camaraderie spilling over the clubhouse and grandstands, the flow of libations, a stack of vouchers, and most of all, the exhilarating spectacle of superior horsepower, we celebrate the sport of kings. We invite you to pony up and come along.

*O*ntario, settled by the British, has prevailed as the Thoroughbred capital of Canada since the earliest contests there in the late eighteenth century. Horse racing first came to Toronto in 1793, to a sandy stretch of land on Toronto Island, when soldiers exercising their horses naturally turned to racing them. The first recorded running of the King's Plate—the oldest stakes race in North America—took place in 1836, in Quebec. In later years, both the King's and Queen's Plates were run in Quebec, Toronto, and Montreal; eventually the prestigious race moved permanently to Woodbine, in Toronto.

The first race in Vancouver, British Columbia, was held on a downtown street in 1889, before spectators bunched in front of the Vancouver Hotel. The winner, Mayflower, was awarded $250, a tidy sum back then. At the same time, the British Columbia Jockey Club had begun clearing land for what would become Hastings Park the following year. In 1910, racing was the featured event at the Vancouver Exhibition, forerunner of the modern fairgrounds that stood beside the track.

The Canadian prairie, a northerly extension of the Great Plains that cozies up to the Canadian border, is a vast and sparsely populated region. Its three provinces, Alberta, Saskatchewan, and Manitoba, are both the breadbasket and the tri-tip center of the country. Farming is still king, and horses are meant for riding, ranching, and racing. Our shared agrarian roots mean that here, too, the provinces are speckled with fairgrounds that hold brief summer meets.

Toronto

BRITISH COLUMBIA

HASTINGS RACECOURSE

(VANCOUVER)

On a clear day at Hastings Racecourse, the view beyond the track is almost too pretty to be true. Looking north, the indigo blue waters of Burrard Inlet sport boats of all sizes. Behind them, the green peaks of the Pacific Coast mountains rise to surprising heights. The picturesque Ironworkers Memorial Bridge frames the view to the east, while the skyline of North Vancouver sits to the west.

The live racing season runs from late April to late November, offering solid purses throughout the season (the fattest of them hitting $100 thousand) coming in the peak of summer and early fall. Two high points of the Hastings Racecourse season are British Columbia (BC) Day in early August and the Championship Weekend in late September. BC Day is a "homebred" contest of seven races, whose purses total nearly $400 thousand. The Championship includes four major races run over the course of the weekend: the Sir Winston Churchill, the British Columbia Breeders' Cup Oaks (Can-G3), the BC Derby (Can-G3), and the Delta Colleen. The races are worth almost half a million dollars. With the 2004 announcement that gaming can be expanded at Hastings Racecourse, management, which has faced its share of recent uncertainties, is anticipating a bright future.

At most tracks, racing's historic feats are celebrated in the naming of stakes and handicaps. Here in Vancouver we clink our Molsons in June in honor of the John Longden Handicap. In 1965, Johnny Longden (1907–2003), who grew up in Alberta,

became the first jockey to win 6,000 races. He did it here at Hastings Park (then called Exhibition Park) and retired the next year, with 6,033 career victories. The British-born rider's career included winning the 1943 Triple Crown on Count Fleet—with a 25-length victory in the Belmont—and becoming the first ever to win the Kentucky Derby as both a rider and a trainer. He also founded the Jockey's Guild in 1941.

For the better part of the past century, this racetrack, within the boundaries of the city's Hastings Park, has been a popular destination for Vancouverites as well as horsemen and jockeys racing the West Coast circuit. Thoroughbreds and standardbreds share the eighty-three-day meet. Hastings Racecourse has a 6 ½-furlong track with a 513-foot home-stretch. There is also a ½-mile training track on site. Address: Hastings Park Racecourse, Vancouver, BC V5K 3N8; phone 604-254-1631/(fax) 604-251-0411; Web site: http://www.hastingspark.com.

ONTARIO

FORT ERIE RACE TRACK AND SLOTS (FORT ERIE)

Perched on the western shore of Lake Ontario directly across from Buffalo, New York, is the town of Fort Erie. Guarding the mouth of the river, this was the site of an important fort built in 1764. A British resupply point, the fort stood until 1814, when American troops destroyed it. (In 1939, the ruins were rebuilt as a tourist attraction.)

Built and inaugurated in 1897, Fort Erie Race Track proved an immediate hit. In 1959, thanks to the efforts of horseman E. P. Taylor, the Prince of Wales Stakes was established as the premier race here. It runs in mid-July as the second leg of the Canada Triple Crown series.

It was 1963 when a little bay colt strode out onto the sandy loam track for his maiden start. Breaking alertly, he quickly made short work of the seven other two-year-olds, his white-striped head bobbing along in front at the wire. Northern Dancer had arrived. The undersized bay blazed across the Canadian racing scene before traveling south to the United States. In 1964, he won the Kentucky Derby and Preakness Stakes before falling short with a third place finish in the Belmont Stakes. His get have since captured important races all over the world, and his lineage has been stamped deeply into the breed, with many dozens of international champions descending from him. Northern Dancer was inducted into the Racing Hall of Fame in 1976.

The track is a beautiful place, the historic stands looking out over the lush infield. Flowers blaze against the manicured hedges, and willow trees grace the edges of the small lake in the center of the infield. In 1999, having survived more than one hundred years in business, Fort Erie finished a makeover, opening its doors to a new 75,000-square-foot casino. Since then, purses have risen dramatically, drawing more horses and fans to the banks of the Niagara River. Fort Erie has a 1-mile track with a 1,060-foot-long homestretch. Its season runs from late April to late November. Address: 230 Catherine Street, Fort Erie, ON L2A 5N9; phone: 905-871-3200/(fax) 905-994-3629; Web site: http://www.forterieracing.com.

WOODBINE (Toronto)

In 1874, the first Woodbine was born. The track backed onto Lake Ontario, allowing horses to be exercised in the lake as a respite from the hard pounding of the track surface. Its inaugural meet was held on October 19, 1875. Canadians thronged the new track to watch a mixture of Thoroughbred, standardbred, and steeplechase races. In 1939, King George VI and Queen Elizabeth attended the track's eightieth running of the King's Plate, the first time British royalty had visited since Queen Victoria sanctioned horse racing here in 1860. In 1956, the Ontario Jockey Club constructed a course they named New Woodbine on Toronto's northwestern edge. In 1993, as the city encroached, the land was sold and quickly covered with houses. With "old" Woodbine closed, the city's racing scene switched entirely to New Woodbine, now simply called Woodbine.

The 13th Breeders' Cup World Thoroughbred Championship races came to Woodbine in 1996, the only time they have traveled outside the United States. The races not only drew a record Woodbine crowd of nearly 43,000 but also brought international recognition to the Canadian horse racing industry. Woodbine sports an interesting configuration; with a concentric ring of three separate tracks—one turf and two dirt—it's the only racetrack anywhere that can conduct Thoroughbred and harness racing simultaneously. With its 167-day season running from April into December, Woodbine is the destination of choice for witnessing Canada's major stakes races, including the prestigious $1-million Queen's (or King's, as determined by the reigning monarch's gender) Plate. It highlights the Festival of Racing, a mid-June weekend celebration including the $1.5-million Pepsi North American Cup and a complimentary track breakfast and tours. Counterpart to the Kentucky Derby, the 1 ¼-mile Queen's Plate showcases the best three-year-olds foaled in Canada.

In 2003 Wando won the June race on his way to sweeping Canada's Triple Crown, which also includes the Prince of Wales Stakes and Breeders' Stakes. Wando was later named Canadian Horse of the Year.

Accomplished horses from around the world regularly stop at Woodbine. In 1964, a huge crowd saw Canadian-bred Northern Dancer win the Queen's Plate, after taking the Kentucky Derby and Preakness. Nine years later, fans thronged here to witness the immortal Secretariat winning the final race of his career on the Woodbine turf. Fun to watch as well have been the ongoing jockey rivalries between Canadian and Caribbean tracks, especially Garrison Savannah in Barbados, which regularly spice up the international racing scene.

In 2000, Canadians approved slots at the racetrack. The machines improved the economics of the facility, field sizes remained good at more than eight horses, and by 2003 the daily purse average had risen to $550,000. Address: 555 Rexdale Boulevard, Toronto, ON M9W 5L2; phone 416-675-7223/(fax) 416-213-2104; Web site: http://www.woodbineentertainment.com.

CANADIAN PRAIRIE TRACKS

ASSINIBOIA DOWNS
(WINNIPEG, MANITOBA)

Racing fans and bettors can always find action in Winnipeg, where Assiniboia Downs stays open year-round, welcoming players to the casino as well as to the seventy-six-day racing meet that runs from May to September. This is central Canada's longest track, a hefty 1 ⅙ miles, with a 990-foot homestretch. In 1970, the richest contest on the card, the Manitoba Derby (Can-G3), drew Queen Elizabeth

II and Prince Phillip to the races as part of Manitoba's centennial celebrations. Despite a rocky interlude when competition from other gambling venues jeopardized the site's future, Assiniboia Downs has recovered. Address: 3975 Portage Avenue, Winnipeg, MB R3K 2E9; phone: 204-885-3330; Web site: http://www.assiniboiadowns.com.

MARQUIS DOWNS
(SASKATOON, SASKATCHEWAN)

The Saskatchewan province's only Thoroughbred racetrack, in Saskatoon, hosts a very small meet at Prairieland Exhibition Park. With an estimated 1.6 million visitors going through the park gates every year, some of those must make their way over to this little track. Marquis offers a mixed card from May to September, with Thoroughbreds and quarter horses sharing the bill on Friday and Saturday nights. Come out on a summer night for drinks and dinner, Terrace level, clubhouse, or tarmac-style. The track is a modest 5-furlong affair, with a 660-foot long homestretch. Address: 2326 Herman Avenue, Saskatoon, SK S7K 4E4; phone: 306-931-7149; Web site: http://www.saskatoonex.com.

NORTHLANDS PARK
(EDMONTON, ALBERTA)

When the premier of the province is a former harness racer, as is Ralph Klein, you can expect a favorable racing climate. Northlands, in Edmonton, Canada's northernmost large city, opened in 1925 as the Edmonton Racetrack but in fact continues the town's nearly 125-year horse racing past. The season hosts harness racing from March to June, and then the ⅝-mile bullring track launches its Thoroughbred meet on or near the summer solstice (late June) and continues into late October. Slot machines have helped the sport, and recent renovations have spruced up the buildings. Edmonton is a pretty spot; the North Saskatchewan River meanders through town on the way to the Hudson Bay; low rolling hills and prairie surround the racetrack and the city. Address: Northlands Spectrum, Edmonton, AB T5J 2N5; phone: 780-471-7379; Web site: http://www.northlands.com.

STAMPEDE PARK
(CALGARY, ALBERTA)

Thoroughbreds open the spring meet here in Calgary, racing around the bullring from April until June and wrapping up the season with the $100,000 Alberta Derby (Can-G3). Then the Calgary Stampede comes to town, and the crowd swells from a couple thousand to ten times that number. With the rodeo's reputation, and slots now on the premises, Stampede is positioned to make changes that will draw more players. Address: 2300 Stampede Trail S.E., Calgary, AB, T2G 2W1; phone 403-261-0214; Web site: http://www.stampede-park.com.

WHOOP-UP DOWNS
(LETHBRIDGE, ALBERTA)

This chunky, cinderblock open-air grandstand, also with a bullring track, came to life as the Rocky Mountain Turf Club. Its specialty is quarter horses; only recently did management introduce Thoroughbred racing. The track sits in eastern Lethbridge, at the Lethbridge & District Agricultural Grounds. Whoop-Up's split meet runs in early summer and again in the fall, generally for a total of forty days. The four-furlong ring is narrow, with tight, banked turns, putting the racing action right in front of you. The crowd is friendly—the track seems to have been named for the atmosphere that is not only welcomed but encouraged. A mixed slate of racing is augmented by slot machines and

simulcasting on the premises. Address: 3401 Parkside Drive S., Lethbridge, AB T1K 6X5; phone 403-380-1900; Web site: http://www.rockymountainturf club.com.

CANADIAN TRAVEL

ALBERTA
CALGARY

With three opportunities to enjoy Canadian Thoroughbred racing clustered in southern Alberta, and the spectacular Canadian Rockies rising just fifty miles west of Calgary, this region offers a nice opportunity to sample its geographic and cultural diversity. Sophisticated, oil-driven Calgary hosted the 1988 Winter Olympics; its location at the confluence of the Bow and Elbow rivers and a population of nearly a million make it one of the largest and most interesting cities in Canada. Stay at the Fairmont Palliser (133 9th Avenue S.W.; 403-262-1234/800-441-1414; http://www.fairmont.com/palliser). The grand era of rail travel is apparent at this lovely downtown hotel, which is connected by a walkway to the Glenbow Museum and the performing arts center. Fine dining is available in the hotel's Rimrock Restaurant. For everything else Calgary, visit these Web sites: http://www.where.ca/calgary.com and http://www.discovercalgary.com.

BRITISH COLUMBIA
VANCOUVER

Vancouver is one of the most exciting cities on the West Coast and arguably the most beautiful. It sits on a peninsula, surrounded on three sides by the inland waters of the Pacific Ocean. Hugged by parks, promenades, and the wide sandy beach of English Bay on the city's picturesque western edge, the city is framed by dense green mountains and peaks to the north. The deep waters of Burrard Inlet bring international maritime trade into the harbor, where luxury liners filled with tourists also dock. In every direction there are things to discover and enjoy, from art galleries to maritime history to wetlands and mountain peaks. Vancouver is a stimulating metropolis that welcomes visitors from around the world; it offers fine shopping and a great nightlife. An elegant address for your weekend is the Wedgewood Hotel (845 Hornby Street; 604-689-7777; 1-800-663-0666), in the heart of downtown. Its rooms are spacious and sumptuous, and the Bacchus Library is the perfect refuge for enjoying a glass of port or cognac. Dinner at the Bacchus Restaurant and Piano Lounge is divine, featuring Italian cuisine at its most tempting. For everything else Vancouver, check these Web sites: http://www.tourismvancouver.com and http://www.vancouver-bc.com.

ONTARIO
TORONTO

Modern skyscrapers and futuristic exhibition centers rise boldly against the western shores of Lake Ontario, where ferry terminals, boat marinas, and city parks edge the water. Founded in 1834, Toronto is Canada's largest city and main commercial center, the hub of the nation's banking, business, industrial, and cultural worlds. The city is a vibrantly creative metropolis filled with interesting, beautiful, and historic districts offering the traveler a boundless palate of places and activities to explore and enjoy. Internationally acclaimed events fill the Toronto calendar. The Toronto arts and theater scene is also endlessly varied. We recommend the Radisson Plaza Hotel Admiral Toronto-Harbourfront (249 Queen's Quay West;

416-203-333; http://www.radisson.com) for your stay. It is a AAA four-diamond-award hotel, with marina, harbor, and lake views and beach access. Dine at the hotel's Commodore's Restaurant or enjoy cocktails at the Bosun's Bar. For everything else Toronto, check these Web sites: http://www.torontotourism.com and http://www.toronto.com.

PHOTO CREDITS

The book's images are copyright Sir Barton Press, with the exception of the images provided courtesy of the following:

COVER

Group of images on back cover (second from right): Buffalo Niagara Convention & Visitors Bureau and James P. McCoy; **(far right):** Mountaineer Race Track and Gaming Resort. **Inside back flap (bottom):** Jan Cavalli. Endpapers: Finger Lakes Visitors Connection—New York.

APPENDIX

317: Tourism Toronto.

THE NORTHEAST

17, 42, 43: Penn National Race Course. **18, 19:** Hoofprints, Inc. **20:** Churchill Downs. **21, 23, 24, 51, 59:** Stephanie Funk. **25, 26:** Bill Denver, Equiphoto. **28 (bottom):** Monmouth Park. **30:** Bob Coglianese, NYRA. **31, 32:** Adam Coglianese, NYRA. **35:** Sackets Harbor Brewing Company. **37, 53 (top):** Finger Lakes Visitors Connection—New York. **39:** National Racing Museum. **44, 45:** Equi Photo. **47, 48:** Winterthur Museum and Country Estate. **52 (left):** Hotel Northampton. **52 (right):** Buffalo Niagara Convention & Visitors Bureau and James P. McCoy. **60:** Kristen Ciappa/GPTMC.

THE SOUTHEAST

73 (far left): Washington DC Convention & Tourism Corporation. **73 (center left), 74:** Churchill Downs. **73 (far right), 83 (top):** Bill Straus, courtesy of Keeneland. **77:** Corbis Corporation. **78 (top), 79, 80:** Ellis Park Marketing Department. **78 (bottom):** Santa Anita Park. **84:** Copyright JJ Zamaiko. **87:** Grayson/Sutcliffe Collection. **89, 90, 91, 94:** Jim McCue/Maryland Jockey Club. **93:** Bob Coglianese, NYRA. **95:** Jeff Coady/Coady Photography. **96:** Charles Town Races & Slots. **98, 99:** Mountaineer Race Track and Gaming Resort. **101 (left):** John James Audubon State Park. **103:** Brian Keller. **104:** Baltimore Area Convention and Visitors Association. **105 (top):** JakeMcGuire.com; Washington DC Convention & Tourism Corporation. **105 (bottom), 106, 108 (top):** Washington DC Convention & Tourism Corporation. **108 (bottom left):** Robert C. Lautman. Courtesy of the Mount Vernon Ladies' Association. **108 (bottom right), 109:** Richmond Metropolitan Convention and Visitors Bureau. **110:** Stephanie Funk.

THE SOUTH

122: Jeff Coady/Coady Photography. **123, 124 (top):** Oaklawn Jockey Club, Inc. **124 (bottom), 125:** Jean Raftery Photos. **126:** Calder Race Course. **127:** Gulfstream Park. **129 (bottom):** Bob Cicero; Florida Thoroughbred Breeders' and Owners' Association. **130 (bottom):** Tampa Bay Downs. **132, 133:** Jessica East & Amy Benoit/Coady Photography. **134 (top):** Evangeline Downs Racetrack and Casino. **137 (bottom):** Lone Star Park. **140 (top):** Clinton Presidential Library. **140 (bottom):** Paul Johnson

Associates. **141:** Greater Miami Convention and Visitor's Bureau. **142:** Santorini's Greek Grill. **143:** Festival International de Louisiane.

THE MIDWEST
155 (center left, far right), 160, 161: Four Footed Fotos. **156:** Benoit Photos. **158 (bottom), 159:** Jim Ansley, VIP Photos. **162:** Hoosier Park. **167, 168:** Canterbury Park. **169:** Beulah Park, Ohio. **171 (bottom):** River Downs. **173, 174:** Copyright JJ Zamaiko. **177:** Evansville Convention & Visitors Bureau. **180:** Explore Minnesota Tourism Photo. **181 (bottom left):** Greater Cincinnati CVB. **181 (bottom right), 182 (top left):** Convention & Visitors Bureau of Greater Cleveland. **182 (bottom right):** Experience Columbus.

THE GREAT PLAINS
193 (far left), 197: Woodlands Race Park. **193 (center left, center right, far right), 205:** Kansas City Convention and Visitors Bureau. **194:** Jeff Coady/Coady Photography. **199 (top), 200, 202:** Bob Dunn. **204:** Terrace Hill. **206:** R. Neibel, Nebraska DED.

THE WEST
213 (left, center right), 217, 218 (top): Gene Wilson & Associates, Inc. **214:** Arapahoe Park. **215, 216:** Trident Network Services. **218 (top):** Gene Wilson & Associates, Inc. **218 (bottom):** Clyde A. Reavis; Gene Wilson & Associates, Inc. **220 (top):** Denver Metro Convention & Visitors Bureau. Photo by Stan Obert. **220 (bottom):** Denver Metro Convention & Visitors Bureau. **221 (top):** Donnie Sexton, Travel Montana.

THE PACIFIC NORTHWEST
227: (far right), 228 (bottom): Les Bois Park. **228 (center):** Adam Coglianese, NYRA. **235:** Boise Convention and Visitors Bureau. **236 (top):** Oregon

Historical Society. **239:** Benson Hotel.
THE SOUTHWEST
243 (center right), 263 (right): Larry G. Fellows/Arizona Geological Survey. **243 (far right), 245 (bottom), 246:** Turf Paradise. **248 (bottom):** The Downs at Albuquerque. **249:** Ruidoso Downs. **250:** Mano Creative/Brian Kanof. **254:** Remington Park. **255, 256:** Lone Star Park. **258:** Manor Downs. **259:** Retama Park. **263 (left):** Four Seasons Resort Scottsdale at Troon North. **264 (center):** Kathy Curley/Navajo Nation Tourism. **264 (bottom):** National Cowboy & Western Heritage Museum, Oklahoma City. **265:** Ron Behrmann. **266 (top):** George D. Herring/National Park Service. **267 (bottom):** Austin Convention & Visitors Bureau. **268:** Dallas Convention and Visitors Bureau. **270:** SACVB/Al Rendon.

CALIFORNIA
284: Del Mar Thoroughbred Club. **296:** Vasser Photo; courtesy Humboldt County Fair. **301, 302, 303 (left):** Getty Images.

INDEX

A

Alameda Country Fair, 294–295
Alberta, Canada, 320–321
Albuquerque, N.Mex., 247–249, 265,
    271–272, 275–276
allowance races, 20
Altoona, Iowa, 194–195
Anderson, Ind., 162–163
Anthony, Kans., 195–196
Anthony Downs, 195–196
antiquarian horse books, 51
Aqueduct Racetrack, 30–32
Arapahoe Park, 214–215
Arcadia, Calif., 290–294
Arizona
    amenities and sites, 263–264, 271, 275
    county fairs, 244
    racetracks, 244–247
Arkansas
    amenities and sites, 140–141, 146,
        149–150
    racetrack, 122–124
Arlington Heights, Ill., 156–158
Arlington Park, 156–158
art, sporting, 77, 83, 291, 296
Ashado, 135
Assiniboia Downs, 320
Auburn, Wash., 231–233
Aurora, Colo., 214–215
Austin, Tex., 257–258, 267, 273, 277–278
Azeri, 122

B

Baltimore, Md., 91–92, 94, 104–105,
    112–113, 116–117
Bathhouse Bet, 159
Battaglia, Mike, 88
Bay Meadows Race Track, 282–283
Baze, Russell, 296
Bejarano, Rafael, 86
Belmont Park, 33–35, 93
Ben Ali, 87
Bensalem, Pa., 44–45
Berkeley, Calif., 286–287
Beulah Park, 168–170
Beyer, Andy, 13
The Big Fresno Fair, 298
Billings, Mont., 216
Bledsoe, Robin, 51
Blue Ribbon Downs, 251–252
Boise, Idaho, 228–229, 235, 238–239, 240
Bol, Manute, 162
Bossier City, La., 136–138
Boston, Mass., 19, 21–23, 48–51, 61, 66

B (continued)

Breeders' Cup, 315–316
British Columbia, Canada, 318, 321–322
Burning Roma, 26

C

Cal Expo, 296–297
Calder Race Course, 124–126
California, 280, 281, 299
    amenities and sites, 300–307, 308–310,
        310–313
    racetracks, 282–294
    state fairs, 294–298
California Equine Retirement Foundation,
    288
Canada, 317–322
Canterbury Park, 166–168
Chalkbusters, 233
Charles Town, W.Va., 96–97, 110, 114,
    119
Charles Town Races and Slots, 96–97
Chester, W.Va., 98–99
Chicago, Ill., 176–177, 183, 186–187
Churchill Downs, 74–76
Cicero, Ill., 160–161
Cigar, 199
Cincinnati, Ohio, 170–172, 181, 185, 189
claiming races, 20
Cleveland, Ohio, 181–182, 185–186,
    189–190
Collins, Rhonda, 164
Collinsville, Ill., 158–160
Colonial Downs, 94–96
Colorado
    amenities and sites, 220, 223, 224
    racetrack, 214–215
Columbus, Neb., 199–200, 207–208, 210
Columbus, Ohio, 182, 186, 190
Columbus Races, 199–200

D

Dallas, Tex., 268–269, 273, 278
Del Mar, Calif., 283–285, 300–301, 308,
    310–311
Del Mar Thoroughbred Club, 283–285
Delaware
    amenities and sites, 47–48, 61, 65
    racetrack, 18–19
Delaware Park, 16, 18–19
Delta Downs Racetrack and Casino,
    131–133
Denver, Colo., 220, 223, 224
The Derby Restaurant, 293
Des Moines, Iowa, 204, 207, 209
The Downs at Albuquerque, 247–249

E

East Rutherford, N.J., 25–26
El Paso, Tex., 273–274, 278
Ellis Park Race Course, 78–80
Emerald Downs, 231–233
Eureka, Kans., 196
Eureka Downs, 196
Evangeline Downs Racetrack and Casino, 133–134
Evanston, Wyo., 216–218, 221–222, 223–224
Evansville, Ind., 177–178, 183, 187
Exterminator, 87

F

Fair Grounds Race Course, 134–136
Fair Meadows, 252–253
Fairmount Park, 158–160
Fairplex Park, 297–298
Farmington, N.Mex., 251, 265–266, 276
Fast Fractions, *130*
Ferndale, Calif., 296
Finger Lakes Gaming and Racetrack, 37–38
Fingers Lakes Region, N.Y., 37–38, 52–53, 62–63, 67–68
Florence, Ky., 85–89
Florida
    amenities and sites, 141–143, 146–147, 150–151
    racetracks, 124–131
Fonner Park, 200–201
Fort Erie Race Track and Slots, 318–319
Franklin, Ky., 84–85
Fresno, Calif., 298
Funny Cide, *74*
Fusaichi Pegasus, *20*

G

Gilcoyne, Tom, 39
Golden Gate Fields, 286–287
Grand Island, Neb., 200–201, 206, 208, 210–211
Grand Prairie, Tex., 255–257
Grand Rapids, Mich., 179–180, 184, 188
Grantville, Pa., 42–43
Great Falls, Mont., 215–216, 220–221, 223, 224–225
Great Lakes Downs, 165–166
Great Plains, *192*, 193, 203
    amenities and sites, 204–206, 207–208, 209–211
    racetracks, 194–202
Great State Post Stake, 137
Griffin, Merv, *287*
Grove City, Ohio, 168–170
Gulfstream Park, 127–129

H

Hallandale Beach, Fla., 127–129
handicap races, 20
handicapping, 32, 199
Harrah's Louisiana Downs, 136–138
Harrisburg, Pa., 58–59, 70
Haskell, Amory L., *28*
Hastings Racecourse, 318
Hawkins, Abe, 137

Hawthorne Race Course, 160–161
Henderson, Ky., 78–80, 101, 111, 115
Hershey, Pa., 58–59, 64, 71
Hollywood Park, 288–290
Homeister, Rosemary, Jr., *126*
Hoosier Park, 162–163
horse racing performance categories, 20
Horsemen's Atokad Downs, 201
Horsemen's Park, 201–202
Hot Springs, Ark., 122–124, 140–141, 146, 149–150
Houston, Tex., 260–261, 269–270, 274, 278–279
Humboldt County Fair, 296

I

Idaho
    amenities and sites, 235, 238–239, 240
    racetrack, 228–229
Illinois
    amenities and sites, 176–177, 183, 186–187
    racetracks, 156–161
Indiana
    amenities and sites, 177–179, 183–184, 187–188
    racetracks, 162–165
Indiana Downs, 163–165
Indianapolis, Ind., 178–179, 183–184, 187–188
Inglewood, Calif., 288–290
Iowa
    amenities and sites, 204, 207, 209
    racetrack, 194–195

J

Jamaica, N.Y., 30–32
The Jockey Club, 55
Jones, R. A. "Cowboy," *80*

K

Kansas City, Kans., 196–198
Kansas City, Mo., 204–205, 207, 209–210
Kansas racetracks, 195–198
Keeneland, 80–83
Kentucky
    amenities and sites, 101–104, 111–112, 115–116
    racetracks, 74–89
Kentucky Derby winners
    Ben Ali, *87*
    Funny Cide, *74*
    Fusaichi Pegasus, *20*
Kentucky Downs, 84–85
Krone, Julie, 164

L

La Reine's Terms, *91*
Lafayette, La., 143, 148, 151–152
Lascaux, France, *77*
Latonia Race Course, 87
Laurel, Md., 89–90
Laurel Park, 89–90
Laws of Handicapping, Sir Mikey's, 32
Leaping Plum, *200*

Les Bois Park, 228–229
Lexington, Ky., 80–83, 101–103, 111–112,
115
Lincoln, Neb., 202, 206, 208, 211
Lone Star Park, 255–257
Long Island, N.Y., 33–35
Los Angeles, Calif., 301–303, 308–309,
311–312
Louisiana
amenities and sites, 143–145, 148–149,
151–153
racetracks, 131–138
Louisville, Ky., 74–76, 103–104, 112, 116

M
Maffeo, John, 298
Manitoba, Canada, 320
Manor Downs, 257–258
Marquis Downs, 320
Maryland
amenities and sites, 104–105, 112–113,
116–117
racetracks, 89–92, 94
Massachusetts
amenities and sites, 48–52, 61–62, 66–67
racetracks, 19, 20–24
Meadowlands Racetrack, 25–26
Miami, Fla., 124–126, 141–142, 146–147, 150
Michigan
amenities and sites, 179–180, 184, 188
racetrack, 165–166
Midwest, 154, 155, 175
amenities and sites, 176–182, 183–186,
186–190
racetracks, 156–174
Minneapolis/St. Paul, Minn., 180, 184–185,
188–189
Minnesota
amenities and sites, 180, 184–185,
188–189
racetrack, 166–168
Missouri
amenities and sites, 204–205, 207,
209–210
Monmouth Park, 26–29
Montana
amenities and sites, 220–221, 223, 224–225
racetracks, 215–216
Montana ExpoPark, 215–216
Mount Hood, Ore., 229, 230
Mountaineer Race Track and Gaming
Resort, 98–99
Munnings, Sir Alfred, 77
Murphy, Isaac, 137
Muskegon, Mich., 165–166

N
National Museum of Racing, 57
NCAA Hall of Champions, 179
Nebraska
amenities and sites, 206, 207–208, 210–211
racetracks, 199–202
New Jersey
racetracks, 25–28
New Kent, Va., 94–96

New Mexico
amenities and sites, 265–267, 271–272,
275–277
racetracks, 247–251
New Orleans, La., 134–136, 143–145,
148–149, 152–153
New York
amenities and sites, 29, 52–58, 62–64,
67–70
racetracks, 30–41
New York, N.Y., 53–56, 63, 68–69
Nordean, Erica, 291
North Randall, Ohio, 172–174
Northampton, Mass., 23–24, 52, 62, 66–67
Northeast, 16, 17, 46
amenities and sites, 29, 47–60, 61–65,
65–71
racetracks, 18–45
Northlands Park, 320–321

O
Oak Tree Racing Association, 286
Oaklawn Park, 122–124
Oceanport, N.J., 26–29
Ohio
amenities and sites, 181–182, 185–186,
189–190
racetracks, 168–174
Oklahoma
amenities and sites, 264–265, 272–273,
277
racetracks, 251–254
Oklahoma City, Okla., 253–254, 264–265,
272, 277
Omaha, Neb., 201–202, 206, 208, 211
Ontario, Canada, 318–320, 322
Opelousas, La., 133–134
Oregon
amenities and sites, 236–237, 239, 241
racetrack, 229–231

P
Pacific Northwest, 226, 227, 234
amenities and sites, 235–238, 238–240,
240–241
racetracks, 228–233
Parsons, Jesse, 126
Pegasus Foundation, 291
Penn National Race Course, 42–43
Pennsylvania
amenities and sites, 58–60, 64–65, 70–71
racetracks, 42–45
performance categories, 20
Philadelphia, Pa., 59–60, 64–65, 71
Philadelphia Park, 44–45
Phoenix, Ariz., 245–246, 263, 271, 275
Pimlico Race Course, 91–92, 94
Pleasanton, Calif., 294–295
Pomona, Calif., 297–298
Portland, Ore., 229–231, 236–237, 239, 241
Portland Meadows, 229–231
Prado, Edgar, 78
Prairie Meadows, 194–195
Prescott, Ariz., 246–247, 263, 271, 275

R

Race Track Industry Program (Univ. of Arizona), 247
Remington Park, 253–254
Retama Park, 259–260
Richmond, Va., 108–109, 114, 118
Rillito Downs Park, 244–245
River Downs, 170–172
Rock Springs, Wyo., 225
Ruidoso Downs, 249
Ruidoso, N.Mex., 249, 266, 272, 276

S

Sacramento, Calif., 296–297
Sallisaw, Okla., 251–252, 265, 273, 277
Sam Houston Race Park, 260–261
San Antonio, Tex., 270, 274
San Francisco, Calif., 303–307, 309–310, 312–313
San Joaquin Fair, 294
San Mateo, Calif., 282–283, 296
San Mateo County Fair, 296
Santa Anita Park, 290–294
Santa Fe, N.Mex., 266–267, 272, 276–277
Santa Rosa, Calif., 295
Santos, José, 33, 34
Saratoga Monument, 58
Saratoga Race Course, 40–41
Saratoga Springs, N.Y., 40–41, 56–58, 63–64, 69–70
Saskatchewan, 320
Seabiscuit bronze, 14
Seattle, Wash., 237–238, 239–240, 241
Secretariat, 93
Secretariat Center for Equine Adoption, 288
Sellers, Shane, 173
Selma, Tex., 259–260
Shakopee, Minn., 166–168, 180, 184–185
Shelbyville, Ind., 163–165
Shoemaker, Willie, 218
Shreveport, La., 145, 153
Sir Barton, 36, 233
Sirucek, Dave, 199
Solano County Fair, 295
Sonoma County Fair, 295
South, 120, 121, 139
    amenities and sites, 140–145, 146–149, 149–153
    racetracks, 122–138
South Sioux City, Neb., 201, 208, 211
Southeast, 72, 73, 100
    amenities and sites, 101–110, 111–114, 115–119
    racetracks, 74–97
Southwest, 242, 243, 262
    amenities and sites, 263–270, 271–275, 275–279
    racetracks, 244–261
sporting art, 77, 83, 291, 296
stakes races, 20
Stampede Park, 321
State Fair Park, 202
Stevens, Gary, 228
Steward, Keenan, 162
St. Julien, Marlon, 137

Stockton, Calif., 294
Stubbs, George, 77
Suffolk Downs, 19, 21–23
Sunland Park, N.Mex., 249–251
Sunland Park Racetrack and Casino, 249–251
SunRay Park, 251
Swaps bronze, 288

T

Tampa, Fla., 129–131, 142–143, 147, 151
Tampa Bay Downs, 129–131
Texas
    amenities and sites, 267–270, 273–274, 277–279
    racetracks, 255–261
Thistledown, 172–174
Thoroughbred Charities of America, 288
Thoroughbred Retirement Foundation (TRF), 288
Three County Fair, 23–24
Triple Crown
    about, 93
    Secretariat, 93
    Sir Barton, 36
Troye, Edward, 77
Tucson, Ariz., 244–245, 264, 271, 275
Tulsa, Okla., 252–253
Turf Paradise, 245–246
Turfway Park, 85–89

V

Vallejo, Calif., 295
Vinton, La., 131–133
Virginia
    amenities and sites, 108–109, 114, 118
    racetrack, 94–96

W

War Emblem, 78
Washington
    amenities and sites, 237–238, 239–240, 241
    racetrack, 231–233
Washington, D.C., 105–108, 113, 117–118
West Virginia
    amenities and sites, 110, 114, 119
    racetracks, 96–99
West,
    amenities and sites, 212, 213, 219
    racetracks, 214–218
Whoop-Up Downs, 321
Williams, Peter, 83
Wilmington, Del., 18–19, 47–48, 61, 65
Woodbine, 319–320
Woodlands Race Park, 196–198
Woolf, George "The Iceman," 293
Wyoming
    amenities and sites, 221–222, 223–224, 225
    racetrack, 216–218
Wyoming Downs, 216–218

Y

Yavapai Downs, 246–247
Yellowstone Downs, 216